PRESENCE
OF
ANGELS

—·◆·▪▪▪·◆·—

A HEALER'S LIFE

PRESENCE
OF
ANGELS

—•◆•••◆•—

A HEALER'S LIFE

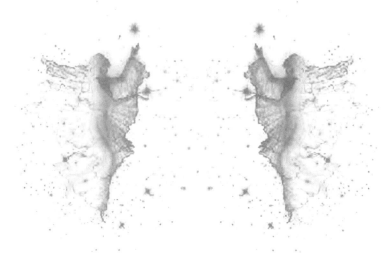

J. C. HUGH MACKIMMIE

KNOWING HEART PUBLISHING

Knowing Heart Publishing, Eureka, Montana 59917

ISBN: 0-9770545-4-3

Library of Congress Cataloging-in-Publication Data in process

All information in this book is for educational purposes only and in no way
comprises a substitute for medical advice, diagnosis or treatment by a
qualified healthcare professional, including Chapter 15, which contains
personal experiences from contributors, and represents the opinions and
perceptions of those who tell their stories. Before embarking on any diet or
exercise program, including those presented in this book, readers should
consult with their physician. Should individuals choose to use any of the
information contained in this book in any way, the author and the publisher
disclaim any responsibility for the results of these actions.

♻ Printed on recycled paper in the United Sates of America

Second Printing, December 2005

Knowing Heart Publishing
www.knowingheart.com

To my beloved wife, Andrea, who, as Mark Twain once said about his wife, edits my books and edits me also. Andrea does both with talent that amazes me. She has shuffled and organized all my random memories and thoughts of my healing life into focus. Without her this book would not have been possible, or it might have come out looking like an elephant with a trunk at both ends. There are those who sparkle in our life like brilliant stars in the evening sky. Andrea is one of these.

And to all my wonderful patients over these many years who have become dear friends, and as close to me as family.

Contents

ACKNOWLEDGMENTS

I am indebted to my close friend, Dennis Vogelhut of Willowhut Publishing, who guided me forward on the road of authorship, generously sharing his expertise and facilitating my creative process, and to his lovely wife and partner, Deborah Willow who graciously cheered him on in this mission.

My heartfelt thanks to my dear friend and brother in spirit, Levon Sagatelyan, for his wise words and loving encouragement along the way.

I extend my gratitude to my fellow authors who encouraged me in writing my memoirs: Cheri Bianchini, Dr. Dan Benor, Winston Cook, Dolora Deal, Dr. June d'Estelle, Jim Gettins, Dr. Jack Holland, and Caroline Sutherland.

Bless all my wonderful and extraordinary friends who urged me to tell my story with special thanks to my old friends, Dave and Jan Semling, for their part in making sure this book happened.

And I thank my family of grown children, who, in the long haul, have been very supportive of their 76-year-old father during his lifetime of healing: Marilyn, Robert, Bruce, Sue, Kim, and Michelle.

Lastly, I bow to all Healers in the world, especially my own great teacher. I have spent a lifetime in healing and been in contact with Healers on all levels. Healing is not an easy calling. At times, we get little support and are labeled "quacks." But in my opinion, Healers are heroes, dedicating their lives to relieve human suffering. They serve in the trenches with Mother Nature as their guide as they pursue their destinies in healing. If Karma is a reality—and it is—they are stacking up golden points in the heavenly book.

PREFACE

I am a healer. Born one just before the roaring '20s stopped roaring and became the Great Depression. My great-grandfather in Scotland was a seer and healer of high standing so these inherited abilities must have passed on down through the bloodline. In this book, I will share my life and endeavor to explain healing from my point of view, as I have lived it. Through my words, I hope to inspire others who heal or wish to become healers, and to encourage those who are seeking to be healed, whether physically, emotionally or spiritually. I am addicted to healing—always have been. To take away pain, to inspire people to change their habits to a more natural way of life, to see people soften and open to loving and being loved, these are the things that have filled my life with joy.

Whatever I can do to facilitate healing on all levels is my purpose in this lifetime. When I flow healing energy, it lights me up inside because I see the wondrous possibilities for health and awakening inherent in each person. I touch the higher energy patterns within each person and fan the flames of Love, Joy and Happiness therein to awaken soul patterns. With this inspiration, lives change by opening to the Creator's infinite possibilities. Thus, our world is changed forever.

The healing energy that flows from my hands into and through people is a loving gift from the Creator, and I happily admit that I have enjoyed every moment of my many years in the healing arts. I cannot steer this energy; I can only pray that each person opens to receive whatever is for the highest good for all concerned. Each time I have the opportunity to bring this gift to others, I give thanks for the privilege of sharing this blessing.

Right now I'm on the last leg of a flight from Montana to California. There I will see those directed by the mysterious cosmic forces of the universe, or by their own inner guidance, to come and see me. Looking out the plane's window, I see below the majestic redwood trees clustered along Skyline Ridge, which runs down the spine of the San Mateo peninsula of northern California.

As the plane banks slowly left to begin its landing pattern, row upon row of houses appear below, revealing the heavily populated area of San Jose. Each time I return, California seems to contain more of everything—houses, traffic and, most of all, people rushing about in ordered disorder like a huge community of purposeful ants. Suddenly, the landing gear drops with a shudder, slowing the plane as it lines up with the runway. Homes surrounding the airport grow rapidly in size as the ground rushes up to meet the plane.

Once in the airport terminal, my rolling suitcase obediently following my lead, I join the throngs of people moving with determination toward various exits. Somewhere in the outer world's traffic congestion, Jim, my longtime friend from Santa Cruz, is driving slowly around the terminal, patiently waiting for me to emerge from the crowd. Hoping to see Jim's smiling face, I begin looking into cars and vans crowding the area in front of the baggage claim exit.

Out of the corner of my eye, I notice the vigilant airport security challenging any vehicles attempting to invade the "No Parking" zone. Soon I spot Jim's van in the lineup of traffic. I wave to catch his eye. Anxious to avoid airport security's stern disapproval of people who are slow to board waiting vehicles, I hurry to his van, open the door, throw my suitcase in back, and climb aboard in short order.

Settling into the passenger's seat with a sigh of relief, I turn to smile at Jim, a middle-age man with a great sense of humor who has the art of getting along with everyone. Jim smiles back warmly. I have to admire his youthful features; he is one of those fortunate people who never show their age. As we drive away, people are still pouring out of the terminal. Jim and I are both people watchers, fascinated by the teeming hordes of airport humanity with endless differences in size and shape, like snowflakes, trillions per acre and no two alike. However, Jim and I are already busy talking a mile a minute, catching up on our separate lives, while Jim expertly maneuvers his van through the heavy airport traffic.

Heading for the Santa Cruz mountains on Highway 17, I understand why scores of accidents and deaths occurred on this road until the highway department constructed a center divider of cement. Countless tire marks adorn the divider. I can only wonder how it would feel to hit that unforgiving barrier and leave my own imprint in black rubber on this forbidding wall of cement and steel. Perhaps some mysterious effect from the famous Mystery Spot, which is close to this highway, accounts for the crazy drivers on this particular road. With little regard for life and limb, drivers zip around each other on sharp curves that require exceptional skill just to stay on the road.

At last we exit and take a frontage road to Jim's home where his lovely wife, Sandi, waits to welcome us. They are a wonderful, loving couple, who share their fine humor and talk together for long hours each day about world events and life's wonders. Jim quickly parks his van beneath the towering redwood trees that surround their home. The side of the house away from the road has a long, expansive deck facing a forest of giant redwoods, stately oaks, madrones, and thick, twisting vines. Standing on the deck, I can easily imagine that I'm looking out upon a Brazilian jungle. In the thick foliage, I see birds and squirrels enjoying their wilderness.

As I unpack my suitcase in the guest room, Jim and Sandi's kindness brings a smile to my weary traveler's face. I know the next three days of energy work will go by swiftly while I am busy balancing energies for old and new patients. Being an older chap now, I can no longer see as many people as in the past. After three days of healing, I will be ready to let down and just relax for a time before heading home to Montana.

During healing sessions, I am a conduit for the "Power," which is my name for the healing energy and the angels who guide me. The Power flows wherever needed to bring peace, harmony and balance to each patient. People come to see me for many varied reasons, and over the years, I have learned there are many levels of healing. The Power carefully calculates exactly what is needed for each person. Some are healed instantly and others more slowly, all according to a divine plan.

In my mind, the goal of the healing that flows through me is soul growth. The ego personality is made up of wishes, wants and desires, all clamoring for fulfillment. But that is not why we are here. We are born into this physical body for soul growth and to balance the great book of life. It is my belief that we all carry our own healing with us as we walk our path through life. My purpose is to facilitate that healing to the extent allowed within each person's karmic pattern and to awaken people to the higher aspects of life. For once touched by the Creator's love, you, and the world as you know it, are forever changed. Your eyes see differently, your heart opens, and your horizons expand beyond all comprehension. Life simply begins living itself through you. God is . . . You are . . .

————•◆•————

After three days of running energy and visiting with my hosts, Jim drops me off again at the San Jose Airport. There I wait for my flight to Seattle, where I have another wait before boarding a connecting flight back home. Once on Montana soil again, I see my wife, Andrea, smiling and waving to me from inside the terminal. Although we will have to drive another hour and a half to our home in Big Sky country, I know I will enjoy the beauty of each mile.

Traveling home through peaceful woods contrasts sharply with the rush of traffic and the bustle of the cities I left just a few hours ago. Driving through national forests, we put on our "deer eyes" to watch for deer, so many and so unpredictable. Many cars in our town have dented front ends from these fickle creatures. Why do *deer* cross the road, not *the chicken*, is our question here in Montana.

Soon I feel the eternal presence of the forest welcoming me home. Its beauty settles me as I return once again from a trip to the outer world. Andrea and I never take the beauty of Montana's magnificent wilderness for granted. When we behold the mountains and the wild creatures that share our life here, we feel that the Creator sees through our eyes and rejoices in His creation. To be dead to life's beauty would be to lose the exhilaration of living in the vastness of the Creator's glory.

As we near our small hometown, Andrea and I both smile at each other, anticipating the greetings of our two cats: he, a rowdy teenage boy with big blue eyes from his siamese heritage, lean and muscular with movements like quicksilver; and she, the queen dowager with penetrating jade-green eyes, wearing a silky black coat, and presenting a matronly figure with movements suited to her elder years. They, of course, both studiously ignore me upon our return as punishment for having deserted them.

Home again, it's time to begin my book and share my experiences.

I know I will flounder and flap forward in this authorship, cows all over the hills while I am supposed to round them up and perhaps get them to step in time, but that is foreign to me. Thoughts and memories and intuition, all join in one vast matrix of energy, tumbling together as though caught up in one of the powerful Pacific waves of Hawaii that surfers love so well. My tenses may wander a bit as I drift from past to present and back again, or my punctuation may take a few side trips off the map, but I hope the reader will stay on the trail as I wind my way through my life of healing.

What is a "preface" all about? The word itself should reveal something to my brain cells. How can I be sure to serve what it signifies? I may be forced to look it up in the dictionary if I don't want to get the buffalo all running away from the camera—a rear shot is not good—much better seen head on. I imagine a cartoon with thousands of buffalo coming at you. One buff says to the other, "Right turn! Quick, pass it on!"

All those running buffalo remind me of the years that Andrea and I lived on the beach in Washington. We loved to watch the flocks of shore birds turn in flight, hundreds of them, all swooping as one, in perfect unison. Often we would see a hawk appear high above the flock. Dropping through the sky like a stone, the hawk would try to grab one of the smaller birds.

Without a moment's hesitation, or calling a meeting for consensus, the birds would instantly break their perfect flight pattern, scattering through the sky and leaving behind a newly created hole for the hawk's surprise attack. Plummeting toward the ocean, and no doubt confused by his sudden lack of prey, the hawk would pull up just in time to avoid a dip in the ocean. But, I digress. It's time to corral my thoughts and plunge forward in telling my tale . . .

PART I

MY LIFE AND TIMES

1

BEGINNINGS

◆ •• ◆

How can anyone understand my burning desire to be a healer? From the moment the Creator touched my heart and awakened this desire, the dream of healing lived within me, never far from my thoughts. But as I awakened to my contract to heal, I didn't really understand the agreement. Had I ever been a free agent with a choice in the matter? Was my healing written in an ironclad contract for this lifetime? Had I signed this contract before birth?

Healing was the compass to guide my ship safely through the fog to my destined port, a course I knew totally in my heart. However, the passengers and crew were constantly demanding a change of course through the turbulent tides of mind and emotion. Perhaps when you see how my headstrong mental outlook tried to knock me off my path, you will see that it is possible for anyone to heal. I think God must have chosen me, with all my shortcomings, to prove this point.

Until we awaken, we cannot remember our contract with the Creator. Nevertheless, it does exist and we are obliged to follow as it moves us through life, here and there, for reasons we can only guess at. Like a leaf in a stream, we rest in quiet backwaters at times. But then we're swept into swirling rapids and plunged over thundering waterfalls until we come to rest once again in peaceful waters downstream.

Each moment of our journey is arranged in life's great symphony by the vast energy flow of the universe. Opening to the limitless possibilities of the Creator, this symphony of life moves through me to heal. And for more than fifty years, I have been a court of last resort . . .

I recall one sunny afternoon when a worried daughter brought her 40-year-old mother to my office. The daughter sat in a chair across the room, at a distance from where I would be running energy. She told me her mother was slated for exploratory surgery in two days.

Silently, I prayed, "Dear God, I pray to be a willing channel of love, healing and grace for this patient. I release her to You for her highest good, asking Your love and blessing for whatever is best in every way for the good of all concerned in a state of healing and grace." These words, given to me by the Power when I was very young, have always been my prayer before beginning a healing session. (The Power is my name for the healing energy and the angels who guide me.)

I asked the mother to lay face up on my treating table. Her face turned white with pain as she followed my instructions. The daughter leaned forward and warned, "Please be careful. My mother can barely tolerate the slightest touch."

"No doubt an exaggeration," I thought. Confidently, I placed my hand lightly on her mother's arm. But my gentlest touch brought screams so loud that they must have alarmed the other patients in my waiting room. They certainly alarmed *me!*

Quickly recovering from the mother's outburst, I stood at the foot of my treatment table and began running energy without touching her. Soon the familiar tingling and warmth from the healing energy filled my hands. After a few minutes, my patient sighed deeply and relaxed. Her face was peaceful and a gentle smile formed on her lips. This is the power of healing. The incredible pain and agony were gone. My patient said, "There's such a wonderful feeling of calm . . . like a wave of well-being moving through my body."

As always, I marveled how healing energies moved through the patient's body exactly where needed to fill the body's many batteries to capacity. The voice that instructs me directed me to sit next to my patient and lay my hands on her abdomen. I did so without question. I could now touch her without causing her any pain, and from that moment, I knew she would be pain-free. Her eyes filled with relief and gratitude, she looked up at me and exclaimed, "I feel so happy now!"

Before I could say anything, the energy in the room began to shift and intensify. When I looked up, I saw row upon row of angels entering the room. The walls of my treating room disappeared as these beautiful beings, clothed in garments of shimmering silver light, appeared. This procession continued until one hundred luminescent angels encircled my patient and me. Love and serenity radiated from their shining countenances. Their presence filled the room with ever deepening peace.

The tallest angel stepped forward to stand across from where I was sitting. She reached into my patient's body and removed the left kidney, which looked like a lump of black coal. From within her robes, this angel brought forth a brand-new, pink kidney. It was glowing and pulsating with life's radiant aura. She gently placed this kidney into my patient's body. I watched in awe. Never looking at me, the angel solemnly went on to replace my patient's heart, eyes, brain, right arm, and left leg. Then she stepped back.

Suddenly, I was lifted to another state of consciousness. It seemed as though I was floating high above my patient's body. Her physical form now appeared to be a vast field of sparkling, colored lights. Effortlessly, my consciousness began to glide slowly downward toward the patient as though I was suspended in a hang glider. At the same time, my perception of her body changed. Now I saw higher dimensional energies forming spindles of light and swirling disks of dazzling, rainbow colors, shimmering in ethereal radiance. I banked right, and glided lower toward these brilliant, vibrating lights, which looked like the city of Paris at night.

As I observed the body's organs, I saw the liver take charge of all the healing operations within the body. The liver was a vibrant magenta color surrounded by a pink, iridescent glow. It was busy instructing the new organs and filling them with loving energy. I sensed the body's joy and gratitude as new cells began to participate in this restored dance of life.

Continuing to glide slowly downward, zigzagging back and forth, I saw large, dandelion-like puffballs of brilliant light begin to float up toward me from the body. These lights increased in number until thousands of spheres of light were rushing up to meet me. Afraid these lights might be guardians prepared to protect the body, I panicked and shouted, "My name is Jim MacKimmie and I'm trying to help this woman!"

The dazzling lights were almost upon me. I held my breath. To my astonishment, they began to pass right through me. Then I heard and felt the delightful giggles of thousands of cherubs as these bubbles of light danced through me. They knew all about me and the healing. Embraced in their love, my heart filled with joy. How silly my fears had been! I joined in their laughter. In that blessed coming together, we became one vast being of light and love. This loving reality was the truth of our existence, our very reason for being, now and forever.

Later that afternoon, the daughter called to tell me that her mother's healing had been a miracle. She said, "Mother came to you a dying woman and now she's like an excited teenager. She's running all over the neighborhood telling people that she's brand-new." I hung up the phone and thanked God for performing this miracle.

———•◆•———

How did I come to be a healer? Destiny is often reached by a winding road filled with unimaginable twists and turns. And so it was in my case.

On a frosty November night in Nova Scotia, Canada, my mother, Corina, was in labor with her seventh child—me. My father, James Alexander Sutherland, was at sea, earning what he could as a marine engineer during the lean years of the late 1920s. I had one sister and two brothers waiting for me. (Three other babies had died during childbirth.) Too poor to have a midwife or doctor present, Mum went through her labor alone while my sister and brothers slept.

Whenever my sister awakened during the night, she heard Mum praying aloud for a baby girl to help with the burden of caring for her family. Then, at first light, my sleepy seven-year-old sister crept close to our mother's bed where she saw me wrapped in a blanket in our mother's arms. I had arrived, Victor Verdun Sutherland born on November 29, 1928.

My exhausted mother opened her eyes to see her only daughter staring down at her new brother bundled in a blanket. Sick from lack of food, Mum couldn't bear the thought that her new baby was another boy, one more mouth to feed when all were hungry. In despair, she threw me with her remaining strength into the dying embers of the fireplace. My sister snatched me back from the embers and prevented an early cremation by dousing the burning blanket with water. After brushing my skin free of ashes, she pleaded with Mum to take me back. She did, and thus, my adventures in life began.

From the beginning, I was different, born with the Power intact within me. And with the Power came the gift that allowed me to see into the future and into people. This gift has flowed through me from my first memory. I just knew things. Watching people's thoughts and emotions was quite natural to me, but seeing into people spooked me. Not in the seeing itself, but in what I saw. People could lie, break their word, and were, in general, not to be trusted. Too often they said one thing, but thought another.

It never bothered me to see death take up residence in someone's energy. We all go through that doorway at the appointed hour. Our time on earth is well-charted, and when our contract is over, we take flight. But it did bother me to see how many people lived their lives in fear. They stayed in the mind, seldom visiting the heart where the infinite energies of the Creator reside.

And yet at times, I looked within others and saw absolute truth and beauty shining forth in loving energies and brilliant colors. It was the beauty of those moments that inspired me to look beyond my bleak outer life in a world caught in the throes of the Great Depression. However, only shadow memories remain from the first three years of my life. Much of what I do know about my early life as a Sutherland, I learned from my sister many years after I had been adopted from an orphanage.

———•◆•———

Far removed from Nova Scotia, I was 29 and living in California when I sent a request for my Birth Certificate to Canada. Little did I know that fate was ready to take me in hand. Across a continent and in another country, an uncle saw my request as it was wending its way through the Hall of Records. He immediately notified my father.

Although I knew I had been adopted, it came as quite a shock to receive a letter from my father and learn that I had another family and Scottish Sutherland clan relations still living in Nova Scotia. I had been so involved in my life of healing that I had never actually given any thought to finding my birth family. I began corresponding with my father. At 76, he wrote to say that he would like to see me before he died.

It took a year for me to save enough money to make a trip to Halifax where I could stay with my sister, Marigold. As soon as I saw her, I knew we were birds of a feather. We understood each other instantly through a deep kinship that our years apart had not diminished. We spent every precious moment talking and sharing our lives. It was she who revealed to me that my great-grandfather had been a well-known seer and healer in Scotland. It was exciting for me to learn that my healing and intuitive gifts had been passed down through our bloodline.

During my stay in Nova Scotia, Marigold revealed that our mother had also been intuitive, and frequently saw things that others could not. Although Mum was sick from malnutrition and in bed most of the time, she insisted the house be kept clean and tidy at all times. Marigold said Mum required all of us to be washed and scrubbed in the hottest water possible until we resembled boiled lobsters. Our family survived by trapping rabbits and fishing. The only fuel for our fireplace came from bits of coal and cinders we gathered near the railroad tracks. During those harsh times of survival, this was true for most families in our area.

When I asked Marigold to tell me more about our mother, she recalled that Mum hated anything she considered unnatural—like prescribed drugs. She was also zealous in her determination that none of her children would ever have immunizations, which she claimed caused much of the sickness in the world. She believed children needed to experience childhood diseases for the body's own immune system to be strengthened.

Recounting Mum's philosophy of health reminded Marigold of Mum's unexpected reaction to an event that took place on one of those rare occasions when Dad was home from the sea. Without telling anyone, my two older brothers dragged me off to the nearby freight yard on a stormy, winter afternoon. The snow was already falling heavily when they took me from the house.

After reaching the trains, my oldest brother, who was eight, carried me piggyback to the top of a box car. Then my other brother, who was seven, climbed up after us. Together my industrious siblings tied me to the roof with a rope. Pleased with their handiwork, they left me to enjoy my rooftop view and headed home through what was now deep snow.

By the time my father noticed his two-year-old son was missing and began asking where I was, the storm had become a blizzard. In the face of my father's growing anger, my brothers nervously reported that Victor was going to California on the train. Dad gave Marigold hell for not keeping an eye on me and they all hurried to the freight yard to search for me. I was easy to spot since I formed a high, snowy silhouette on top of my box car. When they reached me, I was buried under two feet of snow. Dad climbed up, dug me out, untied me, and brought me down.

My rescuers hurried home with Dad carrying me in his arms since my own unbendable limbs were numb with cold. At home, Mum plunged me into a hot bath to get me warm. Before long, I was up and ready for another adventure. Mum's surprising reaction to the whole event was one of delight because this event proved what she had always known—without doctors, without drugs—her children were tough as nails.

———•◆•———

As delightful as it was to meet Marigold, it was quite another thing to face my father when Marigold took me to meet him a few days later. He lived out in the country in a small cottage sided with weather-beaten shingles. When I entered, Dad was sitting in a well-used, overstuffed armchair.

Years spent on an icebreaker in salty ocean air had weathered Dad's face magnificently, forming a fierce terrain of harsh crags and crevices. His forbidding features managed what I identified as a welcoming smile in a face unused to smiles. After pushing himself up out of his chair slowly and stiffly, he studied me for several minutes. It was clear he was more prepared than I was for our momentous meeting. At last he asked in gravest tones, "Son, have you been saved?"

This question—after more than 20 years of separation—forced me to place dear old dad in the same category I place all who are dedicated to their own particular religion to the exclusion of all others. I knew I had better tread lightly, and prepared to agree with him on all counts. This was no time to debate church affiliations and my beliefs. I could see that my interest in comparative religions would not be a selling point for retying the old filial bonds. Cautiously I replied, "Yes, Dad. Of course I've been saved."

Dad squinted at me as if to detect any untruth in my answer. He stiffened slightly, "Have you been saved in the Annapolis Valley Church by the Sea?"

Dangerous waters loomed ahead. Although I already had my suspicions, I asked the location of this church. Dad beamed proudly and revealed—not to my surprise—that it was three miles down the road. He informed me that he was a staunch member along with 11 other devoted servants of the Lord. With pride, he confided that the members of his church were the only ones in the entire world who would enter Heaven to be with Jesus. I wondered what the rest of the world's population would say to this startling news. Nodding my head, I tried to look duly impressed.

My father pleaded with me to stay in Canada until the church met next week so that I could be officially saved in the Annapolis Valley Church by the Sea. He insisted that only this event would allow me to reside in Heaven with himself, the 11 others, and of course Jesus and assorted angels. I said, "I'm sorry, Dad, I have to get back to my practice in California. My plane tickets are for tomorrow."

Dad broke down and wept. Then he stiffened and warned, "Son, you'll surely burn in Hell for all eternity if you don't stay until the church meets again next Sunday."

"I would if I could," I said placatingly. "But I have patients who are waiting for my return. I just can't stay." He looked at me with tearful but steely eyes, shook my hand, and returned to the comfort of his armchair.

This vacation had been like no other in my life. Learning from Marigold why I could see events to come and why healing energies flowed through me was a blessing, but encountering my father with his brittle religious outlook was a blow. I was astounded by my father's rigid beliefs since he was an intelligent marine engineer.

A month after my return to California, my sister wrote to tell me that Dad had split from his church with two other loyal members, leaving the other nine members behind. Thus, only three people—including my dad—would now find salvation in Heaven. All the other slackers in the Annapolis Valley Church by the Sea would now burn in Hell along with the rest of the world's population. I knew that any mention of a previous life might have given him a stroke. As long as he lived, I wrote letters carefully avoiding the "saved" subject. When he died, I'm sure it was without any doubt that he would be swept up into the arms of Jesus.

My joke with Andrea is that when I see God on the other side, my father will be present with his two fellow parishioners. My earthly father will be in charge of the lever that allows you into Heaven, or sends you straight to Hell. He will solemnly pronounce, "Son, it was your choice. I tried to tell you. Now it's too late!" Then he will shove the lever to the gauge's high heat side, and yours truly will go down the chute—without benefit of an asbestos suit—the better to roast through all eternity.

Many would agree with my father and believe their religion is the only true road to Heaven. Strangely, all religions seem to have this belief. One group is in, and everyone else is out. Isn't it just like man to subdivide God? And then start wars to vie for the positions closest to God? Personally, I think it's all nonsense. We are in God's loving heart always and forever while we dream this weird outer world dream called life. All things are one loving thing, and that one thing is the Creator. Nothing has ever existed outside of that awesome loving energy. Won't it be a grand surprise for all concerned when everyone shows up in Heaven, no matter who?

———•◆•———

Returning to my early years, my life took a sudden turn when I was three years old. Exhausted after struggling to give birth to yet another son, Mum died of malnutrition when she was 31. Father came home from the sea, but he was unable to care for his children after her death. He placed his older children with various farm folk to labor for their keep. A nearby family took my infant brother as their own and I was placed in an orphanage. Nothing remains in my memory about the orphanage, except that it most assuredly had no kindly doctor and staff as depicted in the movie *Cider House Rules*.

My clearest memories begin when a wealthy couple, who could have no children of their own, adopted me when I was four years old. Winnie and Bob MacKimmie carefully explained to me that I now had a new last name, "MacKimmie." They said I was going home to live with them. If I had learned one thing during my orphanage stay, it was the cardinal rule: *Do not ask questions!* I had watched other children leave with no explanations, never to return. These were frightening occurrences so I held my breath and said nothing when my new "mother" took my hand.

Listening to my "parents" laugh and chat along as we drove through town helped calm my fears. When we arrived "home," they asked if I would like to have a new first name to go with my new last name. Without hesitation, I excitedly announced my choice, "Jimmie." This name had been dancing in my head all the way home, whispered with promise by the voice of my inner knowing. Smiling, they agreed this was a fine choice and would be my new name. I had to hide my disappointment when I was officially renamed James Chisholm MacKimmie, and not "Jimmie MacKimmie" as promised.

Home was one of the largest houses in Pictou, with many rooms for a young boy to explore, and a maid to be evaded while exploring. Roaming through the house the next day, I discovered bowls filled with chocolates. It was every child's dream come true. (Later, I learned that my new family owned Hamilton's Chocolate and Biscuit factory.)

Bob and Winnie soon discovered that I was a great sleepwalker who continued my explorations at night. They tracked me all over the house on these nightly excursions to see where I would go and what I would do. After wandering dead asleep for hours, I would finally return to my bed. I sometimes wonder where I traveled on the inner planes during my nightly strolls.

My new life was one of unending excitement for a small boy. On Halloween, I accompanied my parents out on an upper story balcony to throw candy down to the children who gathered below for these treats. In November, I had my first birthday celebration. Until I saw my very own birthday cake with four candles carefully placed on its glorious frosted surface, I never knew birthdays were a cause for celebration.

When Christmas came, my first sight of the Christmas tree in the living room frightened me. I thought the tree was on fire when I first saw the electric lights blazing brightly in its branches. Reassured this was not the case, my attention soon went to the gaily wrapped packages under the tree. I could hardly believe all the presents were for me. But the best present of all was being with my new mother and father who were mine to love forever.

Following a severe January blizzard, the MacKimmies bundled me up in a bearskin rug and tucked me into the back seat of their car for my first official road trip. They were anxious to show off their new son ("our adopted boy" was the phrase they used) to friends who had recently moved to the country. My father cautiously edged the car slowly down a road banked on both sides by towering snowdrifts. My eyes wide with wonder, I watched the passing countryside from the back seat, enjoying every moment.

Once we passed beyond the edge of town, the few houses we saw had snowdrifts up to the rooftops. I had never been on this road before and didn't know anyone in my new surroundings. However, I knew instantly that we had arrived at our destination when I spotted an imposing black mailbox standing like a sentinel near the edge of the road. Filled with excitement, I pointed to the mailbox and the house beyond, and shouted with certainty, "That's where we're going to see those people!"

A roar of laughter exploded from the front seat, and my new parents turned to look back at me with amused curiosity. Discouraged, I retreated into silence, burrowing deeper under the bearskin until only my nose and eyes could be seen above the thick, brown fur. I knew without a doubt our destination was the house with the black mailbox. I didn't understand their laughter. Why didn't they *know* that I *knew?*

We traveled on and on. Hours later, after asking directions from several farmers, we arrived back at the house I had identified. And that's where we spent the afternoon visiting. I always "knew," but this was the first strong wave of intuition I can remember voicing to others.

When spring began to melt the snow, Father decided it was time for me to read. He began our new game by using the Sunday newspaper comics. I sat on his lap while he read. My job was to repeat words aloud as he pointed to them. I already adored my father and tried hard to please him. My brain grappled with the relationship between written and spoken words. A few times my confusion ended in tears, but he patiently and firmly began again. Somewhere along the line I made the connection, and we began reading the first book I had ever touched.

From my parents, I learned to treasure books, to treat them with respect and loving care. Then I was allowed to read precious books passed down through my mother's family for generations. I was off and running, eager for more books. With full approval from my parents, I buried myself in books whenever possible. Although children were not known for

reading anything on their own, except comics, I read voraciously for
hours every day.

My favorite stories centered around heroes who saved others no
matter what hardships had to be faced. These stories came vividly to life
in my imagination. I was especially fascinated by the three magical wishes
given when you rescued an animal in distress. Obviously, my first wish
would have been for a thousand more wishes. I was completely frustrated
when the first two wishes were wasted in a foolish and careless manner,
which always seemed to be the case. Now, if only their first wish had
been for a thousand more . . .

2

CALIFORNIA DREAMS

———————◆▪◆———————

S adly, my newfound happiness with the MacKimmies was not to last. As the Great Depression steadily devoured the lives of everyone around us, my new family lost nearly everything. I was terrified when my parents spent hours whispering. Adults always whispered when something bad was about to happen.

Things came to a head when Winnie, who had enough determination for any dozen people, recalled happy memories of California where she had visited relatives in 1903 when she was in her twenties. Once she got the idea of California in her head, Dad didn't stand a chance. In 1933, she finally persuaded him that they should make a new start in Pasadena, California where she still had relatives. As soon as this decision was made, we left Canada behind and headed for California.

My father drove our 1928 Chevy sedan right down the middle of America's dirt highways. In those days, there were few cars on the roads, and the sides of the roads were occupied by lines of men walking, single file, heads bowed in defeat. On one side, they were walking west to look for work. On the other side, they were walking east with the same hope. These lines stretched for miles across America. We saw thousands of men trudging in each direction. Farmers who lived near the roads gave these men what food they could spare.

Looking back, I wonder why we were not attacked by those desperate men and dragged from our car, which was tightly packed with all our possessions. But we passed through state after state and finally arrived safely in California where everything was exciting and new. Having driven on dirt roads all across the country, we were astonished by California's smooth asphalt roads, and fascinated by road reflectors, which we had never seen before. We thought someone was stationed out in the darkness to turn these lights on when your car approached. Dad also had to get accustomed to stopping at stop signs, which we didn't have in Nova Scotia.

We loved Pasadena. The air felt incredibly clean and fresh after our long, dusty car trip. During the year we lived there, I never tired of looking at the distant snow-capped mountains, shining brilliantly in the sun, even in the middle of summer. It seemed that every day brought unexpected adventures. One day, Dad drove us to a spot he had found near Christmas Tree Lane. He stopped the car in the middle of the road. Turning off the motor, he got out and asked us to follow him. He took us over to the side of the road where we watched in fascination as our car moved—by itself—uphill for 50 feet. People came from all over to visit this spot and watch their cars go uphill, pulled by some mysterious magnetic force. I wonder if this magic spot is still there, but forgotten.

Once in California, my intuition began to flow in earnest when one Sunday my parents stopped to watch an outdoor wedding in the park. I was bored stiff until pandemonium broke out in front of the palm tree "altar." This entertaining commotion centered around the groom. Suddenly it became painfully clear. The distraught groom was no longer in possession of the diamond wedding ring destined for his bride's waiting finger. As the hubbub gathered force, both wedding guests and people strolling by, including my parents, got down on their hands and knees to search for the lost ring, which remained stubbornly sequestered somewhere in the dense, manicured grass.

This time when my flash of intuition came, I said nothing to my parents. My first painful experience—when they laughed at my knowing—was still fresh in my mind. Instead, I walked away from where the growing crowd hunted for the ring and there it was sparkling up at me, hidden by thick grass. After handing the lost ring directly to the distressed groom, I was happy to receive the first slice of wedding cake as a reward. The almost married couple were even happier to continue their wedding. I felt vindicated by this visible proof of my intuition, and Bob and Winnie exchanged meaningful glances with each other all the way home.

The next year we moved to Redlands, California, a small citrus growing town east of Los Angeles, primarily so that I could attend Kingsbury Elementary School. Thus began my life amidst the glorious orange groves, which at that time blanketed thousands of acres. In those days, the sweet scent of orange blossoms filled the air for miles in every direction. Summer temperatures hovered in the high 90s, but winters could drop to 28 degrees at night, the perfect hot/cold climate for growing sweet naval oranges.

The Golden State truly earned its name. Local groves produced exceptional oranges, sweet and tasty with the thinnest of skins. I have fond memories of darting in among the trees, moving secretly through the groves like Tarzan through the jungle, free and unseen. Hundreds of fig, apricot, peach, nectarine and tangerine trees had been planted at the bottom of the orange groves to catch the irrigation overflow. I roamed for miles through the groves, and found the very best of these trees. Few ladies bothered canning this perfectly ripe and unsprayed fruit, so every summer the birds and I foraged in the groves and ate our fill.

———•◆•———

How can I describe those times? Nothing much ever happened in our quiet town. Homes were well-tended. There was no litter. People often strolled around the block in the evenings, occasionally stopping to speak quietly with other neighbors who were sitting out on their porches enjoying the balmy air. It was a time when people got along with each other. Children were obedient and—difficult as this may be to believe—even silent upon occasion. "Don't speak unless you're spoken to!" was a message drummed into children by every adult.

Although the depression was in full swing, there was work in California, if you didn't mind low wages for long hours of hard work. The Work Projects Administration came on the scene and men were grateful to find work paying minimum wages. The WPA put in storm ditches, rock walls, and bridges with such fine workmanship that they remain marvels of engineering even today.

In our area, it was a time when beautiful mansions were built and splendid parks were dedicated. At one time, Redlands had more millionaires than any other American city. Redland's local newspaper, *The Facts*, reported on October 23, 1890: "Men have made fortunes (in Redlands), and are making fortunes with a rapidity unknown in any other part of the world."

America was rapidly becoming a kingdom of cars. Automobiles were nearly indestructible. Bumpers were made of heavy steel, and interiors were covered in upholstery that lasted for years. Clothes also lasted for years, as did shoes, but tires did not, so people usually walked to do their shopping and other errands. Small stores—about the size of today's garage—were in most neighborhoods in our town. These stores carried a little bit of everything. The cost of groceries was minuscule compared to today's prices. Bread cost a nickel a loaf. A dime bought 100-pounds of onions. Haircuts were ten cents, and there were no skinheads. Wages were low, but you could rent a house for seven dollars a month.

Southern California was semiarid so lawns were small and located in front, and backyards were usually sand or dirt. Tidy, manicured front lawns were easily watered using a hand-held hose. It was a time when water did not have chlorine or fluoride added to it. Drinkable, delicious water came right from the tap, or gushed from your hose for a cold, refreshing drink on a hot summer day. While watering the front lawn, you could pass the time talking with neighbors or anyone else strolling by.

The serenity of quiet neighborhoods was not disturbed by the roar of lawnmowers or leaf blowers. Mowing was accomplished with hard work and a push mower. Amazingly, leaves were actually raked off lawns and swept off sidewalks with brooms. All these summer activities were underway as early in the day as possible. The moment the sun rose in a blue and cloudless sky, the temperature soared, the better to bake us natives. Since there was no air conditioning, most homes were built with large screened-in porches. Folks sat on their porches, or even slept there, until the early morning hours brought relief from the suffocating, summer heat.

When we said "downtown," we meant the big time. On the commercial side, Sears and Montgomery Wards opened for business and provided enthusiastic customers with catalogues we called "wish books." When the first Safeway opened, it was a big event. We were awed by its enormous size, but today that same store would fit handily in the back corner of any local Safeway. The Pep Boys, an auto parts supply store, welcomed eager shoppers with a large sign overhead with Manny, Moe and Jack (the Pep Boys themselves) smiling benevolently down upon prospective customers.

Best of all, downtown was where we headed for our major entertainment as provided by our local movie house. High adventure awaited inside for a ten-cent admission. And every Saturday, we dreamed our dreams at the movies. Some afternoons we even ventured to the far reaches of outer space and visited other planets with Buck Rogers or Flash Gordon.

Heart-pounding thrills in cliffhanger serials, like *Daredevils of the Red Circle* and *The Purple Monster Strikes* kept us returning, week after week. Why? Because our hero looked done for at the climax of the last episode, and we were anxious to find out how he managed to escape certain death. All week long, we would puzzle among our friends trying to figure out how the hero could possibly avoid his doom. If his escape— as presented in the next episode—didn't measure up, there was general booing from the audience. But the booing didn't last long. In those days, you acted in a civilized manner, or you were banished from the theater.

In our town, everyone knew each other by name. Local coffee shops never lacked for customers or the latest gossip. I recall one small diner where "Mom" and "Pop" cooked breakfast, lunch, and dinner. It had only seven stools at the counter, and impatient patrons squeezed in, ready to claim those coveted stools and share the latest rumors. Standard menu fare was pot roast, vegetables, mashed potatoes and gravy, with pie and ice cream for dessert. This full course meal was 15 cents for portions so large that one could hardly walk when finished.

The first radio on our block was a marvel for all to hear, but promptly at 8:00 P.M. broadcasting stopped and silence again prevailed. People quite simply went to bed. However, just past midnight, you could tune into the Midnight Flyer, a show broadcast from Clint, Texas. This powerful station reached out across the country with blaring ads for hemorrhoid creams and cures for corns. I dreaded the commercials when a booming voice asked, "Do you have an itching, painful, stabbing, irritating rectal condition known as hemorrhoids or piles? If you do . . ." By the time the intrusive voice finished reciting a litany of horrible symptoms, I could almost feel those hemorrhoids.

Advertising in the '30s went to extremes. One enterprising chap from Clint, Texas advertised his guaranteed cockroach killer for 25 cents.

When you received your cockroach killer in the mail, you found two small blocks of wood in the cardboard box. One was clearly labeled: Block A. The other was labeled with equal precision: Block B. Most important, there were classic instructions enclosed: "Position the cockroach between Block A and Block B and bring the blocks smartly together."

The cagey inventor of the cockroach killer surely made millions before the public woke up. Twenty-five cents was a sizeable investment at that time. Finally, the post office stepped in and halted this operation. As news about gullible buyers spread across the country, killer Blocks A and B were swiftly retired from the scene to be buried in the bottom of the closet, or hidden in the back of a kitchen drawer. After that, no one would admit to owning the killer blocks—least of all my mother—fearing to be labeled a P.T. Barnum sucker.

When I was growing up, the post office was an official arm of the government and a force to be reckoned with, as I found out at 11 years of age. I had mailed a letter to Ireland containing a money order for a course of mental exercises to stimulate the mind. The cost of this course was 18 dollars, an astronomical sum of money for a young boy to borrow from his mother in 1939.

Immediately after dropping my letter in one of the large, blue, corner mailboxes, waves of regret began to dampen my enthusiasm. I ran home and asked my mother to drive me to the main post office so I could plead for my letter's return. She agreed and drove me downtown to confront the powers that be. Once inside the hallowed postal halls, I gained an audience with the Postmaster himself.

Mother remained out in the hallway while I entered the inner sanctum. The Postmaster was sitting behind his desk in a substantial oak chair. From his size, I wondered if he ever left his office, except to feed. I took a deep breath and asked if I could please have my letter back, explaining I had made a terrible mistake by dropping it in the mailbox. He didn't blink. Stammering on, I said I would be very grateful if he could see his way clear to returning my letter. I anxiously awaited his reply, desperately wanting to get my money, or more accurately my mother's money, back into my hands.

However, then, as now, a few people with power loved to wield it for their own self-importance. Before the Postmaster even drew a breath to speak, I could see in his narrowing eyes that my letter was already sailing off to Ireland. The Postmaster's chair creaked ominously as he leaned his great bulk forward. To further impress me with his authority, he placed his carefully folded hands firmly on his desk. His chubby, sausage-like fingers barely fit within each other.

After a great clearing of his throat, the Postmaster spoke, "Now James, as soon as you put that letter in the mailbox, it became the property of the United States Post Office." He paused to be sure the importance of his words had sunk into my young brain. Clearing his throat again, he continued, "Son, you no longer have any legal right to that letter. I can only advise that you write to the recipient and ask that your letter be returned unopened, but this entire matter is out of my hands. *That*, young man, (a pause for further throat clearing) is the *law of the land.*"

But I was not prepared to give up my plans for its retrieval without a fight. Seeking to sway his rigid viewpoint, I told him exactly which mailbox my letter rested in, adding that my return address was clearly printed on it. My news was received like a tiny rock bouncing off an elephant, no penetration, no effect whatsoever. No matter how I argued my case, the Postmaster remained silent and unmoved.

Leaning further over his desk, the Postmaster readied himself to continue his lecture while his captive audience squirmed under his penetrating gaze. Unfolding his hands, he spread his pudgy fingers out on his desk. I groaned inwardly as he warmed to his subject. He declared the entire country would collapse and general lawlessness would follow if he bent the rules for me, or anyone else. Droning on and on about the legalities of letters residing within the confines of the United States Post Office, he crushed my every hope. I returned home defeated by my first encounter with bureaucracy.

In a final attempt to regain my 18 dollars, I wrote a threatening letter to the outfit in Ireland, demanding my money back. They responded by sending me a friendly note along with a small booklet containing the course. They requested that I commence the mental exercises described therein. If I was not happy within 30 days, they would cheerfully refund my money and I could keep the instruction booklet.

Convinced I would not be happy, I did the exercises faithfully for 30 days. At the end of that time, I wrote to thank the publishers, agreeing that the information they had sent was worth all the money in the world. And I have continued these exercises faithfully for more than 60 years. While I had the Postmaster fired many times and run out of town on a rail in childish fantasies, that inflexible man unknowingly helped me. If I meet him on the other side, I will have to thank him for sticking to the letter of the law.

———— •◆• ————

Although most of middle America was living out the depression in hard times, I remember my childhood as living in the best of times. People felt safe. Churches were full. All was well with our world. The surface of life was smooth and harmonious. God only knows what went on under that peaceful facade. There were rumors of social improprieties, but only rumors. The lives of movie stars living in our area were portrayed as innocent. There were no tabloids to reveal behind-the-scenes exploits. All were innocent. Everyone in town conformed to social conventions, which gave the illusion that nothing could ever happen to ripple the smooth pond of our little town.

On the outskirts of society were hobos, a familiar and unique lot. One wealthy woman in Santa Barbara opened her extensive property to hobos where they made camp in a "hobo jungle." At night, you could see dozens of small fires as they prepared their evening meals. Hobos lived there for years and I never heard of any violence. The upper crust of Santa Barbara was always putting the squeeze on the old girl to kick them out, but she never gave in.

Later in life, I knew a bank president who took a month off twice a year to become a hobo. He told me this program restored his sanity after all the chaos and confusion of the business world. He said that, if not for his family, he would love to be a full-time hobo and wander the country, much like RV people who roam the country in their motor homes. These snowbirds head for warm areas (like Yuma, Arizona and Truth or Consequences, New Mexico) in the winter months. As soon as it gets too hot to enjoy the desert, they head north to cooler climes. I've met some wonderful characters among these desert denizens. And why not? Older people have learned there's nothing to lose by being themselves.

I remember sitting at senior dances in campgrounds only to be grabbed up by some old gal and danced into the ground. There was one wild character living at Tecopa Hot Springs who dressed like a floozy. She played this role to the hilt every night, but during the day, she passed herself off as her "sister." As her sister, she dressed primly and was ever so proper . . . until the sun went down . . . then her other flamboyant self was back to having a gay old time.

Our own little town was filled with eccentrics who were simply accepted as a part of life in a small town back then. Among the curious characters were two old fellows who owned gas stations near the high school. Their claim to fame was their ongoing competition to sell the cheapest gas in town. But their favorite pastime was gawking at the high school girls who walked by their stations. The girls all knew the game and made a point of sashaying by the stations to flirt outrageously with those two old gents.

For reasons long forgotten, these old fellows were known locally as "Jungle Jim" and "Sleeping Jesus." Mention either name and people knew exactly whom you meant. Both names stuck like glue to those old gophers. I understood "Jungle Jim" since Jim was never seen without his pith helmet. We swore he wore it to bed since we never saw him without it, summer and winter. "Sleeping Jesus" was another matter. I asked around town, but no one knew the origins of this name. Apparently nicknames earned in our youth like "Benny-the-Arm" stick for a lifetime, Mafia style.

Before World War II, business bounced back and forth between Sleeping and Jungle with price being the deciding factor. But during WWII, when gas rationing was enforced, there was an unwritten loophole among the fellows I knew. If you could persuade a girl to go with you when you went for gas—and if she was willing to flirt with Jungle Jim— he frequently forgot to collect your gas stamp. However, Sleeping Jesus was an absolute stickler for making you turn in those precious stamps. It was no contest. If you could convince a girl to play the part, your business went straight to Jungle Jim.

———•◆•———

Once settled in Redlands, we transplanted Canadians were invited by Winnie's relatives to share in a classic slice of American life. From the time I was six until I was 15, we spent every Thanksgiving and Christmas, at Aunt Susan's house for the traditional holiday feast. Thirty people from the clan gathered around the table in celebration. Shirttail relatives filled in spaces between aunts, uncles and cousins. Guests brought their favorite foods and the table groaned from the sheer weight of it all.

As luck would have it, I was the only child at these gatherings. All too often, I had to suffer through comments from various relatives. Usually the words to my mother were, "James doesn't apply himself in school." On these occasions, Ross, Aunt Susan's son, an impeccably dressed, opinionated school teacher, always spoke up to denounce my scholastic endeavors and advise that I should be enrolled in a strict military school to bring my grades up to snuff. I was mortified. The fact he had never been in a military school was ignored. But luckily, before any dire decisions could be made about my future, I would be rescued by Aunt Susan announcing dinner.

Dear Aunt Susan was a hefty woman who appeared to enjoy her own cooking immensely, and Pa was her easygoing husband. As the official turkey carver, he claimed the head of the table where empty plates were carefully stacked high in front of him, waiting for turkey and all the trimmings. Pa interrogated each guest as to light or dark meat, and how much. We shouted our responses since Pa was deaf.

With many a pause to sharpen his big carving knife, Pa skillfully apportioned turkey to each plate. Next, he quizzed each person as to their choices among the other foods crowding our holiday table. Once brimming with food, the plate moved with agonizing slowness around the table, from person to person, finally arriving at its intended destination where it was gratefully received. By the time the entire table had been served, the food on our plates was barely warm. We longed to dig in, but we had to wait for another holiday ritual.

As the food continued to cool, we bowed our heads and waited for Pa to say grace. This was Pa's moment of glory. Unfortunately, grace became lengthier with each passing holiday. He solemnly droned on and on, asking the Creator's mercy on all humanity. But there was no mercy for his captive audience as the food on our plates grew steadily colder. An eternity passed while our heads remained bowed in submission to his oratory. No one dared lift a fork until Pa uttered his final words: "Amen. Let us commence."

After putting up with Pa's sermonizing for several years, my mother did the unthinkable. Halfway through Pa's sermon, she banged the table authoritatively with her dinner fork. I felt like crawling under the table when her formidable, commanding voice rang out, "For God's sake man! The food's stone cold! Let's eat!"

Mid-oration, a shocked Pa sat down . . . hard. His mouth was still open and moving, but no more words came forth, much to the relief of his starving guests. On every holiday following Mother's outburst, the reformed Pa meekly offered a very short prayer of thanks while keeping an ever watchful eye on my mother. If she even shifted in her chair, he began stammering and quickly ended his prayer.

As the meal progressed, food was stuffed down at an alarming rate until we could scarcely move. And I was the first to ask for seconds, and then thirds. No sooner had we finished dinner, when a parade of desserts began: pies of pumpkin, mince, lemon meringue, and coconut cream; hard sauce; plum pudding; and other delicacies.

With the last bite of dessert, everyone sat back and began to talk. The focus turned to everything that adults prefer to talk about: who died, who had tuberculosis (in those days it was tuberculosis, now it would be cancer), who had gotten married and such. We never heard the word "divorce" back then. The unhappy couple simply stuck it out, like a prolonged jail sentence.

Slowly digestion claimed the body's full attention, and conversation faded away. We simply couldn't stay awake. Pa claimed his favorite chair and was asleep in seconds. Head back, mouth open, Pa's lovely snore echoed throughout the house. Guests took possession of beds and couches, others settled down with pillows on the living room floor. Being stuffed ourselves, we didn't even feel the floor beneath us, and Morpheus descended swiftly. Dead to the world, a robber could have come in and taken everything. No one would have been the wiser.

A few hours later, we awoke . . . famished! No other word could cover the gnawing emptiness we felt upon awakening. Our stomachs were still packed with food, but we reunited once more at the table. We gallantly repeated our former efforts with enough gusto to supply fuel to the body for the years ahead. Groggy, but too embarrassed to sleep again, the adults discussed family matters and shared stories from the past.

At dusk, we were given more food to take home in containers. Like everyone else, I *swore* I would never eat again. However, the next day found us hungry once more. Later in physiology classes, I learned that when so much food is dumped into the stomach, it's too much for the liver to handle. The overload brings digestion to a halt. Since nothing is digested, cells receive no nourishment. The result is that you soon feel as though you are starving and need to eat.

Now our hostess was clearly *not* starving. Aunt Susan was a very large woman, but—to the family's constant amazement—she ate almost nothing. My mother was forever trying to convince her to eat larger portions. Since Mother baked the pies, she also cut and served them. When it was Aunt Susan's turn to receive a slice, Susan would put up her hand, and motion to my mother to stop. Susan would insist on a much smaller piece, cautioning my mother, "No, no, Winn. Less than that. Doctor's orders, Winn." Mother would fume and sputter, insisting that Susan would starve herself to death. Since Aunt Susan weighed well over 250 pounds and shook the floor when she walked, her demise from starvation appeared exceedingly unlikely to me.

However, I learned her secret one Christmas when I was extremely thirsty after dinner. I decided to get a drink of water even though I knew the kitchen was strictly out of bounds to all but Aunt Susan. She, and she alone, went in and out the swinging door between her kitchen and the dining room. And she guarded her domain like a rabid Rottweiler. Still, I thought I could sneak in unseen for a drink of water before dessert.

As I was getting a drink from the kitchen tap, I suddenly felt Aunt Susan's thunderous, floor-shaking tread heading my way. I panicked and quickly hid in the generous gap behind her large refrigerator. Luckily, even with a bulging stomach, I was thin. It was a tight squeeze, but well worth the effort since I couldn't imagine what penalty would be exacted for trespassing in the forbidden kitchen. In came Aunt Susan, carrying plates from the table with leftovers of turkey, gravy, mashed potato, and goodies galore. I heard the clatter of plates being settled carefully near the kitchen sink.

Peering from behind the refrigerator, I saw Aunt Susan creep stealthily over to the swinging door. She cautiously pushed the door open slightly to peek into the dining room. Once satisfied that her guests were still settled around the table, she went over to the kitchen sink. Hurriedly,

I flattened myself against the wall, not daring to breathe. Soon I heard munching, slurping, and little moans of pleasure.

I peered out from my hiding place. Stunned, I saw Aunt Susan—she of the small hummingbird appetite—gorging on leftovers. Using her bare hands, she shoveled food directly off the plates and into her mouth. Once she had cleaned all the plates in this manner, she meticulously washed her hands, face and chin to remove any telltale signs of her "meal." Then she resumed her hostess duties by picking up two pies, pushing through the swinging door, and calling out, "Is anyone ready for dessert?"

Like a cat burglar trapped in the act when the homeowner returns, I slipped quietly out the back door. I crept around the house and entered through the front door. I managed to slip back into my chair just in time to watch the now familiar comedy. My mother told Susan she would become skin and bones if she didn't take a larger portion of pie. And Aunt Susan, bless her heart, went into her usual routine, "No, no! Smaller please! Doctor's orders, Winn, doctor's orders!" Recalling the recent kitchen scene, I bit my lip. But the old girl lived into her 90s, outliving most of the others around that table. I can only think genetics had a great deal to do with her survival.

When I was 11 years old, a distant shirttail relative, Mary, came to share our Thanksgiving feast. I noticed Mary did not partake of the stuffing—a personal favorite—or gravy, or any of the wonderful, rich goodies I loved. She took some turkey, veggies, and salad. After the meal, when everyone else headed for their naps, Mary went into the kitchen to wash the dishes, with Aunt Susan's permission of course. I was surprised at her ambition, and she was surprised when I stuck my head into the kitchen to ask if I could help. She readily agreed and I gained entrance into the hallowed kitchen.

After the dishes were washed and put away, she and I took a long walk together through the orange groves. It was one of those beautiful days we always had in the 1940s—blue sky, warm sun, clean air, and not a car on the road. Everything came to a halt on holidays. Businesses closed and folks stayed home to share Thanksgiving dinner with their families. As we walked, we talked about life, food, and how she came to eat so sensibly.

When we returned to the house, much to my surprise, I didn't feel hungry or sleepy. The rest of the family—sleeping off their meal—looked like enormous, basking seals lying all over the house. After the family slowly roused from their naps, they gathered at the table for dessert. Mary and I settled for a slice of pumpkin pie and some tea. She smiled at me, the single sharer of her dining secret.

That night, I slept better, and the next day I was filled with energy, which irritated my mother who was still groggy, feeling the effects of her holiday meal. Later, I walked into town to let Mother take another nap. Everyone I saw looked like they were suffering from H.G.S., Holiday Gorge Syndrome. I was pleased to feel so fit and full of energy . . . thanks to Mary.

A few years later Mary headed for other climes, but she left me with her common sense outlook on healthy eating. I tell patients they cannot fill their car with bricks until the tires threaten to burst and expect a comfortable ride down the road. It's better for the body to cruise along like an empty car, getting good mileage and not needing repairs. And can you guess when the greatest number of strokes and heart attacks occur? If you answered "right after huge holiday meals," then you were correct.

Our body's warehouse can be so filled with goods that the hard-working employees—stomach, liver, gallbladder, intestines, bowel—waiting to sort, file, and break down incoming supplies are overwhelmed. When food supplies clog the warehouse—overloading the aisles and shelves—the delivery system comes to a halt. No wonder belt sizes have increased since WW II. If we could shed pounds as quickly as we spend money, we would all be thin. I've seen patients near death from eating every possible holiday food combination in amounts that would make Henry the Eighth blush. They wonder why they don't feel well, and yet they don't make the connection.

———•◆•———

Even as a young child, I asked questions, usually ones my friends and family didn't want to answer, or even discuss. I wanted to know: Who are we? Where do we come from? What are we doing here? What will happen after we leave this earth plane? What final destiny is in store for us? Why was I attracted to some people, but disliked others as soon as I met them? What were the energy bubbles that I felt and saw around people? Why were some people so disturbing that I had to avoid them, even if others liked them? Questions like these consumed my waking thoughts.

In grammar school, I was shocked to see how disloyal people could be in their affections for one another. I could hear their thoughts and feel their emotions; they said one thing, but their energy bubble expressed something completely different. Since I didn't know any other way of being, I thought all children had the same abilities that I had. I was disappointed to discover no one knew what I was talking about when I spoke of the energies I saw and felt.

A childhood of always being "right" through intuition made it difficult to fit in with my peers or to have many friends. In short, I became a loner when I discovered that what others thought and what they said and did were two different things. Although professing true-to-the-ends-of-time friendship, my friends could change sides in seconds. Their word meant nothing. Now, I know they meant what they said at the time, but it disturbed me that friendship could be so easily betrayed. When I saw the inner motives of my school chums, I knew it would be a long time before I understood the intricacies of getting along in the world.

Once I saw how often my fellow students lied in grammar school, I too learned to pass as a member of this club when needed. Lying was like a true art form. My chums and I learned to tell whoppers with such a perfectly straight face that we appeared completely innocent to adults. However, other kids could see through the charade and were usually eager to give the game away.

Finally, I realized that I could only trust myself and my inner knowing, my intuition. So I retreated inside myself, into the Silence. I kept mostly to myself, except for becoming the class clown. Everyone knew who I was from my antics so whenever there was trouble, all eyes turned toward me. Unfortunately, I was blamed on *every* occasion, not that I didn't deserve it at times.

In spite of my mischievous nature, three angelic beings appeared to me when I was seven. No earthly words were needed. Our communication was heart-to-heart. Their radiant beauty filled my room with shimmering rainbow light. They had come to remind me that I had returned to earth for a divine purpose. My heart opened to merge with their eternal essence . . . Love. Time and life's every limitation dissolved.

I was aware of nothing but their power and glory. For the first time, I was shown my contract to heal and teach, chosen before birth.

When at last the Power spoke, they asked, *"How much do you want to receive in this lifetime of healing and teaching?"*

With all the conviction of a child, I boldly declared, "Everything."

"Unwise, Dear Child. The lessons of many lifetimes would be focused into this one lifetime. Think . . . and choose again."

Deep within, I felt a great wave of certainty about my destiny. I felt compelled to say again, "Everything."

"So be it," the angels replied.

Then the presence of the Power enfolded me. I was embraced by a love far beyond any earthly love I had ever known. Everything about these angelic beings was completely familiar. I recognized their loving, unseen presence had always been with me, in every moment of this life, and before this life began. I knew I would be with them forever, far beyond this present life. When they withdrew, promising to return, I longed to stay in my room and hold fast to my experience. But far too soon what we think of as reality intruded with my mother's call to dinner. And this angelic visitation became a cherished memory.

———— •◆• ————

As my seventh year continued, the angelic reminder of my contract to heal faded. Consumed by the need to be like all the other kids, I wanted a "normal" life, and pursued this goal until my knowing and seeing retreated into the background. Then, without warning, my world fell apart. The school principal came into my classroom and sent me home. There I learned my beloved father Bob had died of a heart attack at 40. I was numb. I couldn't believe it. Grief was beyond me. I felt empty and abandoned. In one awful moment, all my security was gone.

Days turned into weeks and my mother's wailing could still be heard all over the neighborhood. I dreaded that my friends would find out my mother was the source of this continuing uproar. On the inner planes, I knew Dad was still around us. He had crossed over, but he was still in contact. I could talk to him whenever I needed to make sense of all that was happening in my world. But in my outer world, his death was the final betrayal. I became angry with life itself, and my anger began to eat away at me.

My anger intensified when I tried to share my intuitive gifts. You might think knowing the future would be fun, but I had no idea how to use this information to help others, or make friends. My efforts backfired. People were frightened when I told them about future events; they shied away from me. More and more, I stayed in my own company.

During this dark period in my life, school was very difficult for me. One of my worst days came in second grade. Our teacher, Miss Simpson, had us line up with our backs against the blackboard, which covered the top half of one wall. With my hands behind my back, I found a tiny piece of chalk resting on the bottom ledge of the board. I could hardly believe my luck. Using my find, I drew the tiniest of lines, barely a quarter of an inch long, on the freshly washed blackboard behind me.

After taking attendance, we returned to our assigned seats. Sharp-eyed Miss Simpson looked with horror at the tiny mark on her once pristine blackboard. She quickly insisted we line up again against the blackboard in our same positions. She was clearly ready to identify the culprit who had dared to vandalize her blackboard.

Terrified, I tried to find another place in the student lineup. However, my unfeeling classmates continued to shove me in front of the condemning mark. There was no escape. I was trapped. I looked up to see Miss Simpson towering over me, her eyes filled with accusation. In the sweetest voice, she said, "Jimmie MacKimmie, I know you are too good a boy to have made that mark."

Oh, how I longed to disappear from Miss Simpson's penetrating gaze. I couldn't bear to return the stares of my classmates, which branded me a criminal of the worst sort. Miss Simpson continued piling guilt upon guilt in her shame-inspiring voice, "Jimmie MacKimmie, I know that you would never, *ever* make such a mark. You would never *think* of damaging school property. You come from too fine a family to stoop to doing something like this." "Mea culpa!" should have been my cry, but I was a mere amateur in the game of life, and Miss Simpson was a professional.

Suddenly, the bell rang, signaling the end of class. I slunk out of the classroom like the low life I had become in the eyes of my teacher and classmates. Compared to the events of today, it was really nothing.

No doubt today, I would return to shoot the blackboard full of holes, but back then such vandalism was unknown. That load of guilt kept me in line for *years*. Each time I would even think of doing something wrong, Miss Simpson's thin, accusing face would appear in front of me delivering remarks—in dulcet tones—about my goodness.

Who knows? Miss Simpson may have saved me from a life of crime. I might have become a habitual chalk thief, or a serial blackboard vandalizer. One never knows how far all this might have gone, had I not reformed, thanks to her steely gaze and soft voice. "Next time, Miss Simpson," says Karma, *"You* will do the chalking and *Jimmie* will be the teacher." How wonderful it is to dismiss the terrors of childhood with humor, looking back through adult eyes and seeing the truth of those early experiences.

Another grammar school teacher—whose name I have thankfully forgotten—also left her mark. She was trying to explain the mysteries of fractions. When she alluded to a "pie" being divided into sections—as neatly drawn on the blackboard—I was completely in the dark. It didn't make any sense to me at all. Besides, if a complete pie was 100 percent, why did she start talking about a pie that was 150 percent? She stopped and asked if anyone didn't understand the lesson. Anxious to find out what the drawing had to do with fractions, my hand shot up. But my hand was the *only* hand in the air. She glared at me with irritation, "Are you *stupid*, James? Are you an *idiot?* Didn't they teach you *anything* in Canada?"

After this encounter, I never raised my hand again. After class, I discovered none of my classmates had a clue about the baffling fractional pie. I was shocked. Why hadn't they raised their hands? I saw it was strictly get along, go along. Pretend you know, and keep your mouth shut. I wonder how many silent students are terrified because they simply don't know what's going on in class? You must *always* know, or at least *appear* to know.

Later, in college, one of my fellow students was an older man who always came to class impeccably attired. When the professor asked him a question, he simply ignored him and said nothing. The entire class thought he must be a genius who simply wouldn't lower himself to answer. The professors must have thought the same since they never challenged his silence. However, one day he arrived in class obviously inebriated. When he responded to a question, his ridiculous answer revealed he knew absolutely nothing about what we had been studying. We lost a well-dressed student shortly thereafter. But what a lesson. Silence is not only golden, it raises your IQ!

But back to Kingsbury Elementary School . . . Miss Pillsbury, the Principal, was a monster in our eyes. Towering over us, she was a huge ogre with long, sharp fingernails that dug into your flesh when she grabbed you for any act that roused her suspicion. We were all terrified of her. Years later, I saw her on the street and stopped to introduce myself. She was actually a petite, plump woman with a generous bosom and a gentle face. I thanked her for being tough on us. Retired for many years, she appreciated my words since—typical of that era—she had dedicated her whole life to teaching. I told her I was in my first year of practice. She was pleased to learn I had continued my education because she said I had been a real handful in grammar school.

———·◆·———

The summer following Dad's death, Redlands was—as usual—boiling hot. To escape the inland heat, Mother rented a small apartment in Long Beach, California where we welcomed the cool, ocean breezes. Half a block away from our apartment was beautiful Bixby Park with swings, and a small merry-go-round propelled by the riders' feet. But what drew my interest was a beautiful croquette court where a group of old men gathered to play every day. I loved to watch. It was deadly serious as to who played the best game each day. Each player had his own special mallet. Gentlemen, not currently engaged in play, sat on green wooden benches at one side of the court. At the end of the game, all the mallets were secured in a locked metal bin on the other side of the court.

The game and the seriousness with which these old gentlemen played were fascinating to me. After a week, I got up my courage and moved closer to the field of play. I sat tentatively on the equipment bin and leaned back against one of the two huge pine trees growing next to the bin. It was a wonderful, shady spot for viewing the game. The moment I sat on the bin, all play stopped while the gentlemen assessed my presence. Sitting very still, my eyes downcast, I didn't make a sound. After a lengthy pause, they resumed their game.

One morning, one of the players did not show up. Invited to take his place, I was thrilled. I had been sitting on the equipment bin for weeks, studying closely how the game was played. They handed me the absent player's mallet, a marvel of woodwork and inlaid metal. They informed me that I had better not damage the mallet, or ruin their sand court, which was perfectly maintained by the players. After that day, I was allowed to play with them. Although the players talked among themselves, I remained silent. My silence assured them that I was a worthy fellow player at eight years of age.

Croquette proved to be a perfect game for me. I was proud to be accepted as a team member and pleased to find I was as good, or better than they were. Every morning, I gulped down breakfast and raced over to the park. Arriving first at the court, I would pick up pine needles and carefully groom the area of play with a fine rake. The other players gradually arrived on the scene, but they never commented on the efforts of their new groundskeeper. Once the teams had assembled, the ceremony of opening up the bin and handing out the equipment followed.

Overjoyed to be an honorary member of the team, I didn't miss a single day until the last week of our summer vacation. That morning I hurried through breakfast as usual, eager to head for the park. But to my surprise, I couldn't leave the apartment. Some great force held me prisoner in the kitchen for two hours. Mother warned that my friends might not let me play again if I arrived late. Not wanting to end my croquette career, I struggled against this force, but to no avail. When the force finally released me, I raced to the park, praying I wouldn't be kicked off the team.

When I arrived, I saw the park superintendent standing near the court. As soon as he spotted me, he called me over. He pointed out where, an hour ago, lightning had struck the tree I sat against when it was not my turn. My faithful back support had split in two, from top to bottom. Then I saw some of the wickets on the court had melted. The superintendent told me two of the old gentlemen had been killed by the lightning. I was in shock. The old men had become my friends over the summer. The shock of this event stayed with me for years, but I never spoke to anyone about the force that held me captive that summer morning. Later in life, I realized the Power had been watching over me, keeping me safe from harm.

My summer vacation also meant a reprieve from attending church.

However, once back in school, I was forced to attend my mother's church again. It was agony for an eight-year-old boy to listen to dry, boring sermons. I don't know if my posterior has ever fully recovered from those hours spent sitting on hard, unforgiving wooden pews.

When winter arrived, I devised a brilliant plan to speed the torturous sermon along. On Sunday, shortly after sunrise, I entered the church. At that time churches were unlocked 24 hours a day, every day. No one would have ever thought of taking anything from a church. However, I wasn't planning on taking anything. No, since it's better to give than to receive, I was bringing a donation, a dead, very ripe possum. I carefully pried open the heating vent register in the floor, gently deposited the deceased down the vent shaft, and departed.

The day was still wonderfully chilly when Mother and I arrived for morning service. I heard our minister instruct the janitor to turn on the heat. At the first opportunity, I headed out to find a choice spot on a lawn across from the church where I could watch the proceedings. It wasn't long before the congregation came rushing out with a vigor and haste I had never seen before.

Unfortunately, I knew the possum gambit was a one-time deal. Once again I was trapped and forced to listen to long, tiresome sermons. George Burns said, "The secret of a good sermon is to have a good beginning and a good ending; and to have the two as close together as possible." But our minister enjoyed the sound of his own voice and the longer, the better, for his trapped congregation.

To make matters worse, our balding, corpulent minister presented an angry God—definitely the Old Testament version—seated on His golden throne ready to hurl thunderbolts down upon us for our sins. The minister's frightening portrayal was enthusiastically carried on in Sunday school. I concluded that God was far too terrifying to meet in church or anywhere else. I decided to go it alone.

On Sundays, I sat in the very back row, far behind the faithful and close to the back door. Shortly, I would vanish into the outer world. When I saw my mother exit after the church service, it was my cue to flash back and blend with the congregation, as if I'd been there all along.

Once in the outer world, I went to a nearby park where I discovered an entertaining group of old men who had immigrated to America.

Telling wonderful stories in fascinating accents, they gathered every Sunday for lively conversations about life in "the old country." I wondered where this magical place was, but dared not ask my mother, lest my game be found out.

Keeping an ever watchful eye on the church door after making good my escape, I would edge closer to listen to the old men. However, they were wary and stopped talking as soon as I sat down near them. I pretended to fall asleep. Shortly, they began talking again as if I wasn't there. Once used to the child-sleeper, they continued talking even when I opened my eyes to check on the church door. If they glanced in my direction, I feigned interest in the park's pigeons.

Every Sunday, I happily and quietly enjoyed their company. After months of silence, the old men of the park bench assembly were surprised when I finally spoke, asking them what life was all about. From then on, they freely shared their hard-earned knowledge with their attentive listener. Their collective wisdom poured into my inquisitive mind. "Never complain, never explain, never blame." "Accept everything in your life as your own creation." "Life is short, enjoy each day to the fullest." "Treat others as you would like to be treated." These seeds of wisdom, planted so early in my life, bore fruit years later when I was old enough to recognize the truth of their words.

From these fine old gentlemen, I also learned the value of observation without judgment. From what I could gather, judging others always backfired in some mysterious way upon the person who did the judging. My new friends said to look for the good in others, but to watch out for people who were dishonest. They advised me to take my time in making new friends. How well they taught me, but I was too young to follow their sage advice until later in life.

———·◆·———

Before the year ended, my mother was admitted to the hospital. Everyone knew that she was dying. I spent long hours sitting by her bedside, feeling helpless and alone. What would happen to me after her death? Late one afternoon, the minister came to visit her. (This was the same minister whose depiction of God compelled me to seek refuge in the park.) I was displeased when I saw his pudgy, florid face peer into her room, and even more displeased when he entered. Without even a nod in my direction, he approached her bedside. When she turned her head to look at him, he asked, "Now you know, Mrs. MacKimmie, that you don't have long to live. What's going to become of James when you die?"

Mother's eyes filled with tears, but she was too weak to answer. Glancing at his watch, the minister then turned to me, "James, will you accept Jesus Christ as your Lord and Savior?" Under the circumstances, I wasn't up to accepting anything. The minister kept checking his watch. With each passing moment, his face got redder. (Hospitals had no air conditioning at that time.)

Barely concealing his annoyance, he said, "All right, little man, you have five minutes to make up your mind, or burn in Hell for all eternity." Hell didn't bother me as much as his overbearing manner did. After several more precious minutes passed, during which I studied the floor, I finally managed to say, "I don't know."

Sweating profusely, his face flushed crimson, the minister tapped his watch and decreed, "Son, if you don't know now, it's perfectly clear to me that you *will* burn in Hell forever!"

The minister started to leave the room, but abruptly stopped in the doorway. He turned toward my mother, presumably to offer some parting words of comfort, and said, "I'm sure, Mrs. MacKimmie, you've made provisions in your will to continue your yearly pledge to the church after you're gone. If you haven't, be sure your lawyer takes care of this for you before it's too late." Mother was too sick to reply. However, soon after his departure, she became so enraged by his statements that I think she got well just to spite him.

Back home again, Mother declared that church attendance was a thing of the past. What a joy it was for a young boy to know he would never again have to dress up in a wool suit that prickled, a tie that choked, and shoes that refused to bend when walking. Instead, I could wear my well-washed jeans, a shirt, and comfortable tennis shoes. Even better, I had permission to go out adventuring on Sunday. Free at last!

3

DESERT SOLITUDE

———•◆••◆•———

Characteristically, my mother was firmly in control of the situation as she drove with infuriating slowness over a dirt road ridged with brick-hard, washboard ruts. It was Easter vacation and I was nine when my mother, a friend of hers named Nina, and I drove into the Mojave desert. We planned to spend a week at an old homestead, which belonged to friends

As we rattled along, I thought the car would shake apart. Nina pleaded, "Please! Winnie! We're being shaken to death by the ruts. If you would just drive faster . . . say 60 miles an hour . . . the car would ride on the ridge tops. We'd get there sooner . . . without being shaken to death!"

But Nina's pleas fell on deaf ears. No one could tell my mother anything. She continued to poke along, jarring us by apparently targeting every rut she could find. I started nagging her—as only an impatient nine-year-old can—to drive faster.

Finally my nagging paid off, and Mother picked up the pace. Sure enough, we had a smooth ride and our teeth stopped rattling. In her haughtiest manner—which always came into play when proved wrong—Mother informed us, "I just don't know *what* you two were *thinking!* It's *obvious* that driving faster makes the ride more comfortable. You should have asked me to drive faster in the first place." Nina looked at me and raised her eyebrows in disbelief.

Late in the afternoon, we pulled into a parched, dusty yard in front of a decrepit old shack of a house. We went inside the house to investigate our new home. The few homesteads scattered in the Mojave were always unlocked, but nothing was ever taken. Even the burial grounds in the nearby hills, where Indians had been buried sitting up to face the rising sun, had not yet been disturbed.

The interior wasn't in much better condition than the outside, although a proud hand-pump at the kitchen sink boasted the only water for miles around. For years no one ever suspected the bone-dry Mojave had a high water table hidden just beneath the sands. I think the Indians may have known this desert secret, but said nothing, thus protecting their precious water supply from Los Angeles predators for many years.

The living room with its sparse, dusty furniture had a massive rock fireplace. Near the fireplace was an inviting bookshelf filled with mysterious offerings. I desperately wanted to investigate this collection since the desert was a boring place in my estimation. Mother saw my gaze and said, "There will be *no* reading unless it's daylight. There's no electricity. You'll ruin your eyes if you read by a kerosene lamp."

Anxious to settle in, we began unloading the car and moving things into the house. After we locked up our food to keep pack rats from claiming a share, our focus turned to preparing an afternoon feast to celebrate our safe arrival. My job, as carefully instructed, was to take two huge, ripe watermelons out back and put them in the shade to cool while my mother swept the floors and Nina dusted the furniture.

An hour later, I was sent to bring the now cool melons in for our feast. However, instead of finding two beautiful, juicy watermelons, I witnessed dozens of jackrabbits exploding away from scattered melon remains. In the blink of an eye, they disappeared into the vast emptiness of the desert, leaving behind only a few chunks of rind on the sand. I took the rinds inside and explained what had happened. Nina said it was her fault since she had forgotten the desert's voracious jackrabbits.

My thoughts immediately went to my dream .22 rifle, which I wanted in the worst way. Here, at the price of a watermelon, was prey to dispatch. However, Mother had become an expert at dangling my dream rifle in front of me like a carrot on a stick. She told me I could have one if I would get good grades, mind my manners, eat lima beans, and generally engage in all kinds of hated activities. At the other end of this bargain was my rifle. Mother never had to make good on her promise because I never held out long enough in the role of a perfect son. As Mark Twain said, "I have been on the verge of being an angel all my life, but it's never happened yet."

I contemplated my sling shot—the only weapon I possessed—but I knew such a weapon would be a joke to those long-eared, watermelon-eating rodents who seemed to be the only other life in the desert. I didn't count the pack rats who came alive at night, scurrying everywhere until I turned on my flashlight. In the beam of my light, they froze in position. Dozens of beady, black eyes stared back into mine. Light off, the scurrying began again and continued all night.

The next morning to take my mind off jackrabbit hunting, I headed for the fireplace bookshelf where I discovered a Tarzan book by Edgar Rice Burroughs. Holy cow! Gold for the taking! In minutes, I *was* Tarzan, subduing lions and all manner of wild life. My world became the jungle. Tarzan and the great apes lived again in southern California, now making their home in giant pepper trees.

But one thing has puzzled me all these years—Tarzan's "mile-eating lope." The author tells us Tarzan kept his focus on another plane of existence until his mile-eating lope carried him to his destination. I tried to master Tarzan's lope for years. No doubt Tarzan reached the runner's high, but those particular endorphins eluded me.

How Tarzan swung from tree to tree was also a mystery. Who placed vines in position ready for his swing? I always asked that question. Other kids took it for granted, the vines were there. Scampering through tree tops, Tarzan also managed to snare natives from the ground by using a rope noose. Then he pulled them up with such incredible speed that the natives thought he was a god. Using this tactic, he equipped himself with bows and arrows made by the natives. I wondered how could he pull people up with a rope—no matter how fast—without the natives seeing it and realizing he wasn't so godlike after all?

But I had a plan. I would find out how all this was done when I moved to the jungle. Without a doubt, I would live either in the jungle like Tarzan, or on the plains with the American Indians when I finished school. Such is the career planning of a nine-year-old. Imagine my shock when I found out the Wild West was no more, and that Africans lived without benefit of Tarzan. After I learned the awful truth, I was bereft for weeks. Still, those books passed my time on the desert.

In the passing years, I learned to love the desert's solitude. Every Sunday, from early morning until dusk, I walked in the dry, rolling hills far from home. Covered with sage and cactus, they stretched for hundreds of miles. There was not a drop of surface water to be found. At that time, no one thought to drill for water. Dry meant dry . . . no water . . . period . . . end of story.

My dog, Prince, ran free by my side and together we roamed those hills on and on with nary another soul to disturb the silence. If someone came within a mile of us, I would feel that presence as a disturbance in the web of energy that connected me to all things. Pulling the energy web back within me, I waited until the stranger had gone. Then I would send the energy web back out into the universe.

Alone in the desert solitude, I could breathe in its loving energy and feel its living force move through my body while I walked, pondering life's meaning. I discovered the silent, beautiful gifts the noble desert offers to those who seek her treasures, incredible secrets that escape the casual observer. I was alone, but never lonely while I communed with universal energies. Angelic beings walked beside me as dear friends. We traveled together through the hills, as we did at night in other worlds beyond time.

There is something grand in such solitude. Later in life, I read that Einstein said he loved his own company and craved solitude, even from his close family and loved ones. He said these feelings increased as he got older. I heartily agree. We all need alone time and silence to feed our souls. Both are more difficult to find in our busy lives today, but worth the search. As Thoreau wrote, "I love to be alone. I never found the companion that was so companionable as solitude."

———— • ◆ • ————

Reveling in my desert freedom, I'm sure I was a handful for Winnie to raise alone. Mother was strict, but she also had a heart of purest gold. God bless her. With her soft heart, she was never cut out to be a landlady. However, after Father died, she rented out a house they owned downtown. Every month when we stopped by to collect the rent, the window screens were ruined. They were ripped open from top to bottom as though slashed by a sword, and torn wide open as though some great beast had crashed through them.

Each month, my mother would ask her tenant what had happened. The dismayed woman always declared the ruined screens were a complete mystery to her. When she asked her ten-year-old son if he could shed some light on the mystery, he invariably looked down and shook his head. The woman dutifully paid the rent and we left.

Window screens were replaced every month for two years until one day the mystery was solved. As we approached the front door to collect the rent, we saw to our amazement that the recently replaced screens were still intact. Mother raised her hand to ring the door bell. At that very instant, the front window closest to us was thrown open with a loud bang.

Horrified, we watched a huge butcher knife stab through the top of the new screen and slash wildly from top to bottom. This alarming event was followed by the ten-year-old son bursting through the screen wearing a towel over his shoulders, which flowed and flapped behind him like a cape. As his feet hit the front porch a foot from where we stood, he gave a piercing scream and took off running around the corner of the house without ever seeing us.

Before we could react, his mother's head poked through the gaping hole of the destroyed screen. Not noticing her front porch visitors, she yelled after her son at top volume, "Georgie! You'd better not do this at our *new* house. This is a *rental*. *They* pay for screens. When we move this weekend, that's *it!* Get your screen cutting in *now!* I'm not going to let you ruin the screens at *our* house."

This event lives in my memory as one of the few times I ever saw my mother speechless. When our renter turned her head, she came face-to-face with my mother. Shock washed over the woman's face. She pulled her head back through the hole and slammed the window shut. When our tenant opened the front door, she was smiling innocently. She said she was only joking with her son. She handed my mother the rent, and we left.

No notice was given of their intention to move, but the renters vanished that very weekend, leaving the house in wreckage. Mother and I spent the next week cleaning and repairing the house for new tenants. The screen rippers took everything not nailed down, including doorknobs, rugs, and light bulbs. When the woman was finally found, she claimed someone else must have broken into the house and done the damage.

Renters in our area sought my mother out like sharks to blood. When the rent was due, they offered her a heart-rending sob story rather than money. Time after time, tenants literally destroyed her property. We were left to glue things back together after they moved out. After seeing my mother's experiences, I vowed never to have rentals, unless made of concrete and steel with tenants cleared by the FBI. I'm sure Mother would agree with me if she were alive.

———·◆·———

After spending time alone in the desert, I found more peace in school. I understood the need to be silent about what was shown to me on the inner planes. This new understanding prepared me for my next significant spiritual experience. Until this event, I admit I had no fond feelings for God. I blamed Him for the loss of my father, the unbearable hours in church, in fact everything suffered since birth. Whenever I thought about God, the terrifying image painted by the minister reappeared in my mind. And then it happened . . .

When I was 13, the three, glorious, angelic beings of light returned, and the Power enfolded me in the love that has no beginning and no end, the love that is limitless and forever. Their radiance swept through me, dissolving all my hurts and concerns. Taken to another dimension, I received their guidance and was shown the truth of our existence. Again, I was presented with my destiny as a healer and asked to acknowledge my contract. I accepted without hesitation. All at once, I was lifted to the higher planes of existence where the Creator's Light flowed through me in waves of pure, unconditional love and bliss. In one holy instant, I went from doubting His concern for us, to becoming a complete believer in His Infinite Love.

Soon after this experience, the Power stepped in once again to save my life. In junior high school, all the boys raced to a nearby creek bed every afternoon. There we fought for the privilege of being the first to swing from a thick, heavy rope, which was tied securely to a branch high in a giant oak tree that leaned over the creek bed. The lucky victor carried the coveted rope up into another nearby oak tree where he launched from a spot high on its trunk.

It was grand. We soared through the air in fine, Tarzan-like style. Swinging back and forth in great sweeping arcs above the creek bed, we whooped and howled. The creek bed under our makeshift swing was bone-dry with rocks the size of bowling balls, which would have killed us if we had fallen. But we never thought of dying. It was all too much fun. Indeed, youth and death dance a lively dance together when we are young, foolish, and immortal.

One afternoon, I got out of school early and hurried to the creek. I was eager to beat the other boys and have the rope all to myself for a few magnificent swings. In a flash of youthful enthusiasm, I carried the stout rope up the nearby launching tree. Firmly grasping the rope to begin my flight, I was startled when Something grabbed me and pulled me back. (I didn't know then it was the Power, but I instantly recognized the same force that had held me captive in Long Beach years before.) The Something would not let me go! The hair on the back of my neck stood up. I tried to push past my fear. Over and over I tried to hurl myself into the air. But I was unable to overcome the force that held me captive.

Once school was out, the other boys rushed to the creek. Arriving on the scene, they were disappointed to see me already in place since it was a mark of honor to be first. I summoned all my determination and attempted to swing out once more over the creek bed. However, I just couldn't shake the Something, which held me securely in its grasp. Admitting defeat, I climbed down to the jeers and catcalls of my friends below.

Back on terra firma, I was ready to hand the rope over to the next adventurer when the Something told me to pull on the rope. I tugged gently. The weight of the rope—all 25 feet of it—came crashing down, knocking me to the ground. We all gasped when we saw the end of the rope was frayed so badly that it looked like a horse's tail.

My friends were in shock. The oak's rough surface had slowly worn the rope, until at last—with my gentle pull—it ended its career. The boys patted me on the back and congratulated me on my good luck in not taking my turn. But I knew I had received higher help in not making that swing, which would have been my last. I often think of how close I came to ending my life that day, and thank God for this angelic intervention.

———•◆•———

After the school year ended, I took up bowling. One night at the bowling alley, I was observing other players when one of the bowlers, a man of 30, collapsed. A medical doctor, who happened to be bowling that night, stepped forward from the crowd of onlookers. He laid the man on his back. The man's eyes glazed over. He was no longer breathing. It was clear that he had died.

The doctor ordered everyone away, and the other bowlers reluctantly returned to their games. I remained quietly watching the doctor. He bent over the man and swiftly adjusted his neck. When he saw I was watching, he said, "Watch his eyes." I did. The man's eyelids fluttered. Then he took a deep breath, blinked his eyes open, and said, "What happened? I must have passed out. Help me up. It's my turn to bowl."

The doctor ordered the man not to move and asked him for his phone number. Next, he asked me to phone the man's wife and have her hurry to the bowling alley. When she arrived, the doctor told her that her husband was dying. He explained that her husband's death had been delayed by adjusting his neck, but that he would die within half an hour. The physician told her to write down everything her husband could remember about his business affairs. She was writing furiously when her husband suddenly gasped and passed out again. The doctor adjusted his neck again, and he revived once more. But the doctor said each return to life would be shorter, and it was. Now, he said the man would be dead within minutes, and that was exactly what happened.

After the coroner left, I asked the doctor where he had learned this technique. Surprisingly, an old chiropractor had taught him how to delay death by adjusting the neck in this particular manner. All this took place in 1941, long before emergency 9-1-1 existed. It was a time when the sign "Quiet! Hospital Zone" was actually honored, but you were more or less on your own in matters of health. Strange as it may seem today, there were fewer doctors back then and not many specialists.

The doctor's intervention was the first time I'd seen chiropractic manipulation used to induce reactivation of the nervous system, which temporarily returned the person to life. This event set in motion my lifelong interest in the study of the human body and healing. However, when I found no one to talk to about these things that mattered most to me, I sought the comforting solitude of the sage brush hills beyond town.

The sun browned me like a native while I roamed the desert wilderness where silence fed my soul, far from the press of people. Now those hills are covered by houses. Traffic streams through to Palm Springs and Imperial Valley with freeways leading east to Arizona, New Mexico, and Texas. Today the art of walking is sadly neglected. Still, one has to get to the car. With adjoining carports, this may add 30 steps daily. No doubt sometime in the future, when scientists discover that we—their ancestors—walked to our cars and back, they will marvel at our brute strength in being able to accomplish this astonishing feat.

On my desert treks, I also spent time plotting how to get my mother's approval for my dream rifle. I hounded my mother unmercifully. She wisely withstood my badgering until I was 17. Then I persuaded my mother—or perhaps she just wore down—to let me buy my longed-for .22. It was a fine, accurate, single shot. Oh how I loved that gun! I was a nervous kid who could barely sit still for a minute. But when I imagined myself as a great white hunter, I could sit like a stone for hours waiting for a ground squirrel to come into view. When I spotted one, I moved my gun with such slowness to follow their movements that none of them knew I was there. One day I was so still that a fellow wanderer in the desert, a coyote, nearly walked into me. I laughed out loud and he disappeared like a ghost.

Later that day I crouched in position for an excellent squirrel hunt when a jolly little fellow burst upon the scene. A saucy young squirrel scampered onto a small cliff where he chittered away at me as if we were the best of friends. I shot from my hip like a gunfighter while my new buddy dodged about chattering and flicking his tail, cute as all get out. He seemed to feel we were both having a great time.

As he danced ten feet in front of me, his squirrel antics forced me to laugh. Watching him hop about so full of life, twitching his bushy tail as he darted back and forth in our game, I was charmed. When I thought about taking aim and ending the game, I realized that—if successful—my friend would never again joyously dash about his squirrel realm. He was so charming and cheerful I ended my shooting days right there and then.

Fishing was another addiction. When I was young, I could never get enough. As a teenager, my friends and I used to spear fish from a pier at the beach for sport. But not long after my last squirrel hunt, I considered what it must feel like to be swimming along, minding your own business, when a spear suddenly plunges into your body. After that, I let them enjoy their life of swimming through the chilly depths, and only speared them when we wanted a fish dinner.

How strange that I gave up these sports so long ago, and now live in a sportsman's paradise abundant with wildlife, often in our front yard. I have friends—no names—who have given up hunting. Carrying a gun is their excuse for a pleasant walk in the woods. In Montana, wildlife freely roams the countryside, including the plentiful deer who boldly take their share of our garden during the summer. I'm not happy about their dining habits, but it's their world too.

———•◆•———

When not admiring deer grazing in our garden this summer, I took time for reflection. I realized that after my adoption I became sicker and sicker even though I was athletic and active. Unfortunately, Winnie and Bob had been horrified to learn their new son hadn't been immunized. They were afraid their precious boy might drop dead of disease at any moment. Riding on this wave of parental fear, doctors enthusiastically began a series of every shot known at that time. Although I was sick after the very first shot and have hated needles ever since, it was shots, shots, and more shots.

Medical doctors injected me with God-knows-what drugs, which only served to make me sicker. Winnie was sure the next shot would be "the one" to "fix" me—my own, personal magic bullet. But every year my low back pain was worse and I was sick and in bed much of the time. Finally, the doctor taped me up and told my mother I would probably have to wear a back brace for the rest of my life. More pills and shots followed this news, but the pain only increased.

Our money flowed out, injections flowed in, and my skin was forever scarred from the shots. At age 11, I rebelled and told my mother emphatically, "No more shots!" Fortunately, my declaration came at the same time Mother ran out of money. Most of her money had been spent on surgeries and medications for herself, and shots and doctor visits for me. After my father's death, she was always sick and spent much of her time in bed. Five abdominal surgeries did nothing to alleviate her suffering, but she continued to brag about her caring doctors. These same doctors disappeared into the woodwork once her money was gone. No doubt there's a medical facility somewhere paid for single-handedly by my mother. We decided to seek a less expensive treatment for my chronic pain—a chiropractor.

One day, I was in so much pain I couldn't sit still in class. I went to the school nurse and asked to be excused from school to go to my first chiropractic appointment. Little did I know I would get a sermon on the evils of chiropractic. The nurse used every scare tactic she could think of to keep me from going to that appointment. She even warned me that I might get cancer or be paralyzed for life if I went to a chiropractor. I left her office wondering if I should cancel my appointment.

Luckily, I kept my appointment and found that Dr. Wright, the chiropractor, was surely right for me. He had just moved into town the week before and only his treating table had arrived, which explained why there was no office furniture. The energy in his office felt balanced, and the colors of his energy bubble showed a good, honest man trying to help people in pain. He positioned a heat lamp over my back for a few minutes. Then he adjusted my spine, a first for me. A warm glow and tingling sensation spread throughout my body. To my surprise, the terrible nagging pain I had suffered for years was completely gone. I was thrilled to be able to walk and move about freely without any pain. Dr. Wright said that at my age it was easy to return the spine to its proper balance.

When my school wouldn't accept the word of a chiropractor that I could return to sports, I had to brave the same opinionated school nurse to get a permission slip for gym. I thought she would be pleased to see me out of pain. Instead, she was furious that I had gone to a chiropractor in spite of her dire warnings. Glaring at me with renewed venom, she lectured me again on the evils of chiropractic. She declared chiropractors had only a two-week education at most and had paralyzed many people. There were fifteen other students sitting in her office with thermometers in their mouths. They all nodded vigorously, their thermometers bobbing up and down in agreement.

I tried to tell the school nurse I felt fine, and moved around to prove my point. She announced to me—and her audience—my healing was from the fine drugs my medical doctors had been giving me. She declared this chiropractor was, as usual, taking credit for the cure. I shut my mouth and listened to another lecture about quacks and charlatans. Properly chastised, I humbly received my permission slip and left her office. A strange introduction to the profession I would choose to begin my career in healing.

The next week, I returned to Dr. Wright's office. Armed with the nurse's ammunition, I told him he was a quack, a fraud, and that he had stolen our money. I said, "I'm not ever coming back. I don't want to be paralyzed by your dangerous adjustments." He assured me that he had tangled with many a school nurse. He said, "I wish they'd stick to their own field, and not judge things they don't understand."

Dr. Wright asked me to tell him exactly what the nurse had told me. I thought he would be angry. Instead, as he listened to all the details, he laughed until tears rolled down his cheeks. He was so good-natured about the nurse's remarks that I found myself laughing too. When we stopped laughing, he said he had heard such tales many times, but had never found anyone injured by chiropractic.

After taking one treatment a week for a month, he suggested I come in once a month for maintenance, and I did. From Dr. Wright, I had the first relief from the chronic low back pain that had haunted me for years. I felt wonderful and healthy, and we soon became great friends. I no longer had to stay in bed with pain for weeks at a time. Thrilled to be free from pain, I decided to become a chiropractor. When I shared my plan with Dr. Wright, he said, "Son, I believe you'll be a fine chiropractor and a credit to the profession."

In school, I told my friends I was going to become a doctor of chiropractic. At first my school chums laughed, but I was happy to know exactly what I wanted to do with my life. Wanting to help others as I had been helped, I sensed the Power already steering me firmly toward chiropractic college. Always different, I knew I would walk a road less traveled to fulfill my contract with the Creator.

———·◆·———

Surviving junior high, it was on to high school. Caught up in the excitement of my new school activities, I forgot my promise to keep my inner knowing a secret. My first mistake was to reveal visions of coming events to some of my close friends, but these revelations disturbed them. I became depressed and unhappy when no one wanted to accept my gift of knowing.

In school sports, I enjoyed playing baseball. My intuition came in handy since I knew where the ball would come down before the hitter even came to bat. And I was always there to catch it. However, this stunt, which was great fun for me, didn't win me any friends on the team. I felt isolated from my classmates, as though I was separated from them by dark clouds gathering around me.

The negativity I felt rewarded me with more dark thoughts about life. As I tell my patients, negative thoughts invite all their family and friends into your mind. Soon they green-card all their negative shirttail relatives until the world becomes a terrible place and you are miserable. I fought a battle with depression during high school, unable to find a balance between my outer life of turmoil that caused me so much pain, and my inner life of intuition that brought me so much comfort and peace.

However, my spirits got a lift when I met my friend Hugh. He was a few years younger and funny as heck. I was still searching for balance and his humorous outlook on life brought relief from my own darker thoughts. I remember when he got a job selling Dutch Boy paint after he graduated. As a traveling salesman he went to Arizona where he called on a Sherman-Williams paint dealer in a thriving town. He asked the owner if he would stock Dutch Boy paint. The owner turned him down flat. He told him that he only handled Sherman-Williams paint. Hugh shook his head and said, "Boy, I wish I had a hundred just like you."

Every few weeks for two years, Hugh went back to the same store where he repeated his performance of asking the owner if he would consider stocking Dutch Boy paints. After being turned down, he would always shake his head and say, "Boy, I wish I had a hundred just like you."

Finally, the owner blew up. Irate, he grabbed Hugh by the lapels and yelled, "*All right! I've had it!* I've told you for two years now I'm a Sherman-Williams paint distributor. *It's all I carry! Look around!* Do you see anything *but* Sherman-Williams paint in my store? *You're driving me crazy!* Every time I tell you I refuse to carry Dutch Boy paint, you say, 'Boy, I wish I had a hundred just like you.' *What* in the *hell* do you *mean* by that?"

Unruffled, Hugh smiled, "Heck, I *wish* I had a hundred that wouldn't handle Dutch Boy paint. I must have a *thousand* that won't carry Dutch Boy paint."

The owner stopped his tirade and released his grip on Hugh's lapels. Looking at Hugh's smiling face, he started laughing. And he kept on laughing and said, "Hugh, I never heard such a story. Tell you what. I'll split the store. I'll put in half Dutch Boy and half Sherman-Williams." Thus, I learned from Hugh that persistence with a touch of humor can win the day.

Unfortunately, my own humor lost me a few jobs. During World War II, I worked with friends at a Texaco station behind Hudlows drive-in. I was only 14, but since most men were in the service, it was easy to get a job. There were four of us and we worked well together. As soon as a car pulled in, we all rushed out. While one of us checked the tires, another checked the oil and water, another washed the windows and mirrors, and, of course, one pumped the gas and took the money. Now all this worked very well, except when Ed, one of the station owners, was present.

It appeared Ed's one interest in life was romancing every attractive female who drove into the station, especially ones wearing jewelry with intimations of money in the picture. He was quick to flood these unsuspecting women with charm. And the ladies were flattered to receive such personal attention. Whenever a beautiful woman drove into the station, Ed would rush out to the car. Turning back to look at all of us, he would raise his right-hand high in the air, snap his fingers in an imperious manner, and shout haughtily, "Front!" If there wasn't an immediate response to his summons, he would snap his fingers again shouting, *"Boy, I said front!"*

We were required to drop everything and hurry over to work on the car while Ed lounged against the driver's door and smooth-talked the lady. I took this routine for a while and then I complained to his partner. I asked him if we weren't all supposed to work together as a team. He knew immediately why I was asking. He agreed this was how it should work—in theory—but since Ed was his partner, he couldn't do anything about the innocent flirtations. And so the summer steamed on with Ed romancing the ladies day after day.

After a few months of tolerating this nonsense, I saw an opportunity I couldn't pass up. A stunning blonde we had never seen before pulled up in a flashy, red convertible. Seeing Ed sitting in the office, I was out to the car in a flash before he could get his feet under him. Lounging against the driver's door, I raised my hand high in the air, snapped my fingers with a flourish, pointed back at Ed, and shouted, *"Boy!"*

Ed pointed at himself in confusion. I summoned him again, "Yes, *you . . . Boy . . . front!"* Ed got beet red. He followed the other guys out to the car. I casually leaned on the car and chatted with the blonde while my coworkers tried to suppress their laughter. Ed steamed silently while he checked the tires. Soon the lovely lady was on her way, never realizing her part in the performance.

An hour later, Ed's partner called me into the office. While he struggled not to laugh, he couldn't suppress a smile. He said he had to let me go even though I had been a very good worker. Since Ed was his partner, I had to understand that I couldn't continue working there. He said he would have loved to have been present to see the show, which the other employees described to him. We shook hands and he wrote a wonderful letter of recommendation for me.

I know it was a case of cutting off my nose to spite my face. But I still have fond memories of Ed's stunned, red face as he pointed at himself—obviously questioning whether I could have possibly meant him—when I called out, "Yes, *you . . . Boy . . . front!"* Great memories . . .

———•◆•———

When I realized that physical activity lifted my spirits, I joined some high school friends in weight lifting at the local YMCA. At first we didn't know what we were doing, but the "Y" had a workout room with a fine collection of weights we could use when the spirit moved us. Being young and enthusiastic, it didn't take long to build choice muscles in areas that could be displayed to advantage while wearing a T-shirt. None of us stuck to any particular schedule. It took the right mood—or a little female admiration—to return us to the weight room.

In the second year of our hit and miss workouts, Ron, a freshman who got straight A grades, came to watch us lift. He was unquestionably handsome, but his arms were as spindly as sticks. We got a kick out of asking him to pass us weights. We tossed them back and forth quite easily, but Ron struggled to lift them off the floor. In spite of our friendly banter, he began a steady program of working out with weights. His good-natured smiles when we kidded him won us over. We saw how serious and determined he was so we started giving him pointers on lifting.

There were times we wouldn't see Ron working out for *weeks*. Not because *he* was gone, but because *we* were goofing off and weren't there to see him. While we were off having fun, Ron continued his unwavering workout schedule. Little by little, week after week, Ron's perseverence paid off. Ronnie was building muscle. However, what disturbed us even more was that he continued to maintain perfect grades. Watching his steady progress, we became embarrassed at our own laziness and pledged to work out every day. But like alcoholics falling off the wagon, our perfect attendance never lasted.

Within a year, Ronnie had a body any movie star would envy. Once his muscles were in perfect balance, he stayed in shape by playing tennis and other sports that caught his interest. Like most of my fellow enthusiasts, I stopped working out after a while, but Ron's results remain in my memory as a fine example of what can be achieved by sticking with a daily exercise program.

In my weight lifting days, I thought strengthening my body was the way to health. Since my back no longer hurt—thanks to Dr. Wright—I thought my health problems were over. In reality, they were just beginning. I couldn't know I would be facing a devastating illness in my early twenties, a turning point that would force me to change all my eating habits and begin a total health program, which has suited me ever since. But even before this experience, I was diagnosed with polio in my late teens.

Polio was—I believe in my case—from ingesting vast quantities of sugar. Due to this disease, one day my bowel just up and quit, leaving me with a paralyzed colon. A blocked bowel did nothing to improve my pessimistic outlook on life. Since this condition lasted for several years, I was forced to rely on enemas every two days. If there's a god of enemas, my thanks go out for my only relief at that time.

One day walking in the desert, far from another soul, I finally thought to pray and ask God to help my bowel work normally. After I completed my prayer, I suddenly felt the slightest urge. I gratefully answered the call right there and gave heartfelt thanks to God for this miracle. My gratitude knew no bounds as my bowel slowly returned to normal over the next few weeks.

While my respect for all the body organs has grown over the years, I totally acknowledge the bowel's importance. If the plumbing stops working as God intended, the entire organism comes to a halt. The first question asked by any old-time doctor was always, "How are the bowels?" He knew what every plumber knows. When the pipes clog, chaos and confusion result throughout the system.

With the return of my bowel, life became more agreeable. I was so heartened that I began working on my negative thinking. Through prayer, meditation and inner healing, I slowly came to understand that the darkness I lived in was being created moment by moment by my own negative thinking.

In studying ancient philosophers, I learned that mankind has always had the opportunity to be miserable, or to be happy. Using that knowledge, I embarked on a long, slow climb out of the valley of darkness where I had lived for years after my adopted father's death. I discovered the same road down, if taken upward, will return us to a world of sunshine and light. Here, love is abundant and available. Here, our Creator waits for us to come Home. This world exists for all eternity in the upper reaches of our heart, just as the sun shines brightly in a clear sky if you fly above the clouds. In time, I woke up to the joy of living. Like a butterfly emerging from its cocoon on a bright summer day, I eventually reached the light that shines forever within us all.

It is our birthright to lift up through contemplation of the loving thoughts that the Creator placed within our hearts at the very beginning. As conscious beings our spiritual essence flows from our hearts into all life. Now I see humanity as one great family of loving light. We are of infinite value as individuals, but in our connectedness we change the destiny of all creation. When we make ourselves available to help our spiritual family, the flame-that-never-dies burns brightest within our hearts, awakening the Creator's own joy within us. What a great blessing to live and journey together on Mother Earth as we make our voyage home through the starry galaxy.

4

Life's Lessons

————•◆••◆•————

B y the time I was 18, the Power had contacted me three times. Each time I was asked to pledge my life to healing and teaching, and each time I felt more confident in my answer. Healing was the only path for me. I enrolled in the Los Angeles College of Chiropractic in 1947, eager to begin my studies of the human body and its mysterious functions.

When I started college, the idea of chiropractic as a profession was a novel one. I was so naive I thought chiropractic would be all hands-on work. My first awakening came when I read the difficult curriculum and had to purchase 28 huge medical textbooks. I learned our education was actually equal to any medical school in the country, but I also learned no one outside our profession acknowledged this fact.

Years later, when friends asked why I didn't become a "real" doctor, I told them I didn't want to work on reels and fishing poles. (I seemed to be the only one who thought this was funny.) Time and again, I tried to explain my love of natural healing to others, but there was no sign of comprehension. In exasperation, I finally said that I wasn't smart enough to get into medical school. My friends shook their heads in disbelief, but my invented story was the only explanation they were willing to accept.

Once enrolled, my first task was to find a cheap place to live. I found "cheap" readily available in rooms for rent near Georgia Street Receiving Hospital. My first night revealed why the price was so low. The landlord had failed to mention the nearby hospital was the main treatment center for L.A.'s gunshot and knife wounds. Throughout the night, sirens wailed to announce the constant ambulance arrivals. Surprisingly, this nightly serenade quickly became my background for studying and sleeping until I hardly noticed it.

Before I could make any mistakes I'd regret, a couple of streetwise neighborhood toughs befriended me and took it upon themselves to explain life in the big city to this small town boy. They told me not to go out after dark in our neighborhood. And to be sure I wouldn't, they told me they would tie me up in my room if they ever found out that I had missed the curfew they had imposed. Looking at their serious faces, I was sure they meant every word.

However, within a few months, cooking for myself became monotonous and tiresome. I found another room to rent (one which included meals) in a building originally used as a "rooming in" hospital for pregnant ladies. When modern hospitals came of age, this building was reclaimed and given new life as a boardinghouse. There were 12 other tenants, all old men, each quietly sequestered in his own room. Meals were eaten together in the large kitchen. I realized too late that I should have sampled a test meal before settling in. What was presented as food was cooked to death by the landlady who ran the boardinghouse.

On my first night, 12 old codgers plus myself, a lad of 18, headed for the kitchen to have supper. I couldn't believe my eyes when I saw a large, ancient dog of uncertain ancestry already seated at the table. Grossly overweight, he appeared to be dying from old age and God knows what else. He stared back at me with rheumy eyes. Patches of his skin were exposed where clumps of hair had fallen out. Wearing a napkin around his neck, he was clearly ready to eat with us.

Suddenly, there was a last minute dash to the table in an adult version of musical chairs. In this case, the two chairs next to the dog were left for the two last arrivals, one of which was yours truly. The race was no mystery once I got a whiff of the dog's rancid breath. His breath alone was enough to put anyone off his feed. Dinner conversation was accompanied by slobbering sounds made while our canine dinner guest was busy cleaning his plate. One time seated next to this canine was more than enough. After this meal, I too sprinted for the chairs farthest from the dreaded dog. My belated apologies go to those old pensioners; youth was a definite advantage and I never again had to sit next to "Poochie."

One morning a charming young man appeared at the house. With great care and courtesy, he collected Poochie from our landlady. Then he drove off with the elderly dog in the back of his van. A month later, he returned with a lively dog in perfect shape. My first thought was that he had substituted a new, young, vital dog in place of the fat, old, mangy dog he had taken, but my fellow lodgers assured me such was not the case. Poochie had returned.

Over the next three months, I watched Poochie gradually turn into the fat, repulsive mongrel we all avoided like the plague. Just when Poochie looked as though he would not live another day, the same fellow arrived and collected the ailing dog. A month later, he returned the dog, looking as fit as a fiddle. I watched this amazing transformation take place every three months like clockwork. However, no matter how I persisted, the obstinate fellow wouldn't tell me how he managed to restore Poochie to perfect health. Just when I was about to give up, fate stepped in and took a hand.

Again the secretive young man appeared on his appointed rounds. He gently picked up Poochie, and placed him with great care into the back of his van. I watched as this enterprising chap assured our landlady he would spare no expense in healing her wonderful dog. She happily paid him 150 dollars, which would be like 5,000 today. When she started crying inconsolably at the thought of being parted from her baby, I fled the premises.

I was only a block away, ready to step off a curb, when the self-same van careened around the very corner I was standing on. I heard a great thump, which I immediately identified as the dog passenger slamming against the side of the van. Thumps, followed by yelps, continued while Poochie ricocheted from side to side on his wild ride. At last I possessed secret evidence to help me learn the truth behind that hairy hound's healing. I bided my time.

When the young man arrived to return Poochie, I took him aside. I said it was time to reveal to me how he was able to transform the landlady's ailing dog into a completely healthy specimen. Otherwise, I would inform the old lady about his cruel treatment of her precious dog. Before he could protest that he didn't know what I was talking about, I revealed my witnessing his reckless driving. I told him I had heard the dog's yelps from the back of the van. He paled and said he would confess everything, if only I would not reveal his canine rehabilitation methods. I promised, and he began his tale.

The dog handler assured me that by the time he had driven a mile, Poochie was bracing in the back of the van. He swore the dog never lost his footing again. This ingenious fellow rented cages behind the racetrack where each dog was put into a cage with plenty of water, but no food, only an old boot to chew on. Once these overfed, pampered dogs were truly hungry—so hungry they were willing to chew the boot—he gave them a little food.

Within a week, the dogs were pacing in their cages. Then the handler rode his bicycle around the track while he towed the dogs behind him. By the second week, the dogs could keep pace with him and run next to the bicycle. By the third and fourth weeks, they were pulling *him* around the track. The last week, he fed them lightly. And presto, brand-new dogs—muscular, trim, and clear-eyed—ready to return to their unsuspecting owners.

Although I was sorely tempted, I kept my word; I never told my landlady. But I had to bite my tongue when she extolled the virtues of that caring young man and his expensive medicines. What a lesson in getting fit. I thought we could use the same approach with people. Who needs an expensive health spa when you could be thrown into a locked room with an abundance of water to drink, and a fine boot to chew on?

However, even the young man's extraordinary care did not keep Poochie from eventually dying. Mourning her loss, our poor landlady could hardly go on from one day to the next. Then one fine morning our animal-loving landlady opened her front door and there was a genuine bobcat, down from the nearby hills, sitting docilely on her stoop. It was love at first sight. She was thrilled with her new "kitty" and brought him a saucer of milk. With that, "Stubby," as she fondly named him, joined us as a permanent boarder.

Our landlady was overjoyed to have a pet to love again. Fortunately for her, the feeling was mutual. Whenever she sat in the living room, he would calmly curl up at her feet as if the tamest of house cats. She petted him and fussed over him while he basked in her love, and purred in a low rumble that sent shivers down our spines. However, she was so delighted with her new pet that she wouldn't hear of it when we broached the subject of returning Stubby to the hills.

Our lives became a perpetual nightmare. We never knew when Stubby might be on the prowl. That wild bobcat terrorized us night and day. His favorite place of ambush was the long upstairs hallway where he lurked, hidden in the alcoves, waiting to pounce. He bit fiercely, tearing our trousers and bruising our legs. Many clothes had to be discarded because they had been shredded by that beast.

We were terrified to venture into the hallway to get to either of the two bathrooms. My own method of coping was to ignore the urge until there was no choice in the matter. Then I would peek out from the safety of my room. Seeing no sign of Stubby, I would make a mad dash for the bathroom. Once inside I slammed the door shut—safe and sound—or so I thought until I heard Stubby pounding down the hall. He would lunge through the air and crash full force into the door, which shook on its hinges while I prayed for it to hold. It was like a grade B horror movie. Holding my breath, I remained perfectly still until I heard the beast retreat. I listened. The hallway on the other side of the door was filled with an eerie silence. The fiend had gone.

Unfortunately, before I could return to my room, I had to check on the whereabouts of Stubby to see if he had found another hiding place. Opening the door a crack, I was fully prepared to slam it shut if he appeared. There was always great relief in reaching the safe haven of my room, and securing its sturdy door between me and my crafty assailant. I became an expert in tactical cat evasion.

In our eyes, Stubby was good for only one thing: keeping our neighborhood free from stray dogs. It was great entertainment when roaming dogs spotted Stubby sleeping in the sun on the front lawn. Huge, growling dogs—hair bristling, teeth bared—would stalk the napping cat. Suddenly, the roles would be reversed when the sleeper came to life, springing sideways and puffing out his fur, which made him look three times his size.

These exciting encounters always ended with the dog turning tail and running for dear life. Making a final pounce, Stubby would land on the dog's back. Firmly astride, he raked the poor dog with his claws and bit its ear. Once our personal lion had made his point, he jumped off, ambled over to a sunny spot, and continued his catnap. And that particular dog was never seen again on our street.

However, a neighborhood free from canines couldn't compensate for living in fear. Desperate, we even discussed poisoning Stubby, but none of us had the heart to do it. Our landlady just loved that big cat, which, needless to say, never bothered her at all . . . ever. We were at our wits' end with no solution in sight.

One morning I got up to take my usual 5 A.M. walk. I crept out the front door, leaving the rest of the tenants—and hopefully Stubby—fast asleep. Crossing the street in front of the house, I glanced down and could hardly believe my eyes. There decorating the asphalt was Stubby. He had been run over so many times that he now resembled a large hair rug. He was so flat I could have slid him under the front door of the rooming house.

I hurried back to wake one of the old gents. "Get up! Come with me quick!" I urged him. Grumbling and cursing under his breath, he reluctantly followed me out of the house and into the street. However, all was forgiven when I pointed out the flat cat mat. He pumped my hand up and down vigorously, gave me a toothless grin, and asked how I had "done him in." I told him I couldn't take credit for this gift from God.

We quickly summoned all the other old boarders to view the earthly remains of one who had tortured us with teeth and claws for so long. After we congratulated each other on our rescue from our tormentor, we realized we had to break the news to our landlady. When she saw the last vestiges of her cherished Stubby, she cried and cried, saying her baby had been such a dear, sweet kitty. We nodded solemnly in agreement.

Our landlady insisted that we pry Stubby off the asphalt so she could take his remains to the local vet for burial. The vet was horrified when he saw the body. He insisted she was lucky to be alive since this was obviously a wild bobcat from the hills. She refused to believe him and returned home in a huff.

The days following Stubby's unexpected departure were sweet. The luxury of roaming the halls without fear filled us with gratitude. It seems we need life's sharp contrasts to pounce on us once in a while. Otherwise, we can't appreciate how wonderful the simple things in life can be—right here, right now.

Recently a local paper had an article about a chap in Kalispell, Montana who raises bobcats and sells them. (I have to presume they are tamed and quieted before purchase.) The article brought back fond memories of my boardinghouse days and Stubby. For as long as I rented a room there, the landlady spoke fondly of her dear Stubby. Luckily, I left before she found a replacement.

————•◆•————

During my years at college, I watched Los Angeles changing on its way to becoming the smoggy, overcrowded "paradise" it is today. But when I first arrived, there wasn't a bit of smog. Steady ocean breezes blew what little smog existed over to Pasadena. Los Angeles was charming, clean, and filled with wonderfully strange people. When I watched the fascinating character portrayals in the movie *Million Dollar Hotel*, it brought back the colorful characters who wandered the city's poorer neighborhoods. Today these people would no doubt be locked away, but back then they added excitement to everyday life. Some of these eccentrics patrolled their territory wearing sandwich boards. The front typically declaring: "The end of the world is coming" and the back something like: "Eat no meat." San Francisco's Emperor Norton comes to mind.

While my boardinghouse life gave me plenty of time to study, like all the other students, I was ready to take a break and venture into the big city after studying all week. On Saturday nights, hundreds of people gathered downtown in Central Park to enjoy the music and camaraderie. Many local bars had upright pianos with rubber wheels on the bottom. These pianos were rolled outside into the park where everyone had a great time singing along with their old favorite tunes.

Weekends were also the perfect time to attend lectures and meetings in the area. Like me, many of my fellow students were interested in studying alternative healing therapies and philosophy. Idealistic as to the results of chiropractic, we relished every opportunity to explore the cutting edge of healing. We were eager to gain more knowledge and made the most of our free time.

Knowing my interest in nutrition, a classmate asked me to join him at a lecture on health being given by a genuine yogi. The lecture was being held in an old movie theater in Hollywood. At that time, theaters, which had been closed due to lack of patrons, could be rented for cultural events.

When I saw a wizened, little man perched cross-legged on a table at the front of the room, rather than behind a podium, I had to suppress my laughter. If this was a top-of-the-line, genuine yogi, I was not impressed. Once the lecture was underway, I noticed all 60 people in the audience were hanging on his every word. I, on the other hand, was completely bored as he droned on and on in his high-pitched voice about diet and health.

However, I perked up when the speaker said, "He who conquers his stomach, conquers everything in his life." Since I knew everything at 18, I could hardly let his statement go unchallenged. I raised my hand and waited impatiently for his attention. He pointed at me and asked if I had a question. I stood up. "Not a question, a clarification," I said confidently. I went on to inform him and his audience that the mind, not the lowly stomach, directed our lives. Warming to my subject, I cited various authorities, quoting from the Greeks and other scholars to support my case. He listened intently, his head cocked to one side.

After ten minutes, I ceased my oration, the yogi politely asked, "Have you finished?" Convinced I had clarified my case for the mind's precedence over the insignificant stomach, I answered, "Yes" and took my seat. With firm conviction and authority in his voice, he repeated, "He who conquers his stomach, conquers everything in his life."

Stunned, I realized the man hadn't learned anything from my educational speech. It was clear the little pipsqueak had no education, and couldn't recognize the truth when he heard it. When the lecture ended, I left the theater with my school chum, who was obviously bamboozled by this yogi and no doubt confused about life in general. Today I know the lecturer was perfectly correct and I was wrong. I can only apologize to him in spirit because . . . "He who conquers his stomach, conquers everything in his life."

Every day I learned more about the healing mysteries that abounded in early Los Angeles; I wanted to explore them all. When stories of a man named Rappatoni, who reportedly could heal every kind of illness, began to spread through the college, we eagerly discussed the possibilities of his work. A friend's whispered statement—given in strictest confidence—aroused my curiosity. "Check out Rappatoni and his Gravitonic Ray," he said.

What the "Gravitonic Ray" might have been, remains a mystery to me to this day. I never did see it, or hear it explained. But at a meeting,

I heard Rappatoni, man of mystery, declare, "In the wave, lies the secret of Creation." How strangely similar this statement is to what physicists believe today. Scientists say that if you look for a wave, you will find a wave; if you look for a particle, you will find a particle. So scientifically, you find what you are looking to find. In essence, we are interacting with creation every moment as revealed in quantum physics today.

Continuing my search for unusual healing methods, I went to witness "bloodless" surgery. Checking the address, I nodded to the sentries posted in front of the house. In those days, lookouts were always posted to avoid raids by the authorities. Things were very hush-hush because participants were terrified of such a raid. Alternative therapies didn't have the growing acceptance we see today, and fear kept many people from attending such unorthodox gatherings.

Once inside, I was taken to a room where a male patient was lying on his back on a therapy table. The doctor, who was from Germany, opened an elegant, black leather case, which contained a pair of unusual spectacles with colored lenses. After announcing to the observers that his patient would feel no pain, he carefully positioned these glasses over his patient's eyes. He told us the patient's eyes had to remain open during the entire procedure. His assistant was to shine a light through these lenses into the patient's eyes precisely at 30 second intervals.

The doctor began probing with his fingers deeper and deeper into the patient's abdominal area to break up adhesions in the intestines. Although the "surgery" looked painful, the patient appeared to be completely comfortable. At least he was until the assistant also began watching the procedure and forgot to shine the light into his eyes. When the light didn't shine 30 seconds later, the patient let out a bloodcurdling scream. We all jumped and the doctor spoke sharply to the light holder. She quickly shined the light into the patient's eyes. Immediately, his pain stopped. The entire procedure lasted 20 minutes and the patient said he was quite pleased with his "surgery."

A week later, a good friend from Redlands approached me in secret, thus avoiding our small town's enthusiastic gossipers. He told me about a chap charging two dollars for 15 minutes of healing using copper wires. I quickly headed off to see this new method. When I arrived, I was led into a large room, which was empty except for 40 folding chairs and

40 copper wires (one per chair) extending out of the cement floor into the room.

Somewhere encased in the floor's cement was an instrument generating healing energy, which was transmitted through the copper wires. People being treated had copper wires clipped to either an arm or a leg. It was quite a sight. After 15 minutes, people left feeling quite renewed as a result of this strange treatment.

In a few days, I was contacted by my friend again. He told me that the owner of the "whatever-it-was" in the floor had died quite unexpectedly. My friend asked if I wanted to chip in and buy the gadget since the widow now wanted to sell it. I was ready, but my friend called the next morning with startling news. Someone had broken into the old healer's office and jack-hammered the whatever-it-was right out of the cement floor, leaving only a gaping hole. Nothing remained to show what had created the marvelous healings. One more unsolved mystery.

———•◆•———

Early Los Angeles was a Mecca for every new philosophy. During the time I lived there, Paramahansa Yogananda built a sanctuary near the beach for his Self-Realization Fellowship. Many of us went to hear him out of curiosity. When I first saw Yogananda, a quiet man of loving countenance, he was dressed in the traditional, saffron robes of a yogi. He represented India at its best and his disciples clearly adored him.

Surrounded by his Indian devotees, Yogananda lectured weekly at his sanctuary, which is still one of the most peaceful places on earth. After spending time at this oasis of serenity, which thrives in the midst of city noise and confusion, I asked him why he chose to build his sanctuary where it would be forever surrounded by the city's uproar. He answered simply, "Because it was needed. Here it teaches people that Peace can reign in the midst of chaos."

Yogananda taught Kriya Yoga and meditation, explaining their many benefits. Due to his influence, many of us began to meditate seriously. His teachings inspired acceptance and appreciation for all religions. Those who knew him came to have great admiration and affection for him. He was a living example of love and compassion in our time. His book, *Autobiography of a Yogi*, remains a classic in spiritual literature. He died on March 7, 1952. According to the mortuary statement his body had not shown any visible signs of decay when the casket was formally sealed twenty days after his death. Perhaps his body remains so even today.

Further explorations found me attending my first metaphysical service at a new age church. When the minister spoke on Sunday evening, I felt inspired by every lofty principle through his uplifting words. As I was leaving the church, the minister smiled charmingly in my direction. Smiling back, I extended my hand to shake his, only to discover that his smile wasn't for me.

Ignoring me, the minister hurried into the waiting arms of a buxom blonde, who was dripping with diamonds, dressed to the nines, and wearing enough makeup to make her identity a mystery even to her closest friends. Left with my hand outstretched in midair, I used it to smooth my hair back, in what I hoped was a casual manner. Then I casually returned my hand to my coat pocket. The minister couldn't have been more charming to this blonde. He gushed about her fabulous beauty and her generosity in sponsoring him.

I managed to step aside just as the minister ushered the blonde past where I had been standing a moment before. If I hadn't moved, I would surely have been trampled under his generous feet. In spite of the minister's slight, my heart was filled with the joy of having met people who thought as I did. I felt accepted into the fold.

The minister's wonderful phrases about Love had inspired me. I felt transformed. I decided that when I went home next weekend to visit my mother, I would give her a big hug, tell her how much I loved her, and confess my shortcomings as a son. Standing on the curb in front of the church, I was a new man, filled with a grand purpose—reborn!

Now let me explain that Mother and I banged our heads all the way through life. We were two Sagittarians who never backed down for each other. Sparks flew whenever we were together. But after listening to the minister, I felt an attempt to bridge the gap in our relationship was long overdue. I could hardly wait for the weekend to arrive.

Envisioning my presentation, I imagined how my mother would re-act. I was on a mission bordering on the evangelical in my zeal to confess all. In preparation for the great event, I rehearsed by recounting all my past indiscretions to the mirror. The mirror was very forgiving. Encouraged, I revealed my worst offenses. And still the mirror generously forgave me.

A few days before my trip home, I called my mother to reveal that I was coming home for the weekend, ready to make amends, confess my shortcomings, and start over in our relationship. Hanging up the phone, I imagined a reunion that would be perfect in every respect. Our hearts would bond in an outpouring of love and appreciation for each other. Surely we would live happily ever after. I felt certain my life was about to change for the better.

When the appointed day finally arrived, I eagerly headed home. I felt as certain of a warm, wonderful welcome as if the prodigal son had once again returned home, only this time to Redlands.

Entering the house with anticipation, I saw my mother seated in her favorite chair by the living room window. She was knitting quietly. She looked up when I came into the room. However, since she didn't get up, my plans for a warm embrace to start off my program fell through. Ignoring her stony silence—never a wise move—I claimed the center of the room for my confessional. Raising my right hand toward heaven, I began. For 20 minutes, I poured out my shortcomings into the silence.

When I could think of nothing more to confess, I asked if she could forgive me for all the past wrongs I had committed that might have hurt her and everyone else ever born. I waited with tears in my eyes for my mother to speak the words that my mirror had spoken to me, "Are you through, beloved son, standing bravely before me begging for my forgiveness? Come. Let me embrace you."

But it didn't happen that way. Mother continued knitting as she gazed upon my repentant face. At last, she asked, "Are you through?" I nodded. She stopped knitting, reached into her knitting bag, and brought forth an enormous roll of paper. The writing on it was so small that it looked like tiny hen scratches from one end to the other. By the sheer size of the document and the care with which she unrolled it, I was sure my mother had unearthed the original Dead Sea Scroll.

Clearing her throat, my mother began reading aloud, in solemn tones, all my *other* sins, which I had evidently overlooked in my confession. She concentrated on those sins that she viewed as crimes against herself. My determination to stay cool, calm and collected began to ebb. Continuing to unroll her account of my life—and the shortcomings therein—she gathered momentum. My resolution to be loving and repentant through any lightning bolts she might hurl at me—if she was foolish enough to call attention to the *very* few things I had forgotten— faded rapidly under her barrage of blame.

Mother raised her voice anew like a minister at the height of his sermon, ready to condemn all but himself. She fixed me with her steely eyes and went on to bring up incidents so far back that Adam and Eve were not far from the origins of my sins. My firm resolve to not lose my temper vanished. I boiled over with righteous indignation. I yelled, *"You can go to Hell!"* and left.

Today, I'm shocked that I could say such a thing to my mother. But at the time, I was furious that she couldn't see my deep love for her. I was hurt as only a teenager can be hurt when she didn't see our relationship blossoming into adoration for each other. After storming out of the house, I didn't call or return home for a month, even though it had been my habit to come home every weekend.

Of course youth knows everything and waits impatiently for the world to wake up to this fact. Today in my 70s—far older than my mother was when she blocked my end run for glory—I see my foolishness in trying to force our relationship into something it never was. When teenagers burst upon the scene, they're sure that if adults would just get out of their way, they could straighten the world out in no time at all. At least that's what I thought. And dear old mom was my chief obstacle.

Years later in meditation, after she had passed on, I told the Power, "If only my mother could be here, right now, I'd make it up to her. I'd be loving and kind no matter what she said to me." What's even funnier is that I meant every word.

My words were greeted by angelic laughter. The Power said, *"If your mother appeared, you would soon be at each other's throats, just as you were in life. She always loved you in her way, and you always loved her in your way. But you were never destined to live together harmoniously. Your karma was to clash all the way in your life together this time around."*

As the angels continued presenting an amusing portrayal of the true relationship I had with my mother, I finally had to laugh too. I'm ever so grateful that our heavenly guides have a rich sense of humor, or I would never make it through this life. Laughing with the angels brought great relief. I saw my words in the light of truth and humor. Years of pent up emotion were released, and I felt the sweet freedom of forgiveness fill my soul.

Now, my mother has been gone for many, many years. However, one day, when I meet her on the other side, I will thank her for raising me in the best way she knew how. I know I flunked SON, and later I flunked DAD when it was my turn. As hard as we try, I think many moms and dads feel they missed the mark and flunked PARENTING 101.

———•◆•———

While I was busy trying to live life, the angelic ones were busy charting my life's course. During my first year at college, they arranged for my spiritual search to catch the attention of the dean. He called me into his office and advised me to meet with a Dr. Cook, an old educator who lived near the college. While my heavenly guides continued to whisper that this meeting was important, I delayed it many times.

One sunny afternoon, I couldn't ignore my angelic messengers any longer; I headed over to Dr. Cook's apartment. When he opened the door, I knew at once the dear old chap was dying. I guessed him to be in his 70s, a slight man with thin, fine white hair, and the pale complexion of a man who rarely left his apartment. He was neatly dressed in a formal smoking jacket, black silk trousers, and black velvet slippers. Extending a frail, alabaster hand in welcome, he invited me in.

The apartment was a spacious series of rooms built in the 1920s. No doubt thousands of the city's inhabitants were tucked away in such rooms, which rented for very little in the '30s and '40s, but Dr. Cook's apartment was unique. As the good doctor led me to his living room, our footsteps made no sound, cushioned by thick, elegant Persian rugs in soft, muted tones. I was startled to see that every wall had been painted with ethereal angelic forms in deep purples, violets and blues. It was like entering another world in a more heavenly dimension. Stars and planets, painted on the ceilings, glittered above me, creating the celestial glory of some far distant galaxy.

Once we reached the living room, we settled into two comfortable, leather chairs across from each other. Delicate wisps of smoke from a brass incense burner on a carved rosewood table carried the exotic fragrance of sandalwood into the room. I felt perfectly comfortable and at home. Although death's energy surrounded him, Dr. Cook's eyes were still bright with knowing. They held a warm invitation to share my spiritual search with him. The hours passed quickly as we conversed. I was overjoyed to find a mind as eager as my own to explore the secrets of the universe. We pondered life's mysteries, healing, and all things dearest to my heart.

After Dr. Cook had plumbed the innermost depths of my soul's searching, he began to reveal his own life of seeking the eternal truths. He explained he had established inner ties to a powerful mind force by use of a mental formula. With this powerful force to serve him, he had done everything he had ever wanted to do in this life, even creating great wealth when it suited him.

Knowing his time on earth was coming to an end, Dr. Cook wanted to pass on his formula to me, as he had to a very few others. He warned me that the force was without conscience. For this reason, he rarely divulged the formula. I, and I alone, would be responsible for its use or abuse. To emphasize the inherent dangers, he revealed how he came to be facing what we both recognized as his impending death . . .

It began on a lovely summer morning a few months earlier. Strolling along Hollywood Boulevard, Dr. Cook thought about his life. Pondering his fame and fortune, he realized he had come to a crossroads in life. Thinking of the formula, he suddenly knew that he no longer wished for anything in this life. Startled by this realization, he mused aloud, "There's nothing I haven't done or experienced. I must be ready to die now."

The moment he spoke these words, a car appeared from out of nowhere and ran him down. The force—ever alert to do his bidding—had been listening. It simply obeyed by bringing a car to create his death. His perfect communication with the force—which had obeyed him for a lifetime in making his every wish come true—had determined his fate.

As soon as he realized what he had done, he tried to reverse the command. But the inner link he had developed with his personal "genie" would not respond to his pleas. It was then he understood that no amount of repeating the formula would alter the course of his coming death. What had been set in motion by cosmic forces could not be stopped. The door to communication on this issue had slammed shut, sealed forever. He concluded later that the initial shock of the accident had temporarily disturbed his connection with the force.

Dr. Cook saw that I was upset by his story, which gave new meaning to the old saying: "Be careful what you wish for." He reached over and gently patted my hand. He said he had come to terms with his death and it no longer bothered him. Now he was looking forward to exploring the new worlds awaiting him on the other side of the veil. I looked away, unable to face his death with the same composure that he had arrived at.

The sun was close to setting when Dr. Cook offered me tea, back then it was always tea, never coffee. When I declined his offer of sugar, he told me it was just as well since his sugar bowl was empty. However, he said he wanted some sugar for his tea. Still holding his teacup and sugar spoon, he got up from his chair, turned away, and mumbled a few words. Seconds later there was a knock at his door. When he opened it, there was a man holding a bowl of sugar standing in front of his door. Dr. Cook casually dipped his spoon into the bowl and took two teaspoons of sugar for his tea while the man looked on with a dazed expression. Dr. Cook thanked the man, shut the door in his face, and returned to his chair while stirring the sugar into his tea.

I recognized that I had just seen the force in action. Amazed, I asked, "Who was *that man?* Why on *earth* would he be at your door with a bowl of *sugar?*"

"I have no idea. It's not important. The universe is simply answering my request."

Puzzled, I inquired further, "Does he live in your apartment building?"

"I don't know. I've never seen him before. Remember, my boy, he's merely an agent of the universe, here to fulfill my request."

When Dr. Cook told me that money flowed to him, like the sugar, whenever he needed it. I asked how this could be possible. He answered, "Universal Energy has trillions of dollars floating about at all times. All I do is send my request out into the universe using the formula. My request has to be answered. That's Cosmic Law. Your mind is capable of creating anything. Our thoughts are so powerful we could change the world overnight. However, our concentration is so poor that most people can't focus on anything for more than a few seconds. I pray that someday—when mankind is ready—God will reveal the mind's power for infinite good."

Still curious how the process worked, I asked if he had ever questioned anyone who handed him money. Dr. Cook replied, "Only once. I was standing on a street corner in Los Angeles having just used the formula to ask the universe for three hundred dollars. A man came up to me and started to hand me three one-hundred dollar bills. I looked him squarely in the eye and asked, 'Where did you get this money?' With a blank stare, he asked, 'What money?' I said, 'The money you're handing me.' Startled, he looked down and saw his extended hand was holding three one-hundred dollar bills. He tightened his grip and struggled to keep the money for himself. Of course, I did the same."

"Who got to keep the money?" I asked.

"Well, about that time, a passing police officer saw our struggle and ended the battle by taking both of us—along with the money—to court. Since neither of us could prove ownership of the money, the judge kept it. After this, the force refused to obey me for nearly a month. It took all my concentration to get it to respond. And I never again questioned the giver, realizing each one is merely an agent of the universe."

When I left the doctor's apartment, I had been given the gift of his formula with instructions to return when I felt I was ready to take the final step. Putting all my attention on the task before me, I held my unwavering focus on the formula every moment until I felt the force reluctantly stir within me. As instructed by Dr. Cook, I didn't stop. I shifted into the second part of the program, concentrating on establishing my inner contact with the force itself.

When I finally felt close to being directly in contact with the force, it was time to meet with Dr. Cook again. After questioning me about my experiences with the formula, he agreed that I was ready. He explained how to complete the activation of the force. From that moment on, no matter what I was doing or whom I was with, the formula came first. Fueled by my desire to be an open channel for this energy to flow through me, I fixed my attention like a laser beam on the force.

At last I felt the great force awaken and come alive within me. It asked what I wanted and began to move as I directed. It was awesome to feel the force moving through me. At the same time, I felt the ego rejoice and begin suggesting uses for the force. Gradually I realized that I would be able to do anything I wanted to do, and the force would bring me anything I wanted. Heady thoughts indeed, but the semester was ending and I turned my attention to my studies while the force slept impatiently within, waiting to be used.

———•◆•———

With summer's arrival the school year ended, and I headed back home to enjoy my first break after starting college. In exchange for good times with my friends, I broke my inner contact with Dr. Cook's mental force. I stayed up late every night, stopped meditating, goofed off, and ate all the wrong foods. Chicken fried steaks and chocolate milkshakes were my basic food groups along with a quart of Mint English Toffee ice cream to wash it all down. With so many delightful distractions, I completely ignored the force that I had developed so strongly in my mind. Thus, the force began to live a life of its own through me . . . without conscience . . . ego driven . . . and without my *knowing* . . .

The force, whose only purpose was to be available to satisfy my every wish, simply went crazy like a well-trained dog turned loose in the wild. I had no idea there would be a terrible price to pay for my foolishness. My thoughts were on finding a summer job and spending time with my friends. It would all be so pleasant—no books, no classes, no problems. I was young and life was mine for the taking. Forgetting the years of study ahead, I could see myself graduating and working with people to bring them better health.

Unbeknownst to me, the force was in motion to bring me the greatest lesson of my young life. I had neglected it by not giving it any assignments to occupy its energy. Therefore, searching to be of service, this powerful force of universal energy designed its own lesson for me, a lesson to teach me compassion for people in pain and bring me closer contact with the inner Angels of Light.

While final preparations were being arranged for my lesson, I sat on my motorcycle parked just off the shoulder of the road waiting for some friends to meet me. I couldn't help smiling when I thought how wonderful life was at that very moment. I was determined to ignore the inner voice that kept telling me firmly to go home. At 19, I thought I knew better and dismissed the ominous warning. Why should I listen to inner directions on a beautiful sunny afternoon? Then I felt a large, powerful hand push against my chest, trying to hold me back from the coming disaster. When I disregarded the hand, the sensation slowly faded away. And now I found myself waiting for my friends without a care in the world, not knowing my life was about to change forever.

Suddenly out of nowhere, an old pickup truck doing 70 miles an hour sped around the corner behind me. Losing control on the curve, the driver swerved right. Knocking my motorcycle out from under me, the truck hit me squarely in the middle of my back. Instantly airborne from the impact, I landed face down, 96 feet from where I had been hit.

Only my hands were spared from injury when my body smashed against the unforgiving asphalt, my neck broken in two places. Plunged into a world of brutal, agonizing pain, darkness mercifully engulfed me. I was rushed to the hospital—thankfully still unconscious—in an ambulance. The emergency room doctors determined that I would be dead in a few hours. With a prognosis of death, they decided not to transfuse a "dead" man.

When I finally regained consciousness that night, I found myself surrounded by white light. The Guardians of Life appeared in this wondrous light to instruct me in a specific method of breathing. These heavenly emissaries said I must fight to remain conscious and breathe exactly as instructed for the next eight hours. They told me that only by following their instructions would I live to complete my mission. While pain threatened to consume me, I gratefully began the steady, rhythmic breathing, which kept me in contact with these angelic beings throughout the night. Embraced in their love, I was taken to another world far from my body's pain, a world of tranquility, peace and healing.

The next morning, the nurses were shocked to discover that I was still alive. One of the nurses quickly rushed in with my first meal—*a steak!* Not only could I not chew it, I couldn't even tell the nurse what was wrong. My upper jaw—split in two from the accident—literally fell into my mouth whenever I stopped pressing my tongue up against it. The same nurse returned a half hour later. Seeing my untouched steak, she remarked, "Not hungry, eh?" She quickly grabbed my tray and left.

Fortunately, another nurse in the kitchen noticed my uneaten steak, which came back with a report that I wasn't hungry. Checking my chart further, she saw that I hadn't eaten anything since arriving. She put the steak through a meat grinder and brought it to my bedside. When she managed to bring me back to consciousness, I couldn't explain that I could barely open my mouth without my upper teeth falling into it. Somehow I managed to swallow the ground meat whole as she gently pushed tiny bits of it through my closed lips. It was days before my broken jaw was discovered because there was so much concern about my other injuries.

After this agonizing first meal, the doctors decided to set my broken legs since it appeared I might live after all. Later that same morning, a husky nurse entered my room before the casts had fully set. She was in the wrong room and thought she was supposed to turn me over. Grabbing both leg casts, she started to turn me over with great strength and a hearty, "Here we go!"

The nurse only realized her mistake when her fingers sank further into the now bloody casting material and I screamed in pain. Horrified, she backed away and ran from my room. Her forceful attempt to turn me over, twisted the set so that my legs didn't heal well. They were never reset and recast because the doctors were never informed of this incident. The nurses kept it quiet—no doubt to protect their jobs—and I was in no position to inform the doctors since I was unconscious most of the time during the first days of my hospitalization.

For the next week, I drifted in and out of consciousness, more aware of the presence of the angels than the nurses coming and going. Once the doctors were absolutely certain I would live, they met with my mother, solemnly informing her that I would never walk again. However, they hadn't counted on the determination of a teenager and divine intervention.

For three months, I lay immobilized in bed, longing for the day when the doctors would allow me to use a wheelchair. During this time, the doctors removed the casts from my legs every six weeks, but each time the bones were like jelly. It made me sick to watch the doctor move them from side to side while he shook his head. But each night the Power visited me, and their loving presence awakened my desire for further communication with them. They showed me my life ahead, a life in which

I *was* walking. I clung to this vision like a drowning man to a life preserver. Their constant words of encouragement carried me through my long recovery.

Finally the day arrived when my doctors approved a wheelchair. It was a 1918 beauty of woven cane, manufactured for the wounded of World War I. Although my legs remained in casts, I reveled in my new found mobility. Once accustomed to my chair, I could be found wheeling all over the hospital. For months I zipped up and down the halls, thrilled to cruise in freedom all day long. I even managed to sneak out of the hospital a few times to roll up and down the nearby streets since there was little traffic in those days.

My upper body got stronger and stronger, and after a while, I begged the doctors to let me have crutches. If I could just get my hands on crutches, I knew I'd be up and walking in no time. Finally they gave in to my pleas. They warned me not to get my hopes up, and told me that my leg casts still could not be removed. I didn't care. I knew I was ready.

When a nurse finally brought me crutches, my heart started to beat faster. This was *it*. Excitedly, I used the crutches to push myself up out of my wheelchair while she watched. Taking a deep breath, I tucked one crutch under each arm, ready to embark on my new means of travel. I promptly collapsed on the floor unable to bear the pain shooting up both legs. My right leg still hadn't healed, and both legs were worthless after being immobilized in casts for months. Helpless, I cried as the nurse lifted me off the floor and back into my wheelchair.

For the first time I wondered if the doctors were right. Maybe I would never walk again. Only the blessed visitations from the Angels of Light kept me focused on the hope that I would walk again. Inspired by visions of walking, which the angels continued to show me, I decided to try again. Every step was agony and I learned to inhabit a world of unending pain where I met pain's constant companions: hopelessness and depression. Only in the precious moments when I was surrounded by celestial beings of light, did I know my future was assured.

Finally the doctors sent me home. I realized my education had to be put aside while I learned to walk. Months of agony passed slowly, but eventually my determined efforts met with success. Once I mastered the crutches, there was no stopping me. I became an expert at dragging myself around the house by propelling myself forward on the crutches while my plaster legs dragged painfully behind me. As the pain in my legs slowly diminished, I began to feel safe traveling on my convenience sticks. These were lonely times, but I didn't seek the company of friends. I told myself they were busy working or having fun and had no time for someone confined to crutches. Although I wasn't really happy being alone, I didn't realize that my anger over the "unfairness" of my accident drove my friends away.

It was years before I fully accepted any responsibility for my part in the accident by not listening to my guidance. However, as I began to see the truth, there came a day when I felt ready to walk without crutches. Although I hated to give up my safety net, I knew it was time for my legs to try the walking game. I thought I had learned to live with pain, but my first efforts to walk rewarded me with a new level of agony. My legs—still encased in protective casts—simply would not obey me. Despite my best efforts day after day, I began to worry that I might be crippled for the rest of my life.

The months spent struggling to master crutches seemed like child's play compared to forcing my legs to walk. Relying on the angelic visions of my future, I summoned the will power that had brought me this far. Forcing myself to take my first steps using supporting canes, I began to walk with naked intent . . . just me, my canes, my legs, and, most importantly, God. An eternity seemed to pass before I could walk unassisted, but, in time, I left the canes behind. I could walk on my own.

As soon as I could walk without my canes, the doctors removed my casts for the last time. I was shocked to see the spindly appendages that claimed to be my legs. They were thin as willow branches, but I was grateful to see them again. I swore I would never take the privilege of walking for granted. Although it took years for my ankles to flex normally, there came a day when I could walk for miles, up hill and down, as far as I wished.

I truly thought I would never forget the privilege of walking. And for a while after my recovery I thanked God every morning. But somewhere along the way I forgot and began to take walking for granted. Then when I was 55, I got an early morning call from worried parents asking me to visit their 18-year-old daughter in the hospital. She had been driving near Lake Tahoe when she put on the brakes and they grabbed. The sudden stop threw her forward and she hit her head on the windshield.

Although the impact didn't damage the windshield, the blow to her forehead caused paralysis from her neck down. She had been in the hospital for nearly a month, but x-rays and scans didn't reveal any damage to her nervous system.

The next day I went to the hospital and ran healing energy, but it refused to go into her body. The Power told me that I couldn't help her because she had chosen this path for her soul growth. I told her I was sorry that I was unable to help her. When I asked if she ever prayed and meditated, she replied she never had time. I told her gently that God had now given her the time. I encouraged her to begin praying that very day and to keep on searching for help.

Driving home, I pondered why my motorcycle accident had nearly destroyed my body and yet I was walking. This young girl's car accident had done no visible damage to her body or her car, and yet she might never walk again. Remembering my promise never to take the privilege of walking for granted, I renewed my prayers of thanks. Walking up the steps at home, I felt blessed to be walking when every orthopedic specialist my mother consulted said that I would never walk again.

The pain I endured while learning to walk again enabled me to see how I had created my accident by turning my back on the energy force created with Dr. Cook's mental formula. It was rather like patting a grizzly on the head, turning my back, and walking away from the beast without expecting any trouble from that direction. Once I realized what I had done, I never used the formula again. I realized it was too dangerous, and too available to any ego impulse. It was—as Dr. Cook had said—a force without conscience, without heart.

Some things are best left alone. Even *with* a conscience, we are sometimes hard-pressed to do the right thing when faced with the temptations of life. What would you have done in the same circumstances? Would Ultimate Mastery over the physical world sweep you into the realm of ego? Now looking back, I realize how unfit I was to receive a gift of that potency in my early years of development.

Once Dr. Cook died, those people who had activated the mental flow of energy under his instruction ceased having the power to receive whatever they wanted by using his formula. He was the lodestone for that particular energy so that after his death the power of the formula lessened and gradually faded away. Many years later, I tried to reclaim that inner mental pattern of energy, but whatever Dr. Cook had done for me in those early years had simply vanished. He had been the catalyst, but now that particular energy that he activated is gone forever.

5

LIFE BEGINS AGAIN

————•◆••◆•————

Ayear had passed since my accident. It was summer again and I had to find a summer job to help pay for my college tuition. Before long, the perfect job appeared. I became a lifeguard at the Redlands Sylvan Plunge. This gave me a chance to swim every day and further strengthen my legs. The Plunge (built in the early 1900s) was a huge outdoor pool whose water poured in icy cold directly from the mountains. We all had a love/hate relationship with that frigid water in the blistering heat of summer. The pool was kept clean by throwing in handfuls of chlorine once a day. We had to be on the alert to dodge this casual chemical bath.

One of my duties was to teach swimming to children ranging in ages from five through 14. They were charming, or so I thought when I first saw them eagerly arranged around the pool. Our famous Red Cross swimming program was in action for the summer, and I was proud to be a part of it. As the newest instructor, I wanted the kids to like me and thought I should go easy on them. After all, they were only youngsters.

The experienced lifeguards said I was crazy to baby the kids. Sure enough, I watched other students learn to swim under the tutelage of these seasoned lifeguards who yelled and screamed at their charges like Marine Drill Sergeants. These instructors got first class results while my kids used and abused me by spending their class time fooling around the pool. As summer rolled on and none of my 60 charges could swim, I became desperate.

Finally, the turning point came in midsummer. One of the little monsters—as I now regarded them—was a chubby kid named Charlie. All summer, he had been my adversary in a battle of wills. He would *not* stay out of the pool, no matter how I pleaded. Every time I turned my back there was Charlie bobbing about in the water like some enormous walrus. He clung to the side of the pool, eyes dreamily closed, stubbornly refusing to come out of the water.

On this landmark day—after warning Charlie over and over to get out of the pool—I reached down and grabbed him out of the water. With all the frustration of an entire summer lost trying to teach these little fiends to swim, I flung him far out into deep water before I remembered he couldn't swim. The class froze. We all came to the same conclusion at once: Charlie was about to *drown!*

The children began yelling at me to save him. I dove in, swam to where he was struggling, and pulled his thrashing, rotund body back to the pool's edge. As I climbed out of the water with Charlie in tow, dozens of little hands began patting me on the back. They cheered and shouted, "Mr. MacKimmie saved Charlie!"

Evidently the fact that I had thrown Charlie into deep water in the first place had been forgotten in the excitement of watching his rescue. I recognized my chance. I turned and yelled, *"All right you little monsters, line up against the wall. Now!"* To my complete amazement, they followed my instructions. Standing motionless, they were glued to the wall like tiny soldiers frozen at attention. Charlie was still sputtering out chlorinated water when I turned to him and barked, *"You too, Charlie, or back you go into the pool!"*

From that glorious moment on, the children were transformed. They followed my every direction to the letter. One at a time, I had them jump into deep water from the ten-foot board, an exciting event considering none of them could swim a stroke. As each one surfaced, I touched a long bamboo pole to the non-swimmer's chest. Instantly, little hands clamped the pole with a viselike grip. Then I pulled each one to the side of the pool.

When all 60 had gone through this jump and retrieve, I informed them that they would have to stay in the shallow end (nicknamed the "baby pool") until they could swim. By this time, they desperately wanted their parents to see them jump from the ten-foot board into the deep end of the pool. Although there was grumbling among the troops, my edict was all the motivation they needed. Soon they were swimming back and forth across the pool like little fish. Only then did I let them bring their parents on Sunday, a big day at the pool, to watch them fly fearlessly off the ten-foot board in a great show of bravado. By helping them present this awesome spectacle to their parents, I became their hero for the summer.

Years later, when grown men stopped me on the street to ask if I had been a lifeguard and teacher at Sylvan Plunge, I answered "yes" with some trepidation. Most of my life I've weighed in at 155, and some of these inquisitors towered above me with musculature that would have made Mr. Universe envious. To my surprise—and relief—they insisted on shaking my hand. They thanked me for not letting them get away with any mischief and complemented me on my strict discipline. Whenever this happened, I pondered then—as I do now—why strict discipline got the job done when kindness turned my charges into wild, defiant little beasts.

Early in life I discovered I never did worth a darn working for others, and the pool was no exception. In my third summer of lifeguarding and teaching swimming, our new pool manager, Walt, decided to let the mothers of the newest group of fledgling swimmers sit around the edge of the pool. Redlands had produced champion swimmers for years, but the children had always been separated from their mothers during class. Now with mothers ringing the pool, happily sunbathing and dangling their feet in the water, the children looked to them for support and comfort.

Soon it was clear these youngsters weren't learning how to swim. All the instructors were discouraged. Finally I asked the other instructors if I should present our case to the manager. They agreed and said they would back me up. We marched in as a group to confront Walt. After I explained our difficulty, Walt asked the others if they agreed with me. Seeing their jobs on the line, they quickly shifted sides. I was shocked to hear their four voices. "No way." "This is all MacKimmie's idea." "MacKimmie's the only one who thinks your new program won't work." "We don't have a problem." Walt turned to me, "Well, MacKimmie, I hope you have another job. You're fired."

Not wanting to let Walt have the last word, I replied, "Walt, surely you recognized my resignation speech. The way you have it set up, these kids will *never* learn to swim." Then I added a few pointed remarks about the loyalty of friends while the other instructors studied the floor in embarrassment. I held back from using a phrase I remembered a minister saying when the church deacon made an announcement that the minister's services would no longer be required. He explained that the minister was being replaced the next week by a new pastor. This announcement came as a total surprise to the minister. Now standing at the pulpit, sacked, he declared, "Today will be my final sermon. And when I walk up the center aisle on my way out, I hope you will *all* feel free to take advantage of the mistletoe pinned to the seat of my pants."

———·◆·———

Once my lifeguarding days were over, I had to find another summer job. Fortunately, I found one working the pick and shovel detail at a pottery plant outside of town. I enjoyed getting my body in shape since I knew I would be spending most of the day sitting in class during the coming school year.

On my first day, I was surprised to find out that people came from miles around to watch one particular forklift operator move ceramics from one place to another in the warehouse. Famous for his skill, he loaded his forklift an impossible seven tiers high and almost burnt rubber taking off. The stacked ceramics always appeared in danger of crashing to the cement floor. Flying through the factory at full tilt, "Lucky" turned corners at ever higher speeds.

All the workers had side-bets going, sure that Lucky would crash a load, but it never happened. It was as though he became one with the forklift. Totally in charge of this balance game, he would twitch the back end of the forklift after each daring maneuver, and the ceramics would magically settle back into place. A marvelous showman, he was as astounding as the finest athlete, making the impossible seem easy.

Each morning various molds were poured full of soft clay. Once turned out of the mold, these future ceramics were carefully arranged to air-dry. Toilet bowls and tanks, sinks and other ceramics filled the factory. Before firing, these forms were so fragile that they would shatter instantly from the slightest tap, like a delicate, china cup dropped on the floor. Although no one would ever admit bumping them, a few had to be discarded every day.

Once dry, the clay forms were sprayed with a colored glaze and run through the kiln on a slow tour at 2,100 degrees. After firing, they were incredibly tough, but it was days before they cooled down enough to be handled again. At that point, they were inspected to catch any flaws before shipment.

Part of my job was to truck the flawed seconds out to a cliff where I threw them off the edge to destroy them. They broke when they shattered on rocks 30 feet below or crashed on the piles of other broken ceramics. Amazingly, I would sometimes hear a resounding "bonk" when they occasionally bounced off another ceramic and high into the air. I would look over the edge of the cliff and see that the piece I had just thrown was still intact. When that happened, I had to hike down and break up the recalcitrant reject with a sledge hammer. I marveled at the strength of this clay, which would have shattered from the slightest tap before firing.

When I think of the incredible transformation that took place in the kiln, I'm reminded of the human soul. It is likewise transformed by the fires of life—perfectly designed to test each soul—until it is steadfast to its inner purpose. Thus, our soul becomes a finished ceramic, able to withstand the slings and arrows of outrageous fortune that befall us in daily life. Faced with trillions of decisions to make in our brief lifetime, I think that all of us who choose life in this dimension have earned gold stars in heaven.

———— • ◆ • ————

In the fall of 1949, while I was preparing to return to chiropractic college, the Power appeared again to ask if I wanted to ease the burden of my journey. Ignorance and youthful enthusiasm bubbled to the surface. I thought I had already experienced the difficult times of my earthly existence. In my view, I had traveled every potholed road imaginable. Brimming with confidence, I asked again for everything. And the Power graciously designed more lessons for the years ahead. But back to my education . . .

Glad to return to my studies, I appreciated our outstanding professors. I remember Dr. Regerdie, our instructor in psychiatry. At the front of the room above his desk was a sign near the ceiling that declared on one side: "It is later than you think," and on the other side: "Things are not as they seem to be." The sign was hinged in such a manner as to show only one side at a time. Often when we asked a question during his lecture, he would use a long pole to flip the sign so that it would show one side or the other. We were amazed at how many of our questions could be answered by these two statements. I thought there should have been third side reading: "Man, know thyself" to complete the sequence.

Dr. Rake was our brilliant physiology instructor. We fondly called him Dr. George. He would enter the lecture hall promptly at 8:00 A.M. Running swiftly, briefcase in hand, he headed for a high wooden stool placed at the front of the room. Our attention was always on Dr. George from the moment he began his unusual entrance.

Gathering speed, Dr. George would mount the stool like a professional rodeo rider. Then, doctor and stool would both slide across the polished floor. With a practiced eye, he zeroed in on his target. The stool came to a halt just behind the podium. Setting down his briefcase, he began his lecture without missing a beat. Students from all over the college gathered to watch his ever increasing skill in this event. As he gained more confidence, he rode the stool with one hand in the air like a cowboy riding a bull. His other hand held his briefcase. Watching him slide into place behind the podium, perfectly relaxed and at ease, was an amazing show.

However, one day his performance came to an abrupt halt. Dr. George dashed in and leaped full tilt upon the stool, which promptly split right down the middle. We watched in horror as the legs of the stool shot out sideways, leaving the good doctor with his feet spread far apart on the floor, and his more delicate anatomy pinched firmly between the stool's two top halves. His face turned chalk white. We rushed forward and carefully helped him extricate himself from the stool remains. He went on with his lecture—a testimony to his fortitude—and limped heroically out of class after dismissing us.

For a week, Dr. George resembled a large capital "A" in slow motion when he walked. I winced every time I saw him walking gingerly around the college. We were astonished when—like any good cowboy— he decided to ride again. But he added a new wrinkle to his performance. When he entered the lecture hall, he first tested the stool vigorously in every direction.

Once the stool had passed his thorough inspection, Dr. George left the room. A moment later, he came dashing in as of old. Jumping astride the stool at top speed—briefcase in one hand, the other in the air—he slid expertly across the front of the room to land in perfect position behind the lectern. His valiant return to the saddle brought cheers and thunderous applause from his students who had assumed his riding days were over.

Staying after class to inspect the infamous stool, I saw it had been wired together so securely it could have withstood an atomic blast. However, as the semester went on, I noted that Dr. George still tested the stool vigorously before each ride. A good lesson for us all to look before we leap.

In 1949, Dr. Nilsson, our superb anatomy professor, acquired new, surplus refrigerators from the Navy for the school's dissection laboratory. This was a great improvement over the old formaldehyde method of preservation. With refrigeration, the bodies remained perfectly preserved, and we could work on them for hours every day. I found the study of the human body incredibly fascinating, and anatomy quickly became one of my favorite subjects.

In the lab, we worked on hundreds of cadavers and were soon accustomed to dissecting all parts of the human body. However, I was saddened to realize that once our miraculous life force was gone, only inert matter remained, mere vestiges of our former humanity. I knew the wondrous spark of life had to be a gift from a higher power since any endeavor to rekindle it, once gone, came to nothing. I was already looking forward to helping my future patients realize the full potential of their own gift of life.

As part of our chiropractic education, we also studied the process of human creation with comprehensive courses in obstetrics and gynecology. After a professor showed our class several public health reports, which documented home births as having lower mortality rates than hospital births, I was astonished to learn that home births were considered unorthodox and were discouraged by medical authorities. Every mother-to-be was encouraged to have a hospital delivery by a medical doctor.

After being in practice for years, one lady chiropractor from my obstetrics class began delivering babies for poor Mexican women living in the Los Angeles barrios. She was Spanish and wanted to help poor people in her community with home deliveries. I learned later that—although she had no complaints from her patients and had been trained in obstetrics—the authorities took away her license for delivering babies without a medical degree.

Years later, I met a physiotherapist who had home-delivered more than 5,000 babies until he was arrested for practicing medicine without a license. I asked him how he had delivered so many babies with no complications and nothing but praise from the mothers. When he shared his approach, it made perfect "common" sense to me.

The therapist told the prospective mother that he would stay at her home until she had delivered and her baby was breast-feeding in her arms. As soon as the mother felt her time was near, he actually moved into her home! He assured each anxious mother-to-be that there was absolutely no hurry in giving birth. Knowing the therapist was right there and ready to help deliver the baby in God's good time, the mother had a sense of complete support and relaxation in the birthing process.

A wonderful bond developed between the mother, the therapist, and the coming baby. There was no stress about getting to the hospital, no drugs to hurry the delivery so the doctor could attend another patient, and none to slow the delivery until the doctor arrived. The therapist said that his only job was to keep the baby from falling on the floor. After the delivery, he had the mother breast-feed her baby. This caused the large blood vessels, which had fed the baby in the uterus, to constrict automatically.

As in the case of the lady chiropractor, no complaints were ever made against the therapist by his patients. What a strange world we live in. Why can't every patient freely choose his or her own care? Having access to whatever care is chosen should be as divine a right as breathing clean air and drinking pure water. Why does this choice sometimes become a battlefield, as in the movie *First Do No Harm?*

———•◆•———

During my second year in school, there was a shortage of nurses in Los Angeles. In contrast to the war years, there were finally enough doctors to minister to the medical needs of society, and hospital surgeries exploded in numbers. I started working as a nurse at the largest hospital in Los Angeles. Although I wasn't Catholic, most of the hospital staff belonged to that faith.

Sister Geraldine ruled the nursing staff with an iron hand like Hitler (minus the mustache) and scared the hell out of everyone, including me. Thankfully, she took a shine to me, which made my life easier. I attended college during the day and worked 12 hour private-duty shifts at night, a draining schedule. Fortunately, nursing supervisors kindly took pity on college students and allowed us to study when routine hospital activities slowed in the late evening hours.

At first, I was terrified. I worried constantly about making a mistake. The older nursing supervisors told me I was too conscientious, but I wanted my patients to be comfortable and have the best possible care. Veteran nurses carefully explained that if I followed specific orders— exactly as given by the doctor—and the patient died, it was not my fault. Somehow that idea did nothing to calm my nerves. During the three years that I nursed pre- and post-surgically, I never rested easily. I began to suspect, what I now know. In most cases, Mother Nature can *prevent* what drugs and surgery can only attempt to correct.

While I was working as a nurse, it continued to disturb me that the medical profession did not accept chiropractors, no matter what we accomplished in the way of pain relief. Like a fool, I thought I could change that view. I mentioned the merits of chiropractic to the hospital staff. What a mistake! They told me I was crazy and proceeded to tell me stories of chiropractors paralyzing people for life. I felt right at home as though I had gone back in time to the school nurse's office for another lecture on the evils of chiropractic.

However, I talked to some of the nurses after hours. Half of them said I was totally correct, but they were afraid of losing their jobs and being blackballed from nursing if they supported my view. My coworkers urged me to become a "real" doctor, another familiar notion. I decided to keep my mouth shut about my career choice. The staff relaxed, sure they had converted a potential quack into a promising medical student. I went along since what they didn't know wouldn't hurt them—or me.

After I had gained more experience, I was assigned to work for six months on the psychiatric ward, home to 40 patients in separate rooms. They could be out of their rooms during the day as long as they didn't leave the ward, which was separated from the main hospital by large, heavy double doors. I thought this interesting assignment would give me another perspective on healing. Things were going smoothly on my first day until the official bedtime when the other nurses casually asked if I would put a petite, older woman to bed.

"Simple enough," I thought. I didn't notice that my fellow workers made no move to put any of the other patients to bed. Studying the tiny woman before me, she appeared to be in her 60s, and looked as frail and withered as a dried autumn leaf. Thin, pale arms revealed IV puncture marks from her long stay in the ward. I smiled and told her that it was time for bed. She calmly turned around and started down the hall. I frowned. She was clearly headed in the *opposite* direction from her room.

Before I could react, my elderly patient suddenly took off running. As she gained speed, my fellow workers shouted wildly, urging me to catch her before she made it through the doors leading to the main hospital corridor beyond. Ignoring the growing laughter of the other nurses, I raced down the hall after her. I was determined to catch her before she escaped. When I caught up with her, I tackled her from behind, throwing my arms around her upper body. With amazing speed and strength, she bent over, lifting my feet off the ground, and raced on.

Now I was being carried on her back while she sprinted onward with all the determination of a football player headed for a touchdown in the final seconds of the Super Bowl. My struggling only served to increase the old girl's resolve to escape into the hospital. A mighty battle ensued. Her goal was in sight, and my thrashing about on her back didn't even give her pause. I dared not let go.

In a last desperate attempt to stop her, I threw my body weight backward with enough force so that I was again on my feet, and she was off hers. Once she didn't have any purchase on the floor, victory was mine. She instantly calmed down as though her mad dash for freedom had never taken place. We quietly headed back to her room where she meekly allowed me to put her to bed for the night.

When I returned to the nursing station—still unnerved by my recent skirmish—the other nurses were in hysterics. I was forced to listen while my coworkers laughed and described my mad dash down the hall as I desperately tried to stop our patient's flight to freedom. My initiation over, I was welcomed onto the ward as one of the gang.

Every full moon, the nurses asked me to help put leather restraints on the patients for the night. They told me their patients reacted to the moon's influence, thus the word "lunatic." I thought this was all superstitious nonsense. But one night when the patients started acting crazier than usual, the head nurse told me to go up on the roof for a look at the night sky. From my vantage point on the roof, I saw the full moon rising over the eastern mountains. After that, I was convinced. Experts may say people are not affected by the full moon, but we learn as we go along, and the experts always seem to be the last to wake up to the facts of life.

I enjoyed my new assignment, but secretly agreed with my co-workers who said that a few of the psychiatrists were crazier than their patients. Since I got along well with the psychiatric patients—probably since I have a few of my own quirks and wouldn't life be boring if we *all* didn't have a few—I was soon transferred to the highest security section. Here the patients, who were considered dangerous to themselves or to others, remained locked in their rooms at all times.

Since there was little interaction with the patients, my new duty seemed boring until one day a new priest showed up on the ward. He was replacing one of the assigned priests who had gone on vacation. Normally the priests performed all rites with the security door firmly locked between themselves and the inmate/patient. A small window-like opening in the top of the door was used for these rituals. However, this newly assigned priest pompously insisted that he was going into each room to attend his new flock. Unwilling to heed our warnings, he haughtily pronounced to us lowly mortals that he was completely protected by God. We could hardly argue this point with a priest.

Exuding confidence and religious supremacy, the self-important priest ordered us not to—under any circumstances—interfere with his ministry as he visited each patient. We opened the first locked door and he headed into the patient's room while we huddled safely outside. As he began to offer religious succor, the uncooperative patient grabbed him by the throat and proceeded to choke him to the floor. Instantly, the priest began kicking and screaming while the patient—now on top of him—started scratching and biting his captive.

Against the holy father's order, we quickly headed in before any serious damage could be inflicted upon God's anointed. By the time we subdued the patient, the priest's face and neck were bleeding and his cassock was ripped in several places. The next day, sporting mummy-like bandages and wearing a new cassock, the subdued priest quietly performed the rites of the church standing well back from the window of the locked door. We heard no more lofty talk of heavenly protection during his temporary assignment.

——— • ◆ • ———

By the time I returned to regular ward duty, I was completely familiar with hospital procedures. I began questioning what I saw happening around me. Why were certain people allowed to make such momentous decisions in our lives when we were sick and incapacitated? Who could judge how and when our own fire of life may be extinguished?

I recall a Japanese man hospitalized on my floor who had shot himself in the head. He owed $150 and thought if he killed himself, he would no longer be a financial burden to his family. However, when his next door neighbor, a medical doctor, heard the shot, he rushed over and literally stuffed the man's exposed brain back into his head.

Once admitted to the hospital, the patient's temperature spiked up and down between 80 and 112. When his temperature went up, nurses poured dozens of bottles of rubbing alcohol over him and positioned six huge floor fans, blowing full blast over his body, to cool him. When his temperature dropped to 80, they encased him in heating pads to bring the body temperature up again. Per doctor's orders, this routine went on for three days and nights. Attending specialists hovered whenever the family visited. He died on the fourth day.

A bill of $35,000 for around-the-clock care went to his family. (I can't begin to imagine what this bill would look like today.) I was nursing down the hall and saw all of this firsthand. Even after the man's death, the specialists crowed about how they had kept him alive and very nearly saved him. Another nurse showed me the hospital chart. In her eyes, this patient had been legally dead for three days since his brain wave had remained flat during his entire hospitalization.

During my years of nursing, I was surprised when other nurses confided to me how many doctors were in the dark about their patient's condition. However, the nurses told me that doctors covered their lack of knowledge in graceful ways as they had to present an appearance of total knowledge concerning the ills of humanity. One nursing supervisor complained that some doctors were such paragons of self-importance that they had to have their lofty place in the hospital hierarchy acknowledged by all us lesser mortals. In those days, an M.D. was a god and knew everything about healing. He was the final authority and had no feet of clay.

About this time, I had the good fortune to make friends with a wonderful older nurse who told me that when she first started her career, doctors would not open a closed hospital door for themselves. They would stop in front of the door and wait for a nurse or one of the staff to come by and open the door *for* them. This unwritten law actually caused her dismissal from one hospital.

My friend explained that she was on her way to answer a patient's call button in another part of the hospital when she saw a physician standing in front of the door she needed to go through. He was at the front of a line of nurses, waiting for one of them to open the door for him. He was too grand to open it for himself, and none of the nurses would step forward to open it for him. My friend went to the head of this Mexican standoff, threw the door wide open and asked the doctor, "Did you break your arm?" She was fired the same day even though she was a superb nurse who always put the needs of her patients first.

Whenever I found time, I enjoyed hanging out in other hospitals, which were wonderful places to observe patients firsthand. In those days, no one paid much attention as to who came and went in the wards. I wandered in and out of hospital rooms with wonderful opportunities to talk with patients about their conditions and treatments. When I had an opportunity to ask doctors difficult questions in chemistry, physiology and pathology, they were surprised to find a nurse knowledgeable in these areas. I was also interested in blood work and enjoyed talking with the technicians about their work. They too were surprised when I could discuss their speciality in detail. These experiences gave me a great appreciation for my education, but I never forgot that our chiropractic education wasn't recognized by other professions. To them, we would always be "quacks," plain and simple.

I was young and innocent when I first started nursing. However, I soon developed a cynical attitude toward drugs and surgery when I saw them used and abused in the 1940s to the disadvantage of the patient. It was then that I pledged to ally myself with Mother Nature in my future healing practice. While drugs and surgery have become the accepted methods in our ongoing attempts to heal the body, alternative therapies offer a more natural way. They return the responsibility of health and healing back into the patient's hands where it belongs. After all, who knows more about a body than the person who lives in it 24/7?

————·◆·————

Nursing for top medical specialists gave me insight into the standard treatments for mankind's common ills. Intuition was a mainstay for old-time medical practitioners. By actually taking the time to talk with the patient, doctors got a gut feeling about the cause of the patient's illness and the remedy. Today, most doctors rely on sophisticated diagnostic testing. They have given up the compassionate art of listening to the patient for clues and findings that may not appear in modern test results. Despite modern medical technology, the body remains a mystery. Today's medical approach to ill health continues to be the relief of symptoms. Seldom is there a search to find the deeper, underlying cause of the patient's sickness and disease. Americans have become a nation of pill takers, looking for the magic bullet to alleviate any and all symptoms.

At one time, I too thought the magic bullet was a reality. I recall one evening when I was babysitting for one of the hospital surgeons and discovered his son was running a high fever. Since aspirin was the magic bullet for fevers, I called the surgeon for permission to give his son an aspirin. Over the background noise of the party, the surgeon shouted, "That fever has a purpose. It tells us that Mother Nature is already on the job. Just give my son plenty of water and let him rest."

When the surgeon returned home, he told me that he didn't believe in childhood vaccinations. In his opinion, chicken pox, measles, mumps and the like were simply a normal part of growing up. Like my birth mother, he thought going through these diseases provided a child with a strong immune system. He was a wonderful doctor who cared more for his patients than for money, and I resolved to pattern myself after this fine physician.

On another night when I was on duty at the hospital, a mother and father brought their newborn baby into the emergency room. I was a friend of the older doctor on call that night and he called me in to see the preemie. I gasped when I saw her. She was the tiniest baby I had ever seen. Her delicate fingers, curled tightly around her mother's thumb, looked impossibly small.

Today preemies are placed in incubators and many different therapies are available to save their lives, but back in the '40s, technology had nothing to offer these worried parents. Desperate to save their baby, they looked hopefully at my medical friend. He put his hand on the father's shoulder and told them to take their little one back home. He instructed the father to hold and rock the baby for as long as he could, taking care to keep her warm at all times. Then the mother was to take over and do the same.

The parents were to continue taking turns so that one of them was always touching, holding and rocking their baby 24 hours a day for the next month. The good doctor explained that their constant, touching care was her only chance for survival; otherwise, she would die. And she *did* survive thanks to a wise doctor's sensible advice, and to her loving parents for following his advice.

Today more people are aware of the increased disease and death rates in children who are not touched and held when they are young. Before the nuclear family became a thing of the past, people used to be affectionate, hugging each other without fear of disapproval. I used to pick up little children in the park, swing them around, talk and laugh with them, but today such activities might land one in jail. Society is so fragmented that we have become strangers to one another. As a consequence, our immune systems suffer for lack of human touch.

Touch is so very important throughout our lives, especially during those moments before we cross over the great divide between this life and the next. While I worked as a nurse, I was blessed many times to be with patients making their final transition. Loving angels would appear and touch those about to depart. As soon as this took place, the patient's face would light up, having received God's grace.

Cherished relatives and friends who had crossed over also gathered around the bed to bring their loved ones home. Often my patients introduced me to the family gathering from the other side. I was always happy to meet "Aunt Mabel who died last year," "Grandpa Ed who died 40 years ago," or "my best friend, Sam, from kindergarten, who died when

I was ten." On their part, patients were grateful to have someone accept the presence of their precious spiritual family, who waited at their bedside to take them home. After being present at these joyful reunions and seeing the breathtaking beauty of the other side, I know it is a cause for great celebration as patients near the end of their old life and embrace their new life's beginning.

——————•◆•——————

Back at school, the day finally arrived for my internship at the school's clinic to begin. I was thrilled to start working with people. When I arrived at the clinic on my first day, several clinicians standing outside the front door warned me not to allow any dogs into the waiting room. I noticed a spaniel lurking nearby in the bushes, but I thought their warning must be some prank played on every new clinician. I wasn't about to play the fool on my first day. Nodding briskly in their direction, I started through the door.

Before I could close the door behind me, the spaniel bolted from the bushes and darted past me, racing through the waiting room. He dived into a treatment room and made a flying leap onto an adjusting table. I couldn't believe my eyes when he carefully positioned himself with his head in the face cradle. The clinicians, who had followed me in, laughed and said I would have to adjust him, or he would never leave. I wasn't about to be made a fool of a second time. I tried to look confident and stepped forward to forcibly remove the animal. When I started to take hold of him, he growled loudly, making it clear he was ready to hold his ground.

A group of senior clinicians gathered in the treating room to watch the show. One of them explained that the spaniel had been afflicted with terrible arthritis until last semester when one of the interns adjusted him for a joke. The dog's arthritis was so relieved that he now hovered outside the clinic, waiting for any opportunity to get further adjustments. Once I gave the dog his adjustment, he jumped down and headed outside. After this incident, I was careful not to let the dog get past me. I noticed he never tried to get in when patients were going through the door. No, he would wait until he saw the white of our lab coats to make his move. Smart dog!

The last two years of school were the most enjoyable because we finally treated real live human beings. These were the first patients we treated on our way to becoming drugless doctors of chiropractic. We quickly discovered they were not some strange animal called a "patient," but living, breathing human beings who required real solutions to real problems.

At first I thought the patients we saw at the clinic were committed to chiropractic since they poured in every day. More likely it was the low fee of 25 cents that brought them in. This fee covered all diagnostic tests, x-rays, psychiatric screening and every test imaginable. Since few people had money for medical treatment back then, most folks simply kept on struggling through life in spite of their problems.

In the clinic, we came face-to-face with every condition we had studied. We were very thorough and our studies served us well during our years of clinical practice. While it was wonderful to be helping people, we had to follow strict protocols that didn't include using intuition in diagnosis. So, I packed my intuition away for the time being.

One of our regular patients arrived every Thursday morning like clockwork. Poor Mr. P. shuffled into the clinic wearing tattered overalls and worn shoes that had seen better days, but those days were long gone. After his weekly treatment, he slowly took the world's oldest wallet from one of his torn pockets. Giving us a melancholy look, he reluctantly asked how much he needed to pay. We replied, "That'll be 25 cents, Mr. P."

When he opened his battered wallet, we watched expectantly for moths to fly out. Searching his wallet for a quarter with studied slowness, he mumbled about old age and tough times. We always felt sorry for him and sent him on his way without charging him. "Don't worry Mr. P. You can pay us next time," we said. As he carefully restored his wallet to his pocket, he muttered, "Thank you, boys. Thank you." When he shuffled off, we felt glad to have helped the poverty-stricken old fellow. In those days, people worked hard for low wages and we often waived the payment for those in need.

However, the true state of affairs was revealed to me one Thursday morning when I was on a break from the clinic. Walking on a quiet side street, I noticed an immaculate Fleetwood Cadillac, which was parked in the shade on the opposite side of the street. It was a giant of a machine, coal-black and perfectly waxed. Stooping to tie my shoe, I glanced up just in time to see Mr. P. striding along on the other side of the street, no doubt coming from his regular appointment at the clinic. I was amazed by the spring in his step. He hardly looked like the old man who shuffled in every Thursday. But I was even more amazed when he stopped behind the Cadillac.

Mr. P. looked around cautiously. He couldn't see me because a hedge on my side of the street blocked his view and I was still crouched after tying my shoe. Quickly, he opened the trunk of the magnificent vehicle. Peeking over the top of the hedge, I saw him take off his ragged duds, which were hurriedly deposited, along with his shabby shoes, into the car's trunk. Then, after carefully looking around again, he donned a beautifully tailored suit with all the trimmings, including gold cuff links! The glossy shoes he put on would have made a Marine Drill Sergeant proud. With a satisfied look, he snapped what was no doubt a Rolex on his wrist, combed his hair, got in the caddy, and drove away. This well-rehearsed charade took less than five minutes. The only thing missing was a chauffeur in livery. I could hardly wait to get back to the clinic and report to my fellow interns that we'd been hoodwinked.

When next Thursday arrived, we were ready. While Mr. P. was giving his pauper performance at the clinic, a group of us found his Cadillac, which was parked in the shade on the same side street, just as before. Leaning casually against the doors of his big caddy, we waited for our prey. We watched with enjoyment as Mr. P. approached. Walking briskly, he was already unbuttoning his overalls when he saw us and froze. He quickly dodged behind some bushes. We pretended we hadn't seen him.

From time to time, Mr. P. popped up furtively from behind the bushes while he waited for us to leave. We didn't budge. Instead, we talked on and on, as though we had no place to go and weren't in any hurry to get there. Glancing surreptitiously in his direction, we caught Mr. P. checking his watch. Obviously he had an appointment to keep, and we were not moving, no matter what.

At long last, Mr. P. vacated the bushes and walked up to us. Victory was ours. We greeted him with mock surprise. He looked down sheepishly, "Well, boys, you caught me." He admitted fooling the clinic for years. We then told him to park his beautiful Cadillac right in front of the clinic when he came for his next appointment. And he did, in the shade of course.

To our surprise, Mr. P. repaid the clinic for every treatment he had received as a freeloader. Later, he confided to us that he relished this game; he couldn't resist fooling people with his pauper disguise. And we enjoyed setting the trap that snared the millionaire mooch.

PART II

IN THE FLOW

6

AWAKENING AS A HEALER

———— ·◆··◆·· ————

y the time I graduated in 1952 as a doctor of chiropractic, I understood the great importance of cultivating a positive, happy frame of mind. Even thousands of years ago, focus was the key: "As a man *thinketh* in his heart, so is he." (Proverbs 23:7) We can see ourselves mired in life's mud, or we can focus on the beauty of mountain peaks. Our lives sparkle like diamonds when we acknowledge the everyday miracles around us: a child's smile, the morning sun's first rays, the setting sun's last caress, the brilliance of the evening stars, rainbows shining in the mist, the first flowers of spring, or the laughter of friends sharing our adventures in life. Every day we have the opportunity to embrace life and choose how we will view our world.

Once I realized that the first few seconds upon awakening determines our course for the day, I promised to begin each day with a smile and happy thoughts. However, as Marcus Aurelius no doubt discovered when he pledged to think on God more often than he breathed, this was a task more easily said than done. But I kept at it. My deepest desire was to be used by the Creator as an instrument of His healing, and I knew every uplifting thought would help me to open to God's healing energies. I thought of Edgar Cayce's words when I started out in practice: "Dear God, here am I, do with me as you will."

My career began when I joined a chiropractic clinic in Compton, California. I was delighted to have my own treating room and enjoyed seeing patients on my own. However, I was startled to discover that whenever I touched a patient, a strange, tingling sensation started in the tip of my right little finger. Subtle at first, this feeling became stronger until I couldn't ignore it. My fingertip felt as though someone was squeezing it.

At first I paid little attention to this strange phenomenon, but with each patient the feeling became stronger and stronger. Finally I concluded this ever-present sensation must be part of my role as a healer. Once I acknowledged this connection, the feeling became even stronger as though to tell me that I was on the right track. During my first few weeks at the clinic, I paid close attention to this energy as it became more intense. By concentrating, I was able to move this unusual energy over to the next finger. Then the energy began to move from finger to finger while I was treating until my entire right hand was "activated" by this energy.

After my right hand was filled with the energy, my patients reported feeling "something" that produced heat or tingling inside their bodies while I was treating them. Patients also said they felt an inner sense of well-being and peace during the treatment, a feeling that continued after they left. At the same time, I felt a heightened awareness while treating people. The more I could "just be" during treatment sessions, the better were the results. At times angelic beings appeared while I was running energy, usually encircling the patient and me. At other times, my angelic helpers stood behind me to flow healing to the patient.

Hoping to increase the healing flow, I focused on moving the energy to my left hand. This process went smoothly since my right hand was already activated. Within two months, the Power—as I called this healing energy and the healing angels—flowed equally from both hands. I was overjoyed to find that whenever I lifted my hands, this loving flow of healing poured forth effortlessly.

Soon I realized that everything I had learned in school was only a small part of the story of health and healing. I also saw that the Power knew exactly where the energy was needed for each person. As the healing flow energized the etheric batteries in the patient's body, I began to see and feel these battery centers. I came to understand that each of us is electrical in nature. Through every moment of eternity we are broadcasting millions of frequencies from every cell in our body while, at the same time, we are receiving energy patterns from higher levels of existence. I discovered that we are all connected within, as one vast being of living light, working together in multidimensional splendor throughout the cosmos.

As if I wasn't already properly humbled by watching the Power in action, I suddenly found my mouth saying things that were totally different from my own thoughts about a patient. It was disconcerting, but these words, which spilled unbidden to patients, were always right while my careful conclusions from diagnostic tests might be wrong. Thus, I was pressed into being a steward of the healing, which was obviously taking place with little assistance from me. When I saw my first patients getting well, I sat in silent gratitude and acknowledged God as the source of all healing. I realized my practice would always belong to God and Company, and I was an employee of the firm.

Part of my contract to heal was to tell each patient any intuitive information I received for them exactly as given by the Power. I never thought this would be a difficult assignment. However, patients started asking me for *more* information about what I had revealed to them when I didn't remember ever giving them *any* information at *all*. I was sure my patients were mistaking me with someone else who *had* given them this information. However, so many patients insisted I had told them about coming events in their lives that I finally accepted my part in passing on these mysterious transmissions from the Power.

———•◆•———

Later on I came to understand that intuitive information came through me without ever being processed by my conscious mind. The messages simply didn't touch my memory banks. However, I learned from my patients that the Power spoke volumes through me to give them information they needed to help them or even save their lives. I found out later that my patients told friends they sent to me, "Be sure to listen to every word he says. Everything he says is important and has deep meaning." If this is so, all credit goes to the Power as I am only a messenger service.

At times the Power tapped me lightly to reveal a brief glimpse of future events. I remember an ex-football player weighing 230 pounds—all muscle—coming in for treatment on his low back. He was a very handsome fellow with a kind and generous nature. We were both pleased that after running energy, the pain from his old football injury was gone. A news flash breezed in as he was leaving, and I said, "I hope you like Florida."

Looking at me strangely, he said, "I don't have any plans to go to Florida. I love California."

"Well, it looks like you'll be leaving for Florida soon and will be there for three years." He told me later he thought I was crazy at the time, but a week later he called from Florida where he had been transferred because of business.

Occasionally, the new Florida resident came in for energy work when he was back in town. One day he asked where he was going next since his Florida job was ending. Again a message drifted in. I told him he would shortly be in Hawaii where he would love every minute of his stay. And that's where he went next.

Two years later, I was shocked when he came in looking like death warmed over. He had been hit by a bus when he was out taking a walk. Unable to recover his health after the accident, he remembered me and booked a flight to the mainland. It took nine treatments to return him to health, but he was in high spirits when he left again for Hawaii.

Three years later my Hawaiian patient called and said he was dying again. I said he'd better get on a plane and come over. As soon as I saw him, the Power told me he had been cooking in some kind of non-stick cookware that he was sensitive to. When I asked how long he had been sick, he said six months. I asked if he had purchased any new cooking utensils, he said he had bought some non-stick pans six months ago. I told him to switch to stainless steel. He did, and, within a month, he was well once more.

My patient loved Hawaii and vowed he would never leave, but in his eighth year on the island, he called to ask how long he would stay there. I told him that 10 years to the day from having set foot on the island, he would sicken of Hawaii and return to California. Two years later he called for an appointment. When he came in the next day, I asked, "So, how are you enjoying Hawaii?"

Shaking his head, he answered, "I'm not. I went to the beach to play football with my friends last week, and much to my surprise, every-thing felt dead for me. It was like all the joy of living in Hawaii had vanished. I enjoyed it for 10 years, just like you said, but then I felt compelled to leave. I packed it up and flew to California. When I called you yesterday, I was in Oakland."

While I was treating him, he asked, "So where am I headed next?"

I paused, "Hmm . . ." My patient looked at me expectantly. Buying time, I added, "Well . . ." Hearing nothing from the Power, I finally responded, "How about *Oakland?*" And we both laughed.

———·◆·———

In the beginning, I asked my patients to shut their eyes so they would not see my hands over them as I ran energy. I was worried what patients might think if they opened their eyes and saw my hands moving above them. After I became more recognized for my healing work, I grew bolder and allowed my patients to watch the process, which was easier all around.

Surprisingly, I found the energy also flowed from my feet, but it seemed rather impractical—if not downright rude—to take off my shoes and point my toes at a patient. For a time I tried flowing energy from my forehead. I stayed with this experiment until I could send healing from the middle of my forehead, or what is referred to as the third eye. I imagined this would be an exciting step up, but headaches started and wouldn't stop until I moved the energy back to my hands.

I watched as the Power brought in people who were unable to find help elsewhere. It wasn't long before I was comfortable seeing difficult and unusual cases. However, I was surprised when a beautiful, young woman in her early twenties came into the office holding her hands high above her head. She seemed to be holding her head up by pulling her long, thick, dark hair upward like a rope. I couldn't blame the other patients in the waiting room for staring. I quickly guided her into my treatment room. Once we were in private, I asked her what was going on.

The young lady explained that trauma from an accident, which had occurred years before, still caused her acute neck pain at times. Whenever her pain returned, she was forced to hold her head up by her hair. This relieved the pressure on her neck from the weight of her head, but she was embarrassed when people stared at her. Nonetheless, when her old injuries flared, this brave lady would carry her head to a chiropractor to begin a series of neck adjustments. She was new to our town and wanted me to start giving her adjustments to relieve her current suffering.

I had already discovered that adjustments were far easier for the patient if I moved energy into the area first. Putting my hands on either side of the young woman's neck, I ran energy. Before my eyes—without any adjustment—God healed her neck. We were both stunned by her instantaneous relief. She said her condition had always required many treatments to relieve her pain and restore her neck to a normal, flexible state. Tired of being seen as a freak with her hair-held head, she asked if I knew any way to keep her neck pain free.

We discussed her diet. I explained that a healthy diet could bring the proper nutrients to all the cells of her body and allow rebuilding of her neck. My patient excitedly started on a program of improved nutrition and never had another neck problem. Her greatest thrill was the freedom to cut her hair now that she no longer needed it to carry her head. It was the first time I had the thrill of treating someone ready to listen and anxious make the changes that lead to health.

————·◆·————

Every day I was more comfortable running the energy, until it became the most natural thing in the world. Patients became accustomed to my method until I hardly gave it a thought. However, one day a woman I was treating asked, "Are you related to Dr. Saunders?"

Puzzled, I replied, "No, can't say I am."

"Well, you look and sound just like Dr. Saunders from Oklahoma," she insisted.

"Really? I don't have any relatives in Oklahoma that I know of."

"I have to tell you. It's eerie. When I close my eyes, I have the same feeling of energy pouring into me that I felt when I saw Dr. Saunders years ago."

Curious about her statements, I couldn't pass up the opportunity to ask about her experience. She told me that when her husband was dying from throat cancer, they decided to go to Oklahoma so he could have one last visit with his relatives. Taking a break from their family gathering, they left the city to go for a walk in the woods where they were surprised to see a long line of people moving slowly toward a cabin in the distance. Intrigued by this unusual procession, they decided to get in line. Of course they wondered why in the world people would be waiting in line out in the middle of the woods. By talking with other people in line, they learned that everyone was in line to see a medical doctor, named Saunders, who helped people with serious diseases.

The couple waited in line for an hour until it was their turn. When the cabin door opened, a slight, older gentleman asked them in. After they were inside, he quickly bolted the door behind them. They were surprised to see that the doctor was toting a double-barrel, 12-gauge shotgun. Seeing the unspoken question in their eyes, he explained, "Yes it's loaded. And believe me, it keeps people away who want to steal my secret healing formula."

The doctor beckoned them over to the table where a mysterious black bottle held the formula. Squinting closely at her husband's neck, he calmly remarked, "Cancer, eh?" Together, they responded, "Yes."

Dr. Saunders unscrewed the lid of the black bottle. Using a small brush, he painted the husband's neck with the mystery bottle's thick, black goo until the cancerous area was completely covered. Then he bandaged his patient's neck and told them to return in a week. He instructed my patient to tie her husband's hands at night because he must not, under any circumstances, scratch the area on his neck.

The doctor warned that it would itch terribly for the next seven days. Due to the doctor's insistence, she agreed. However, she was sure this precaution wouldn't be necessary, saw no need of it, and didn't do it. But that night she woke up when she heard her husband tearing at the bandage in his sleep. She quickly tied his hands and did so every night after that.

A week later, when they returned to the good doctor in the forest, he removed the bandage and congratulated them on not disturbing the site of the cancer. They were shocked when he took a firm grip on the cancerous tissue with a hemostat and began pulling. The doctor pulled until the tissue loosened and came free along with a mass of long, twisted tentacles of tissue, which reminded her of seaweed.

However, the fearful thing was not the cancerous tissue that had been removed, but the awful gaping hole left in her husband's neck, a horrible wound, which looked as though it would never heal. The doctor told them not to worry; he assured them this hole would fill in as it healed. Again he painted the area with his incredible formula, applied bandages, and told them to come back in two weeks.

When they returned, the doctor removed the bandages. All that remained of the wound was a faint difference in skin tone. Over the years, from time to time, patients with similar stories have asked me if Dr. Saunders was my father. I had to answer, "No." But I always added that I would have been proud to have been his son.

———— •◆• ————

About the time that I learned of Dr. Saunders, I decided to join a small clinic in Redlands. By moving to this clinic, I would be closer to my mother who was in her seventies and needing more care. Although Mother had lost her wealth during the depression, she never lost her commanding air. Her imperious presence alone was usually enough to intimidate people. As she was fond of reminding me, she was only 13 when she was put in charge of Hamilton's Chocolate and Biscuit factory, the family business in Nova Scotia. Her control had been absolute until her brother came of age. These years of authority left no doubt in her mind as to who should be in charge in all situations.

Two years after Dad died, Mother announced that she was going to trade in Dad's car for a brand-new Chevy. I was shocked when she insisted she was ready for the road since she had never driven in her life. The unsuspecting dealer sent someone to collect Dad's '28 Chevy, which had been gathering dust in the garage.

On the day her new car was ready, we took a taxi to the dealer to pick up her shiny, new Chevy, parked on the street and ready to go. Riding in the passenger's seat, I was white knuckling it all the way home. Where Mother learned her driving skills, I'll never know, and all went well until we pulled up to the house. Mother forgot how to stop and took out half the garage—knocked it flat—before she remembered the brakes.

Mother forbade me to ever say a word to anyone about this event. I recognized her tone and nodded obediently. She phoned the showroom to inform the manager she needed a new car—exactly like the one she had just purchased—to be delivered to her immediately. Before the manager could ask any questions, she hung up.

Shortly, the manager arrived at our house with the new car. He was shocked to see the previous new car, which had so recently left his dealership, "parked" amidst the debris of the garage. Observing the extensive damage, he asked, "What happened here?"

Mother glared at me with Sagittarian fire in her eyes. I stared up at the sky as though nothing unusual was afoot. Without batting an eye, Mother said, "A bee tried to sting my eye and I lost control." She looked right at me while telling this whopper. Hitler's gaze would have been friendly in comparison, so I said nothing.

The manager shook his head and said, "I'll see if I can get the other car started." Fortunately, he could. He backed the car out into the street and drove off, still shaking his head. Within a few minutes, we were driving off in our second new car of the day. We maintained an uneasy silence on this first outing, and I never dared speak of the "bee" incident to my mother on that day or any other. Luckily, her driving slowly improved. Eventually she found the brakes *all* the time and actually became quite good at stopping.

However, by the time I moved to the Redlands clinic, my mother was having "good" days and "bad" days. It was not a "good" day when she drove over to San Bernardino to take her driver's test. With the driver examiner in the passenger's seat, she drove right through a red light on a busy Saturday morning when the crosswalks were bulging with people. Once they saw her coming, like fish spotting an oncoming predator, they scattered, leaving a hole for her to drive through.

The speechless examiner watched in horror as Mother increased her speed through town—posted at 35—until she reached 50 miles an hour. She barreled through another red light while people in the cross-walks parted like the Red Sea to let her pass. The terrified examiner screamed, *"Stop! Pull over!"* Getting out of the car, he told her she had just failed the driving test, but could retest in a week. She eyed him haughtily and drove off in a huff.

Later that day, shaken by his recent brush with death, the examiner called me and described his hair-raising encounter. "In my mind I saw horrible headlines, which reported that dozens of people had been injured or were lying dead in the streets while I did nothing to stop your mother. All this flashed before my eyes while I was in the car. I couldn't even walk when I got out of the car. I swear an hour must have passed before my legs would hold me up. I'm retiring in two weeks after 35 years as an examiner." He paused, took a deep breath and continued, "Dr. MacKimmie, by law your mother is allowed another test, but not by *me*. I will *never* get in a car with your mother again; someone else will have to go in my place for her driving test."

In spite of my pleas to pull Mother's license before she killed someone, she did get her second chance. As luck would have it, she was having a good day on her next try, and returned home proudly waving her renewed driver's license. "I *told* you that other examiner was a fool!" she crowed triumphantly.

On good days she would drive judiciously and precisely 5 miles an hour *under* the speed limit. Aggravated drivers passed while she shouted after them, "Go it, you speeder!" On bad days, she would speed along cheerfully passing every car on the road while yelling, "Out of the way, you slow poke!"

A few years later, I convinced her to give up driving. To the relief of all the citizenry, she began taking taxis. However, she made up for the loss of her license by telling the taxi drivers how to drive every moment of every trip.

———•◆•———

When I first returned to Redlands to work at the clinic, my next door neighbor, Ethel, avoided me. As a child I had always been into mischief and her view of me was colored by those early days. However, one day she called me over to the fence between our yards. Leaning over the fence, she confided that she was thinking about having gallbladder surgery. She said she couldn't stand the terrible pain whenever she ate anything.

I was completely taken by surprise when she asked if I had any ideas how to avoid the surgery. Smiling, I told her that if she would stop eating chocolate and drinking coffee, go to bed early, drink lots of water, and take an early morning walk every day, she would not need the surgery. From the look on her face I could tell that she didn't actually expect me to have any thoughts on the subject at all. She looked at me curiously, thanked me, and headed back to her house.

The next week Ethel came to my office suffering terribly from horrible gut pain. When she asked if I could do anything to relieve it, I said I'd certainly try. After treating her, the pain left. She surprised me when she said, "You know, I followed the advice you gave me last week. And actually, my pain stays away as long as I don't touch coffee or chocolate. Unfortunately, I love them *both.*"

For six long months, Ethel debated whether or not to have the surgery. Her surgeons assured her that—once her gallbladder was removed—she would be able to eat anything she wanted without any problem. I told her God had a purpose for every organ in the body. When she looked uncertain, I told her that if she had the surgery, she would probably gain weight and not feel as healthy as she was feeling now by watching what she ate. I advised her to pray about her decision. Each time Ethel saw me, she would say, "If only I hadn't known you as a youngster, it would be easier for me to be under your care and follow your advice."

One day Ethel spotted me in the yard and called me over to say that she was ready to take my advice and pray about the surgery. She had arranged to spend time alone in a mountain cabin to seek her answer. I promised her that God would present her with the answer while she was on her retreat. As she walked back to her house, she glanced over her shoulder at me, apparently puzzled by my statement about receiving a personal answer from God.

However, when Ethel returned from her retreat in the mountains, she was eager to share her experience in the forest. On the third day of her retreat, she was sitting on a log crying when a scruffy, bearded man with a large backpack tramped out of the woods. He came over, sat down beside her, and asked why she was crying. She blurted out that she didn't know whether or not she should have surgery to remove her gallbladder. She found herself telling this total stranger that her chiropractor had told her that her gallbladder would be fine if she would stop drinking coffee and eating chocolate, drink lots of water, go to bed early, and walk every day. But she didn't know whether to follow this advice or have the surgery.

Suddenly, Ethel realized she was miles from civilization, sitting on a log beside a burly, bearded stranger. Before she could leave, the hiker declared she should listen to her chiropractor. He told her to forego the surgery, casually adding that if she had the surgery she would put on weight and feel terrible. Of course, she couldn't let this go, "Who are *you* to tell *me* what to do?"

The stranger revealed that he was a prominent surgeon in Hollywood who operated on movie stars. He told her that gallbladders were under siege, and as soon as one star had a gallbladder removed, the rest wanted to follow suit. Feeling helpless when stars insisted on unnecessary surgeries, he hiked in the mountains to relieve his stress. He told Ethel that she was "damn lucky" to have my advice because it would help her avoid unnecessary surgery. Then he hiked away and she never saw him again. I'm sure Ethel has passed on by now, but she was a patient for many years and never had any more gallbladder trouble. After her experience, she always followed my advice because she knew God *had* answered her prayers that day in the mountains.

————•◆•————

Like Ethel, every patient must make personal decisions concerning their health. This was made clear to me again when I was asked to make a house call on a patient who was a tree topper by trade. Tom was only 30, but he was bedridden due to a massive heart attack. Terrified of dying at this young age, he lay in bed, pale and frightened. His doctors had told him that his heart was failing rapidly and there was nothing more they could do for him, except to give him painkillers to keep him comfortable until the end. They sent him home from the hospital so that he could die in familiar surroundings.

When I arrived, Tom's grieving wife took me to his bedside and left the room. I ran energy while he lay in bed gasping for each breath. A half hour later, Tom and I walked into the kitchen together. His wife was stunned to see him out of bed and walking again.

In front of his wife, I told Tom—just as I had instructed him during his treatment—that he must eat perfectly for the next 30 days. I reviewed the strict dietary program he needed to follow so that his wife could help him stay on it. I told them that if Tom would follow this precise nutritional program conscientiously, I believed he could restore his heart and recover totally, but the decision to follow these guidelines was his, and his alone.

For three weeks, Tom followed the dietary program exactly. He and his wife expressed their gratitude many times. Much to everyone's surprise, Tom rapidly regained his strength and returned to topping trees. At the end of the fourth week, I drove past Tom's house and saw his wife standing in front of their house. She was dressed all in black and crying. I knew instantly that Tom had gone off the strict diet I had given him and died. I stopped to offer my condolences. As I was leaving, I turned back and asked, "Alice, what was it that Tom ate that killed him?"

Alice hesitated for a moment and then sobbed, "A neighbor baked Tom a three-layer chocolate cake with chocolate icing, decorated with 31 maraschino cherries on top for his thirty-first birthday. I begged him not to eat any of it. At first, he said he was just going to eat one cherry as a treat for his birthday."

"But he ate it all, didn't he?" I asked.

"Every bite . . . and all the cherries *too!*"

Shaking my head in sympathy, I said, "Tom died within an hour after he finished eating the cake . . . right?"

Alice nodded. Her eyes filled again with tears and she asked, "Why couldn't he follow your advice when he had been doing so well?" Sadly, I had no answer for her. This was the first time I had seen a patient doing so well who then slid back into illness, but sadly, it was not the last. In talking with Alice, I came face-to-face with the most devastating aspect of being a healer. My patient had followed my advice and gotten well, but returned to his old bad habits, which recreated his illness. Only later in life, did I learn the ways in which karma reveals a deeper explanation for every event in our lives.

————— •◆• —————

Not long after talking with Tom's wife, a lovely, young Spanish girl of 18 came to see me. As I was taking her history, I noticed a peculiar, yellowish liquid of some sort oozing from her scalp. I knew she had to be aware of this strange condition since she kept dabbing her face and neck with a handkerchief to prevent the liquid from running down. I asked if the doctors had identified this abnormal substance. She said the doctors didn't know what it was, but this strange liquid had been seeping from her head for a month. She was hoping that I could make it stop.

Leaning over her head, I smelled the baffling substance. It was *urine!* I've never seen such a thing again in all my years of practice. I asked if the doctors had said anything about her kidneys. She nodded, "My doctors just released me from the hospital. They said my kidneys are failing and I have to start dialysis treatments since I can't urinate on my own."

I ran energy into her kidneys. After a few minutes, the urine stopped oozing from her scalp. Suddenly she asked if she could go to the ladies room. When she returned, she was smiling broadly and told me her kidneys were working perfectly for the first time in months. I instructed her to drink a gallon of pure water every day and asked her to return in two days. She was delighted with this simple guideline and promised to follow it. In two days she returned, grateful for her healing, and I was as grateful as she was to have seen God perform this miracle.

———•◆•———

About the same time that I treated the Spanish lady, one of my patients went on a family vacation to Mexico. At the last moment, they decided to take Granny along. She was 89, but very spry. The family spent a month traveling through Mexico, camping, and having a wonderful time. Nearing the American border at the end of their vacation, they decided to camp out one more night before leaving Mexico. In the morning, they were shocked to discover Granny had died during the night.

Holding a hasty family conference, they agreed they were all terrified of being detained at the border by the Mexican authorities. They knew that any delay would prevent them from getting Granny back to the states for a proper funeral. In discussing possible solutions to their predicament, they finally came up with a creative idea. They piled their tents and sleeping bags up on top of the station wagon with one addition. In one sleeping bag—carefully zipped up—was Granny. Using all their rope, they secured everything—including Granny—to the roof of the car. They hoped this pile would appear to be too much trouble to untie and search.

Plastering the smiles of happy tourists on their faces, the family—and Granny—passed safely through the border. They were so relieved to be back in the states that they decided to stop in San Diego at a restaurant to have a late breakfast. To their horror, when they returned to their station wagon in the parking lot after breakfast, everything on top had been stolen—including Granny.

My patient said everyone in the family watched the San Diego papers for months, but no news item ever appeared about an unidentified body turning up. Finally the family reported Granny missing. After seven years she was officially declared dead. Eventually the family saw this event as a colorful, even humorous, episode in their family history; they came to refer to it as the cheapest funeral ever held. Since it had been many years since Granny's unusual disappearance, her granddaughter thought it would be safe to share her story with me.

As we imagined those thieves coming across Granny in the middle of their plunder, my patient and I laughed until tears ran down our faces on the day she shared this adventure. If only all of our difficult problems would resolve themselves so easily, and end with laughter. Wherever you are Granny, enjoy the smiles you provide whenever your story is told, and know that you are remembered fondly by your camping family.

———•◆•———

As many times as I've smiled when thinking about Granny's final adventure, every day in practice was an adventure. I could never predict what God might have in mind for my day. One Saturday morning, Theresa, a 90-year-old Italian lady, brought her 92-year-old sister, Maria, to see me. Maria didn't speak any English, but she chattered away in Italian during the entire session. Perhaps she was telling me all her health problems, I'll never know. However, Theresa kept interrupting her. Maybe she was translating, but she never slowed down long enough for me to ask her. She told me everything that was wrong with Maria. Taking it from the top, she had cataracts, glaucoma, headaches, deafness, sinus problems, arthritis, heart failure, emphysema, stomach ulcers, kidney stones, gallstones, constipation, hemorrhoids, varicose veins, swollen ankles, and had suffered several strokes, etc. Did I miss anything?

While running energy on Maria—through a nonstop stream of Italian and rapid fire interruptions in English from her sister—my constant prayer to God was to please let Maria leave my office before she passed on to her heavenly reward. Finally the treatment was over, and Theresa took Maria home.

A week later Theresa phoned me, "Well, you sure fixed my sister." My heart nearly stopped. Sure that Maria had passed on, I was about to offer my condolences. But before I could respond, she continued, "When we got home, Maria fell asleep. She didn't move for 23 hours, and we thought she might be dead." As soon as I heard the word "thought," I knew I was off the hook.

Theresa went on, "When she woke up the next day, she went out to the orchard, climbed a tripod picking ladder, and picked our biggest fig tree until it was bare. Now Maria's outside and wants to dig up our backyard for a garden. She's always loved gardening, but our yard is a third of an acre, and I can't get her to *stop!"*

The next time Theresa brought in Maria, I was instantly immersed in a stream of Italian from Maria. Right on cue, Theresa started interrupting. She told me Maria could see like an eagle now and had thrown away her thick glasses. Her aches and pains were gone, her hemorrhoids and varicose veins had disappeared, her lungs were as clear as any young person's, and she had energy to spare. In fact, as Theresa continued her report on her sister's newfound health, I thought I would like to be as healthy as Maria, myself.

For better or for worse, Theresa began sending in all the old ailing people she could round up. My waiting area started looking like a critical care unit at a rest home. Of course I had long since learned that the healing energy did what it wanted and there was not much I could do about it. Some folks had evidently signed up for instant healing, while others had to work to achieve results, and others experienced just enough to impress them that "something" was taking place.

I tried to explain to Theresa that her sister was very fortunate to have received God's gift of healing, but not everyone would receive this gift. Theresa just smiled, "You can do it, Dr. Jim. I know you can." Theresa was never discouraged and continued to find people for me to help, even when I couldn't help all of them. Happily her sister continued to have wonderful health until she left this earth. No doubt she is now happily working in God's heavenly gardens.

It was always interesting to treat people who didn't speak English since their problems remained a mystery to me if they didn't bring along a translator. Fortunately, the Power never needed a translator. I recall another older Italian gentleman who didn't speak English and lay very quietly during the treatment. When he returned the next week, he brought his wife, who did speak English, with him. He kissed my hands and said, *"Miraculo, miraculo!"*

Turning to his wife, I asked what was going on. She happily held up two x-rays. When I checked the dates, one had been taken a month before his first energy treatment from me, which clearly showed that emphysema had damaged 99 percent of his lungs. The current film showed perfectly healthy lungs, as if he was 16 years old. Now I understood.

Agreeing that it was one of God's great miracles, I pointed to his current x-ray and said my new Italian word, "Miraculo." He and his wife nodded happily. I smiled and patted him on the back. After they left the office, I thanked God again for the privilege of witnessing His miracles, which change our lives in those magical moments of grace.

7

ON MY OWN

————◆••◆————

After being at the Redland's clinic for six months, I realized my healing gift would deepen when I opened my own office so I prepared to take the plunge at 24. Unbeknownst to friends and family, I was terrified. However, I saw no escape from the inevitable. With five years of chiropractic college behind me, a degree from the State of California, a hometown crowd of friends expecting me to do well, and a mother spreading the word all over town about her son's future success, what else could I do? Like Joan of Arc, I marched forth onto the field of battle and rented an office downtown in the old Fox theater building.

In spite of my apprehension, I was anxious to be on my own, ready to let my intuition fly free. The knowing, my companion since birth, has flowed information from a world beyond our five senses for as long as I can remember. Unfortunately, I usually based my youthful decisions on the marvelous workings of my mind, which was trouble all the way. However, I was unwilling to turn the reins over to my untested, inner guidance system in those early days.

While my angelic guides promised intuitive instructions for healing and teaching, they warned me that I wouldn't receive divine guidance if I chose to follow mental patterns, instead of heart patterns. They explained that the two roads of life looked exactly alike, but I would know the road of heart by its inner sense of peace. The Power told me I would have to wrestle my way through life and the trials of my emotions just like everyone else. My instructions were to stay centered in the heart and ask for help whenever I was in doubt about any course of action.

I have always had one foot in another world, an inner world of knowing that surpassed all the knowledge and intelligence of my outer everyday world. Intuition, that sudden knowing without thought, has been with me from the beginning of my life. And I have found it to be infallible in every way when I pay attention to it. Through it, the characters of people, their inner selves, were revealed to me even though I tried to judge people from what they *said* was true about themselves.

In college, I remember "knowing" that President Truman would win, not Dewey, in the famous 1948 elections, that solid knowing came to me in an instant. My college friends offered to bet me 100 dollars to my one that I was wrong. I laughed their bet off and refused to wager since I knew the enemies I would create as soon as Truman was announced as the victor in this race. The Chicago Daily Tribune had already printed an issue with the unprophetic headline: "DEWEY DEFEATS TRUMAN." Still, it always amazed me that people got upset when I was right instead of being curious enough to ask me how I knew.

When I started out in practice and my first truly difficult case came in on a Friday, I was grateful that I had all weekend to prepare before the lady's next appointment. I studied the x-rays, blood tests, case history and every scientific article I could find on the particular symptoms of this lady. Finally on Monday, when the patient came in, I spoke to her with total authority on my findings. For a moment, what sounded to me like complete gibberish came from my mouth, then my speech shifted, and, to my shock and surprise, the words that followed presented a totally different view of her condition.

These findings, which proved to be totally correct, had nothing to do with my original conclusions, which were off the mark, but had been the best my studies could come up with. I was quite surprised when the same thing happened for the patients that followed. At the end of that day, I thanked God, as always, for His healing gift. I also thanked Him for this new aspect of intuition to help my patients, which floated into my mind and pronounced the truth of each condition in a rather blunt manner. It became a joy to cooperate with intuition whenever it manifested for the patients.

Although intuition has always been correct, answers came only when necessary, and not because I could ever summon them at will. In my private life, I am left to my own devices whenever I depend on my mind alone to solve my personal problems. Intuition has never allowed me to use its findings to avoid learning from the problems of everyday living; I still have to manage finances and perform daily tasks on my own.

I wish I could will intuition to flow into my daily life at all times, but it is a thing in and of itself, appearing when it wants to, and not necessarily when *I* want it to. However, I leave the inner door open for intuition to enter, always remembering that it cannot be commanded. When it does come from time to time in my personal life, it's usually to rescue me from my own stupidity—at the last possible moment.

Intuition is without thought, appearing out of the blue. Bang! And there it is in all its truth and glory and there's not much one can do about it. It speaks as though God Himself is speaking. The best I could do in my healing practice was to stay in neutral where the intuitive energies could reach me and instruct me how to help those coming to me. Intuition does not come from our thinking mind. It just is! All the analysis in the world is feeble in comparison to our inner knowing, which comes when we relax and yield to the heart.

A lifetime of leaning on intuition has proved it to be a wonderful companion; however, it is as independent as a cat and lives its own life. I share that life. At times, when I think the answers need to be there, they may or may not come forth. Although intuition remains a puzzle that I have not solved in my 76 years on the planet, I thank God for it every day. Intuition is the Ace card in my deck of life.

To give you an example how intuition can strike at any moment, often when you least expect it, let me tell you about an incident that happened several years ago. A wonderful friend of mine in Oregon has a muffler shop. Ever since I have known him, he has always found the time to help older people when they have mechanical problems with their cars.

While visiting with him at his shop one day, I watched him interrupt his muffler work over and over again when senior citizens stopped by to ask him about their car problems. He would stop his work, listen patiently to these older folk and then advise them on what the problem might be. I asked him if all this extra time involved wasn't a problem in running his muffler business.

My friend agreed that it was slowing his work down. He proclaimed that in the future when older people came in with car problems that had nothing to do with mufflers, he would tell them to run along as he was a muffler man, not an automotive mechanic.

As I was leaving, I turned, smiled and asked, "What if an older lady came in with a strange sound in the right front wheel and asked you what could be wrong? And you found after looking at the wheel that the lug nuts holding the wheel on were bad . . . as in two out of the five were broken off and the other three were loose? Would you tell her to run along since it had nothing to do with mufflers?"

"Absolutely," he replied confidently. "I'd tell her that I only do mufflers and that she needs to go to a regular car mechanic to solve her problem."

The next day my friend called me. He said that an elderly lady came in shortly after I had left. She asked what could possibly be wrong with her car since there was a terrible noise in front on the right side. He dreaded looking at her right front wheel after my questions. When he did, the condition was exactly as I had said it would be: three loose lug nuts and the other two broken off.

Knowing the answer, I asked, "Did you tell her you were a muffler man and that she'd have to run along and find someone else to fix her car?"

"Good God, no! I couldn't let her drive off like that. I went to the junk yard for a wheel assembly, installed it for her, and got her safely back on the road."

———·◆·———

When I first started listening and paying attention to intuitive messages in my practice, it was like sensing a delicate thread just barely brushing across my face. However, as I followed where my guidance led, my intuition became stronger and stronger. The fine thread turned into a string, then into a rope, and finally into a strong cable of intuitive strength that I could rely on.

This knowing intelligence never insists, but it is always right. Intuition is like a radio that receives countless frequencies, and, thus, offers many different programs, which are flowing through us every moment. With practice, we learn to listen to our inner radio and tune *out* the world's constant clatter. By being open and focusing on one unique frequency, we can access information about healing, or any other subject, as needed in the moment.

It is while the mystery of life's next moment remains unseen that intuition can burst forth into consciousness. Intuition is like a tiny snowflake landing on your hand. It is without weight and dissolves quickly if you have not trained yourself to be aware and acknowledge its presence. By activating our inner listening, we attune ourselves to respond to these inner cosmic signals and embrace the great changes in our lives. The Power has assured me many times that this ability will be tapped by everyone in the future.

Whenever I think about intuition, I think of Doug. The first time I saw him as a patient, he explained that he had been so jittery that he went to a psychiatrist to get medication to calm his nerves. His doctor suggested a new experimental drug from Switzerland. However, he would only give Doug a month's supply, and *only* on the condition that he would return in a month to report his reactions. Doug agreed.

The next morning Doug took his first pill. Within seconds, he stood straighter and quite literally knew everything: what people were thinking, what stocks would go up, what real estate was going to increase in value and how to buy it. Doug effortlessly made a million dollars before he returned to the psychiatrist. He was eager to tell the doctor about his new, perfect life. Expecting the doctor to be thrilled for him, Doug revealed that he felt like a god on earth, that everything in his life now flowed effortlessly, and that he was making fortunes every week.

Alarmed by Doug's ecstatic report, the psychiatrist insisted Doug was manic and demanded the return of any remaining pills. Doug meekly turned the bottle over to him. Throwing the suspect pills into his desk drawer, the doctor took new pills from his supply cabinet, and gave them to Doug. The doctor assured him these pills would produce identical results, but without creating this strange euphoria.

As soon as Doug woke up the next morning, he took his first new pill. Within minutes, he felt his nervousness beginning to return. When he finally came to see me, fearing that he would soon become his old anxious self, there were tears in his eyes. He told me that he hated the doctor for changing his medication. The warm, tender love Doug had found for humanity while taking the original pills had washed away, leaving him a hollow shell of his former godlike self.

Doug said he would rather have been an ordinary person forever than to have experienced that month of power and bliss, only to have that state taken from him. While running energy to bring him into balance, I could still sense that incredible state of well-being within him, but it was fading. The Power told me I wouldn't be able to return him to that glorious high plane of existence. Although the treatments slowed the exit of that extraordinary state, it gradually receded until it vanished completely. Gone the perfect posture along with his confidence and optimism. Gone his intuition for buying stocks and real estate. Gone his knowing what others were thinking.

To have been touched by the gods, even for a short time, is to feel life in its fullness. But to lose that love brings unbearable pain. Imagine being a billionaire one moment, a tramp the next. Although I felt sorry for Doug, I believe his experience shows that this state *does* exist within us all. And one day we will each find it, *without* needing intuitive pills. What delays our awakening is a mystery. As fledglings grow feathers to fly, we are still growing our spiritual feathers, which will lift us to the next level of the soul.

I believe that everyone has intuition; it has been on hand to save our lives since time began. It is within the new level of consciousness that is coming now in our evolution. As we surrender ourselves to the changes that are upon us, we will find that our intuition can lead us through life, while the mind must follow as a good servant does.

When intuition speaks, it is best to follow, for it is always right. However, personal desire, or any emotional attachment, stops intuition's true wisdom from coming forth. While the flow of intuition may appear to have no rhyme or reason, this inner wisdom knows all when we stand aside and allow it a free reign. Then, what we know vaguely, or not at all, is fully revealed to the intuitive senses. Intuition is judge, jury, and the verdict all in one without needing any evidence, coming to its conclusions with a speed, accuracy, and total knowing that are superior to all thinking.

Although intuition may at times appear illogical, nevertheless, it illuminates my healing practice. It is a gift from the divine intention of the universe, directing me to tell patients what is wrong and what corrections need to take place for healing. It is God's grace in action. Often it speaks through the Power at the very last minute, sometimes changing the course of treatment on the spot. But I am used to this after a lifetime of having guidance thrust upon me. As an observer, I remain mystified but grateful for the divine help intuition provides in healing.

Before I forget, Doug's story reminds me of a patient who had gone to an 80-year-old chiropractor in Palo Alto a month before he came to see me. The old doctor had just finished mopping the floor of his treating room when Frank arrived at his office. He asked Frank to lie face down on the treating table. As the doctor started to approach the table, he slipped on the wet floor and went flying through the air. The old boy's elbow landed sharply on Frank's neck, on the atlas vertebra to be exact, the first vertebra of the spine. Frank passed out. When the doctor managed to revive him, Frank, like Doug, stood straight and tall for the first time in his life and felt like a young boy.

In the weeks following this accidental adjustment, Frank's depression left, his digestion was perfect, his sinuses were clear, and he could run easily for miles. He slept soundly at night and all manner of creative ideas came to him during the day. Filled with gratitude, Frank called the doctor to tell him what had happened since his unusual adjustment via the old boy's elbow. The chiropractor convinced him that the area would be strengthened by a series of adjustments. Frank went back and the doctor proceeded to administer the first one. Instantly Frank slumped back into his previous condition. God's miraculous adjustment was gone. When Frank came to see me, he said he felt as though he was living in hell after being in heaven. It's an old lesson. If it ain't broke, don't fix it.

———•◆•———

In my practice, I found—as many have before me—that opening an office did not automatically bring patients to my door. I thought a life of service to others naturally meant my own life would be as smooth as glass. I cut loose from all responsibility and assumed that God would provide for my needs, as long as I did my part to help those who were sent to me. That's what I thought, but that isn't what happened.

To my surprise, I was required to balance my own books. No one magically appeared to do it for me. And as I went along, I learned that among the sheep are a few wolves ready to fleece you. And worse, once in a while Little Red Riding Hood turns out to be the Big Bad Wolf, whether you like it or not. After a few months of financial difficulties resulting in near starvation, I realized that no matter what your God-given talents, you are still responsible for using discrimination in your life.

It wasn't long before I felt overwhelmed. I was starting from ground zero with no patients, but I still had to pay the rent, furnish my office, and put my business together. I wanted to pray for a miracle, but my mind took command and threw me into a state of depression. Looking through the darkness that filled my mind, I couldn't see daylight.

Finally, at the end of another day spent in an empty office, I hit bottom. I thought it might be time to bow out of life since my wife and I didn't have any children yet. Hiding in the deepest, darkest cave in my mind, I slammed the door shut, and crawled under the black, mental rock I had created when my adopted father died. It was cold and lonely there, but so familiar that it seemed comfortable and warm to me.

I didn't think to ask for help. When I was young, I thought asking for help was a sign of failure and weakness. It was years before I understood that asking for help is part of the surrendering process, which allows our heavenly guides to communicate with us and flow into our lives.

Imagine my surprise when a sweet, loving voice spoke to me in the blackness of my cave. The voice asked me to open the door a bit to allow a little light in. I waited stubbornly in the dark, not saying anything. The angel spoke again in gentle tones, *"Dear one, we promise to bring the light in if you will just open the door to your cave. The tiniest crack will do. Then we can help you."*

I sulked, "If you cared about me at *all*, you would *drag* me out of this dark hole into the light."

And instantly, it was done. Suddenly I was enveloped in the most glorious light. God's grace surrounded and filled me with a feeling of ever deepening peace that flowed through every cell in my body. Filled with joy I shouted, "Thank you. I will never, ever get down *again!*"

An angelic chorus quickly asked, *"Is that a challenge?"*

"Yes! Nothing can ever possibly bring me out of this heavenly bliss."

Foolish words! Instantly, I was returned to the blackness of the hellish cave I had created so long ago. Before I could put up a wall to stop them, thoughts of suicide came boiling up in my mind. The angels said, *"Dear One, when you are up, you cannot imagine down. When you are down, you cannot imagine being up."* I saw the wisdom of their words.

My guiding angels gently reminded me, *"Whenever you are in any kind of trouble, all you need to do is ask for help. We are always available, but it is entirely up to you to ask for that help. By asking for help and by giving thanks for that help, you flow harmoniously with the Divine Intention of the Universe."*

The angels lifted me far enough out of my mind's shadows so that I could close the office and go home. I got in my Volkswagen beetle and headed for home, which was a huge barn of a house surrounded by thousands of acres of orange groves. This ancient farmhouse would no doubt have burned to the ground in a second if fire had even looked in its direction, but I loved the quiet and isolation of the groves. At night, there was a stillness I could breathe in like air, which nourished the deepest part of my being.

As I was driving home, the angels interrupted the dark thoughts circling in my mind, *"Would you give us a laugh please?"*

I was astonished, "Can't you see I'm depressed to the point of suicide?"

They replied, *"Of course, but we cannot bring joy and happiness into your life if you do not offer us a portal . . . a gateway into your heart. For you, laughter has always given us a wonderful welcome mat. We can easily enter your life on the sound of your laughter."*

It took all my strength to croak out a depressed, "Ha." But my voice sounded dead, even to me.

After a few moments, the angels spoke again, *"Hmm, well, that was a beginning. How about giving us another ha?"*

Deciding to go one better, I said, "Ha, ha."

"Wonderful. Now, why don't you add another ha to the two and give us a triple ha?" The angels continued to stack one "ha" upon another until I was actually laughing so hard I couldn't drive. I had to pull over and stop at the side of the road where I laughed until my stomach hurt.

Life was once more filled with hope, and I was forced to admit to my angelic guides that I felt wonderful. If only I'd had the understanding to continue feeding that state with more happiness. In my mind, the angels would sustain me in that glorious state forever. But as I returned to my old mental patterns, the joy slowly slipped away.

The story of this angelic encounter is one I often share with patients to illustrate that our moods are not thrust upon us. We invite our moods into our lives with the acceptance of our thoughts. As Shakespeare wrote so eloquently in Hamlet, "Assume a virtue, if you have it not." Following the Bard's wisdom, I encourage patients who are treading the heavy path of depression: if you do not have a virtue, assume one, until it becomes you and you become it.

Assuming the virtue of happiness works especially well for all of us. Over the years, many patients practiced the virtue of happiness until it became them. Then they spread their happiness to others. Thankfully, happiness is delightfully contagious.

———·◆·———

And so my office doors were open, but I had no practice. I was rattled. The hordes of patients I envisioned crowding into my waiting room had not yet appeared. Of course, I can imagine what those first few patients thought when they walked into my office and saw me for the first time. At 24, I was a very, very young looking professional who barely needed to shave once a week. I hardly looked like a wise and confident healer.

One day as I sat in my empty office pondering my choice of careers, I looked up to see an attractive woman in her 40s enter. I will never forget her. She was wearing the highest spike heels I had ever seen. They clicked sharply on the floor as she approached. Before she could say anything, I asked, "How can you possibly manage to have healthy feet when you wear such incredibly high heels?"

She smiled, "Every night I fill one pail with very hot water and another with ice water. I soak my feet, first in the hot water, then in the cold, and keep switching back and forth every two minutes. I do this for ten minutes. Then I wiggle and twist my feet and toes in every possible way for five minutes. After this, I dry-brush my legs vigorously from the knees down to the tips of my toes until my legs glow. A final twisting of my feet using my hands and I'm done. If I do this faithfully, I never have any trouble."

The lovely lady hesitated after her explanation and asked if I was busy. Waving my hand around the room to indicate its discouraging emptiness, I said, "I've only treated a few patients since opening my own office." She nodded sympathetically.

I sighed and continued, "Actually I was thinking of doing some *other* type of work for a living just before you came in. Being a chiropractor is a tough climb. Most of the fellows I went to school with have another part-time job to make ends meet."

She smiled gently and said, "If you have time, I'd like to tell you my story."

Smiling back, I replied, "I have nothing *but* time. Please. Go ahead. Why don't you take a seat?"

She sat across from me and began, "I'm hoping my story will encourage you to stay in your chosen profession. I'm a saleslady and I travel all over the country. Whenever I see a chiropractor's office, I go in. If the office is busy, I leave. But if it's not busy, or the chiropractor is very young, like you, then I stay and tell my story."

Intrigued, I leaned forward in my chair wondering why her story would encourage me. She continued, "Eleven years ago, I fell and injured my back terribly. I was rushed to the hospital where I was x-rayed and sent to an orthopedic doctor. He and three assistants studied the x-rays and put me into a full body cast."

"I was horrified," she continued. "I told them I had to walk a great deal in my work so they refashioned the cast to come up under my armpits at the top and just past my hip bones at the bottom. They supplied me with drugs for the pain and crutches to help support the weight of the body cast. This stopped every other activity in my life, except work. I had good insurance and went to appointments with the orthopedic surgeons every week for a year."

"During that year, the cast was removed and replaced three times. As I was leaving from the third recasting, still in the same horrible pain, one of the orthopedic surgeons offhandedly mentioned they planned to do surgery on my spine soon to fuse several of the lumbar vertebrae. In shock, I started to leave when the doctor casually added that my back would never be flexible again after the surgery."

"The surgeons all warned me that if I ever removed my cast, my back would be injured again, beyond repair. Above all, they warned me never, never, *ever* go to a chiropractor. If I did, they said I would be paralyzed for life without any hope of ever walking again and there would be nothing they could do for me then."

I grimaced, remembering the terrifying sermons on chiropractic given by my high school nurse. The woman nodded as if to acknowledge my unspoken thoughts and resumed her story, "I was in such hellish pain that even the drugs didn't touch it. I swore I'd kill myself if I had to go on living this way. Walking down the street, I thought of all my suffering from trying to sleep in the cast. I looked up and saw a sign with the infamous word 'chiropractor' on it. At that moment I decided I could hardly be in any *more* pain and if I *did* become paralyzed, at least I would be rid of my miserable iron maiden, which I wore day and night. And so I went in."

"Before the chiropractor could say anything, I told him how nervous I was just being in his office. Then I explained what I had been going through with the orthopedic surgeons. He talked to me for a long time about chiropractic. Then he suggested removing the cast so that he could adjust my back. To this day, I don't know why I agreed, but I did. He asked me to wait while he went to his car for a pair of pliers. When he returned, he started in on the cast and carefully removed it. My God, it felt good to be free of that monster, but I was suddenly terrified to move. I was afraid that if I moved, I *would* be paralyzed."

Thinking I could see where her story was headed, I started to speak. She quickly put her index finger to her lips to stop me and continued, "After reassuring me that I could move, he gently adjusted my low back and hips. Lo and behold, I was now totally out of pain. I felt such a rush of joy and happiness that I hugged him. After he told me that I should be out of pain from then on, he advised me not to go back to the orthopedic doctors. He said they were no doubt doing what they thought was best and it might hurt their feelings if I told them about seeing a chiropractor. When I left his office, I felt wonderful. After months of agony, I now had absolutely no pain."

I started to congratulate her on her victory when she stopped me again and went on with her story, "The next day, I was so angry I simply couldn't resist going back to the orthopedic surgeons. Furious, I gave them both barrels. After I finished, I waited for their apology. Instead, they told me that it would have been easy for them to have taken off the cast. But by removing their cast too soon, I would be paralyzed within a few weeks. I was terrified and begged them for help."

"The surgeons said any pain relief had been from their perfectly applied casts. They said the chiropractor was no doubt a poorly educated man who might have a mail order degree. Their recommendation was to have the cast replaced immediately in preparation for their proposed surgery, which would spare me from any future pain. Above all, they warned me not to have any further contact with the 'quack' chiropractor. After blasting them with my tirade, I was so grateful that they would still consider helping me, I almost got down on my knees and *begged* them to reapply the cast. Before I knew it, I was encased once more in my plaster prison."

"Within hours, I was in complete agony again. When I complained to the doctors, they told me it was my own fault. They said removing the cast had caused terrible damage. Now I would have to wear the cast to rest the involved area before they could schedule surgery. They gave me prescription drugs to ease the pain until surgery, which would now have to be postponed for many months, all due to my mistake. And I bought it . . . hook, line, and sinker."

My visitor asked if she could have a glass of water, which I quickly brought to her. I was anxious for her to go on with her story. After a drink of water, she began again, "Four months later, I was downtown—still immobilized by my body cast and in terrible pain—when I looked up and saw a familiar face. Strolling toward me, was the quack chiropractor who had removed my cast. I quickly ducked into a store and hid behind a rack of clothes. I couldn't believe it when he actually had the audacity to follow me into the store. He confronted me and asked if I had gone back to the orthopedic doctors again. Before I could answer, he said the doctors must have frightened me into another body cast and no doubt planned to do surgery in the future."

"I was furious. I told him that my orthopedic doctors said he was a quack and a fraud with a mail order diploma, out to hoodwink the unsuspecting public. He laughed and suggested that I let him remove the cast once again. When I said I didn't want to be paralyzed for life, he said he would write me a note stating that he would care for me the rest of my life if that happened. I really don't know why I agreed, but I went back to his office and let him remove the cast. Once he adjusted my back again, I was out of pain. In fact, I've never had any more back pain. And he actually *did* write me that note."

At this point, my remarkable visitor reached into her purse and took out a folded piece of paper from her wallet. She carefully unfolded it to show me the note written by the chiropractor who had given her back her life. Putting the note away, she encouraged me to stay with my chosen profession. "Believe me, young man, eventually people will find out how much you can help them and then your office will be filled with grateful patients."

I have never forgotten this wonderful saleslady whose incredible story inspired me to stay in my profession. Dear lady, you are no doubt on the other side by now, but I'm sure God blessed you for the hope and encouragement you gave so freely to young chiropractors starting out in practice.

———•◆•———

Shortly after the traveling saleslady told me her inspiring story, I found myself once again waiting in my empty office when a famous movie star from the 1930s came through the door. The poor fellow was leaning heavily on crutches and wearing a grotesque body brace from his neck to his tailbone. Although he was 72 years old, I recognized him immediately—or thought I did—until he told me that he was not the movie star, but his stand-in and best friend.

"Believe me, Doctor, the glamour of Hollywood life didn't mean anything to me after I fell 42 years ago and ruined my back," he said. "I take drugs for the pain, but I still suffer night and day. The doctors have tried many different treatments over the years, but nothing's helped," he sighed. "I've worn this monstrosity for 42 years. I have to wear it even at night or the pain is intolerable. Today I noticed your office sign and thought I'd come in and see what you could do for me."

Like the saleslady, this gentleman had decided there was nothing to lose by going to a chiropractor. After he leaned his crutches against the wall, I helped him remove his back brace. It was a corset-like affair with metal ties and hooks. It looked more like a medieval torture instrument than a medical appliance. I helped my new patient lay down on my treating table and began the flow of energy to bring circulation to his spinal tissues. Although I was not touching him, he said, "It feels as though you're applying warm oil to my back. It's very soothing."

When I touched his low back, my patient suddenly started crying. I stopped and asked, "Am I hurting you?"

Sobbing, he answered, "No, no. I'm *out of pain* for the first time in 42 years. These are tears of *joy.*" After the treatment was complete, he continued sobbing quietly for a few minutes Then he took my hand and said he felt wonderful. Holding his crutches and brace under his arm, he left the office, shaking his head and muttering, "I'm 42 years too late . . . 42 years too late."

When he left, I was higher than a kite, basking in the bliss that often accompanies healing. The gentleman returned the next day to thank me once more. He stayed to quiz me about the healing power that had taken away his pain. I told him of my beginnings and my contract with the Power. He was quite amazed and so was I when I thought about it. Usually several treatments would have been necessary for complete healing, but in his case, one treatment had been just the ticket. Occasionally, I saw him in town and was glad to know that he was able to live the rest of his life without pain and without being in that horrible contraption.

The following week, a sign painter came in to see me. Although he was only 30 years old, he was shaking so badly that I had to help him into the treatment room. He jittered and lurched around uncontrollably. I thought he might break through my walls when he crashed into them. He showed me his x-rays, taken at a large Los Angeles hospital, which revealed a tumor the size of a golf ball in the middle of his brain. His pale blue eyes were clouded, their whites a sickly gray. I helped him remove his shirt, and positioned him on my 200-pound examination table, which literally vibrated from his spastic movements.

Afraid my new patient would convulse and fall off the table, I held him down while examining him. The energies in his body were in total chaos. I didn't know what else I could do to help him, so I ran healing energy into his body. As I was touching him, it suddenly it felt as though 220 volts of electricity ran through me and into him. Fearing to move my hands and break this powerful contact, I froze in position and surrendered to God and His Healing. In a few minutes, my patient's violent convulsions stopped. I continued to hold the contact. As I watched, he closed his pale, sickly eyes. His entire body relaxed, and his breathing became steady and peaceful.

Moments later, the painter opened his eyes again, I was startled to see they were now like deep blue diamonds, sparkling with health and energy. The whites of his eyes had become pure white like a child's. Amazingly, a deep, tropical tan began spreading over his pale skin. It started at his hair line and moved slowly and steadily down his face, neck, arms, and chest until it reached his waist. Within minutes, he looked as though he had just returned from Hawaii.

Suddenly my patient pushed my hands away and stood up. Posturing like a body builder, he flexed his arms and declared, "By God, I'm healed." Completely bewildered, I said, "Lie down and let me finish your treatment." He ignored me, grabbed his shirt, and ran out without paying. A week later, he returned with his wife and paid me. They were anxious to tell me what happened after he left my office the week before . . .

Ready to go back to work, the painter drove to where he was employed as a sign painter. There he climbed a tall ladder and began the delicate work of lettering a sign. Other workers informed the boss who came out screaming, *"Are you crazy? Your brain surgery's next week. You damn fool, get down from there, before you fall down!"*

When the painter reached the ground, his boss demanded, "What the hell is that brown stain on your face and arms?" My patient said he really didn't know what it was. His boss tried removing it with paint and lacquer thinner, but without success—he still looked like a Hawaiian native.

Immediately, the boss insisted on driving his employee over to the hospital for new x-rays. When the new x-rays didn't show any tumor, the doctors declared his problems had been psychological, even though all prior x-rays had shown the tumor and surgery for its removal had been scheduled. His wife interrupted to say that all their neighbors thought he was crazy too, even when he showed them his before and after x-rays.

———•◆•———

After these two miraculous healings, I was ready for miraculous healings to occur with *every* patient, *every* day. However, I was also starting to realize that the Power was in control and I had no say so as to who would be healed, how that healing would take place, and what the final outcome would be. I spent many months pondering the healing and my part in it. Should I try to contact great healers from the past? Would my thoughts during the treatment have an effect? Should I try to influence the energy?

Putting all questions aside, I decided to declare my professional status to the world by having my name emblazoned in gold on the frosted window of my front office door. I hired a delightful black man to do the lettering. He was a true artist in his chosen profession, and looked like Uncle Remus from Walt Disney's *Song of the South*. Arriving promptly at 8 A.M., he quickly started his task. Having never seen such lettering done before, I could hardly believe the steadiness with which he held his fine brush. Finally he stopped and laughed out loud, a marvelous, deep belly laugh. "Doc, I'm afraid I'm going to paint your *nose*. It's closer to the door than *mine*." I laughed and continued to watch—from a distance—with fascination.

Once the lettering was complete, we stood side by side to admire his beautiful work. My name on the front office door now shone with radiance, like sunshine dispelling clouds on a rainy day. Although I had paid him, he remained in my doorway, looking shyly down at the floor. I inquired, "Is there something else?" He hesitated and then asked, "Do you think you could do anything for my heart trouble?" I replied, "I can try. Let's go into my treating room."

As soon as I touched him, the Power told me that pork was poison for him, and especially affected his heart. The healing angels told me many times as I sat quietly flowing energy that if he would give up pork, his heart problems would stop. I gave him the news and he solemnly nodded. He smiled as he felt the energy pouring into him. In a few minutes, his own energy radiated with renewed vitality. He thanked me many times, and swore on his Bible, which he always carried, to give up all pork.

Whenever I saw my friend on the street, I waved and we would stop and chat a bit. Before we said goodbye, I always reminded him, "No pork." He would laugh out loud. I loved to hear his wonderful, rich, rolling laugh that made his whole body shake. He always assured me that he was doing just fine. One day he told me he had gone to the clinic to have his heart checked. It was perfect and the doctors had taken him off all his heart medications. I congratulated him and he beamed proudly.

However, a year later, he came to see me looking as pale as a black man could possibly look. I helped him into the treating room since he could barely walk without holding onto the furniture. When he was on the table, I touched him and saw pork energies swirling around him again like poisonous vapors. I declared, "You've eaten pork."

Opening his eyes, he quickly grabbed his ever present Bible, and held it up, "Doc, I *swear on my Bible* I haven't had *any* since you treated me last year."

I looked at him sternly, "My friend, this morning when your wife was cooking her morning bacon, she left the kitchen. As soon as she was gone, you snapped off a tiny piece of bacon the size of my little fingernail, and popped it into your mouth. Five minutes later you had heart pain and felt as though you were going to die. Am I right?"

He nodded sheepishly, "Yes, but how could you *know?*"

"Because you *did* it."

"I know I did it, but how do *you* know I did it? You weren't *there,"* he countered.

"If you *didn't* do it, then I wouldn't be *seeing* it, right here and now in front of us."

Startled by my revelation, he looked nervously around the room, as though his kitchen might suddenly appear out of thin air. Still mystified, he asked again, "But, Doctor Jim, how can you know what *happened* when you weren't *there?"*

I explained, "All of us have the ability to gather information from other places. In your case, when I asked to be shown exactly what caused your recent heart symptoms, the morning scene in your kitchen appeared, floating in front of me just as though I was watching it on a colored television screen. Remember God knows everything and I'm just being used as an instrument to help you regain your health."

When I began to run the energy, he immediately felt power and strength return to his heart and he was healed once again. I told him that he must stop eating pork for the rest of his life. He raised his Bible and pledged never to touch pork again. What a sweet man and what a blessing to help such angelic people.

———•◆•———

Of course, not all my patients were angelic. Among my first patients, I had the dubious honor of treating crafty Miss Fox who came in to see me once a month. She was 71, petite, and as bright and sharp as her namesake. On each visit, she was ever so pleased to present me with a bag—thank God for plastic—which contained her morning bowel contribution. I took the bag from her as carefully as I would handle a bag of rattlesnakes and placed it on my desk with great reverence. She then went on with great enthusiasm to tell me everything about her movement: when it happened, how it looked to her, and what she felt at the time.

After Miss Fox reviewed the history of her offering, she would solemnly ask for a stool study. As a county patient, I knew she had no money to pay the hospital lab for such an expensive study. Happily, Miss Fox was one of my healthiest, older patients and the contents of the bag—clearly visible through the plastic—showed a bowel that worked normally.

Rather than hurt her feelings and bring attention to her impoverished situation, I said the contents would be examined later. Said "exam" was to toss the bag in the garbage bin behind the office building. To prevent leakage, I always took the extra precaution to double-seal the bag in more plastic before dropping it in the bin. (My belated apologies to the environment, but this took place long before environmental concerns.)

One day after my usual subterfuge, Miss Fox stormed in later that afternoon. Holding her specimen—obviously retrieved from the garbage— she glared at me, ready to accuse me of my horrible crime. Outraged, she demanded to know why I had taken the liberty of dumping her offering without proper testing.

I knew that, per county regulations, her penniless situation forbade all laboratory tests unless critical so I said, "Miss Fox, in this scientific age, do you really think we have to take stool samples *out* of a bag to examine the contents?" Her glare vanished. She brightened and blushed like an embarrassed teenager. I was once again her hero. Paying homage to my scientific skill, she took my hand, looked up at me with her bright eyes, and promised never to doubt me again. I breathed a sigh of relief at having spared her feelings once more.

———•◆•———

It does my old heart good to think of those past times. My early years of practice brought out The Lone Ranger in me when I made house calls on county patients. These calls gave me an opportunity to see everything in the disease line, and I loved every minute of it. Imagine, I was paid a whopping $1.25 per month for each patient whether I treated them daily, weekly, or once a month. Hardly a princely sum—unless you were fasting and didn't need to buy food—but it couldn't have been better in terms of experience.

However, county bureaucracy—in its infinite wisdom—shifted gears and determined that an M.D. without county patients would be assigned to each chiropractor. It was his job to approve the magnanimous $1.25 payments after reviewing the patient records. I was annoyed when most of my requests for payment were denied by the medical overseer.

After thinking over an approach to this problem, I sent a letter to the reviewing physician explaining that I was about to draft a letter to all my county patients. This letter would suggest that he was a better choice for their care since he was medically trained and would attend to all their ills. I went on to inform him that he would no doubt be receiving calls from my many county patients as soon as my letter went out with his contact information. Smiling to myself, I wrote that I knew he would give these patients the same fine care that his private patients received. Mysteriously, I began seeing his official stamp of approval on all my county patient records, followed by the county's prompt and generous $1.25 payment for services rendered. The medical doctor involved was evidently willing to forgo the stupendous fee of $1.25 per patient per month when he envisioned his office filled with county patients, all clamoring for his time and attention.

I had dozens of county patients, equally as sharp as Miss Fox, and I had to dazzle them with my footwork to find answers for all their various needs. After all, they had seen *Marcus Welby, M.D.* on television where the wonderful world of Doctor Welby happily revolved around his patients with nary a distasteful mention of money. I was surprised that the good doctor didn't mow their lawns, shop for them, and rock them to sleep. However, he did have time to spend endless hours sitting and chatting with the fortunate recipients of his care. And after all, if it was on television, it had to be like real life. But in real life, medical care does not always result in happy endings . . .

One day, a friend's wife gave their young daughter some raisins to eat and sent her out to play. It never crossed the mother's mind that their yard had recently been sprayed with DDT. (It was a time when DDT was used liberally to prevent mosquitos from taking over during warm summer months.) Looking through her kitchen window, she saw her daughter spill some raisins on the ground. Her daughter picked them up off the ground, popped them into her mouth, and began chewing. Instantly, the mother remembered the recent spraying. She yelled for her husband to get their daughter while she called the hospital.

Once in the emergency room, the anxious parents watched while a young doctor took charge. While they looked on, grateful to have prevented their daughter's death, the young man began pumping their daughter's stomach. Unfortunately, before turning off the suction pump, the doctor began pulling the tube out of the girl's throat. He didn't see the solitary raisin still hanging on the tip of the tube when he turned off the machine. The instant the doctor turned off the pump, it released the raisin, which fell back into the little girl's throat. Suddenly, their daughter was choking to death.

Horrified, the parents screamed at the doctor to do something to save their child. The inexperienced doctor became hysterical. He was unable to take action and the poor girl choked to death while her helpless parents watched. Tragically, when the report came back from the lab, no DDT had been found on the raisins. (This sad event took place long before the Heimlich maneuver, which was not introduced until the 1970s.)

Mistakes of this magnitude rarely remain a secret in a small town. I remember another case of a woman in Redlands who was an absolute fireball before she had surgery. We all admired her vitality and zest for life. She loved to dance all night and lived each day to the fullest. However, when she went for her annual checkup, her doctor said she needed a total hysterectomy immediately, or she would die. She argued that she felt terrific, but he was adamant. Frightened by the thought of dying, she agreed to the surgery.

Six months after the operation, I saw the lady downtown. She had gained 100 pounds and had facial hair at 37. All her marvelous energy had disappeared. Now she was tired all the time. She told me—and anyone else who would stand still—that her surgeon was a butcher. After causing several scenes at the hospital, she was banned from the premises. However, she would sneak in during visiting hours to scream out her message. Pursuing the surgeon all over town, she swore at him whenever she caught up with him. When she couldn't find him, she haunted the street where he lived and yelled obscenities at his house. This happened years ago. Now both the surgeon and his patient have passed on. Still, I can't help wondering what they have to say to each other—if anything—in the afterlife.

———·◆·———

Unlike this surgeon and his patient, the relationship between doctor and patient is hopefully one of trust and mutual respect. But even early in my career, I feared that medicine was becoming a business instead of a sacred trust, which was—and is—my view of bringing health to others. I think the "business" side of medicine was behind the nickname "Old Money Bags." This was the name one of my older patients found out she was being called behind her back by her medical doctors. She learned this one day when her doctors made the mistake of using this title before she was fully under anesthesia. They didn't realize she could hear them discussing their *"next* surgery on Old Money Bags" while they prepared to operate on her.

After she recovered from her surgery, she stormed into their office. She told them she had heard their unflattering nickname while she was "out." Her doctors denied this with such passion that she finally accepted these claims of innocence. However, when I treated the lady, she confided to me that she had serious doubts about the sincerity of their claims.

I first met this lady when I treated her after she had undergone a double mastectomy. Her upper arms were so swollen with blocked lymph that they resembled two watermelons. It took three treatments to help the lymph system drain. Then she crowed that the clinic couldn't understand how her arms had returned to normal so quickly. She was so pleased that she passed on the news of her recovery to her friend, Doris.

Doris was also recovering from a double mastectomy when she

came to see me. Her arms were like two huge sausages. The skin was tight, filled with liquid, and very tender, which can typically occur after the lymph nodes have been stripped away. She timidly asked if I thought the energy she had heard about might help. I said, "Let's try and see." After the treatment, the pain in her arms was gone. When she said she was feeling very sleepy, I told her to go home and rest. She returned the next day thrilled that both arms were perfectly normal and eager to tell me her story . . .

At home, Doris decided to watch television before going to bed, but she kept hearing a loud, disturbing drip . . . drip . . . drip. She searched every room in the house for the cause, but found nothing amiss. Deciding to ignore the irritating drips, she turned up the volume on her television. After watching for two hours, she got up to go to bed. Suddenly, she realized that her arms were normal. She was startled to see two large pools of liquid on the floor, one on either side of her chair. The drips had been liquid being released from her arms. She mopped her floor and went to bed a happy camper.

Over the years I have been blessed to restore lymphatic function for many patients to what remained of the lymphatic system after their surgeries. Two years before we met, Aunt Martha, who joined our family via marriage, had both breasts removed, along with lymphatic ducts and large sections of the pectoral muscles. When Martha's symptoms returned with a vengeance, she decided to ask me for help because advice from the medical side had been to go home and get her affairs in order. Happily, with the flow of healing, her symptoms disappeared within a few weeks. She began to put on weight and felt well again. Like many patients, she said, "If only I'd known you *before* the surgery."

A few weeks later Martha called laughing and said, "You're going to *love* this. I've just received a letter from the hospital addressed to *me* as *deceased!*"

I laughed too and said, "Thank your lucky stars that you're alive to laugh about it. I'd toss the letter out and thank God for keeping you around." However, she couldn't leave well enough alone and called the hospital to tell them, "I received your letter saying that I'm deceased. But I'm just fine and doing very well at 80, thank you very much."

The very next day, a young M.D. came knocking at her door and requested to interview her. He explained that the hospital wanted to gather some additional information since her condition had been fatal, but now, instead of being properly deceased, she described herself as "fine." She informed him that she had gone to a chiropractor and had recovered in a few weeks.

With the eager doctor standing next to her, Martha phoned me to ask permission to give the young doctor my name. Martha said her visitor wanted my name so the hospital could send me patients who needed similar help. He assured her that the doctors would be happy to see their patients get well. The Power gave me the perfect response: "Martha, I'd like you to tell him nicely that I've said 'no' and judge his reaction. If he takes the news well, then send him over to my office and I'll explain exactly what was done for you."

Soon after hanging up, Martha called back to report that the doctor's wonderful, courteous, ingratiating manner disappeared when she wouldn't reveal my name. Turning red as a beet, he yelled hysterically, *"You damned old fool! Whoever he is, he's a quack, a charlatan, and a fraud. And one day we'll catch up with him!"* We both had to laugh at his sudden personality shift. Martha was always 16 in her heart and lived well into her 90s, so I believe she had the last laugh.

———— • ◆ • ————

Every day in practice I learned something new. I clearly remember one strange house call, which woke me up in ways that were completely beyond my studies in chiropractic college. After finding the address I had been given on the phone, I went up to the front door of a large home with a huge screened porch. Two middle-aged women came to greet me at the front door. They brought me into the living room and explained that the patient was their 70-year-old mother, an ancient age to me at that time. Now in my mid-seventies, I look at this as quite the prime of life.

When I asked to see the patient, they told me she was in the attic, two stories above the main floor. I found this hard to believe. It was July and the day simply boiled, as only a summer day in Redlands could boil. Following the daughters up the stairs, I found that each step brought us into territory that was several degrees hotter than the step before it. When we reached the attic, it was stifling, easily over 120 degrees.

Trying to recover from the sweltering climb, I glanced around the attic and realized there wasn't even a fan to move the heavy air. I thought I would pass out from the heat. When I wiped the sweat out of my eyes, I spotted my patient lying on an army cot, panting in the heat with a *blanket* thrown over her frail body. Looking up at me, she seemed barely alive. Strands of thin, white hair clung to her damp forehead.

Outraged, I told the daughters they must help me take this poor suffering soul down to the main floor at once. (In those big old houses you slept downstairs in the summer; the upper floors were much too hot.) The daughters obstinately argued that if their mother wasn't kept in that hot attic, she would go into convulsions and become completely helpless. I had one word for them, *"Nonsense!"* Afraid that my patient might die before I even had a chance to treat her, I shouted, *"I am ordering you to help me carry your mother downstairs!"*

Like a well-trained military unit, we each took hold of the cot with Mom riding on top and started down the stairs. One flight down, where it was slightly cooler, Mom suddenly went into convulsions, nearly scaring me to death. Shaken, I thought, "Here I am just starting out and one of my first patients is having convulsions." Without waiting for the daughters, I lifted the convulsing woman off the cot and raced back up the stairs to the attic.

To my surprise and relief, once she was back in that inferno, she came right out of it. The daughters brought the cot up and we settled Mom in the attic once more. I thought I would expire any second from the heat, but I stayed in the attic and flowed healing energy to her. Actually, I prayed and asked God to flow healing to her before I passed out. After thanking the Almighty for His healing, I headed downstairs while I could still walk. Although people may have been healthier in the days before the modern convenience of air conditioning, I would have paid good money to have had one in that attic.

Three days later, I was called back. The daughters were very pleased; Mom was now down one story and doing fine. I tried to bring her down to the main floor for treatment. But she went into convulsions again, and we hurriedly carried her back up to the second floor for treatment. After this healing session, she was able to move down to her bedroom on the main floor. After the attic heat, the main floor felt almost cool at 90 degrees. The third treatment cleared the rest of her mysterious problem and that was the end of her convulsions. What caused them? I never knew, but God was kind enough to heal her and release her from them.

Mom and her two daughters were delighted with her progress. For the first time in years, Mom could work in her garden, which had been her passion. Unfortunately, one day while she was working outside, she got a small speck of something in her eye. A local clinic removed the particle, but insisted on giving her penicillin. She told them she was allergic to penicillin so they gave her another antibiotic.

By the time I saw her the next day, her eye was swollen shut and the size of a softball. Running energy normalized everything, and her eye returned to its usual shape and size. By this time, I had gotten to know the old girl quite well as we chatted along. She said she knew I was a healer and wanted to share an experience from her childhood in Minnesota . . .

When Mom was 12 years old, she had a goiter the size of a large grapefruit hanging from the front of her throat. It was held in a cloth sling, tied like a hat ribbon on top of her head. One morning while she was eating breakfast, a neighbor lady came over. The woman said she was a Christian Science practitioner and asked if she could give her a prayer treatment to remove the goiter. My patient knew nothing about healing, but she thought it would be nice not to have the goiter's mass hanging from her throat so she agreed. While my patient continued eating, the neighbor sat across from her, closed her eyes, and quietly prayed for 20 minutes. Then she thanked God aloud for the healing and left.

After breakfast, my patient noticed a strange sensation in her neck. She took the sling off and looked at her neck in a mirror. The goiter was gone. There was only a large, empty flap of skin hanging loosely from her neck where the goiter had been. By morning the excess skin had also disappeared and her neck was perfectly normal. She said she had wanted to tell me this story ever since her attic healing.

Astonished by her story, I asked if this incredible healing had changed her life. She looked at me with surprise, "No. *Why?* Should it have? Why would you ask that?" I quickly responded, "No reason, just wondered." And I *did* wonder. I know I would have been mighty impressed if it had happened to me. Such a healing would have changed my view of the world forever. How could solid goiter tissue disappear in minutes? God's miracles are endless, and that was surely one of them in my opinion.

————·◆·————

Mom's story affirms the attitude I hold in my healing work: No Limitations! My belief is that anything can be healed, with no limitations. Why? Because God set it up that way. If there is any doubt about the power of healing, it lies with the patient, for I believe in God's miracles and have witnessed them for a lifetime.

Miracles have been all around us since the beginning of time. Life itself is a miracle. The mystery is why some people choose to heal while others delay their healing adventure or choose another path for their journey through life.

I've observed thousands of miracles while running energy and I've also observed the people who have been blessed with these miracles. Some people change in every aspect of their being, while others simply carry on with their lives as though nothing remarkable has happened. Indeed, there are times when I can't put together how patients reach their conclusions after their healing experience . . .

One Saturday morning a man named Floyd came into my office. He was wrapped in so many ace bandages that he looked like a mummy. I unwrapped him and examined his swollen lumbar tissues. As I ran energy, I visualized it normalizing the blood flow in his low back and removing toxins from the area.

After a few minutes, Floyd declared his pain was decreasing. Ten minutes later, he was out of pain. Floyd cautiously stood up and walked slowly around my treating room. A smile of wonder lit up his face, "Doc, it's a miracle, my back feels better than it has in my entire life." Before he left, I showed Floyd some gentle exercises to do in the morning upon arising. He came in for one more treatment. At that time, we both agreed he was perfectly well. After I told him he didn't need to come back unless his back bothered him again, he shook my hand and thanked me for getting him well.

A year later, I was surprised to see Floyd sitting in a wheelchair in the park. I went over to where he was resting under a shade tree. Dismayed to see him so incapacitated, I asked what had happened. He sighed and said his low back was in trouble again. I couldn't imagine why Floyd hadn't called me since his treatment had gone so well the year before. I asked what he was doing for his back. He said he was on disability and taking drugs for the pain. He added that he'd been in his shiny, new wheelchair—paid for by the insurance company—for the last few months.

I asked, "Are you in pain right now?"

Floyd nodded, "Well, yeah. But the drugs keep the pain down as long as I don't get out of the wheelchair."

Pondering this strange turn of events, I inquired, "Did the treatment I gave you last year stop the pain?"

"Boy, it sure did, Doc."

"Floyd, I thought you were doing fine when I released you. You certainly didn't need a wheelchair or even a back support."

He looked at me steadily, "Yes, Doc, your treatment fixed me up fine. My back was perfect for six months. I felt like a kid again. I could do anything. It was great. When my back started to bother me again, I thought about coming to see you, but my insurance wouldn't pay for your treatments."

"I don't understand. Why do you want to be in a wheelchair taking pain pills when you could come to me and get help?"

"Doc, are you hard of hearing? My insurance doesn't *pay* for your treatments. *Get it?*"

"I think I've got it. You were in terrible pain when you first came to me . . ."

"Right."

"And after I treated you, you were out of pain and could do anything. Your back was perfect and you felt better than you ever had in your life."

"Right again, Doc."

"But the insurance company won't pay if you come to me. Right?"

"Hey Doc, I think you've *got* it. My insurance won't pay for you. That's a fact."

"OK, so now the insurance company is paying your disability, covering your drugs for the pain, and they paid for a wheelchair."

"Doc, you finally have the picture."

"Floyd, did they say anything about you getting well?"

"Oh, the orthopedic doctors say they'll need to do surgery to get me back on my feet."

When I asked if he had a written guarantee from the surgeons that he'd be back on his feet after the surgery, we had a good laugh. After we said goodbye, I walked on leaving Floyd sitting in his wheelchair under the shade tree. On my way back to the office, I tried to make sense out of our conversation. I found it hard to understand his outlook. It still puzzles me after all these years.

Months later I made a house call to see Floyd after his back surgery, which hadn't gone well. He was now resigned to being in a wheelchair for the rest of his life. The energy wouldn't flow when I tried, so we just chatted about life in general. He spoke fondly of the days following my treatment as the best days in his life.

Although I wanted to ask why he had never come back to see me, I didn't want to see the strange way he looked at me while explaining that his insurance wouldn't pay for my treatments. I'm still astounded by his logic that the better choice was to stick with what his insurance covered, even though it wasn't helping him at all. Little did I know that this would not be the only time I would hear this same reasoning, which made no sense to me at that time. And still doesn't!

8

HEALER HEAL THYSELF

———————————◆··◆·———————————

Unfortunately, while I was helping my patients get well, my own health deteriorated. Constant abdominal pain became my daily companion. Still I vowed there was no way that I would ever be taken to a hospital, unless it was feet first. And the universe jumped right in to make sure it happened just that way. I collapsed and was taken by ambulance to the hospital where I was diagnosed with liver cancer. The doctors also informed me that I was facing diabetes. To complicate these conditions, I was still suffering from the effects of polio, contracted when I was a teenager.

My youthful thoughts of immortality evaporated. I was terrified. When I asked to be released from the hospital, the doctors agreed since they had little hope for my recovery. Frightened and powerless to heal myself, I sought the help of an old healer, Dr. Verona Tovy, a local chiropractor.

When I described what had happened to me, Dr. Tovy laughed as though she had never heard anything so funny. Without hesitating, she told me exactly what was wrong with me. Suddenly, for the first time, I came face-to-face with a clear understanding that what I was eating could actually be *causing* my pain and poor health. This was far different from the nutrition classes I had taken in chiropractic college. This was *real!* We were talking about *my body* and *my pain!* I was in shock when she told me that my cancer came not only from what I was eating, but also because it was cooked in aluminum. She informed me that I was very sensitive to this metal and would have to start cooking in stainless steel, or cast-iron.

As soon as I arrived home, I changed everything in my life that Dr. Tovy had pointed out as causes of my illness. I began by putting away every piece of aluminum cookware and using the one stainless steel pot I found stored in the back of the cupboard. However, as I started to feel better, I decided the old doctor must have hypnotized me into believing her. I smugly brought out the old aluminum pots and pans, which were so easy to use, and reverted to my old diet. To make a long story short, I had to be carried back to her office, sick as a dog.

When Dr. Tovy saw me in her office again, she laughed even harder. Then she smiled and said, "Jim, my boy, it's time to either get on, or get off."

"I don't understand what you mean."

Putting a reassuring hand on my shoulder, she explained, "You can either choose to live and fulfill your contract to heal, or die, and come back in another life and take up where you are leaving off in this life. The universe doesn't really care which option you choose since it has all eternity to bring perfection into being." Realizing the truth and wisdom in her words, I nodded and decided to get with the program.

Meeting Dr. Tovy was a major turning point in my life. With cancer, diabetes and polio motivating me, I set out to reclaim my health. I gave sugar the boot, said adios to all dairy products and soft drinks, bought stainless steel and cast-iron cookware, began drinking all the water I could, started exercising, and went to bed at an earlier hour. As I stuck to my new regime, my health slowly returned.

Shortly after I began my journey toward health, a woman came into my office complaining of severe abdominal pain. The pain was constant, and, to add to her discomfort, she had diarrhea, day and night. She and her husband owned a large ranch up in the hills, but it had been years since she had left the house without worrying whether she would make it back before the next wave of diarrhea hit.

As soon as I touched the woman, aluminum's hideous buzz floated up from her entire body in a wave of dark energy. Having cleared my own body from its effects, I now found it easy to detect aluminum sensitivity in others. I asked her to stop using underarm deodorant containing aluminum, stop using any cooking utensils made of aluminum, and stop using aluminum foil for cooking.

In my practice, I have found that some people are not sensitive to this metal. However, many either are, or *become* sensitive after an illness when the immune system is not up to snuff. (I have treated a few patients so sensitive to this metal that they could not even touch aluminum keys and had to replace them with brass.) As a part of my patient health guidelines, I asked patients with critical health issues to stop using aluminum cookware and start cooking in cast-iron, stainless steel, or glass to see if this change would help eliminate their problems. It usually did.

The lady rancher came in for three treatments, but I always felt the telltale aluminum buzz when I touched her. I couldn't understand why the aluminum energy was so persistent when I thought she had followed my instructions to stop all contact with aluminum. After the third treatment, I suggested she continue her search for help since she was no better. I asked her to contact me if she ever regained her health so I could learn how to help others. She promised she would, and we parted good friends.

Ten years later, the lady returned, but her appearance had changed so dramatically that she had to tell me who she was. Now she weighed 250 pounds, which was more than double her weight when I first treated her 10 years before. In attempts to relieve her pain, doctors had removed most of her thyroid, most of her colon, part of her stomach, both breasts, and finally performed a total hysterectomy. I thought, "Poor lady, not much left to take." She and her husband had even moved to Tumwater, Washington in her search for health, hoping that the water there might benefit her condition. But nothing helped.

Just when I was wondering why she had come to see me, she told me that three months ago all her pain had stopped and her diarrhea had ceased so that she could now travel and do whatever she wanted. Anxious to know how she had finally gotten well, I said, "I'm so happy for you. Where did you find your miracle?"

Bursting into tears, she said, "When I came to see you ten years ago, my mother had just given us a full set of aluminum cookware for Christmas. I simply couldn't hurt her feelings when you told me to dump my aluminum cookware."

When the lady rancher finally stopped crying, she told me the rest of her story. It seems that her beloved mother—the giver of all that fine aluminum—died three months ago. My patient immediately thought of the advice I had given her ten years before. She threw out all the aluminum and bought stainless steel cookware. "Within days, I was well," she sobbed. I gave her a hug and suggested that we rejoice and thank God for her new healthy life.

———•◆•———

One other unusual case of aluminum poisoning comes to mind. I had finished a 12-hour day and was closing the office when a man called to ask if I would make a house call. He said his wife had been in bed for years with terrible pain, and someone had just told them about me. While many patients say they have been in bed for years, this is usually a figure of speech. However, when I arrived, I was astounded to find the lady of the house in a bed surrounded by everything that belonged in their kitchen. Stove, refrigerator, sink and counters ringed her bed. This bizarre arrangement had been ingeniously constructed by her husband, a baker by trade, so that his wife could "live" in her bed, which had a strategically placed trap door for bed pan use.

The wife said she hadn't left her bed/kitchen for 20 years. As soon as I touched her, the bitter taste of aluminum filled my mouth and the uncomfortable buzz of that metal coursed through my entire body. While I was running healing energy, I saw that all the pots and pans, hanging above her bed, were aluminum. It reminded me of my mother's vast array of aluminum cookware, which had, in part, brought on my own years of sickness. Giving the couple my best pitch, I suggested they dump the aluminum and shift to stainless steel, glass, or cast-iron.

When I visited the couple a month later, they *both* met me at the door. Grinning happily, they took me on a quick tour of the house. All kitchen appliances had been returned to the kitchen. Touching the lady's skin, I found her energy was perfectly clear. They were both as grateful as I was for her newfound health. It was delightful to see her bustling around and making up for lost time. And so I happily went on my way, thrilled by another wondrous renewal of health.

Two years later, the baker called and asked if I would make another house call. A deja vu nightmare awaited me; once again their kitchen had been rebuilt around her bed. After two years of perfect health, the baker's wife was in bed again, and so ill she wanted to die.

As soon as I touched her, the aluminum buzz shot through my body, creating the familiar, bitter taste in my mouth. Noticing an enormous teapot on the stove, I lifted it up to check the bottom. On the bottom of the pot, clearly stamped, was a large emblem showing that it was aluminum. I asked, "Is this a new teapot? I don't remember seeing it before."

The baker's wife proudly announced, "Yes. My mother left it to us after she died. I keep it boiling all day long so we can have tea whenever we want."

"Do you realize that it's aluminum?" I asked.

"No . . . no," she protested loudly. "It was my mother's and she always told me that it was stainless." They both gasped when I turned the pot over and showed them the emblem.

After I finished running energy, the lady's face glowed with renewed health again. When I checked back in two weeks, it was like magic, the bedroom was a bedroom once more. Receiving their grateful hugs and thanks, I said God in His love had given us all a gift. As I was leaving, I thought how curious it was that another mother's "gift" had come with a legacy of illness. It was so clear in their minds that the pot was stainless. I don't think they would have believed otherwise if they hadn't seen that it was clearly stamped "aluminum" on the bottom.

————•◆•————

No doubt the mind does play tricks on us or we believe what someone else has told us, but sometimes seeing *is* believing. One afternoon, a tall, gaunt, grim-looking fellow came into my office. He stood there shaking his head and looking puzzled, "I'm sorry to bother you, but whenever I pass your doorway, I feel as though a giant magnet is pulling me in. I've resisted it with all my might. Today, I decided to come in and find out why this happens. So, here I am."

This fellow, who looked like the grim reaper, said he was a spiritualist minister. I told him I was a chiropractor. He asked if I had any clue as to why he felt so compelled to come into my office. I said perhaps he needed treatment. He agreed and we went into my treating room.

As soon as I touched him, I felt a serious lung condition, one of long standing. I told him his lung problem had been making him sick for many years. The minister nodded. I ran energy into the area. He immediately felt better and his solemn features softened. Despite his grim appearance, I found him to be a gentle, kindly chap. Before he left, he surprised me by inviting me to a seance, which was going to be held later that week at his home.

On the spur of the moment, I decided to go to the minister's house on the appointed evening. I'd never been to a seance and my curiosity got the better of me. Having once read that Abe Lincoln held seances in the White House on many occasions, I felt in good company. It was just getting dark when I entered the minister's home. I joined the other guests seated in the dining room where chairs had been arranged in a circle.

Checking out the room, I saw the windows had been blacked out with heavy curtains. I could hardly see the other 20 participants, which suited me just fine. A few moments later, the minister's lovely wife appeared. She explained that her husband was the medium and would be with the group soon. I would have been spooked right out of my chair when he entered if I hadn't already met him. His cadaverous face was ghostly white in the darkness, and loomed above us like a disembodied spirit until he took his place in the center of the circle.

Everyone else seemed to know what was expected, so I just followed along. We joined hands in the dark and sang old, familiar hymns. It was all very jolly and relaxed. I was curious and ready to enjoy whatever came next. Suddenly everyone stopped singing. By tacit agreement, silence filled the room.

After a brief pause, a soft, childlike voice spoke. Each person had the opportunity to ask questions while the minister, who was the source of the voice, gave loving advice to each member of the gathering. I got a kick out of the proceedings, but the other participants were deadly serious. Such was my introduction to the world of seances.

Contacting folks who have died and crossed over into another world wasn't my cup of tea, but the minister and his wife were clearly devoted to helping others. After the seance ended, the minister took me into his study and handed me a beautiful, colored photograph of a red rose in full bloom. He instructed me to study the photo. I did so, said it was lovely, and handed it back.

Putting the photo back into my hand, he said, "Examine it again, more closely. You're looking, but not seeing." I stared dutifully at the photo, admiring the deep, ruby red of the perfect rose, and returned it to him once more. He insisted I take it again, "Turn the photo around, study it with your eyes, but more importantly, see with your heart."

Beginning to wonder if I should look for the nearest exit, I took the photo in hand again and focused intently. Suddenly, there appeared within the rose, 18 angelic faces. Joyful cherubs gazed back at me, peeking out from each velvet rose petal. Cherub eyes watched me in glee. I could almost hear their giggles as I turned the picture slowly around in amazement. Adoring, laughing, cherubic faces, gathered around the center of the rose, smiled back at me. Stunned by the transcendent beauty that now appeared with such clarity, I felt like a perfect fool for not having seen their radiant, jubilant faces in the first place.

Reluctantly handing it back, I asked the minister where he had gotten this extraordinary photograph. He smiled, pleased that I had at last seen the angels of the rose, and said, "A few years ago, I had a new roll of film in my shirt pocket when I attended a prayer meeting. On my way home after the meeting, I remembered the film. When I took it out of my pocket, I sensed energy coming from the package. I examined the package closely, but the plastic wrap was clearly intact. Rather than loading the film in my camera, I felt compelled to send the film in to be developed without ever opening the package. When the film came back, only one photograph had been developed. This remarkable red rose with its angelic gathering."

Anxious not to leave this extraordinary photograph behind, I asked if I might borrow the film to have a print made, but the minister explained he had promised the angels he would never make copies. In fact, this was the first time he had allowed anyone else to touch the photo.

———•◆•———

The story of this incredible rose reminds me of Lucy, a patient from Riverside who had a remarkable ability. She could take a freshly cut rose and preserve it perfectly in a vase of water for three months without ever changing the water or using preservatives. The rose continued to look as though it had just been picked and its glorious scent filled the room. Her friends were fascinated by her ability, and so was I.

After months of questioning, Lucy finally confided her secret, "It's actually very simple. I talk lovingly to the rose every day."

Still curious about her talents, I asked, "Why is it you never have to smudge your orange grove to keep the oranges from freezing when the temperature drops below freezing? I know your neighbors have to smudge."

"That's simple too. I walk through my 40 acres of oranges every day and send love to all the trees. I tell them how much I appreciate them and ask them not to freeze. And they never do."

Immediately, I saw a flaw in her program, "But what happens when you go away on vacation?"

She smiled, "I shut my eyes and walk the grove in my mind. It's just as easy to flow love to them when I'm away as when I'm with them."

Intrigued, I asked how she came to have such an unusual talent. My patient happily revealed events that had occurred when she was a child . . .

When Lucy was a little girl, her father bought a house in Texas. It was built on alkali flats where nothing, but *nothing*, would grow. Being wealthy, he hired scientists to improve the soil. Organic soil and manure were hauled in, but still nothing grew. One day, on a whim, he stopped a passing hobo and hired him to put in plants behind the house. Wherever the hobo planted, it looked like a jungle compared to the rest of the barren flats surrounding the house.

As a child, Lucy found this strange man, who could make things grow, fascinating. He told her plants were alive and needed love to thrive, just like people. Soon she was walking the rows with him every day. She paid close attention to the hobo as he planted, and learned to talk to the plants herself. However, one day her father saw the hobo apparently talking to himself and asked, "Bo, who do you think you're talking to?"

The hobo replied, "Why, I'm talking to the plants I put in for you, Sir. I want them to know I love them. I tell them to grow beautifully and flourish."

Horrified that he had allowed this man, who was clearly insane, anywhere near his daughter, he shouted, *"Pack up your things. I want you out of here right now! You're fired!"*

For as long as Lucy lived on those alkali flats, the hobo's plantings grew beautifully. However, the rest of the property remained barren, no matter how much money her father paid to have the soil amended. Through the wisdom of a passing hobo, Lucy learned that love's blessing is the most powerful compost in the world. Imagine if we all applied this technique in our everyday life.

About the time I heard Lucy's story, I was with a research group that used special cameras to take pictures of drops of water. Some drops were blessed—in the same way that grace would be said over food—and some drops were not blessed. As seen in the developed photographs, the unblessed water had no radiance, but the blessed drop of water glowed for 24 hours. We discovered that it didn't matter who said the blessing or what words were used. Intention was the key, and I'm sure Lucy's loving intention was the key to her ability.

———·◆·———

As I went through life, I continued to learn from my patients. When Manuel, a math teacher, brought his wife in to see me, the poor lady had been suffering for thirty years from chronic bladder infections and what would now be called Chronic Fatigue Syndrome. After his wife was well in a few treatments, Manuel said, "It's clear that you are a true healer. I want to tell you my story. I've never told anyone else, but you have to promise that you won't tell anyone until after my death." Curious, I agreed. We shook hands and arranged to meet back at my office that evening.

That night, after getting comfortable, Manuel smiled and began his tale by first describing the small Mestizo village where he had grown up in Chihuahua, Mexico. There, as a young boy, he had encountered a fierce "white" Indian warrior over six feet tall, who towered over the tallest Mestizo man in the village. Once a month, the warrior, who wore bandoliers of ammunition across his chest, came down from the mountains into Manuel's village to trade blocks of pure gold for ammunition. By listening to the village elders, Manuel learned that the warrior belonged to an entire tribe of such imposing men in the mountains.

Manuel's family lived near open air huts where the trading took place. In the center of these huts was a post with a nail driven into the top. This nail served as a skewer to hold papers on which were written

the names of sick people in the village. When the formidable warrior
came to the village, he made his trades, gathered the papers from the nail,
and returned to the mountains. His stern visage did not permit questioning, and everyone knew not to follow this warrior. The few who tried did
not return.

For unknown reasons, this solemn warrior spoke only to Manuel.
After many months, Manuel finally worked up his courage and asked why
people were healed—no matter what their condition—the day after the
warrior returned to the mountains with the papers. The warrior studied
him intently for several moments. Seeing Manuel's sincerity, he said that
he gave the papers to the shamans of his tribe when he returned and they
performed a healing ceremony.

The healers sat in a circle and placed the papers in the center. Each
shaman visualized a triangle of energy. At the top of the triangle was God;
the "patient"—represented by the name on the paper—was another point
of the triangle; and the third point was the shaman. When this visualiza-
tion was held by all the healers, they declared in Spanish, "I release you."
And it was done. By releasing the energy of the person to God, the
healing was complete and total.

The warrior then placed his hands on Manuel's shoulders—something he had never done before—and said, "You must *not* tell the secrets
of our healing ceremony to anyone here. You and your family are destined to leave Chihuahua and live in California. There you will find one
person to tell. This person will not reveal these things until the time is
right and the world is ready."

Manuel told me his parents brought their family to southern California in order to escape the soldiers of Pancho Villa during the revolution
in Mexico. Fascinated by his story, I leaned forward to shake his hand,
"Thank you, Manuel. Your story affirms my own belief that all healing is
from the Creator. Don't worry. I won't tell your story until it's time." And
so it was that I received the secrets of Manuel's youth.

———•◆•———

A few weeks later, Manuel called and said he had to see me. When
we met at his home, he said he had to tell me about his brother, Ben,

who was living in San Diego, so that one day I would tell others. And so he began his account of his brother's adventures . . .

Ben had been a desperate alcoholic for years, but his lowest point came late one night when he sold his children's blankets and clothes for wine. After he realized what a terrible thing he had done, he hitchhiked to Redlands. He went to Manuel's house, stole a gun, and drove off in Manuel's car. His plan was to return to San Diego, say goodbye to his unsuspecting wife and children, drive out into the desert, and kill himself. Unshaven and covered in his own vomit, he drove the lonely highway back toward San Diego. It was during World War II when you could drive the highway all night and see only three or four cars.

Suddenly, in the middle of the highway halfway to San Diego, an elderly man wearing a white suit appeared in Ben's headlights. Ben swerved to avoid hitting him. At the same time, Ben's right foot involun- tarily slammed on the brakes. As the car skidded to a stop on the right shoulder of the road, Ben felt every hair on the back of his neck stand up. He struggled to move his foot back to the gas pedal and get back on the highway as the ghostly figure approached the car. However, Ben was frozen, unable to make his escape.

When the stranger reached the car, he opened the passenger's door and got in without a word. It was as if this distinguished gentleman had been waiting all along for Ben to pick him up. After a few moments of intense silence, Ben's new passenger spoke in a quiet, calming voice, "You know, Ben, you're not going to kill yourself. Now, let's drive to San Diego."

Ben's unexpected passenger continued talking as they drove on through the night. Ben felt as though he was in a trance, soothed by the gentle rise and fall of the man's voice. The stranger explained that he was one of many who served behind the scenes to bring peace to the world. He said, "When we travel across borders, we need no identification. As peacekeepers working for the betterment of humankind, we are never stopped or questioned. No one notices us because we travel shielded by a cloak of invisible protection. But it is not time for us to reveal our work to humanity . . . yet. Whenever mankind becomes greedy, selfish, and totally power hungry, then angelic intervention must take place. Then we are called upon to avert the disasters that mankind is so fond of creating."

Ben's eyes remained glued to the small section of highway ahead illuminated by the car's headlights. Afraid to look at the stranger because he might not actually be there, he was even more afraid that he *would* be there. The stranger went on to detail Ben's life from birth to death.

Just outside the San Diego city limits, the mysterious stranger told Ben to pull over and stop the car. After Ben did so, his passenger said, "Ben, I'm going to leave you now. I want you to drive into the city and pick out any street corner to stand on. Wait there until you are approached by two different men. One of them will offer you a wonderful place to live for five years, and the other will give you a fine job. It doesn't matter what corner you choose."

"But I . . ."

"Just listen, Ben. This *will* happen," the stranger said. "Once these two men have completed their business with you, go to any supermarket and buy groceries for your family."

"But I don't have any money," Ben protested.

"I know, Ben. Just tell the cashier that you will pay the store later."

Finally, the old gentleman got out of the car. Leaning back through the car's open window, he said, "If you ever need to contact me, focus and think of me strongly. I will appear."

Ben started to drive off in a daze. When he looked back in his rearview mirror, there was no one anywhere behind the car. Ben rubbed his eyes and decided he must have had some strange, waking dream brought on by his ambitious consumption of alcohol before taking Manuel's car. But, figment of his imagination or not, Ben couldn't shake the words of the old fellow out of his mind.

Early morning risers were already enjoying the sun's first rays by the time Ben reached the city. Figuring he had nothing to lose, Ben picked a corner for his assignment. Soon after taking his position, a man came up to him, shook hands with him vigorously, and handed him keys to a large downtown hardware store. As if it was the most natural thing in the world, he smiled at Ben and said, "I need you to report Monday to manage my store." Ben took the keys, thanked him, and the man strolled away whistling.

Shortly, another man walked briskly up to Ben. Smiling widely, he patted Ben on the back, put house keys in Ben's hand, and said, "I've got a large house in La Jolla. I need you to live there for five years with your family while I'm with my family in Europe. Don't worry. All the maintenance costs have been paid, including gardeners for the yard work." Astonished by his good fortune, Ben thanked the man who handed him a piece of paper with the address and walked away.

By this time, Ben was smelling pretty sour, his beard was long past the five o'clock shadow mark, and his clothes were wrinkled and soiled. However, since things were following the mysterious stranger's predictions, Ben decided to test his newfound luck further by heading for a nearby market. After the cashier loaded Ben's purchases into two large grocery bags, he hesitantly told the cashier he would pay later. In spite of his appearance and foul odor, the cashier smiled warmly and said, "Pay when you can."

The next day, Ben moved his stunned family into the spacious La Jolla home. Ben never drank again and arrived promptly at the hardware store on Monday morning to become its new manager. From the beginning, he used his time wisely, generously loaning money to local people in distress, and keeping careful records to ensure each loan was repaid.

However, a few years later, Ben got into a financial bind that seemed impossible to solve. Recalling the old man's words, he went into his office, closed the door, sat in his chair, shut his eyes, and thought strongly of the old man. Ben was sure nothing would happen, but when he opened his eyes, the old gentleman was sitting in a rocking chair on the opposite side of Ben's desk. He looked just as Ben remembered him. Rocking in the chair, his benefactor spoke quietly, "Ben, the next time you contact me it had better be a life and death situation. Your little financial problem will resolve itself in three days. I was in a very important meeting with world leaders in New York and must return immediately."

Ben replied, "I'm sorry. I *do* understand. Thank you for coming." His remarkable visitor nodded and Ben turned away for a moment. When he turned back, no one was there. Only the chair, still rocking very gently, indicated that the old man had been with him.

Ben ran out and asked his employees if anyone had seen an old man leave his office. They said they had heard a conversation behind his closed office doors, but no one had come out into the store. Ben went back into his office. He sat in his chair and puzzled why destiny, through the old man's intervention, had given him his second chance. He decided that part of the reason must be to help others get their second chance, and he vowed to continue helping the people who came to him.

When Manuel finished telling me Ben's story, I thanked him and asked if he would introduce me to Ben so I might arrange a meeting with this mysterious old man. Since Manuel had told his brother everything I had done to help his wife, he felt sure Ben would arrange such a meeting.

However, whenever I reminded Manuel about his promise, he told me that it had slipped his mind. One weekend when I was talking with Manuel, he said, "I know. Why don't you come over right now and we'll call Ben?" Suddenly, my intuition told me that my meeting with Ben's old man was not to be. I released Manuel from his promise, and kept mine not to reveal these stories until after Manuel's death. Now I am passing on Manuel's stories as he gave them to me.

———•◆•———

My patients' stories continued to fascinate me. Actually, I sometimes felt I was more interested in the stories than those who *lived* through them . . .

I remember Will as the most henpecked husband I ever met. He could do *nothing* right in his wife's eyes, and his father-in-law continually berated Will by telling everyone he was stupid. Will did have a leisurely southern drawl, which required infinite patience in his listeners, but he was a lovely human being and I enjoyed his easygoing manner.

One day he mentioned that while he was in the army, he had been stationed in London during the blitz. Although he had never been to England, he was astonished to find he knew his way around London as if he had been born there. Since he could find his way back to the base even at night during the blackouts, his army buddies—amazed by his infallible sense of direction—always took him with them when they went drinking in the London pubs.

However, his army pals never dared let Will drink. If he joined in, he was sure to wander out of the pub in a daze when they weren't looking. Once in that trance-like state, Will would roam through London until he found a certain street, which felt like home to him. On that street, there was a house as familiar to him as his own name. All the cracks and bricks in the walk leading to the front door were like old friends.

Standing in front of the door, Will would reach for a large brass key, which he *knew* would be in the right pocket of his coveralls. But when he looked down—expecting to see blue coveralls and a lunch pail in his hand—he was stunned to see army khaki, and no lunch pail. At that point, the hair on the back of his neck stood up and he could hardly breathe. After looking at the door for a few seconds, he turned his back on the door and hightailed it back to the base as if his life depended on it.

When I heard his story, I asked, "Will, didn't you want to open the door and see what was on the other side?" He shook his head and drawled, "Whah, Doc, ah wooden open that doah fer all the money in the worl." Although I tried to get Will to talk more about this mystery, he would never speak of it again. I know wild horses wouldn't have kept me from opening that door and stepping through.

———— •◆• ————

Every day at the office brought new adventures as I got busier. While sometimes it was easy to find out what caused the patient's problem, at other times the mystery remained unsolved, even *after* healing took place. I recall one quiet Saturday morning when a woman came in with a truly startling appearance. It was no doubt planned by the Great Divine Director of Life that the office was empty when she came in, for her sake as well as that of my other patients.

I looked up and gasped. Standing in front of me was a petite woman whose head was the size of a large pumpkin. And I'm *not* exaggerating. Her eyes were narrow slits, barely visible, hidden in the puffy flesh of her face. Her ears were small bumps, which looked as though they had been stuck on as an after thought. I was surprised she could even speak through the tiny opening that served as her mouth.

Recovering my composure, I talked with my new patient about her strange condition. She said she had been this way for two years. Her history didn't reveal anything unusual. The blood studies she showed me were normal, but obviously *something* was very wrong. By this time, I had learned not to rely on lab tests as the last word in diagnosis. Too many patients who came to me sick, or dying brought in perfect blood studies. Other patients came in with test results that made me question when there would be funeral services, only to have them report that they felt wonderful and had always been healthy. While this wasn't typical, it happened often enough to show me that lab tests might—or might not—reveal underlying cause factors.

Taking a deep breath, I prayed and began running energy. After the treatment, I sat with her in prayer, trying to pin down the cause of her strange condition. After she left, I was still puzzled until I received an intuitive message, but the lady had already left my office.

Early Monday morning, there was a knock on my office door. I didn't have any patients at that early hour so I was surprised to see a slim, attractive woman standing in the hallway when I opened the door. She smiled broadly, came in, and took a seat in my waiting room. I asked if I could help her. She laughed and looked at me expectantly. Apparently she was waiting for me to recognize her. Her laugh was absolutely familiar, but I finally confessed I didn't remember her. She laughed again, "I'm the bigheaded woman." Amazed by her incredible transformation, I sat down across from her and asked to hear her story . . .

After seeing me two days ago for her first energy treatment, she had gone directly to her home in Riverside. As she was going up her front steps, her children were looking out the window, but they didn't recognize her. When they finally realized it was their mother, they began screaming, "It's mama and her head's all right!"

She told me that she had called many churches and TV stations about her healing, hoping to put me on the map, but never had a call back. I told her the Power had things other than fame and fortune in mind for my healing practice. Just as she was leaving, my intuitive hit resurfaced. I asked, "By any chance, do you have an electric bug killer, the kind that plugs into the wall?"

She replied, "There's one in my front room. Why do you ask?"

"When did you install it?"

"Let me think. Two years ago."

"And your condition started when?"

"Oh . . . 2 years ago . . . you don't think . . ."

"Well, that could be what caused your problem."

"Hmm, maybe so, but how could your healing work so fast? By the time I reached home, my head was back to normal. Besides, why weren't any of my children affected?"

"That I don't know. Some questions just remain part of God's mystery."

After this lady's experience, I was even more convinced that *anything* could cause *anything* and healing could occur for *any* condition. Surprisingly another lady came in with a similar problem. She was lovely and very petite to her waist, but her legs—which she described to me as huge tree trunks—were enormous, heavy, shapeless things.

It was shocking to see such a delicate lady have legs so swollen with excess fluid and tissue. She was 75 and said her legs had been this way all her life. Her adoring husband said her legs meant nothing to him, but she noticed he gazed admiringly after ladies with shapely legs. Since I had previously helped her daughter with health problems, she decided to take a chance and come in for a treatment.

I began running energy, focusing the healing on her legs. When she returned to my office two hours later, she was walking on legs as slim and shapely as any Hollywood starlet. I nearly fell over in surprise, far too surprised to nonchalantly say, "Oh yes, this sort of thing happens all the time."

The next day she came by the office wearing the shortest miniskirt I had ever seen. It had been purchased by her admiring husband and was perfect for her new figure. When she said her new legs were the greatest miracle of her life, she glowed with happiness. While her husband and I admired her new "gams," she paraded up and down the office like a model on a fashion runway. After her husband went out, she pulled me aside and asked anxiously, "Will it last?" When I asked Upstairs, they said, "Forever." I passed on this happy news and she beamed with joy. Curiously, she had never lost an ounce of weight from the treatment.

———— • ◆ • ————

Often healings made such changes in people that friends and family hardly recognized them. Mrs. H. was one such case. Well-known in our town as a reliable babysitter, she would only work for medical doctors. Anyone else was turned down flat. Before I knew this, I asked her to babysit for us since I knew she had managed an orphanage for 10 years and was both capable and trustworthy. She huffed up and told me that as a mere chiropractor I didn't come up to her standards. After she explained that she only worked for the medical profession, I was properly humbled.

Mrs. H. was a large woman with painful, swollen knees. She only managed to get around by leaning heavily on two stout crutches. One day the local podiatrist, who knew me well, suggested to her that I might be able to help. Since Mrs. H. only went to medical doctors, it was with great misgivings that she came to see me. In examining her swollen knees, I touched every area on both her knees. Suddenly, she burst into tears. I quickly asked, "Am I hurting you?"

Shaking her head, she replied, "No, it's just that no other doctor has ever actually touched my knees. It feels surprisingly comforting."

After hearing this, it was my turn to shake my head. "If they haven't touched your knees, what *have* the doctors done to help you?" I asked.

With a heavy sigh, she answered, "Oh, each doctor takes x-rays and prescribes pain pills."

After several more treatments, the swelling was gone and Mrs. H. could walk normally with no discomfort and without her crutches. She was very grateful to be rid of the terrible pain, which she had endured for years. After her last treatment, she confided, "I have to tell you, Doctor MacKimmie, my greatest joy in life is that people don't *recognize* me now that I don't need my crutches and can walk normally. I'm sorry about what I said before. I'll babysit for you whenever you need me." Those were wonderful words to hear. It is a heavenly feeling—as any parent knows—to go out knowing your children are in capable hands. What a wonderful woman, and steady as a rock.

After I came to know Mrs. H. better, she told me about the ten years she spent running an orphanage. There was an M.D. on staff when she first took the job, but she discovered that the government funding wasn't enough to feed the children adequately and pay the medical man, so she let him go at once. She also arranged for the children to work for a farmer in exchange for fresh goat milk. There were three happy results from her plan: the children's allergies disappeared along with bills for cows' milk and the doctor's salary.

Mrs. H. had hundreds of children in her care and they were like a huge family. However, in 1939, bureaucracy changed how the orphanage was to be managed, and she left. With her wonderful years of experience, she became a much sought after babysitter. In her opinion, corn starch was the best thing for powdering baby bottoms. From then on, I advised parents to dust babies with corn starch at diaper time. At home, we kept it in a large glass jar with holes in the lid and sprinkled it on all six as they came along. Mrs. H. didn't believe in the commercial baby powders of the day. "Lots of stink for lots of money" were her exact words.

One day, Mrs. H. called me; she was crying. When I asked what was wrong, she tearfully replied, "I'm so embarrassed, but I don't know where else to turn for help. My two dachshunds are my only children. I've been taking them to the veterinarian for months. They've had cortisone shots and antibiotics, but they haven't gotten any better. Now the vet says they're going to die." I could hear in her voice how precious her companions were to her and agreed to make a house call that morning. Breaking down again, Mrs. H. sobbed, "I don't think I'll be able to bear it if I lose them."

When I arrived, sure enough, both dogs, old as the hills and white at the muzzle, were dying. But they were not far enough gone to stop them from snapping at me whenever I tried to get near them. I quickly asked Mrs. H. to help me wind cotton bandages around their jaws so that I would survive unscathed. After I treated them, Mrs. H. said softly, "I think they look better already." I smiled, but I thought it might be wishful thinking on her part. As I left, I prayed for the poor old fellows to either improve, or have a quick and painless passing.

Mrs. H. called the next morning, her voice filled with excitement, "During the night, I heard so much commotion downstairs that I thought a robber had broken into the house. But when I got to the top of the stairs, imagine my surprise to see my dear old boys gallop by down below. They were *playing* for the first time in months. I went downstairs and found chalky dog feces in long rows on the hearth. It looked just like limestone to me. I let the boys out into the backyard and they did their business. They're just like new. Thank you so much."

Just as in humans, when the plumbing is blocked, the life force drops lower and lower. I was thrilled that the energy treatment had restored happiness and joy to her household. Mrs. H. is gone now and her precious dogs also, but I know they are together in heaven. Perhaps in heaven our dear animal companions will be able to talk to us. I hope so.

They give us so much love and pleasure in this life that it would be wonderful to converse about old times when we see them again in the hereafter.

———— • ◆ • ————

It didn't take long in practice to discover that you couldn't please everyone. Dear Estelle was close to 40 when I treated her, young in my current estimation, but even at 40 she was like a little old lady about everything. She drove her friends crazy with her prickliness. A friend suggested that she come to me for treatment because she had lost her sense of smell when she was a child.

With a few treatments, she regained her sense of smell, but then her friends came in and gave me hell. Why? Because all she would talk about was the smell of fruits, flowers, air, earth, etc. She drove them crazy describing smells. No one could go shopping with her because she would stand in the produce section and rhapsodize over the particular scent of one fruit over another. No doubt she was making up for her years of olfactory deprivation, but her friends never let me forget the headache I had created for them.

As time went on, I was blessed to see many miracles. When they came, they were spectacular. Of course, they occurred when they darn well pleased. There was nothing I could do to speed them up, or make them come at my bidding. Not being in control was tough on the ego and it took some getting used to. I discovered the ego is a tough, humorless character who loves to lead us around by the nose.

My life's study and work have been to open to the healing energies of the universe. Over the years, I tried to push, pull, cajole, threaten, plead, ask, and demand, but nothing ever changed the steady flow of healing, except to stay out of the way. Walking down the street, I enjoyed seeing the unique energies within each person. I could recognize every health problem, but I had no control over who came to me for help. Certain people were brought to my office for reasons I couldn't possibly understand while the same energy kept other people away, often those were the very people I was sure I could help.

When I first saw miracles in my practice, it was easy to think that maybe I was the healer. Believing that the works and words of Jesus would give me more insight on healing, I studied the New Testament closely. About this time, a friend joked that what I really needed was a sparkling wand, a cape, and low lighting in my treating room. We laughed and I told him that if I thought it would help my patients, I was willing.

But before I came to the point of wand-waving and cape-wearing, my ego was firmly persuaded to take a back seat. This happened one afternoon while I was busy flowing energy to a patient. Suddenly the firm voice of the Power resounded inside my head, *"What are you doing?"*

Without thinking, I answered aloud, "I'm healing."

My startled patient looked up, "What?"

I put my hand on my patient's shoulder and said, "Quiet please! I'm listening!" A chorus of angelic laughter (no doubt only heard by me) echoed through my treating room.

Then the Power spoke again, *"Don't be foolish. You never healed in your life. God heals who, why, when, where, and how, for reasons you will never understand. It is none of your business. Furthermore, if you keep thinking that you are doing the healing, we will find someone else to heal through."*

Stunned by this announcement, I asked inside how to continue my healing practice. The Power answered gently, *"Remember that you are simply a conduit. You are James C. MacKimmie. The 'C' stands for 'conduit' and that is all you are. We bring the patients to you, God heals, and you take the fee and make the appointments."*

I inhaled sharply from this major jolt to my ego. Hearing that God did the healing and that my role was a minor one, I was both shocked and relieved at the same time. Since healing was my entire life, I thanked the Power for this lesson in humility and agreed to be God's instrument. As I felt the angelic ones leaving, I wondered just what I was basing the rest of my life on and called after them, "Remember, from now on *you're* responsible for everything that happens in the patient's healing process."

The angelic chorus responded gently, *"We always have been!"*

Their parting words filled my heart with peace, and I continued treating my patient while I contemplated the important lesson learned. It has taken a lifetime of lessons to understand the perfection of every event as it takes place. The universe is perfect, exactly as it is. And everyone in it is perfect, exactly as they are.

Some folks live a lifetime and never learn to accept life lovingly, as it occurs in the moment. They will return lifetime after lifetime, until this lesson is learned. Each person you meet is playing a part in the play called "Life." If you play *your* unique part lovingly, and allow others to play *their* unique parts, then you are acknowledging the perfection of the universe. Realize that life never changes. You change, through your reactions to life. These were lessons I began learning from a very dear friend.

I first met Harry five years after my Dad, Bob MacKimmie, died. I was 12 and quickly latched onto Harry as my substitute father. For all the years I knew Harry, he willingly listened to my strange ideas, hopes and dreams. Harry's support meant the world to me throughout high school, college, and after I started my practice. However, on the day I told him how grateful I was to be able to share my thoughts with someone who understood me and what I was here to do in life, I had a rude awakening.

To my surprise, Harry told me that he really didn't understand what I was talking about most of the time. I was crestfallen until he put his hand on my shoulder and said, "But, Jim, it's all so interesting. And you're so darn enthusiastic about it, that my advice is to keep on following whatever's leading you through life. Of course, you might fall off the mountain, but then again there's always the chance that you'll make it all the way to the top and have a good, long look around. So, just keep on trying for the top of that mountain." And, thanks to Harry, I *did* keep trying.

———·◆·———

My practice was humming along the summer Harry's brother died in a logging accident in Oregon. Harry drove up for the funeral, which was held in a redwood grove. After he returned, he told me he could barely hide his disgust when he saw the young, baby-faced clergyman approaching through the morning mist. Harry had driven trucks all over the country and had seen most everything. So when this inexperienced preacher, who looked as though he had just graduated from high school, climbed onto a big redwood stump to address the small gathering, Harry's first thought was, "What can this kid, who's still wet behind the ears, tell me that means anything?"

I was nodding in agreement when a sudden glow came over Harry's features. He grabbed my arm and said, "Jim, to my complete surprise, the words of that young minister changed my life forever." I didn't have a clue as to what he meant, and I didn't ask, but I would soon find out.

Before the funeral, Harry and I went out for tacos every Friday night. After dinner, we headed over to the Elk's club to watch the boxing matches broadcast from Los Angeles. After that, we would drive around while we groused about the apparent crookedness in city politics. We always felt better for these nights out. They were like an addiction; we depended on them to establish our place in the world around us.

Whenever I talked with Harry during the week at his gas station, we would discuss everything that was wrong in the world. We both saw the negative side of life and actually enjoyed jawing about how rotten things were in the country. But all that changed after Harry returned from his brother's funeral. Harry was a new man, friendly and cheerful to all. He refused to say anything bad about anybody or anything. Suddenly, he was everyone's best friend. Soon I noticed cars lined up to get gas at his station. There was no gas shortage; people just wanted a chance to chat with Harry.

Exasperated, I finally demanded to know just what the young minister had said that was so impressive. Harry beamed and happily quoted the young minister, "My friends, we only get out of life what we put in."

"I don't get it. That's it?"

"I tell you, Doc, it hit me like a ton of bricks."

"What did?"

Harry repeated, "My friends, we only get out of life what we put in."

"Sorry, Harry, I don't feel a thing. Would you mind saying it again?"

After hearing it for the third time, I shook my head, "I still don't get it. It doesn't do *anything* for me."

"I know, Doc . . . I know. Even though I've heard it hundreds of times before in my life, it never meant a thing to me either until I heard it at my brother's funeral."

The change in Harry was very evident, and it drove me crazy. Now, he quoted the young minister on every possible occasion. Every time I turned around there was Harry saying, "My friends, we only get out of life what we put in." And each time he spoke these words, he lit up like fireworks on the fourth of July. I felt as though I had been left at the side of the road in the mud, while Harry drove cheerfully down the highway of life.

I decided my friend had become a first class bullshitter, but I also saw he had become very popular. From the day of the funeral, he became loving, kind, and considerate to his fellows. One morning he said, "You know, Doc, my life was dismal and depressing before my brother's funeral. But after I heard the minister say . . ."

Desperate to stop him, I grabbed his arm and said, "Harry, it's OK. I know those words by heart! *Please!* Don't say them again!"

He looked at me and smiled, "Well anyway, Doc, afterward, I realized my life was so depressing because all I ever put out into the world was negativity. If I wanted joy and happiness, then I'd have to speak only good of people, smile first, and spread only good news. That way I'll get back from life what I'm putting into it."

Although I saw that Harry's change was heartfelt, I hated to lose my companion in the complaint department. Now I was alone in my preferred pastime of complaining about life. Whenever I saw Harry, I grumbled about his new attitude. He suggested I become a lifter-upper and see how good it felt. I steadfastly remained in the dumps. However, Harry simply refused to join in when I tried to point out all the negative events in the world.

Discouraged, I even gave up my practice of starting my day with positive thoughts. Instead, when I wasn't looking, my morning garden of happy thoughts filled with weeds. My ego had me in a grip of steel. The past rose up to haunt my thoughts; I remembered every hurt and wound suffered; in reality, I was at war with myself.

Harry continued to say uplifting and cheery things, even to me. Feeling alone and miserable, I could not lift myself out of the mire. I was drowning while Harry was in a lifeboat, warm and safe. However, I was unwilling to see that my attitude kept me out of the boat. I felt totally abandoned. When I drove by the station, he would wave, smile broadly, and call out, "Hey, Doc, how's it going?" I would glare back, say nothing, and drive on.

Whenever I stopped at the station for gas, I called Harry a bullshitter to his face. He laughed, "Well, Doc, it may be bullshit, but it's happy bullshit, and I'm happy to share it." Harry seemed to laugh all the time. I saw that his happiness made others happy, which made him happier, and his life just kept on getting better and better all the time. When he saw my grim face, he would call out, "Hey, Doc, it's a great life! Jump on board! Be happy!" Then he would laugh and start telling jokes until I had to laugh too.

Every evening I stopped by while Harry was closing the station for the night. I tried my best to snap him out of his irritating love and good cheer. While I tried to return him to the truth of life—as I saw it—he persisted in trying to show me the happy side of life, "Come on, Doc, put a smile on that face of yours." It was impossible not to see that his optimistic attitude had changed everything in his life for the better. Harry told me that he now had an inner peace he had never thought possible before.

And then it happened. I came up with "The Gooch Plan." It was perfect, a way to show Harry exactly how false his perceptions of life had become. Old Man Gooch was 91, and was generally considered the Scrooge of our town. A multimillionaire with ranches and property all over the world, he never parted with his money for anyone or anything. Every morning he walked past Harry's gas station on his way to breakfast in town without ever smiling or talking to anyone.

One morning on the way to the office, I stopped by the station and casually told Harry that I would become a true believer if he could make Gooch smile. Harry shook my hand enthusiastically and said he would begin his campaign immediately. I smiled inwardly, knowing I was safe from ever having to make good on my promise. In all the years that Gooch walked past Harry's gas station, his stone face had never changed. He looked as though he had seen everything in the world twice, and disapproved of it both times.

Each morning when Gooch walked past, Harry bellowed out, "Good morning, Mr. Gooch." Gooch glanced over at Harry the first time this happened, but the next day, and from then on, not so much as a flicker of recognition. Mount Rushmore's presidents had more animation.

After a few weeks, Harry called me down to watch his early morning performance with Gooch because he was certain he had seen a slight smile on that stern visage the day before. I held my breath and watched closely as the old man walked by, but I saw nothing resembling a smile coming from across the street after Harry's salutation. Confidently, I told Harry he hadn't a prayer of winning Gooch over. But Harry refused to give up.

A month later, I received another call from Harry. He asked me to come down early to the station again, certain that Gooch had acknowledged his greeting. Observing from my favorite vantage point next to one of the pumps, I was gratified to see that there was no discernable acknowledgment from Gooch. I was actually beginning to enjoy this comedy and found myself heading for my office early in order to stop by and watch the show. Harry continued to shout out friendly greetings, but Gooch never broke his stride, or looked in our direction. Other people, who had heard of the bet, started coming to the station in the morning to see if any progress was being made. I continued to tell Harry that it was a lost cause.

Two months later, I was with Harry as he called out his usual, friendly, morning greeting, and as usual got zero response. He turned to me and said, "Jim, I'm a desperate man, here goes nothing . . ." He dashed out to the curb and yelled after Gooch's retreating back, *"Hey, Gooch, you old bastard, how are you?"* Stunned by this new greeting, Old Stone Face stopped in his tracks. He turned and actually looked Harry in the eye before turning away and continuing his walk to town.

Encouraged, Harry turned to me and said, "Doc, I'm sure he's ripe for change." Relieved that I hadn't seen any hint of a smile, I replied, "Harry, give it up. Old Man Gooch is *never* going to change. You might as well realize that people never change, and the world never changes either." Harry said nothing.

Another month passed. Confident that Harry was fighting a losing battle, I hadn't even bothered going by the station. Then one morning Harry called and woke me up, "Come by the station as soon as you can." When I arrived, I was stunned to see Gooch with his arm around Harry's shoulder. He looked like Harry's Siamese twin brother. My mouth fell open to my knees.

While Harry waited on cars, the old man stood a foot away, waiting anxiously for him to finish. Any time Harry wasn't busy, Gooch was barnacled to his side. When Harry went to the bathroom, the old man would patiently wait outside the door for Harry to come back out. Poor Harry seemed to be aging with each passing minute.

As soon as Harry saw me, he ran over, grabbed me by the shirt, and pulled me into his office. Glaring, he said, *"You're* to blame for this. Now Gooch wants to give me a ranch in Arizona and make me a partner in his business." Before Harry could say another word, we were interrupted by old man Gooch, peering in at the doorway and wearing what I had to admit was a genuine smile.

All that summer, the old man was the first to show up at the station in the morning, and the last to leave at night. Harry smoked cigarettes, and it was Gooch who was always at hand with a light. All day long, he hovered near Harry, and I was forced to own up to my part in creating this disaster for my friend. By the time Harry's friends were thinking of ways to slow down this one-sided love affair, Gooch went to meet his maker. But I know he died happy, having found one best friend in this world. Once Gooch was laid to rest, Harry's health improved rapidly. And thanks to the failed Gooch Plan, I had to enroll in Harry's happiness program, which helped this healer heal himself.

As Harry had wanted me to change my attitude, I had tried to get him to change his diet. However, as an old time trucker, he loved fried-foods and coffee strong enough to melt steel. He never drank much water, and spent the evening watching TV while enjoying boxes of chocolate with his wife. Both Harry and his wife loved Boxer dogs; they had five over the years. Each received chocolate treats every night, and each died of heart problems at age two. I suggested too much chocolate was at fault, but Harry said their dogs all loved chocolate treats every evening as much as he and his wife did.

Years later, Harry died after three open heart surgeries. It was a great loss to our community. At his funeral, hundreds of people came to speak of his kindness and how he had changed their lives. He was truly a prince among men. He helped me maintain the balance in my life by getting me to laugh at myself. Whenever I got down, Harry would say,

"Doc, you look lower than whale poop today." As I measured myself against that image at the bottom of the ocean, we'd have a good laugh and I'd be back on track again. God bless you, Harry, my happy friend.

9

A HEALER'S TEACHER

————————•‒••‒•‒————————

Would it shock you to meet a man who knew everything? A man who could look into your very soul? I searched the world over, through letters and in person, hoping to find a Master Healer who would know me to the very core of my being. For years, I envisioned such a person tapping me on the head to awaken further powers of healing within me. Filled with a desire to treat thousands a day, I dreamed this dream. And for as long as I can remember, I knew there would be an old man in my life who would become my great teacher. I searched and searched until I tired of searching and finally let go. Then God took over and it happened . . .

Having given up my search, I was irritated when Fred, a close friend, persisted in asking me along whenever he went to visit an old man in Long Beach, California. Fred nagged me for a year to go with him while I steadfastly refused. My dream was ready to come true, but I was dragging my feet. To further ruffle my feathers, Fred quoted this mysterious stranger all the time. One day when I couldn't stand it a moment longer, I confronted him, "Fred, I don't want to hear what some *old man* has to say. I want to hear what *you* have to say."

Fred replied, "Why would I give you my opinion? I've never found a source of greater wisdom than this old man. Why shouldn't I quote him? If I can ever express more wisdom than Mr. S., I will, until then, I can only quote him."

With great reluctance, I finally agreed to go with Fred to meet this

179

paragon of wisdom and truth. I was secretly hoping our meeting would, once and for all, lay the matter to rest, and put an end to Fred's incessant quoting. Ready for anything—or so I thought—we drove to Long Beach where we parked in front of a small, tidy house, a few blocks from Bixby Park. Fred knocked on the front door and a strong voice called out, "Enter."

Fred led the way through the house to the living room. Glancing around as I followed him, I saw elegant furnishings from the early 1900s, befitting a gentleman of the old school. Faint traces of pipe tobacco in the air mingled with the delicious aroma of what smelled like a fine beef stew, coming from the kitchen.

Walking confidently ahead of me, Fred entered the living room. Peering over his shoulder, I saw an older gentleman sitting in a rocking chair puffing on a pipe. He nodded toward Fred, who then introduced me. The Old Man turned toward me and our eyes locked. I nearly stepped back from the power in his eyes. His first look pierced my soul, probing its very depths. In that instant, I saw that he knew all about me and my life, what I had gone through, and what I would go through in the future. In my heart, I knew he knew, but I resolved to ignore the impact of those penetrating eyes.

Taking a seat near the Old Man, Fred initiated a quiet conversation with him. Across the room, I remained standing, leaning against a wall with my arms crossed, trying to convince myself that I really didn't have that much to learn from anyone. While they talked, I studied the Old Man. His wavy hair was intensely white and his piercing eyes were chestnut brown. Formally dressed in a suit and tie, he was wearing unusual high top, laced shoes, which I learned later were made from kangaroo skin.

Clearly, Fred was entranced by every word this elderly gent uttered. Being 24, I thought I already knew everything so I wondered what—if anything—he could ever offer me in the way of wisdom. The actual words running through my mind were, "I wonder what this old goat *really* knows?"

Instantly, the Old Man stopped talking to Fred, turned toward me, and answered, "This old *goat* knows a lot more than *you* do." I was dumbfounded that he had read my mind. I had heard of people having such abilities, but experiencing it first-hand was totally unnerving. In my mind, I exclaimed, *"Oh My God!"*

Without hesitating, he voiced my thought, "Yes . . . Oh My God!"

The next few minutes went on forever. Every thought I had, he spoke aloud. Thoughts raced through my mind and the Old Man calmly voiced each one. I never uttered a word, and Fred apparently knew better than to interrupt the Old Man as he verbalized my thoughts. I was soon drenched in sweat although I tried my best to appear cool, calm and collected.

No matter where I hid in my mind, the Old Man was right there beside me. No sooner would I slam a mental door shut, then he would appear on my side of the door. Once I gave up and stopped trying to run, he left me to my own thoughts. Grateful to have survived, I took a few deep breaths, hoping that I didn't appear as unnerved as I felt.

At this point, the Old Man said, "A quart can only hold a quart. I'm not about to spill truth all over the ground. You're both full up. Another time." Fred got up and we said our goodbyes. I was thrilled to escape. No other human being had ever made me feel so unsettled. I realized I had met a man with powers beyond any I had ever imagined.

Just as I was about to walk out of the living room, the Old Man banged his pipe firmly into a heavy glass ashtray to get my attention. As I hesitated, he asked if I would like to know my worst fault. Without thinking, I answered, "Yes." This was the first and *only* word I had spoken during our visit. Timing his reply for maximum effect, he slowly added tobacco to his pipe, relit it, and took a few puffs, "You talk too much."

Stunned by his observation, I was speechless. I had spent the entire time there deliberately contributing *nothing* to the conversation between Fred and the Old Man. Then he added, "If you ever get into trouble, it will be from giving your opinion and the luxury of having the last word." I didn't appreciate hearing this because I knew it was all too true. Clearly he saw into me—warts and all—and I agonized on the way home while I thought about his parting words.

After I arrived home, I rambled on and on about the Old Man to my wife. Now, like Fred, I found myself quoting him constantly. For the next two weeks, my energy level was so high, I quite simply "buzzed." Only after I had been to see him many times, did I make the connection between being in his presence and the high energy buzz I felt after seeing him.

Everything else in my life took a backseat while I explored this amazing opportunity to learn from the Old Man. Each time I saw him, I came to life and glowed in the days that followed. My energy was raised to a higher vibration than I had ever experienced before. This sustained high made it difficult to sleep, but that was a small price to pay for all the positive changes happening in my daily life. Months passed before I began to understand the depth of the Old Man's great power and appreciate the importance of his teachings and the effect they would have on my practice as a healer.

———·◆·———

In ordinary conversation, the Old Man spoke with a thick cockney accent, which I strained to decipher when we conversed. But if I asked a question requiring inner knowledge, he would close his eyes for a few seconds to access the source of all knowing. When he opened his eyes again, he answered in a delightful Elizabethan style with words so refined and beautiful you thought an English scholar was speaking. If he chose to dictate an answer, his command of the English language was so perfect that he corrected errors his secretary was about to make before they could be written down. As one of his scribes, I can report that he never allowed any errors to make it onto the page.

The years I spent with the Old Man were like interacting with some ancient wise man from the stars. He had been given great gifts from the Creator, powers and energies that would shock most people. He could appear simultaneously in three different places and heal people thousands of miles away. When people came to him for healing, he knew instantly what was wrong with them without a word ever being spoken. Able to foresee future events, his predictions all came to pass.

When the Old Man was younger and actively healing, he healed on a scale not seen for two thousand years. People often asked him asked if he was Jesus returned. He would solemnly reply, "No, Jesus is the Master." The Old Man adored Jesus and said he had been blessed to be in the Master's presence many times. He told me, "Jesus is the most beautiful, perfect being imaginable. The Master is ever at our side, closer to us than our thoughts. His heart is the center of the universe; His heavenly wisdom radiates glorious colors, which make the brightest rainbows appear pale.

From His lofty brow streams forth a loving light, which fills the universe." The splendor of the vision he shared with me remains forever in my heart.

During his lifetime, I believe the Old Man was the world's greatest healer and teacher of wisdom. Miraculous healings were attributed to him and he brought to the world a unique method of healing, which has saved thousands from illness. In my own lifetime of searching for other healers, I never again met his equal in healing or wisdom. He was a master, strong in every way with no tolerance for weakness, except in children and those suffering from illness. Everything in his life had to be done his way. He followed no one . . . read nothing . . . studied nothing . . . he just *knew* from the highest level of inner knowing. As the life force *is*, so he *was*.

Miraculously, my mentor helped nearly all the people who came to him for healing. With one look, he knew if he could heal the condition or not. If he could not, he would tell the person to look elsewhere for healing. Occasionally he saw that healing would interfere with karmic patterns so he would say that it was not within his power to help.

If a phone call was made to the Old Man when someone was bleeding to death, he could stop the bleeding instantly with the power of his mind. But this miracle ceased as soon as the person was taken through the operating room doors. The Old Man said the operating room was not his domain. In his view, surgery was the doctor's province, and once through the surgery doors, it was the doctor's help the patient needed.

I was surprised to find that the Old Man looked at healing as a job, plain and simple. He knew what was wrong and went about fixing it with a no-nonsense attitude. Conversation between the patient and himself wasn't tolerated. If patients dared to ask personal questions, he rapped them sharply on the head. After instructing them to be quiet, he told them that nothing they said would help in their healing. He warned that if they uttered one more word, they would have to leave and he would never help them again. And he meant it. Strong tough words, but he healed hundreds of people each day in his prime and had no time for talking, which he said weakened the healer and diluted the healing.

———·◆·———

A small group of young men met with this master healer every few weeks. I felt blessed when I was invited to join them. Simply being in his presence was living proof that a life centered in love and wisdom was possible. Here in our midst was a human being with the gifts of prophecy, healing, and inner knowing. In sharing his wisdom with us, he unveiled truths that we had spent years looking for in ancient texts. In a few brief words, he revealed the wisdom and truth of life itself in all its glory.

We were constantly amazed to find that the Old Man knew everything; he could tap in and download any information from Universal Knowledge whenever we asked. Concepts that we knew vaguely, he knew totally in each moment from the Source of All Knowing. He accessed events and information from the past, present, or future whenever he wished. I learned from older members of the group, who had been with the Old Man in the early 1940s, that they had asked him about the outcome of World War II. He told them not to worry since the United States would end the war by "frying" two Japanese cities in the summer of 1945. They couldn't imagine what he meant until after it happened, exactly as he had predicted.

When asked about atomic energy, physics, or any other subject of a scientific bent, he answered with amazing revelations. Even when his answers flew in the face of current scientific theories, he was always right, which later research confirmed. Much of what is considered scientific fact today, he revealed to us in detail 50 years ago, before these facts were even notions within the scientific community.

The Old Man advised us to keep our head in the clouds and our feet planted firmly on the ground. He said it was important to do both at the same time. In this way, higher energies would flow through us to inspire us and those around us. If we were too grounded, we would lose our heavenly inspiration and guidance. But if we were too heavenly, we would be of little earthly use to anyone. I returned home after each meeting filled with incredible energy, pledging to follow his wise words.

According to the Old Man, life was simple and God was simple, but human beings were very complex. He counseled us to simplify everything in our lives. In his view, specialization of any kind obscured life's big picture. By separating life into smaller and smaller pieces for minute examination, the pieces, like the shattered fragments of a broken mirror, lost all meaning.

When we asked him to tell us about God, he said, "As there is a creation, there must be a Creator. But no human being is capable of describing the Creator. To describe something, you must be greater than what you are trying to describe. And the Creator is far greater than All That Is."

Nothing remained hidden from the Old Man, no matter how hard we tried. Everything we did, or did *not* do, he saw and would tell us about it if we asked him. He knew everything about everyone in the group. Although I never spoke to him about my personal life while I was in the group, he knew my life from birth to death. I soon discovered he knew more about me than I knew about myself. He knew who I was, my purpose in life, my past and my future.

Whenever we gathered at his home, he always spent time foretelling future events for members of our group. One afternoon it was my turn, and the Old Man asked what I wanted to know about my life. I responded, "I don't want you to see *for* me. I want to get my information *directly* from the Source of All Knowing as you do."

Uneasy silence gripped the room. The Old Man puffed away on his pipe while we awaited his reply with apprehension. Finally he smiled, "Ah, we have a *teacher* here." A wave of relief and nervous laughter went around the room and he went on to the next person.

At our next gathering, he foretold future events for everyone in the room but me. When I realized he had skipped me, I interrupted and asked for a look at my future. He laughed, "Look for yourself. You wanted to contact the Source. Do so . . . do so. Get your answers from the Source." Disappointed, I was silent for the rest of the meeting. I had crossed the line. I realized he would never again reveal what the future held in store for me.

However, after the meeting, the Old Man took me aside as the others were leaving. Putting his hand on my arm, he said, "You've made a wise decision. The others will be without guidance after my death if they don't develop their own inner contact. Universal intelligence is all around us, ever available. *Everyone* can tap into this soul wisdom. Go into the inner silence and connect with the Source." While I recognized the value of finding my own inner guidance, I knew I would sorely miss his treasured counsel and forward visions of events to come in my life.

———— •◆• ————

Meeting after meeting, I learned more about living life. Adamant that we keep both hands on the steering wheel of life, our teacher insisted we should never allow anyone else to steer for us, or even advise us on our steering. When we asked him to clarify this idea, he said, "By waking up to the fact that you are each responsible for everything in your life, you can learn to focus in the moment. Your lives are perfect in every way, exactly what you have signed up for. Power over others is nothing, but power over your own ego personality is everything. Surrender to the power of the soul, which will direct your life. Then you will be in harmony with all that you experience."

One afternoon, the Old Man told us that God wanted us all to be millionaires. Mystified, we shook our heads and looked at each other, wondering—if his statement was true—why weren't we all rolling in money? "Ah, you doubt this," he said. "Realize that only your thoughts and attitudes block your participation in the abundance of God's storehouse, which is open to everyone." Of course, we immediately asked how to shift our thoughts and attitudes. I will never forget the power of his answer, "He who creates, sees the end of all things mortal, and begins to live a life of Light. As you see, so shall it be. See it completed before you begin."

After he directed us to write these compelling words in our notes, he said, "If you meditate on the meaning of this truth, it will lead you to a place of awakening where all things will be revealed unto you." We eagerly asked if he would instruct us in meditation. He nodded and went on, "Meditation consists of three parts. Quiet the body. Quiet the mind. The third part will take care of itself."

Continuing our instruction in meditation, the Old Man told us that position was not important at our early stage of development. We could lie down or sit comfortably in a chair. The important thing was to tell the body to shut down and be quiet. So the foundation was to find a comfortable position and then quietly maintain that position. Easier said than done as anyone who has ever tried to sit without moving for any length of time can tell you. "You must not give in, even when you are tempted to move and relieve the body's tension," he cautioned. "The body always wants to rebel and move around at first, but in time it will obey."

Once the body was still, he instructed us to quiet the mind by focusing on the breath rising and falling, or on a single word—such as love or peace—to pin the mind on one target. "After quieting the body and the mind, meditation will spontaneously arise from the silence of your inner self," he explained. "You all have a point of contact within the stillness of your inner being." In that place, which he called the "soul-mind," the wellspring of our love is in perfect communication with our Creator's heart. Over the ages, teachers have called the soul-mind by other names such as: the oversoul, the higher self, the true being, or the greater part.

Assuring us that contact with the soul-mind would bring miracles into our lives, the Old Man counseled us not to labor at meditation. "Relax into meditation. This state is your birthright and the natural province of your inner being. Once you have achieved stillness of the body/mind, the soul-mind will engage and flow through you to bring about the shifts of energy you are seeking." And these shifts did happen for those of us who followed his teachings, but most of his students were far too busy with their outer lives. A few members of our group, who consistently fell asleep during meditation, were told they needed sleep more than they needed inner guidance.

Our teacher said, "Those who spend their lives in hours and hours of meditation are wasting their life. Our present time is in such a state of acceleration that to meditate more than 20 minutes twice a day is to hide within the practice itself." As he suggested, I began meditating at the same time each day because we are creatures of habit and the physical body loves routine.

————•◆•————

How many of us dream of a kindly, loving teacher who will show us the path of self-realization? I had found my mentor, but he was un-yielding and brooked no nonsense. I admit that I resented his harsh manner. Unlike my dreams of a kindhearted teacher, the Old Man's nature was like an ancient oak tree, strong and rigid in ways that would never change. I quickly acquiesced to his firm, implacable temperament. Only once did I have the nerve to ask him to repeat himself. When I posed my question a second time, he scowled and said, "I only speak *once*. Never question me a *second* time after I have spoken." And I never did.

Guarding his solitude and anonymity, the Old Man never reached out to anyone. However, he made himself available to seekers of truth so I returned to Long Beach as often as possible to spend time alone in his presence. I cherished those inspirational hours when I brought my questions to him and basked in the wisdom of his answers. He revealed many secrets of the universe, as many as he was allowed to reveal to a novice thirsting for wisdom. I learned from my teacher that we all have awesome and incredible powers residing within us. When I asked him why we all settled for so little in life, he replied, "Ask much, get much. Ask little, get little. Most people ask too little."

Grateful for the Old Man's teachings, I used every precious moment with him to ask questions about life: Why are we here on the earth plane? Where did we come from? Where are we going? What is our divine purpose? What is healing? At group meetings, my fellow students were focused on their personal problems, but, when I was alone with him, something inside drove me forward in my quest to connect with the source of his wisdom.

Everything happening in our world now, the Old Man told me long ago. At times, he foretold events that I doubted would ever come to pass. But through the years, I've watched his mysterious predictions come true in ways that I could never have imagined. When he told me in 1955 that children on drugs would bring weapons into their schools to shoot teachers and other students, I was shocked! I couldn't believe this would ever happen, but I lived to see Columbine. He often spoke about the first decades of this present millennium when—out of darkness—the great spiritual consciousness of the Golden Age would blossom. Then we would know as reality the transcendent life we have only imagined in our dreams.

My mentor was inside the circle of light, a true healer and mystic. Not knowing it would be years before I fully grasped his wisdom, I tried to swim along beside him. Perhaps if I had met him later in life, I could have admitted how little I knew about healing and life. After surviving life's school of hard knocks, I now feel ready for his teachings. What I wouldn't give to be with him again and hear his words of wisdom today. Having awakened to the ego's desire to neatly box up knowledge and file it away in the mind's library for safekeeping, I see how this mental process sidesteps the path of wisdom.

Looking back, I can see what a great obstacle my youth was to the wisdom he presented to me and how often it blocked my progress. Youth knows so little, but thinks it knows everything. We all need to steer our lives, but we are such poor drivers. And does age improve us? The Old Man said that most people are frozen in their thoughts and attitudes by 40 years of age, determined to shut the door on anything new that comes their way. I've found this to be true. Sadly, some people are as stiff as starch and will never change no matter what. Clinging to the known in our search for comfort and security, we give up the flexibility of youth, which the Old Man said could be ours forever. Today I know that only in the unknown do we awaken to the true power within.

However, just as leopards can't change their spots, humans don't usually change their nature. I recall visiting my teacher one day with a friend in tow; he was a man who had no fondness for animals and avoided them at all costs. But I didn't think about that fact as we entered the living room, even though the Old Man had told me on several previous occasions that something was amiss with a person who didn't like animals.

As always, the Old Man's beloved companion, an ancient terrier named Jack, was lying in his usual place on a small, dark pillow at his master's feet. Black, except for his white muzzle, and thin as a rail, Jack was as cantankerous, crotchety and ill-tempered as they come. He seldom moved, content to lie on his pillow, looking as though he was carved out of wood. I've always gotten along well with animals, so Jack and I reached an understanding on my first visit. I left him alone and he graciously allowed me into his territory to share his master's company.

Smiling mysteriously, the Old Man patted Jack's head and said again that one could plumb the depths of a man's soul by observing how he related to animals. Hoping to impress the Old Man, my friend walked over to Jack. After offering a few ingratiating and encouraging words to Jack, he tentatively reached out a wary hand to pet the dog. Jack responded to this maneuver by growling and baring his teeth. Laughing, the Old Man said, "My friend, you can't fool an animal." And so it was. I'm sure this was the first and last attempt by my friend to present himself as an animal enthusiast.

———•◆•———

Each time I visited, the Old Man would talk with me for about an hour. After he stopped, I could not get him to continue, no matter how I tried. When his listener's mind could hold no more, he declared that only the ego wanted to go on and on. The soul-mind knew it was time to stop and go home. I dreaded hearing him say, "A quart can only hold a quart." These words signaled the end of a session, and, once uttered, nothing could induce him to speak again. But my mind always wanted more, even though I was bulging with his wisdom and had no room for more.

Once when he fell silent, I thought to outwit him by quickly asking him to continue. He continued by saying, "A quart can only hold a quart." Seeing my disappointment, he added, "You're full up, my boy, and overflowing. Like an automobile, there's no use spilling wisdom all over the ground when the tank is full. Come back when you have used the fuel of wisdom that I have given to you. It's dangerous to try and absorb more than your mind can hold."

After being in his presence, it took days to sort out my thoughts and feelings. He taught in such simple ways that I could easily understand how Jesus taught through parables. Although my teacher's lessons were brief, I felt their effect for months afterwards. However, like a fool, I continued to weigh his power and abilities with my mind. Only when I was older, could I see the futility of the mind's workings and comprehend the true depth of his teachings. Now, I too am an old man and understand that this wisdom is within us all. However, it needs silent nurturing. And we seldom spend the necessary time in the silence within to access this wisdom in its fullness.

One afternoon, I told the Old Man that I thought his life and his powers of healing were quite wonderful. He stopped smoking his pipe, leaned forward in his chair and looked into my heart with his penetrating eyes. Jack lifted his head from his pillow and added his look to his master's so I knew I had better listen up.

The Old Man shook his head and said, "You are mistaken, my boy. Healing is hard work." That said, he leaned back in his chair and began puffing thoughtfully on his pipe once more. I nodded to show that my teacher's words had hit home. Sensing that things were now back to normal, Jack put his head back down on his pillow to continue his nap. At that time, I didn't have a clue as to what was required of a healer-to-be. Today, I know that many healers with a few years of experience behind them ponder whether they would ever have taken the healer's path had they known what it encompassed.

A few weeks passed and I thought it would be safe to bring up the subject of healing again. Cleverly—or so I thought—I worked the conversation around until I was ready and then posed my question, "How can I become a great healer?" Jack rolled on his side and growled in my direction. He seemed to sense that I was treading on thin ice again.

Without hesitating, the Old Man said, "The ego is so strongly in charge of most people that their desire for fame and fortune stands in their way. Although all my power came to me in one night, let me remind you that my gift was the culmination of countless lives spent in pursuit of healing and wisdom. You too have been climbing the mountain in past lives. Understand that your body is your spiritual essence in physical form. Stop trying so hard and let your soul-mind direct your life moment by moment. You will find it is an effortless process."

With his guidance, I recognized that I had been a healer in many previous lives. I came to understand that healing is an apprenticeship, and like many other life patterns, it takes lifetimes of dedication to shift into higher levels. While the desire to help others has always been my driving force, I had to flex and bend to adapt to a healer's life, not at all what I had in mind when I began my career in healing.

———•◆•———

Alone in the Old Man's presence, I soaked up his wisdom as best I could. However, each time we met, my mental patterns were put to the test. Being a primary energy person himself, he saw how attached I was to the mind and its workings. He explained, "Your heart's inner wisdom will guide and direct your life perfectly, but your mind is a troublemaker. Your mind is so proud of its great knowledge, but your soul, certain of its destiny, waits patiently for you to discover the true knowing that abides within your own heart as wisdom. The heart leads, you must follow."

Through his knowing, my teacher saw that I too would have the capacity to "know" if I would give up the mind and seek the source of all wisdom within myself. "The reason you can appreciate the reflected truth in books is that it matches perfectly the primary truth already residing in your heart," he said. "Books are like the moon reflecting the light of the sun; they are only a reflection of the primary wisdom in your heart. The Creator placed the answer to life itself into each person's heart, long ago, before the beginning of time. Never allow reading to block the portal leading to the primary source of inspiration within your heart."

However, I found it difficult to accept that the mind had to be a servant of the heart. Countless times, the Old Man admonished me, "Stop the search. Otherwise, you will spend lifetime after lifetime in distraction following other people's thoughts and findings. That is all secondhand information. Don't be tempted to follow others. Listen to your heart. Run your *own* popcorn stand. The Creator made you an original. Be one!"

Unfortunately, reading was my cherished addiction. Having indulged in books as companions for years, I saw no reason to stop. Book after book beckoned with promises of life's elusive secrets. One more book and I knew all would be made clear to me. I was determined to think my way into fame, fortune, happiness . . . and my teacher's wisdom. Yet, the answers to life and healing continued to elude me.

Healing was what I was born to do, but I thought my mind was my ally. I leaned on it to give me comfort and security on my journey through life. In a fever of activity, I read authorities in every field in an attempt to satisfy my thirst for knowledge. Willing to embrace the author's viewpoint—particularly when it agreed with my own—I filled my mind with endless bits of information. Soon my mental library was so full of facts, there was little room for the higher wisdom of the heart my teacher spoke of. I prided myself on knowledge, forgetting that the inner wisdom that brings spiritual awakening is the ultimate goal of our lives.

Looking back, I wonder why I couldn't accept his infallible perception that I needed to surrender my mental hold on life and open to the heart's wisdom. To wake up at *any* time before death is desirable, but to wake up *early* in life would simplify our journey. Why couldn't I have taken that great leap, dumped my mental library, and emptied myself so that the Old Man's wisdom could fill my heart? But I was proud of my photographic memory and quick mind. I couldn't see that my mind clouded the path to the wisdom I sought. The mind, like a life preserver, serves as a safety net when you are swimming in the vast sea of knowledge. But when you enter the domain of the soul in search of deeper wisdom and eternal truth, it is useless . . . so many intellectuals . . . so little wisdom.

However, my teacher wisely used my intellect as a gateway into my heart by providing teachings that my mind could appreciate, which also penetrated my heart. Each time we met, he placed me on top of the mountain of wisdom where I could see forever. However, soon after leaving his home, I would slide down into the familiar world of my thoughts, filing his wisdom away in my mental vault, instead of living it from my heart.

After the Old Man saw me return over and over again to the mental plane, he said, "One day you will find your true being within your own heart. Why? Because you will wear down using your mind to climb straight up the mountain. You will seek and find a gentler path, which also takes you to the top and has the same magnificent view. This path will be an effortless ascent through your heart. But don't worry. Until that time comes, your humor will keep you afloat."

And my humor had to work overtime when I first met my teacher. I was establishing my practice, had a family to support, and my adopted mother needed more care every day. Finding balance amidst these stresses was never easy. Helping people was the center of my life, but I thought I had to be the Ultimate Healer 24 hours a day. I bled for my patients even though the Old Man told me this was a disservice to the patient and to me. He was right, of course, which I learned the hard way after I burned out.

My patients always came first. In retrospect, I see that it was foolish and unfair to my children, who grew up with me being absent most of the time. Like many, I would like the chance to live my life over again. I would spend those precious years with my children and allow patients the freedom to do what they wanted instead of me cajoling and pleading with them to eat right and follow the rules of health.

The Old Man advised me, "Give each patient a *little* help and a *little* advice to see if you are planting seeds of health in a garden of fertile soil, or if your seeds are falling on rock. I know this is not an easy task for one of your nature who wants to share the wisdom of health with everyone. Like watering a garden, wait and see if your wisdom takes root. If so, give your patients a little more information to gradually teach them a new way of life and health. Then step back and observe the results before further planting."

———— •◆• ————

Often I arrived at the Old Man's house seeking help in resolving some current problem. One morning I arrived all worked up over some new crisis, a crisis I can no longer remember, which suggests its great importance in the scheme of things. But I'll always remember his sage advice. Lighting his pipe, he said, "Give everything its due consideration, but refuse to worry. Worry agitates the body terribly and stops the flow of divine healing energy that revitalizes the body's energy fields. You are never down until you lay down and stay down. Ask for help and be prepared to follow the guidance you receive." I knew he was right, and I laid my emotions to rest, at least for that day.

Curious, I asked my teacher if *he* had ever been discouraged. "Only when I see man's inhumanity to man. You know as well as I that we are here to love and help each other. There is a time ahead when there is the possibility of abundance for all, a time when humankind can flow together in love and harmony. When this time comes, the consciousness of all beings will have the opportunity to lift and merge with the soul-mind in love, truth and wisdom."

At other times, I would arrive bursting with excitement about some new success in my healing practice. Before I could even speak, he would say, "Don't let anything get you up and don't let anything get you down. Both states are equally dangerous. We are on the earth plane to flow into neutral, to bring positive and negative together as one. Thus, the swinging pendulum of the emotions comes to rest."

My mentor told me that most people did too much, ate too much, drank too much of what they shouldn't, thought too much, and stayed up too late. In this regard, his instructions were simple: "Enough, but not too much." In his view, most people choose too much or too little, with too much usually being the winner. Like Goldilocks, we would do better following the "just right" rule. The middle of the road gets us where we're going without the difficulties we encounter on the road of extremes. His favorite word on this subject was "surfeit." He suggested we make this word our middle name as a reminder not to drift into excess in any area of life.

In the game of *enough* but not *too much*, surfeit was a difficult lesson for me to learn. I could never eat just *one* orange and be satisfied. This was especially true during the summer that I spent working in one of the orange packing houses when I was a teenager. Surrounded by fifty thousand acres of luscious oranges, my fellow workers and I ate so many oranges that some of us broke out in rashes. We quickly cured ourselves by abstaining from citrus, but as soon as our skin cleared, we were back into those delectable, mouth-watering fruits.

It was a company rule that the most perfect, thin-skinned oranges were to be set aside for V.I.P. specialty orders. But somehow a few of those enormous, golden beauties found their way into our private stashes, which were hidden in the exposed basement rafters of the packing house. Like a treasure hunt, the challenge was to ferret out your friends' stashes to eat while keeping your own safely hidden. Recalling those delectable oranges, I realize it was a long time before I learned the lesson of surfeit.

One afternoon I asked my teacher why he thought so little of formal education. He said, "Education is the greatest block to wisdom on the planet because clinging to other people's ideas blocks your own innate wisdom. If you honor your primary energy pattern, your heart will present you with primary wisdom. Be still and listen. Go within and unite with the eternal truths in your heart." Wonderful advice for an older gent, but I was young, eager and ready to heal the world.

On this same afternoon—like many that had gone before—I was secretly hoping my mentor would pull out a wand, tap me on the head, and presto I would be the greatest healer in the world. Why not? It sounded good to me. I had little idea of the responsibility that goes along with being a healer and the dangers of the ego. (All that, I would learn in the years ahead.)

As I was getting ready to leave, he began speaking of the 14 angelic beings that surround each one of us. I breathed an inner sigh of relief. For the first time, I knew that I was not crazy. I told him that I had felt these beings around me and had seen them around others. He nodded and the dam broke. I found myself telling him about the angelic beings who are my wise and dear soul companions this lifetime.

Remembering the Old Man lived close to Bixby Park, where my death by lightning might have occurred, I told him how the Power had saved my life that summer when I was eight years old. Nothing I revealed surprised him. He informed me that my life had been spared many times from death in the past and would be again in the future since I still had work to do in this life.

Never wanting to pass up any chance to advance in the healing field, I nerved myself to make another approach. I glanced down at old

Jack, napping peacefully at his master's feet. While Jack snored loudly, unaware that I was about to introduce the subject of the Old Man's healing once more, I ventured, "I would give anything to heal hundreds a day as you have." The Old Man shook his head and sighed, "You foolish young man, one day you will find out how demanding a life of healing really is." And, in time, I did.

———•◆•———

The next year, I began taking a list of my most difficult patients when I went to see the Old Man. Next to each name I wrote questions about the condition. I found that his sage advice always relieved their pain and returned them to health. As I described their problems, I could sense his impatience. Finally, he said, "I can't waste time listening to their problems. Just *think* of each person and I will give you the remedy for each condition." After that, I thought of each patient and he answered by telling me what caused the problem and the remedy, simple solutions that brought incredible healing. By the end of each visit, I had written a list of what to do for each patient.

With his advice and the healing energy from the Power, even difficult patients were getting well. It was heady stuff when I was able to advise patients how to heal their conditions. I never saw him wrong. My ego soared, but my teacher also warned me about this aspect of healing, "Remember, my boy, the ego is a troublemaker, a wily adversary, and seldom tamed."

I vividly remember the day I presented Mrs. A.'s case to him. The lady had first come to see me before I knew the Old Man. At that time, she was carried into my office on a stretcher. She told me she had been bedridden for seven years. Although she had been to all the professionals in town and undergone many tests, nothing revealed the cause of her condition. Her abdomen was swollen with 60 pounds of excess fluid and she was in terrible pain. As my first genuine unsolved mystery, all I could do was run energy and pray for her healing. Even though she was carried out, she walked into my office the next week. Within a few weeks, she was fine and thrilled to get her driver's license again. She was a sweet, lovely, and very grateful lady.

However, three years later the 60 pounds of fluid returned overnight, along with intense pain. I decided to present her difficult case to the Old Man to see what simple remedy he would recommend. Once in his presence, I thought of Mrs. A. and her problem as he had instructed. My teacher closed his eyes for a moment. When he opened them, he pronounced, "No more little green apples." I knew better than to question him. When he gave a remedy, it worked without fail.

The next day I saw Mrs. A. and announced, "You must not eat any more little green apples."

Her eyes opened wide, "Oh, but I *love* them. I've been eating them all summer."

"I know, but you're going to have to give them up."

"Well, if that's what it takes . . ."

"It is," I assured her.

In the morning, she called, excited to tell me that her abdomen was completely normal and all her pain was gone. However, a few years later, I received another call from Mrs. A. The swelling and pain were back. Summoning my most professional voice, I declared, "No more little green apples for you." She admitted having eaten some at a church social. Her condition was back the very next morning. She stopped the apples, but this time there was no improvement. I drove down to see the Old Man, sure that he could help. Just when I was about to explain what had happened and ask his advice, he said emphatically, *"No!"*

"No what?" I asked.

With grim finality, he declared, "No, I will *not* help this woman. I only speak *once*. Her current condition is her own fault for going against my original advice. If I keep rescuing her, she will simply continue her bad habits. If she forgot once, she will forget again, and in the end, since she cannot control her appetite for what is destructive to her body, she will find a way to blame *you* for her problem."

"But . . ."

"Focus on patients who are willing to follow directions."

"But we all make mistakes." My statement brought only silence and a severe look that cut off further discussion. And that was that. I couldn't budge him. In his strict code, if his instructions weren't followed to the letter, he moved on to people who would follow orders as given.

Although Mrs. A. had gone against the Old Man's instructions, I couldn't stand by and watch her suffer. When he declined to offer further assistance, I worked with the energy flow to help her. I carefully explained to Mrs. A.—as the Power had explained to me—how the healing flow of energy worked. "At the time of treatment, a contract is made with the body. When we ask the body to shift into patterns of health, the patient makes an inner promise to follow a new regime of better foods, more water, happy thoughts, and exercise that will support the new health blueprint," I said.

Mrs. A. nodded and I continued, "But if the patient returns to the old bad habits, which originally created the condition, the contract is broken and the symptoms are usually quick to return. In my experience, the body—having been betrayed once—is then far more reluctant to accept healing energy. In such cases, it often takes the body much longer to heal again. Sometimes the only way to persuade the body to accept the healing energy is for me to contact the body's inner intelligence and plead for a renewal of the contract. It's also very important for you to apologize to your body. So, do you understand why it's going to take you longer to heal this time?"

Taking my hand, Mrs. A. said, "I'm sorry I didn't stick to the plan. It won't happen again. I promise you and I promise my body too." And so we began to recreate the health she had cast aside by going back to her old habits. In Mrs. A.'s case, it took three months of weekly energy treatments to renew her health.

Through the years, I have watched the Power take people to the top of the mountain of health where they are shown what it is like to be perfectly well and filled with the joy of living. However, if the patient deals with the body incorrectly, then it's a swift slide back down the mountain. Most patients get into trouble by returning to what is familiar in their lives. Unfortunately, people crave their comfort foods even when the result of eating those foods is pain and sickness.

Usually, it's a rush to consume those tantalizing, ooey, gooey baked goods, or the stimulation of that first cup of coffee in the morning. Maybe some ice cream and candy are added to the pile, or perhaps it's off to chips and sodas. Hungry yet?

What follows is the wake-up call of pain. And so, we must begin again. I say "we" because I was there myself many times when I was young and foolish. Perhaps that's why I could never keep to the Old Man's rules. Over and over he told me to treat only those who would listen and follow instructions exactly. He insisted that I should speak only once and move on if the patient didn't follow the program 100 percent.

However, like most of us, I know what it is to pick myself up—pledging better habits as my life's companions—and start walking the road of health once again. If we make mistakes, we know it. Others are not to blame for our choices. We alone are at fault. If we remember how good it was to feel healthy and how painful it is when we ignore the rules of health, we can start over again. It's best to pick yourself up, dust yourself off, and begin the climb once again.

——— ·◆· ———

My first direct experience with the Old Man's healing work came when he first treated me. The familiar pain in my low back had returned with a vengeance, brought on by stress and overwork. With his unique treatment, he relieved my pain in minutes. I was so impressed that I dedicated myself to studying his method of healing, which he called Creative Healing.

I learned that he had been taken one night by angelic guides to another dimension. There he was shown precise contact points on the human body, and taught a specific way to treat them. Over the years, I have often used the Creative Healing approach and found that it brought wonderful healing and relief from pain for my patients. This technique takes time and effort, but it's worth it to see people come out of pain. I have often had patients start crying because they are so happy to be pain-free for the first time in years.

Yet, as much as I valued the Old Man's work and admired his incredible control and focus, our two methods were different. I knew that my destiny was to surrender to the healing energy flow as it had been given to me long ago. Recognizing the healing power I had been born with, the Old Man never intruded on my chosen path. I believe that you are born to heal, learn to heal, or healing is thrust upon you. I was born with the healing energy, but I believe healing on higher levels was thrust upon me when I met the Old Man.

Surprisingly, after learning the Old Man's healing method, one of my first patients was my mother who was sick much of the time. I gave her one treatment with Creative Healing and she was restored to wonderful health. Her mood swings and painful indigestion were gone. Mightily impressed, I was eager to try my new skills in my practice.

My opportunity came the very next day. I was surprised when a woman came in carrying her husband in her arms. This lady was solid, muscular, and looked like she weighed 150 pounds, but her husband was a small man with a slight build and probably weighed 100 pounds all wet. When he told me he was a truck driver, I found it hard to imagine him ever being able to see over the dashboard. From years of driving nonstop for long hours, he suffered terrible low back pain and was now facing surgery as a last resort. His wife placed him gently on my treating table.

The poor man was in such excruciating pain that I couldn't even touch him at first. I began to flow energy into his low back, but after a few minutes, I decided to use Creative Healing. His wife said she needed to run some errands and would be back in a few minutes. When I completed the treatment a half hour later, the trucker stood up and gasped, "My God, my pain is *gone*. I feel terrific." I wanted to get down on my knees and thank God because his low back was the worst I had ever seen, and I thought I had seen the very worst at the clinic in Los Angeles.

The fellow said he felt so good he wanted to stand outside and wait for his wife. A short time later, he came back into the office to tell me that he had walked around the block, felt wonderful, and was now determined to walk into town since he felt so good. He asked me to tell his wife to drive east on our street and look for him resting on a bench or curb if he tired of walking.

Two hours later, his wife finally returned from her errands to pick up her husband. I explained that he was walking east on our street and told her to drive until she saw him. When she couldn't find him, back she came. She called the police from my office and soon everyone in town was on the lookout for the missing trucker. His wife was afraid he might have collapsed and been taken to the hospital.

The police finally spotted the trucker striding along like a young boy several miles east of town. He asked if they would give him a lift to my office where his wife was waiting. Back in my office, he realized he had left without paying because he was feeling so good. After paying, he gave me a grateful hug, and I was filled with the joy of helping others. Such was my sendoff in the Old Man's wonderful healing method.

The Old Man taught me that God's healing is infinite and we should not limit God by our thoughts. In his eyes, for a doctor to tell a patient there was no hope was a crime. "Divinity is humankind's birthright," he declared. "Never let our fellow man—professional or otherwise—tarnish our crown of gold. If we limit healing to what our minds conceive, we restrict the Creator's power to lift us into life's higher patterns of health and happiness. In our choosing the path of light and love, we agree to be of service to our fellow man. Thus, we fulfill our contract with the Creator and allow his infinite blessings to flow through us to all mankind."

One day, my teacher told me that when I was silent during treatments, I would be astonished by the miracles. "Silence allows your power to build up, like a steam engine," he explained. "Once you have built up a mighty force of steam energy, then you can let the energy out in tiny spurts exactly where needed. Don't ever reveal your plans until they are made manifest. You leak energy when you tell other people your plans. The way to keep a secret is to *keep* it."

To date, I'm still looking for a way to treat in silence since I enjoy talking with my patients. However, I have tried the silent mode a few times. In fact, the morning after I had received his sage advice, silence was forced upon me. I was on my way to the office and saw a violet banner, lying tangled on the sidewalk. It was six feet long with bold capital letters in gold that declared: *"SILENCE."*

Amused by the Power's not so subtle humor, I couldn't resist putting the banner on the wall of my waiting room. I meant it as a joke, but every patient assumed the banner was not only a message, but a requirement. After reading the banner, none of my patients spoke during the treatment so I couldn't very well say anything either. I have to admit it was an incredible day, but I took the sign down at the end of the week and have been chatting along with patients ever since.

———•◆•———

During the final years of his life, the Old Man had to stay in bed much of the time. After his death, I recalled that he hardly ever drank anything except dark ale or the blackest tea. I never once saw him drink water, and, in his later years, he suffered terribly from kidney problems. Through his suffering, I saw that all the wisdom in the world cannot spare you from poor health if you don't take care of your body and drink lots of good, clean water.

A month after the Old Man's death, two close friends of mine saw an elderly fellow working two stories up on a ladder. While he shingled the building, he cried and sobbed as though his heart was breaking. Moved by the man's obvious distress, my friends stopped and asked if they could help. He replied, "Nothing can help *any* of us now. The greatest healer in the world died a month ago. Before I saw him a year ago, I was frozen with arthritis and confined to a wheelchair. I couldn't feed myself, open a door, or walk. Look at me now. I'm like a teenager, flexible and able to work again."

One of my friends asked if the healer was the Old Man. When she named him, the old gent was astonished and climbed down to talk with my friends. He said no one knew this great healer's name because he had asked to remain anonymous in his old age.

When my friends reported this meeting, I marveled at God's wonders in arranging for my dear friends to be walking by just at that time so they could share stories about my old teacher. While they had given me *some* credit for truth in the stories I had told them about the Old Man, after meeting the shingler, I was given full recognition as a teller of true tales. Like Edgar Cayce, they broke the mold after the Old Man. That his work lives on is his blessing to humanity.

A year after his death, the Old Man appeared to me. Even from the other side, his penetrating look carried authority. He asked, "Are you still searching for wisdom outside of your own heart?" Knowing he would see the truth of the matter anyway, I replied, "Just a little." He shook his head and walked away.

Another year went by and he reappeared. As if no time had passed since asking his question the year before, he demanded, "And *now?*" Squirming under his gaze, I answered, "Just a *very* little." He turned his back, walked away, and never approached me on this subject again, no doubt seeing that I would have to wake up on my own.

Many more years passed before I finally accepted his judgement that the path to soul growth was an inner journey through the heart. On my soul journey, I came to realize that all mental patterns, while appearing to be absolutely essential, once digested, were as insubstantial as cotton candy, and never satisfied me. Like all of life's illusions, the mind feeds a part of our life, but the heart is the center of the universe. In time, I had to dump most of my hard-won learning and allow the heart energies to take their rightful place at the head of the parade. For it is only in our hearts that we are one with the Creator, and, thus, experience divine oneness in all its magnificence.

10

MOVING ON

———— ◆ ·· ◆ · ————

The years rolled on and I had been ten years in practice when I was given my marching orders. It was Sunday morning at 1:00 A.M. when a powerful hand from another dimension grabbed the front of my pajama top and pulled me straight up in bed. From the darkness of the bedroom, an authoritative voice commanded, *"Move to the San Francisco Bay area as soon as possible."* Then the unseen hand dropped me like a limp rag back on the bed. When I asked the Power about this order, they said, *"Do whatever it takes to move to northern California as The Voice has instructed you."*

In the morning, I described this strange turn of events to my wife. Born and raised in Redlands, she didn't want to leave her family and friends. I could understand her feelings, but I knew I had to follow this guidance. When I explained my dilemma, she said, "Go if you need to, but I'm not leaving." Over the next few months, I tried to fight the order to leave, but I felt like a puppet on a string, pulled by forces beyond my control. A divorce followed, and I moved to northern California.

Once again I began my healing practice without any patients. The "booming" practice I had purchased in San Carlos to get my start had exactly one patient even though the seller had given me a list of hundreds. As soon as I announced my arrival, I discovered that these patients had either moved, or were already working with other practitioners. With four children in Redlands to support, I ate rolled oats three times a day, which I cooked on a hot plate in my tiny apartment above my office.

Living by myself, I hadn't made any friends as yet so when the holiday season approached, I was feeling mighty sorry for myself.

By the time Christmas Eve arrived, I was as far down in the dumps as I could go. Tired of sitting alone in my apartment, I went downstairs to my office and started sorting through the office cabinets. To my surprise, I found a bottle of whiskey left by the former practitioner. I poured myself a shot and drank it down. I hadn't had any alcohol for years so the whiskey went straight to my head. In a few minutes, I was no longer adrift and feeling sorry for myself. My lonely world retreated. Another shot, and I was feeling no pain; life was good.

Suddenly, I was startled by someone pounding on the front door. Looking up at the clock, I saw that it was after 7:00 P.M. I couldn't imagine who would be at the door so late on Christmas Eve. Using my chair for balance, I struggled to my feet and managed to get vertical. I wove through the office to the door and opened it. Even through a whiskey haze, I could see the gentleman at my door was bent over in a grotesque posture. "Something I can do for you?" I risked asking, wondering if I *could* do anything besides answer the door.

He moaned and said, "Yes. In all the Christmas excitement at home, I picked up a heavy package and threw my back out. My regular chiropractor is out of town so I've been driving all over trying to find someone to help me. I was just about to give up and head for home when I saw that your light was on. I'm in so much pain that I thought I'd stop to see if you could help me."

From my perspective, I could have used a little help myself since the room was spinning. However, I led the way to my treating room, occasionally touching the walls for balance. If my unexpected patient noticed anything amiss, he said nothing. From the moment we entered my treatment room, I don't remember anything, not even treating my patient.

On Christmas morning, I woke up in bed with a splitting headache. Slowly, vague memories of the previous evening arose from the murky depths of my recovering brain. I sat up with a start, suddenly recalling the man knocking at my door last night. Had I treated him? Did I help him? Was he still downstairs in my office? Questions flooded my mind, but I had no answers. I went downstairs where all I found was silence. Entering my treatment room, I was relieved to find myself alone.

As I started to leave the office, I noticed a note on my desk: "Thank you so much for taking me in and helping me. Now that I'm out of pain, I'm going home to enjoy Christmas Eve with my family." Under the note was payment in full. I thanked God for His help and decided that abstinence would be the path for me. However, before I die, I intend to find this man during my panoramic life review (which we all have before we leave this life) so that I can see exactly what went on that yuletide night.

———•◆•———

With the new year, the energy shifted for me. Patients began to seek me out as the healing revealed itself to be ever stronger. My practice began to build, and life was once more worth living. I relaxed and started to enjoy the beauty of the San Francisco Bay area.

A few months later, I was blessed again when I hired Mabel, who was then in her 50s, as my first secretary. She was petite with beautiful white hair and a sweet, motherly face. However, despite her kindly appearance, she ruled the outer office with an iron hand and never put up with any nonsense. Working together in the office, it was easy to see that her faith in the Creator's plan was the center of her life.

Whenever I became too concerned about any problem, Mabel would pat my arm and say, "Turn it over to God. We're not equipped to handle anything without His Help." She was very intuitive and we shared a wonderful time in the office during the years that she worked for me. Even when she approached the century mark, she was sixteen in her heart, an inspiration to all who knew her.

One morning after treating 30 patients, I caught sight of myself in a mirror as I passed. It was clearly time to either get a haircut or have someone round up some dog tags for me. After eating a hasty lunch, I told Mabel I'd be back soon and ran down the street to the nearest barbershop. I'd never been to this barber before, but I figured I could get a quick haircut and be back to my office before the afternoon patients started arriving.

Entering the shop, I noticed a number of old men sitting in the chairs against the wall. As soon as I learned that these retirees were regulars who occupied these chairs every day to observe the barber at work and discuss world events, I jumped into the waiting barber chair and asked for a haircut. As the barber began his formidable task, I explained that I was on a very tight schedule and in a hurry. The old men settled back to watch the barber snip away while they continued discussing how to solve the world's problems.

After clipping away for five seconds, the barber held the clippers above my head and asked the standard first haircut question, "So, what do you do for a living?" All eyes from the audience turned toward me. Being new in town, I knew I was in dangerous waters. From past encounters, I knew that if I said I was a chiropractor, half the gallery would hate me and the other half would want to ply me with their symptoms. Like being a Democrat or a Republican, either answer would find me in hot water. I took a deep breath and said, "Actually, I'm a typewriter repairman."

As the barber resumed his task, he clipped more slowly. I tentatively reminded him that I would be late getting back to work. Suddenly the barber stopped cutting altogether and asked if I could look at an old typewriter he had in the back room. Stunned by his request, I tried to think of a way out of my predicament. My brain raced while the clock ticked away and the observers began muttering that I should take the time to check out the typewriter.

"Is the typewriter electric?" I asked, feeling trapped in my web of deceit.

The barber shook his head and said, "No. It's not."

Breathing an inner sigh of relief, I responded in what I thought was a friendly manner, "Too bad. I'm an expert with electrics, but I don't know a thing about manuals."

Bad move. The old men of the wall gallery muttered hostilely under their breath. The barber returned to cutting my hair. But he began jerking it this way and that as if to express his annoyance with my unsatisfactory answer. Meanwhile, the wall contingent berated me loudly for not helping out. Seeking another escape route, I apologized, "I'm sorry that I'm in such a hurry today. I'll have to come back another day when I have more time and take a look at it." The natives were still restless, but the promise of "another day" seemed to settle them and I was able to depart without being unmasked.

Back at the office, I looked nervously at my reflection in the mirror.

Gazing back at me was someone with the worst haircut that I had ever seen. It was me! Mabel restrained herself from asking what in the world had happened to me on my lunch hour, but her eyes said it all.

When the next day dawned, I was up early and set out bravely—without benefit of a hat—to find another barber to repair the unforeseen consequences of my recent subterfuge. Once my new barber finished laughing at my wild-looking topside, he smoothed it out and became my trusted barber for many years. From then on, I took my chances and revealed my true profession when asked. Sir Walter Scott summed it up: "Oh, what a tangled web we weave, When first we practice to deceive!"

———•◆•———

A year had passed since I had moved to the Bay area, but I was still feeling the pain of my divorce. I tried to focus on my practice and appreciate the wonderful new patients I was meeting. One day a charming Russian lady came in. Like thousands of others, Veronica had walked across China to leave Russia during the revolution. From China, she journeyed to California, eventually settling in Monterey where she became a language professor. Because she had suffered nerve damage as a result of her trek across China, she came to see me every two weeks for several months to get relief from her physical pain. During that time, we became good friends.

Veronica, having suffered great emotional pain herself, saw that I was having a difficult time in my personal life. She told me she had been forced to leave her children in Russia when she fled. For years, she had tried to get them to America, but it was impossible. I told her about my divorce and how much I missed my four children. "Don't worry," she counseled. "Dr. Pain and Dr. Time will heal you."

Every two weeks when she came for her appointment, she would ask me how I was feeling. One day she asked, "Have you laughed since your divorce?" I answered, "No." She patted me on the arm and said, "You will . . . you will. One day you'll hear something funny, laugh out loud, and feel guilty about enjoying yourself. But don't feel guilty. This is the beginning of living a normal life again and freeing yourself from the pain of your divorce."

Sure enough, one day I heard a very funny joke and laughed out loud. Instantly I remembered what Veronica had told me. Suddenly I did feel better, in fact, I felt happier than I had in months. Looking up at the perfectly blue sky decorated with feathery white clouds, I felt joyful and thanked God for returning me to a life worth living. When Veronica came in, I told her what had happened. She smiled, "You see, I told you Dr. Pain and Dr. Time would cure you. I thought I'd never get over the loss of my children, but even that was possible. No matter how painful the emotional crisis is, time heals all sorrows."

"Thank you for helping me," I said and gave her a hug.

As Veronica was leaving my office, she stopped and turned back. She smiled and asked, "Would you be popular?"

Taken aback, I answered, "Of course."

Veronica arched one eyebrow and shared an old Russian saying, "Arrive a little later, leave a little sooner, stay away a little longer." Great words of wisdom from a very wise lady.

———•◆•———

When I was first in practice, I was upset when my patients didn't listen to me and became sick again. I quickly learned that it wasn't any fun to burn out helping people who were determined to return to their old bad habits. They headed back into their illness with the bit clamped firmly between their teeth. However, in time, I found a more neutral place where I could accept their sometimes odd decisions (at least odd to me) and bless them on in their choices. I came to understand that some people feel they have no other choice but to slide back into illness because it is so familiar to them.

At times, I watched healing be given to a person who wasn't ready to accept the gift. Jane was one of these patients. Dragging her right leg and holding her right arm tightly curled to her chest, Jane hobbled in using a cane with her good left hand. Her face sagged on the right and her mouth drooped so that it was difficult to understand her when she spoke. The stroke had happened years before, but someone sent her to see me now. She drove an hour to get to my office in the country.

Within minutes after I began the healing work, Jane's tightly curled right arm straightened for the first time in years. She cried out in amazement. I stepped around to her feet to continue running energy. Suddenly her right arm began to whirl around and around in a huge circle like a giant windmill. I'd never seen anything like it before. By the time her arm stopped whirling a few minutes later, my patient's eyes were bulging with surprise. Jane asked, "What's going on?" Actually, I was wondering the same thing myself.

Acting as if such events were commonplace, I was trying to come up with some reasonable explanation for Jane when the windmilling action of her right arm started again. This time it appeared as though someone was trying to pull her off the treatment table by her whirling arm. She shouted, "If this keeps up, I'm going to end up on the *floor!*" At that very instant the whirling slowed and then stopped. She cautiously edged her way back to the center of the table.

For once in my professional life I was at a loss for words. I was trying to think of some wise words to say when Jane exclaimed, "My God, it's going to do it again!" This was the third and last time, and the most spectacular. The movement was vigorous, powerful and much faster. We both started laughing over this unexpected happening. We were just starting to get used to this unusual phenomenon when the human windmill stopped. As instructed by the angels, I told her she needed two more treatments to complete the healing work. She agreed that she would come back in a week.

When she breezed in the next week, her walk was perfect, her arm totally functional and her speech was clear. She happily declared that she was totally healed. While I ran energy, my angelic companions told me that the third treatment was still needed to lock the balanced energies in place. This would ensure that there would be no recurrence of her condition. I told her that without one more treatment to seal the energies in place, she would have a recurrence of her condition later on.

Jane grimaced and complained, "You know, doctor, it takes me an hour to get to your office and another hour to get home. Why don't you move your office to a more central location? (No doubt she meant more central to her.) Besides, it's *obvious* that I'm healed."

The angels spoke again and I passed on the message, "Jane, if you don't make the effort to take the third treatment, I'm told that your condition *will* return in two years. When that happens, you would need weekly treatments for a *year* to return you to the health you're feeling right now. I have to suggest that you come back one more time for your last treatment."

But Jane knew better. She was riding high and laughed at my concern. Before she left, she had to show the patients in the waiting room her wonderful newfound health. She showed them how she had been before the treatments and then marched around the waiting room to show how easily she could move now.

Two years later Jane came in dragging her right leg. Her right arm was once again useless and curled to her chest. Leaning heavily on a single crutch, she could barely walk. Her speech was so slurred that I had a difficult time understanding her.

While I ran energy, Jane told me that she had been perfect for two years, but now she agreed that she was much worse than when she first came to see me. She thought I would be impressed because she had moved further away and had driven five long hours to see me. Holding her head high, she proudly informed me that she was now willing to make the sacrifice and drive this much longer distance to see me three times and be restored to perfect health.

Reminding her of her last visit, I said, "Jane, if you'll recall, I told you that if you didn't come back for the third treatment, you would need weekly treatments for a *year* to be completely healed. And that's how long it will take to return you to the health that you experienced two years ago."

She pursed her lips together tightly, "Hmm. You're right. I do remember you telling me that . . . *Say!* . . . I can't drive 10 hours round trip every week for a *year!* If three treatments don't do it, then I'll go with a wheelchair. That's where my doctor says I should be anyway." In Jane's case, the Power stood firm. Three treatments did not return Jane to the miracle of health she had thrown away. I pondered, if not karma, then what?

When observed from a higher perspective, both the path of healing and the path of self-destruction are entered through a state of grace unknown, except to the soul itself. We on the earth plane are attending a school where all lessons learned are of equal importance to the soul. Patients who can't follow instructions are not only my biggest frustration, but also one of the reasons I believe so strongly in karma. What else explains why people turn away from what might be their one chance for healing, unless there were more important lessons to learn from their illness.

———.◆.———

There's no way around it, we are creatures who follow our whims. Sometimes there's nothing sensible about what we do. Taming the mind is like trying to break a wild stallion, and it's a great step forward when we call a halt to the mind's wild plunges. During our lifetime, our choices contribute either to health or disease. When disease takes precedence in our lives, changes are vital. If you can control your diet—rather than letting your diet control *you*—wonderful things can happen.

When I ask patients to give up their favorite foods, which are usually the source of their illness, I suggest that they pray and ask for help in giving up these foods. At the same time, I stay on the alert, knowing that wily patients, given half a chance, will fudge on their diet program if they can get away with it. I ask patients to imagine their favorite foods on one end of a scale, their health on the other, and make a decision as to which one is more important . . .

Henry, a man of 34, came in wheezing terribly from emphysema. He told me the condition had made his life miserable for seven long years. I lectured him on the importance of drinking lots of water, which seems to be a lost art in America. Then I insisted he stop all milk products and recommended that he read the book, *Milk: The Deadly Poison*, an excellent, well-researched book by Robert Cohen.

As I watched Henry's energy field, I was happy to see the warning about milk products take hold in his mind. I saw him every week for four weeks. However, each time he came in, coughing and gasping for air, milk remained stubbornly fixed in his energy patterns. But when I questioned him, both he and his wife swore he hadn't had a drop of milk since he first became a patient.

When Henry came in for his fifth energy treatment, he was very discouraged, and so was I. His breathing was just as labored as ever. He wheezed and coughed while he lay on my treating table. I touched him and again felt milk in his body's biofield. Quizzing him produced the same results. He and his wife swore that no milk products had touched his lips since my first warning.

Then in a flash the angels showed me the problem and I smiled. "So, Henry, what did you have for breakfast this morning?" I asked, knowing full well what his answer would be.

"Cereal," he wheezed.

"And what did you put on your cereal?"

"Cereal milk," he managed before coughing painfully from somewhere deep inside his chest.

Seeing that Henry was ready for my final blast, I said, "And where does *cereal milk* come from Henry? . . . Does it come from *Mars?* . . . Or does it come from a *cow?*"

Henry hung his head, "A cow."

By this time Henry's breathing was ragged from the effort of answering my questions. "Doc, you don't mean I have to stop my *cereal milk?*" he panted.

"Yes, Henry. I do mean it. If it comes from a cow, it's causing your breathing problems," I said and rested my case.

"Doc, I never would have come to you if I thought I'd have to give up my cereal milk. I love it," he wheezed.

"Henry, all too often we love the very foods that are slowly killing us. Advertising has brainwashed us into believing that all true Americans must eat cereal with milk on it for breakfast. You can still have your cereal, just put water or diluted apple juice on it instead of milk."

After thinking it over Henry got angry at the thought that this small amount of milk might be his only problem, "Doc, I'll stop it right now."

A few weeks later, Henry's emphysema was a thing of the past. He could breathe perfectly under all conditions. I asked the angels why they hadn't shown me the cereal milk vision during the first treatment. The Power said, *"Henry was not ready to give up his cereal milk when he first came to you."*

Timing is everything, even in healing. I smiled and decided that Sherlock Holmes had nothing on Detective MacKimmie's heavenly band of investigators.

————— •◆• —————

Every cell in the body is highly intelligent and in communication with every other cell. Unfortunately, the cells have no control over what the owner eats. Anything and everything are fed to the body simply because they taste good, but try pouring a can of soda pop into a car's gas tank and see how well it runs. . . .

Danny was 18, an incredible athlete and long distance runner. He had just started college when his dad called. The father asked if I could see his son at their home since his boy suffered from colitis and had gut pain all the time. When I talked with Danny at his house, I asked what he liked to eat. Smiling, he led me back to his room where he showed me an impressive storehouse of chocolate bars and soft drinks stashed under his bed. I was stunned. He grinned happily and said, "This way, whenever I get hungry during the night, I don't even have to get up. I've got all my favorite foods right here to snack on."

After viewing Danny's hoard of goodies, I was ready to hear anything when I asked what *else* he ate. He told me that he preferred hot dogs washed down with coffee for his "regular" meals. Somehow I was not surprised by this revelation. I advised him in the strongest possible terms to start eating *real* foods and drinking *water*. And he replied in the strongest possible terms: he flat out refused.

Weeks later, Danny's dad called again. Danny was in the hospital and scheduled for a colostomy the next day. (His bowel hadn't moved in nearly a month.) Danny's father asked me to visit Danny in the hospital. After checking in with the healing angels for their instructions, I went to the hospital armed with organic bread, honey, meat and some spring water. I ran energy and fed him as much as he could get down of those foods followed by as much spring water as he could drink in order to get the bowel in motion again. Within hours, the bowel moved properly and he was sent home.

A few days later, Danny called to tell me that he had been visited at home by members of the local colostomy society after he didn't have the surgery. Assuring him that—with all the new skin tapes and bags—his life would be completely normal after the surgery, they encouraged him to go ahead with the operation. They explained the surgery was no big deal and described the glories of belonging to the colostomy society. The most important factor being that he could eat whatever he wanted from then on without gut pain.

After he shared this with me, I said, "Danny, you'd be crazy to have unnecessary surgery. You're one of those fortunate people who can avoid this operation by simply changing your diet. You don't cut off the front of the car if a tire is flat. Just fix the tire." When I finally convinced him to eat correctly, his colon symptoms disappeared in one month.

Being a bright young man, Danny managed to stay on the diet for many years. However, eventually he "forgot" how sick he had been, a story I've heard frequently in my practice. He returned to eating only hot dogs and raced headlong down the sugar trail with chocolate and soft drinks to round out his diet of choice.

When Danny hit the top of his pain threshold, he called me. Expecting a plea for help, I was startled when he said he had investigated colostomy surgery again. The society painted a rosy picture of his future after surgery. Danny said, "I'd like to give the surgery a whirl. Everyone's told me that sugar has absolutely no effect on the body and has nothing to do with my condition. Besides, I *hate* trying to watch what I eat all the time, and I won't *have* to after the surgery." Hearing the words of a true sugar hound, I didn't argue this time as he continued extolling the virtues of the operation.

I moved out of the area before Danny had his surgery so I don't know how he enjoyed the outcome. As far as I'm concerned, it takes a person with great fortitude to face a lifetime with the bowel hanging outside the body. I had one patient who always referred to his colostomy as his "baggy bowel." If a person is lucky enough to be among those who can control the problem with proper nutrition, I don't understand choosing surgery, but to each his own. Some people are hellbent in one direction. Like alcoholics, they have to crash before they wake up and walk the road of health. I often wonder what happened to this young athlete, now a middle-aged man. Wherever you are, Danny, I hope that you're happy.

———•◆•———

While everyone wants better health, not everyone is willing to make the changes that bring the change to health. Fortunately, the Creator takes over the reins as soon as the prayer asking for help is offered by the healer. I've had my share of dying people who were lifted from the grave by God's healing, but who dragged their feet all the way; somehow they felt compelled to sabotage the healing flow by continuing their old bad habits.

Usually when the healing doesn't impact the patient in a positive way, I find that the patient has not been following instructions. It's disturbing to watch patients use their freewill choice to go against advice that will help them in their healing process. These same patients freely admit later that the recommendations—if they had been followed—would have allowed their bodies to heal. Some people follow the guidelines beautifully, others follow when they think of it, and a few, unwilling to change, will fight the program all the way. My greatest frustration comes when people don't follow instructions as given by the angelic ones . . .

Rob, an ex-Marine, had terrible knee problems when he first came to see me. He had been a runner but now he couldn't enjoy running or hiking anymore. In fact, he couldn't even go up stairs without hanging onto the handrail. After a few energy treatments and replacing the disc patterns into proper alignment, his knees returned to wonderful working order. During his last treatment, the healing angels said emphatically, *"He must never run again!"*

"Simple advice to follow," I thought. At the end of the treatment, I explained, "Rob, you're going to have to give up any thought of jogging or running in the future. It would be too hard on your knees. It's time for you to enjoy life by walking. Anything else will cause serious problems for you." Delighted to be active and free from pain, Rob managed to follow this advice and didn't have the slightest twinge of pain in his knees.

Several years later, Rob phoned me from a U.S. Marine Corps base in southern California. He had retired at 40, but was at the base visiting friends when he learned there was going to be a marathon. Two hundred young Marine recruits were going to be running in this race. I was dumbfounded when he asked if he could run against these new recruits. I could hear the excitement in his voice.

"Are you *crazy?*" I shouted. "Think, Rob, *think!* Those boys are in their *teens* or early twenties. Your knees will *never* take it."

"Gee, I guess you're right. I just thought that maybe . . ."

"Rob, I'm telling you. Don't do it!"

The day of the race Rob called again. "Hi Doc, I've been thinking . . . Are you sure I couldn't run in just this *one* race?"

"Well, if you want your knees to be just like they were 10 years ago when I first treated you and you couldn't go up stairs or walk without pain, then go ahead. But let me tell you something: you *will* cripple yourself if you do."

"Oh, oh . . . ok, Doc, that's all I needed to hear."

The next day he called me. I knew before he spoke that he was lying in bed in the base hospital in terrible pain. His voice was shaky when he said, "Doc, my knees are so swollen they look like two basketballs. Can you bring them out of it again?"

I ignored his question. My frustration came pouring out, "Rob, did you win the race?"

"Yeah, I came in 50 feet ahead of the pack."

"Uh-huh. Did you get a medal?"

"No. A trophy cup."

"Wow, how big a cup?"

"I guess it's about seven inches tall."

"Isn't that amazing? Is it inscribed? To you *personally* I mean."

"No. They gave me five dollars to have it engraved."

"That's wonderful, just wonderful."

"But Doc, what about it? Can you fix my knees again?"

"Rob, your knees aren't important. You *won! That's* important. Tell me, how are the other runners doing? The recruits I mean . . . the ones who lost."

"Well . . . fine I guess. But what about my *knees?* I can't walk. I think they might be worse than when I first came to see you. Can you fix them?"

"Now Rob, pay attention. Forget about your *knees. They* aren't important. That cup you won, now *that's* important. Why I bet you couldn't buy one of those at a trophy shop for under . . . say . . . 10 dollars? Now if you come to my office, I want you to bring the cup to show me and be sure it's been engraved so I know it's the genuine cup that you won."

Finally, Rob caught on, "I'm . . . I'm sorry, Doc. I should have followed your advice. With all this pain . . . I know now . . . it was a stupid thing to do."

"Well come on in when you get home and we'll see what we can do."

Long story short, Rob did come in a week later. God was kind enough to permit healing of his knees once more. However, I told him that if I heard of him running in any more races, I didn't want him to come knocking at my door. He said, "No way, Doc. I've got it now and I've got it good."

———— · ◆ · ————

I love to treat knees and I've treated thousands. Of course, I'd rather treat knees before surgery, but I've treated many after the knife has done its work. I once overheard a young man talking with his girlfriend in a hospital corridor as I was walking past. His voice trembled with fear, "I don't think the doctor understands. To him, it's just one more knee operation, but to me, it's my *life!* What if the operation doesn't help?" I understood. Any thought of permanent disability is frightening.

Knees appear to me like huge batteries; each one has its own individual energy bubble wrapped around it. Knees are such friendly folk—so cooperative and open to help—that it's easy to talk with them. As one of God's most incredible engineering jobs, they are usually happy to return to God's perfection in short order after being treated with energy.

As soon as I learned the Old Man's treatment for knees, I discovered that my hands already knew the technique as if I'd been doing it forever. By using his technique and running energy, I was delighted to find that patients who came in with knee pain were often able to walk without any pain at all after the first treatment. I tell patients that cement floors are tough on knees. This is particularly true for women. If you have a choice in the home or workplace, a wood floor is much kinder to your knees and legs.

When the jogging craze hit, I witnessed the incredible damage to unsuspecting knees. People seemed to have an almost religious fervor to follow their newfound passion. A lively fashion parade, in which appearance meant everything, could be observed all day long as hundreds of joggers took up the torch and proudly jogged up and down El Camino Real. Car exhaust fumes swirled around them while they ran in pursuit of health. Meanwhile, on back country roads and mountain trails, deer and quail enjoyed peace and quiet, grateful these runners had found their niche elsewhere.

One day an elderly man came in for a knee treatment. As we talked, I learned that he was from Bombay, India. When he got up to leave, I asked if he was visiting friends in the Bay area. "Not at all, my boy, I came to see you for my knee. You healed my cousin's knee five years ago and he's been fine ever since. When I couldn't find help for my knee in India, I remembered my cousin's knee and made the journey to see you here in California."

Assuming the gentleman would be enjoying his stay in California, I asked how he planned to spend his time while he was in the states. "Oh, I'm not staying. I have a flight back to Bombay at noon." It was 10:00 A.M. and he was leaving my office to go straight to the airport. I smiled and wished him a safe journey. When I realized he had traveled over eight thousand miles each way to see me, I had to resist this golden opportunity for the ego to take over.

Three months later, the traveler phoned to say he was doing wonderfully well and had convinced another 1,000 people to follow my nutritional advice. He said if I would come to Bombay, he would hold a parade for me. After we hung up, I enjoyed a few moments of imagining what it would be like to have my own parade. Then I told the ego to go sit quietly in the bleachers again.

———·◆·———

Since more than 80 percent of the population suffers from low back pain to some degree, I was grateful to alleviate pain and restore normal energy flow for patients with this problem. I recall a Saturday morning when an exquisite Chinese lady came into my office. She was so graceful and charismatic that a hush fell over the waiting room. My usually talkative patients were silenced by her beauty. It seemed as though a Mandarin princess had stepped out of another century to grace the hushed room with her lovely presence.

While I examined her, she told me she had suffered from horrible low back pain for most of her 36 years. After I finished the flow of energy into her back and body, she suddenly clasped my hands in hers. Her musical voice was gentle and pleasing, "We Chinese say a person is a 'god of gardens' if that person has the gift of growing beautiful gardens. You are a 'god of low backs.' For the first time in my life I have no pain at all in my back. I know with certainty that I will never have back pain again." I hated to see her leave; her magnetism was overwhelming. I can't remember ever meeting another human being with that kind of charisma. And my patients must have thought the same since they continued to talk about her for months afterward.

At this time, I was living among the redwoods in a cabin above Palo Alto. At the end of my busy day, I would drive home on Skyline Boulevard as fast as my car would take the curves. I never noticed when I stopped admiring the beauty of the trees against the clear blue sky on my drive to and from the office. But somewhere in time, the beauty vanished. However, one day the Power's angelic voice commanded, *"Stop the car."*

"Why?" I asked as I pulled over.

"It's time to look around."

After getting out of the car and looking up and down the road, I responded, "So?"

"Do you see the beauty that you saw when you first came to north-ern California?"

"Of course," I answered, but I wondered if I really did.

"Look again. See from your heart. Appreciate what you see. One day this area will be filled with cars, people, and noise. Then it will be too late. The beauty and peace you love so much will be gone."

Heeding their advice, I looked around. The awesome beauty of the trees embraced me. I apologized to the trees and the quiet and the clear blue skies for ignoring them. After that I made a point each day to look and listen and enjoy the beauty both driving home and on my way to the office.

Once I reached the office, I never knew what the day's healing energy would bring, and not knowing was always an intriguing part of life's ongoing play . . .

When Greg came to me, he was in his 40s, but his life force was just barely enough to keep him alive. While I ran energy to him as directed by the Power, he declared that I was his last hope After this one treatment, I never heard from him and didn't see him again for a year. Then one day Greg stopped by the office unexpectedly. He looked wonderful and appeared to be in excellent health. To my surprise, he insisted on calling me "leader," and claimed that my treatment had saved his life, changing it forever.

However, when Greg told me that he now had the ability to put people to sleep by just holding their hand, I laughed. He insisted this gift was the result of my one treatment from the year before. I politely told him this was utter nonsense. Not deterred in the least, he informed me that as the "leader," I was obligated to lead others and change their lives. His part was to arrange all this and he was ready with big time plans for me and my healing practice.

Since I had three minutes before my next patient, I decided I would show Greg the absolute absurdity of his claim and asked him to prove his gift. He took my hand and told me to close my eyes. Before I knew it, I was asleep, only waking up when my secretary came in to announce the next patient. It was such a deep sleep that I had no memory of even *going* to sleep. I felt as though I had slept for 12 hours. Greg was elated and ready to take on the world, with me in tow.

My secretary stood in the doorway with her arms crossed over her chest. She skeptically took in the strange scene before her. I was yawning after my recent nap and Greg was rubbing his hands together with glee. Taking an instant dislike to Greg, she glared at him and told him he was a trouble-making jerk. When I tried to explain my experience, she insisted I was crazy too. She promptly sat in a chair and dared Greg to put her to sleep. She was one powerful lady, a woman who was always in control and never allowed anyone to move her around.

Greg took my secretary's hand. Within a minute, she was snoring comfortably in the chair with her head down. I knew this was the last thing she would have done if she had been in control of the situation. When I woke her up a few minutes later to bring in the next patient, she too awoke as if after a full night's sleep. Stunned that she had no memory of going to sleep, she said she felt as if she had been sleeping for hours. Greg said he hadn't found anyone he couldn't put to sleep since I had first treated him a year ago.

A few days later, Greg came back and asked me to make him a healer, like me. I told him he was crazy since he already had a wonderful gift. I suggested that he open a sleep clinic for people who couldn't sleep without taking drugs. By letting business leaders get a drugless sleep during their lunch hour, I thought he could help any number of these chaps and would become quite famous for his work.

"Imagine," I said, "a clinic with beds in small cubicles, all filled with sleeping business tycoons. They'd have the opportunity to have their minds totally refreshed by going to your clinic. Think of the hundreds of insomniacs you could help." But Greg wanted to heal just like me. Trying to explain that I could never do what he was doing, I said, "You're incredibly lucky to have your own special gift." But I never could convince him to use his gift in this way.

11

PESCADERO, WHERE'S THAT?

—————•◆••◆•—————

Ten years after moving to the Bay area it was time to move on again. And for the second time in my life, the powerful hand grabbed the front of my pajama top at 1:00 A.M. on a Sunday morning and pulled me straight up in bed out of a sound sleep. The same powerful voice spoke in solemn tones, *"Go over to the coast and buy a home today."*

That same morning found me sitting in a real estate office in Half Moon Bay. But every property the agent showed me in the listing book made my gut tighten. She said there was one home in Pescadero, but argued that it was too far off the beaten track. She didn't want to make the long drive to show it since she was positive I wouldn't buy it. When I protested that I was interested and would like to see it, she got as angry as a wasp in an air conditioner and stomped out of the room. As soon as she left, I looked at the listing, wrote down the address, and left the office.

Once outside, I thought, "Pescadero, where's that?" After spotting it on the map further down the coast from Half Moon Bay, I got in my car and headed south to find this town with a population of 125. Several miles in from the coast, I recognized the house I had seen in the property listings and understood the realtor's words: "It's off the beaten track." However, the same powerful voice spoke loudly, *"Turn In."* I did. When the owner came out of the house with two snarling Dobermans straining on their leads, I wondered if I was about to be attacked for trespassing.

The voice commanded, *"Get out of the car!"* I worried about the wisdom of this latest piece of advice, but I did so. The owner, who seemed to be holding the dogs with all his strength, yelled, "Get the hell off my property or I'll turn the dogs loose."

The voice ordered, *"Buy it now!"*

I ventured, "I'd like to buy your house." The angry owner blinked for a moment and then snarled, "You don't even know how much it is."

"How much is it?" I asked. When he told me, I said again that I would like to buy it. I didn't see inside the house that day; the angry owner refused to show me anything. He went inside to call his next door neighbor who was in real estate. She hurried over minutes later with the necessary papers. While standing outside signing the papers, I explained that I would be selling a property to cover the down payment. Since she wanted to buy a property where mine was located, she wrote me a check for the down payment on the house. I then signed the check over to the owner. By the end of the afternoon, I owned a home on the coast as directed by the commanding voice.

Early the next morning, the real estate neighbor called, "I must have been *crazy* giving you that check. I don't know my neighbor all that well . . . and I don't know you *at all!* How do I know that you even *own* any property?" I reassured her that I did and we met that day to see my building. After she saw it, she agreed it was worth the money, and the deal was done. When she came to know me better, she told me an inner force made her write the check. Years later, after I understood how financially sensible she was, I knew it was indeed a miracle that she had ever parted from a penny to a complete stranger, let alone enough to make a down payment on a house.

———•◆•———

Many years later found me getting a divorce—an occasional happening in my life—and I was very disheartened. My ex-wife was a very fine cook and I had been spoiled. There appeared to be only two choices. Taking my meals at the local eateries was one option; however, I knew that in most restaurants food preparation "from scratch" usually meant scratching open a can. My other choice was to take myself in hand and cook three healthy meals a day.

Most men are helpless when it comes to taking care of themselves or others. Left alone, we almost starve to death, the sink piles up with dirty dishes, and dirty laundry decorates the house. Empty tins fill the trash can, and—since men rarely remember to rinse the cans out first—a feast of smells soon pervades the neighborhood. Then we wonder why dogs tip over the garbage can. I have done it all too, gentlemen. So, valuing my health, I bit the bullet. Like most of my male patients, I fell apart when I crossed the kitchen threshold. However, after a few panic-stricken days stumbling around in the unfamiliar territory of the kitchen, I learned to cook healthy meals for myself.

But my lessons in self-responsibility weren't over. A few years down the road when I thought life was going smoothly, I woke up to find a drawer of unpaid bills. I had trusted others in my employ for six months without ever checking the books. I was about to start writing checks to pay these bills when I discovered that my bank account had also been cleaned out! In a panic, I checked my wallet and discovered that I had only eight dollars in cash to my name. Said staff was gone, but the problems resulting from the unpaid bills felt insurmountable. Where to begin? I was devastated and spent most of the night with my head in my hands wondering how to get out of this mess and praying for help.

The next morning, bleary-eyed and deeply depressed, I asked God for a miracle as I walked across Pescadero Road to my mailbox. Inside the mailbox, which was usually stuffed full, I found a single, ordinary envelope. I studied the printing on the envelope; it must have been typed on the oldest typewriter on the planet. Individual letters were blurred or incomplete, but what drew my immediate attention was the startling return address, which read simply: "From the One Above."

Then I saw the address: "To the One Below, Pescadero Road." I blinked in surprise and opened the envelope. It contained a note obviously typed on the same ancient typewriter: "Never fear. You are totally loved and supported from heaven." My heart soared when I read these words. Completely mystified as to the sender, my spirits lifted and I felt the stirring of hope. Encouraged, I sold everything I could think of to raise cash and started working day and night to pay off my debts and return my business to the black side of the ledger.

Two weeks later another solitary envelope arrived in my mailbox. It was again "From the One Above." I instantly recognized the type and opened the envelope. Enclosed was another message: "You are loved beyond all knowing and will be guided, directed, and protected in all that you do." I gave thanks for this message and continued to get my financial life back on track. A life without mistakes is not possible, but a life of learning from them *is.*

Another, now familiar, envelope arrived again two weeks later, and I opened it like a starving man approaching a banquet. The note read: "Your healing work will lift you to the stars." Two weeks passed, and another envelope appeared with the following message: "You are never alone. We are always with you."

I looked forward to 14 days passing in hopes of receiving another message. Two weeks later, there it was waiting in the morning mail: "Your future is assured. Have no fear. We are with you forever." These inspirational words carried me forward until another two weeks had passed when I received the next and final message from "The One Above," which read: "Live in the moment forever embraced by our love." The envelopes stopped coming as suddenly as they had begun. Thankfully, by that time, I was out of the financial ditch and on my way to reclaiming my life, having learned to use discernment in business matters. I never found out who sent these notes but I bless this unseen angel with all my heart.

I include this story to illustrate that we all have help in all situations from unexpected and wondrous sources. The whole universe will help us in our hour of need if we just remember to ask for help. Like walking on water, once you do it, you will have great faith that you *can.* Problems are God's opportunity to come into our lives. Prayer was my mainstay during this terrible and peculiar time in my life, as it is the center of my life now. There are times when I think we shouldn't even attempt to brush our teeth without praying for divine help.

———— • ◆ • ————

A great saint once said man's destiny is not to be this thing or that thing, but just to *"Be."* Today I'm more accepting of things that would have driven me crazy when I was younger. I've seen the foolishness of trying to force life to change so that I can be more comfortable.

When I think of acceptance, I think of a lady who came from Washington state for treatment. She had been bleeding vaginally for two years when she remembered that I had helped her when she had been living in California so she drove down to see me. While I was running energy, I kept having such a strong impression of her mother that I asked, "How's your mother?"

My patient burst into tears. When she finally stopped crying, she said, "She lives just down the street from me—at least she has for the past two years—and she's driving me crazy."

The Power gently posed a question for me to ask. I put my hand on my patient's shoulder and asked, "How would you feel about her if she was someone else's mother?"

In a burst of anger, she spit out, *"I'd hate the old bitch!"*

Shocked by her own outburst, she sputtered, "Oh God, *why* did I *say* that? She's my *mother*. I *have* to love her." But her bleeding stopped for the first time in two years.

After the Power showed me a vision of her future, I counseled my patient to meditate and flow love and forgiveness to her mother. I explained that her mother would die soon and it would be best for both of them to find peace with each other before that event took place. She thanked me and drove home to Washington. As soon as she got home, she phoned to tell me what had happened on her trip back.

On the drive home, she stopped to rest in Lithia Park in Ashland, Oregon. Enjoying the quiet beauty of the park, she contemplated a small waterfall. While she pondered the meaning of life, a beautiful mallard duck came into view floating on the water just above the falls. Suddenly he was swept over the falls into the quiet pool below. Then he took flight, flew above the falls, landed on the water, and repeated the adventure of being swept helplessly over the falls. This happened over and over. It was always an effortless free fall with no attempt on the duck's part to do anything but enjoy his plunge.

As she watched this show, she thought about how relaxed the duck was and wished that she could be that relaxed amidst the chaos of life. She prayed for an answer to her daily problems. Once more she saw the duck floating down toward the falls. As he was swept over the falls, the duck looked directly at her and a voice in her head said clearly, "Just *Be.*"

Startled, she waited for the duck's next trip over the falls. Again the duck looked directly at her and again the voice spoke in her head, "Just

Be." And each time the duck was swept over the falls, the voice gave this answer to all of her problems, *"Just Be."* And so my patient found—as we all find—that to *Be* in each moment is the key to inner peace.

———— ·◆· ————

Many years ago, I thought if I could have a getaway place, it would help me sort things out and learn to "just be." I bought a tiny place at Bolinas; it was the smallest real estate property on the California coast. The entire lot was only 16 feet by 16 feet, but the cramped space of the tiny cabin was all I needed for my getaway. A friend, who had the building skills I lacked, helped me make the best of the hundred-year-old structure.

One morning at Bolinas, I entertained the thought of leaving all my troubles behind—one way or another—while I walked barefoot on the beach in the cool morning air. I realized where my thoughts were headed, and in that moment, I stopped and prayed, "Dear God, I need a miracle. I don't think I can go on without one. And I need it now!" Nothing happened. I waited patiently for an angel to appear, a sign in the sky, or a bolt of lightning to end my misery. But nothing.

Downcast, I continued my walk on the beach when an unexpected, shallow wave tossed something onto the beach; it landed right at my feet. Bending down, I picked it up. It was a four-sided piece of redwood, nine inches long. Words had been carved on all four sides. Turning the carving to read each side, I was amazed when I read the words: "Be Still"—"and Know"—"that I"—"am God." Like a fool, I had already forgotten my request for a miracle. I was sure someone must have dumped a barrel of these carvings somewhere out at sea. I ran up and down the beach, searching in vain for more carvings.

When I got back to my cabin, I prayed to solve the puzzle of receiving the carved message. The Power spoke as a dear friend would, *"Don't you remember your cries for help this morning when you said you had to have an answer in the next few minutes or else?"*

It seemed as though a lifetime had passed since my beach walk that morning, but I answered, "Yes, I do remember."

"The carving brought you the message you so desperately needed. But immediately you questioned the gift the ocean placed at your feet."

"Then all I need to do is to be still and remember God."

"Always this is the Path. Do you not see the synchronicity of this event? Do you know the trouble taken to bring this gift to you at that moment in time? Dear One, you have seen so many miracles in healing, is one more miracle in your own life so difficult to accept?"

"Sorry, I guess I'm a little slow on the uptake."

"That piece of wood was given to help you and all those who will hear your story in the future."

"Thank you. I understand."

"And see the humor in all this. We greatly enjoyed watching you scramble all over the beach looking for more carvings. You were searching for what is already in your heart. Being human, you seek confirmation from the outside, but the Great Teacher is within, as it is for everyone. Know that we will never forsake you. We are with you forever, even unto the ends of time."

A few days later, I shared this event with a dear friend and showed him the redwood carving, he smiled and reminded me of guidance that has been handed down through the ages by various teachers in many religions:

Be still and know that I am God.

Be still and know that I am.

Be still and know.

Be still.

Be.

———•◆•———

In my opinion, human beings can learn a lot about "just being" from animals. Some may disagree but I have always seen that animals have lovely souls, from elephants and whales on down to hummingbirds.

In my California practice, children often brought their pets with them for healing. I found myself running energy on dogs, cats, birds, fish and even pet snakes. And why not? We are all creatures designed by

God's love and nourished by love. To paraphrase Mark Twain, when you help an animal in distress, he won't bite you later on as a human will. Apparently Sam Clemens saw more in the loyalty of animals than in man's fickle nature.

Years ago, Andrea and I watched a documentary about the life of a quadriplegic who could only move his head. He had a small Capuchin Monkey trained to care for him. The monkey did everything, from shaving him and brushing his teeth to cooking and feeding him. It was amazing. We were impressed by the obvious devotion of this fellow's little simian companion. At day's end, the man turned on his television using a chin-button remote on his shoulder and began to watch television for the evening.

The monkey, having served all day without complaint, settled in to watch beside his master. But one day—while the television blared away—the monkey reached out his paw, turned the man's face toward his own, and looked deeply into the man's eyes. It was a soulful look that touched our hearts. Anxious to get back to watching his program, the man pulled his head away from the monkey's paw.

After a few moments, the little monkey reached out and gently turned the man's face toward him so that they were again looking into each other's eyes. The monkey touched the man ever so softly on the cheek with his other paw. But the television watcher impatiently turned back to his program. While we watched the documentary, we saw how capably the monkey served his master, but we also saw that the monkey wanted companionship. It was heart-rending to watch the monkey being ignored for the artificial companionship of television. He longed for what we all need in life—love, a kind look, and words of appreciation.

————•◆•————

However, I do recall one time when I saw man's best friend, a faithful canine companion, take off in a totally unexpected direction. It was while I was still practicing (but not as a typewriter repairman) in San Carlos. Having been there long enough to become part of a community where everyone in the neighborhood knew everyone else, one day I took a different route on my early morning walk.

As I was walking past a grassy field, I noticed a blind man standing in the middle of the lot. He was holding a long leather lead high in the air above his guide dog. While the dog prowled around the empty lot to do his business, his owner gingerly fed out the lead. However, every time the dog moved closer to his owner, the man rapidly pulled in the lead's slack as though his life depended on it. Carefully looped high overhead in his left hand, the lead resembled a cowboy's lariat and his dog was the ornery cow on the end of it. Intrigued by this strange scenario, I started using this new route every day and sure enough, the same peculiar performance took place in the empty lot every morning.

Finally, I asked a neighbor what was going on. Surprised that I didn't know the story behind this daily event, he explained, "Frank's eyesight started failing when he was 30 and now he's totally blind. He always used a cane until he decided to apply for a guide dog. But the trouble is that he and dogs don't get along. So as soon as he got his beautiful, well-trained guide dog, a war started. The question seems to be who's the 'boss' and who's the 'employee' in their relationship."

Shaking my head, I asked, "OK, but what's the story with Frank holding the lead so high up in the air?"

My neighbor continued, "Oh. That's the funny thing. Right from the start, the guide dog instinctively knew his master didn't like dogs and resented their association. It all came to a head on the day the dog seized an opportunity to make his feelings known. This was before Frank learned to hold the lead high in the air. He took the dog to that empty lot for a bathroom break. You won't believe how crafty his dog was. First, it walked to the very end of the lead. Then it quietly crept back to where the lead was laying on the ground. With a target shooter's accuracy, the dog carefully positioned himself over the lead and pooped on it."

I started to laugh and said, "You're kidding."

"Oh no, I'm not! And then the dog quietly crept back to the end of the lead. When Frank was ready to leave, he reeled in the lead only to find his hands covered in fresh, squishy, fragrant dog poop."

"I can't believe it," I remarked.

"It's the truth. Unfortunately, Frank's idea of trying to settle this dispute was to punish the dog by hitting it with the lead. I saw him repeatedly lash out at the dog, but the dog easily dodged Frank's hysterical attempts. After that, Frank kept the lead high overhead, and even so the dog sometimes beats him at this game."

Now I understood the need to keep the lariat lead far from offending doggy deposits. Over the next few months, the dog sulked more and more and became less and less cooperative until the guide dog people exchanged that dog for a new, younger dog. They hoped—as did his neighbors—that master and dog would bond from the start. But it was not to be.

In a few months, the new dog took up the habit of the previous dog, as though he had heard about it on some Doggy Hotline. This dog was younger and more agile, and Frank began losing every skirmish at the empty lot. He resorted to carrying a wet sponge and paper towels to clean his hands since he couldn't catch the dog before the canine took action.

But this wily hound added a new trick. The dog started leading his master into traffic, and jumping back at the last minute to leave his unsuspecting owner in the path of oncoming cars. We nervously organized a neighborhood dog watch. Whoever saw the dog guiding Frank into traffic would yell, *"Frank! Look out!"* There were many hair-raising escapes during this new battle of wills. It was an uneasy time in the neighborhood since we were never sure who was going to win the day. We all breathed a sigh of relief when Frank went back to his faithful cane, leaving the dog victorious.

———•◆•———

I wonder just how many animals are more clever than we might give them credit for based on their looks. Percy was certainly one. He was a docile, laid-back Basset Hound, and didn't look as though he had a clever or deceitful bone in his body. His main job seemed to be to lie around and look baleful as the faithful companion of Clarice, who had been blind for years and lived with her mother. Percy wore a bell so Clarice would know where he was in order not to trip over him. Driving in traffic with her mother behind the wheel made Clarice nervous so she asked me if I would treat her at home, instead of at my office.

I was just approaching the front door when I met Clarice coming out. She asked if I could wait a minute while she sprayed Percy for fleas.

Since Percy was scratching vigorously, I decided it might be a wise move to wait. She took Percy around to the side of the garage where she carefully positioned him against the wall. To my amazement, while she readied a huge can of flea spray she was carrying, Percy silently edged back several feet without so much as a jingle from his bell. The result was that Clarice sprayed exactly where Percy was *not*. Clarice sprayed and sprayed as though every flea in the world had targeted Percy.

By the time the fumes cleared so I could see, Percy had maneuvered himself soundlessly back to the spot where Clarice had originally placed him. And Clarice, very pleased with herself, patted him and gave him treats for being such a good dog. Meanwhile, Percy continued to scratch away at his copious fleas since not one molecule of spray ever struck him. He was already in reverse gear when Clarice raised the can, and safely out of range while she soaked the side of the garage until it dripped with aerosol spray.

When I returned a month later, Clarice was standing outside on the front steps, giving the house painter hell. New paint on the side of the garage was peeling off in great long strips. Clarice made it clear she wasn't going to pay him until the area was repainted. I knew that generous applications of flea spray on that side of the garage were causing the problem, but Percy looked up at me with mournful eyes as if to ask me not to say a word. And I didn't. Eventually the painter brought an industrial strength paint so tough that not even flea spray could dissolve it. Other than not wanting to be sprayed into the ground—and who could blame him—Percy was a wonderful and loving companion.

And if it's always best to have the goodwill of a dog then I'm in good shape. The dog in question was as small as her breed comes. Trixie was a four-year-old Chihuahua whose hind legs had been paralyzed since birth. Her owners had taken her everywhere but had never found any help for her condition. Every day they carefully padded her back feet with cotton batting and taped them so she could drag her legs behind her without scraping her feet on the ground.

Trixie's loving owners brought her to me as a last try before they faced the awful decision to put her to sleep. As soon as I met her, I knew why they had not been able to make this decision. She was as much love as God could have squeezed into so small a package, and happily gave me a vigorous tongue-licking when I reached down to pet her.

Once a week for the five weeks before Christmas, I ran energy on Trixie. Then one day, I received a Christmas card with her paw print and words of thanks from her owners. They reported that Trixie was now running around normally, happy and free. In their words, it was the very best Christmas present they could have received and I received a paw-printed Christmas card every year from Trixie from then on.

———•◆•———

Not to leave out our feline friends—our cats would never forgive me—I was treating a foreign consulate family in San Francisco who had a magnificent cat named Blackie. A beloved member of the family, he was the center of attention at all times, admired by all who knew him. Regal and handsome, I always saw his black, shiny, contented self purring happily in the arms of one of the two daughters, who were seven and nine.

The day before the family was to leave for reassignment in Los Angeles, the girls called. They were both crying and asked if I could save Blackie. When I got to their home, Blackie was lying on a pillow in the front room looking very sick indeed. The sheen of his beautiful black coat was gone, his eyes were closed, and his breathing was slow and ragged. Blackie didn't move when I touched him. I lifted the skin on the back of his neck. It had no tone at all and felt like rubber. When I let go, a patch of his hair remained in my hand, but he never moved or made a sound.

The girls looked at me with anxious eyes while I ran energy through Blackie's motionless body. After five minutes, he raised his head and looked around as though he wondered why he had been napping. I was still running energy when suddenly Blackie looked up at my hands. His eyes opened wide and the pupils dilated until his huge yellow eyes became as black as his coat. He exploded out of the house at high speed right *through* the screen door. What could I say? The girls were heartbroken, and the family had to leave the next morning for the long drive to Los Angeles. I knew it was little comfort for them to know that Blackie had revived. The family called before they left to say that they had looked everywhere for Blackie, but he was nowhere to be found.

Three years later, I was doing a research project in Los Angeles, and decided to look up the consulate family. When I called, the mother asked if I had time to stop by so we could catch up on all that had happened since their move to L.A. When I entered the front room, the first thing I saw was a magnificent black cat lying on a thick Persian rug.

Thrilled to see the family had found a gorgeous replacement for their lost companion, I asked the new cat's name. The girls were overjoyed to tell me it was their beloved Blackie. Neighbors had found him hiding under their deck a few days after the family had left and recognized him immediately. The excited family didn't hesitate a minute when they got the call. They drove all the way back to San Francisco to get their beloved friend. It was heartwarming to see him in flesh and fur. As sleek, beautiful and adored as ever, he stretched out and purred for his admiring audience.

Thinking of cats, I remember neighbor Joe's hay barn in Redlands was a haven for every stray cat in southern California. But Joe never argued with their homesteading as they kept the mouse population down. One day I stopped by to pay Joe a visit. The newest batch of kittens—a continuous byproduct of the feline population—took off running as if their lives depended on it, except for one calico kitten. It hopped around like a rabbit, its back legs frozen together. The poor thing could hardly move around. After Joe asked if I treated cats, I was glad to run energy on the crippled kitten. Suddenly the kitten looked at me as if I'd pulled its tail. With its back legs working normally for the first time, it dashed wildly away. Joe and I laughed while we waited for the farmyard dust to settle.

When I visited Joe the next week, I had on dark glasses. While we stood outside the barn talking, Joe's extended family of cats and their kittens basked luxuriously all around us, soaking up the warmth of the July sun. It was a scene of perfect tranquility . . . until I took off my sunglasses. My calico patient's eyes looked directly into mine and grew round as saucers. Then she tore off in high gear, sending hay and dirt flying in all directions, which resulted in a great scattering of the cat community.

As kittens became cats, the story was always the same. I could walk around the farm all day long if I wore my dark glasses. But the instant I took them off, one calico would explode into action and disappear hellbent for leather, causing a frantic exodus of felines in every direction. This performance was so astonishing that Joe would ask me to stop by if he had visitors so that I could demonstrate the calico's explosive exit from the farmyard as soon as I removed my dark glasses. It never failed to amaze the onlookers. Joe and I both laughed and wondered what she saw in my eyes that stirred the memories of her first run in life after the energy healed her.

—————•◆•—————

Cats and dogs were the usual, but I did have one experience with a horse that brought to mind Edgar Cayce's view that all health problems could be healed, without exception. A neighbor in California owned a two-year-old Arabian colt named Ramar. The owner was heartsick because the horse had recently broken his femur and would have to be put down. However, the veterinary college said they were extremely busy and couldn't get there for some time. At that point the owner decided to ask me for help.

Ramar was the most beautiful Arabian horse I had ever seen. The owner showed me the x-ray and told me that Ramar represented an unbroken bloodline of thousands of years, which would end if he didn't sire any offspring. I shook my head when I saw that the femur was broken through completely. Hobbling toward us on three legs, the colt's back leg clunked and clacked as he moved along. The owner held Ramar's head while I ran energy using a light contact on his broken leg.

The next day when I was driving by the ranch, I saw Ramar standing out in the front pasture. He looked so peaceful and regal, like a statue of equine perfection. I stopped and ran energy from across the field. On the following morning, I was driving past the ranch and saw Ramar again, standing motionless in the same pasture. Stopping to run energy for a third time, I thought what a shame that such beauty would soon be no more. After that I didn't see Ramar out in the pasture. Since I didn't hear anything further from the owner, I presumed he had been put down.

A year later, I happened to stop by the ranch. Galloping easily around in a nearby pasture was an incredible stallion. He was magnificent and looked as though he was performing for movie cameras, running just for the sheer joy of running. As I watched, mesmerized by the grace of this horse, the ranch owner strolled over to where I was leaning against the fence watching.

I asked where he had purchased such an exceptional stallion. He answered, "Why, that's your patient. That's Ramar!" I gasped at this wonderful surprise. "Yes," the owner continued. "By the time the vet arrived to put him down, he was doing fine. When we took another x-ray, it showed only a fine line where the break had been. He'll never race but he'll continue the bloodline." I was thrilled for the owner and his beautiful stallion.

Later that summer, I had the opportunity to help one of God's smallest creatures when I was attending a wedding in Saratoga, California on a Saturday afternoon. I'd been so busy at the office that I hadn't had a chance to eat all day. I surveyed the scene at the reception with the eyes of a starving man. Not seeing any food, I took a glass of wine, which went straight to my head. In short order, I was feeling no pain.

Following the large crowd further into the beautiful home, I saw a hummingbird frantically flapping and beating its wings against the high vaulted ceiling. Trapped, the tiny bird was near exhaustion. It looked as if it was going to end its life fighting against the unforgiving ceiling. In my wine fog, I boldly swept a woman's stole off her shoulders, gathered it up, and shot it heavenward in the direction of the hummingbird.

Unbelievably, the stole neatly captured the little bird. Catching the stole easily as it came down, I extracted the bird and returned the stole to its astonished owner. I held the diminutive flyer delicately as I ran energy to revive it. Soon its tiny eyes opened. It looked around curiously at all the guests, who had gathered around to see this wee adventurer. I carried the bird to a large, open window and tossed it lightly toward the heavens. It flew away to the sound of the crowd cheering. For that moment, I was the hero of hummingbirds.

———•◆•———

While living in the quiet mountains above Palo Alto, I enjoyed the peace and quiet of the beautiful redwood forest surrounding our house. Our dogs and cats may have had close encounters with wild things that roamed the woods at night, but indoors we slept peacefully, unaware of such nocturnal events. However, one night my wife shook me awake to listen to strange shuffling sounds near the front of the house. We thought it might be a burglar at work—maybe more than one. I crept quietly to the front double Dutch doors, opened the top half, and snapped on the outside light. I immediately ran back to the bedroom, and got my wife to show her our intruders.

The burglars were wearing masks all right, but they were also wearing fur coats. A family of raccoons had found our dog and cat food bowls. We laughed in surprise at our uninvited dinner guests. That first night we thought it was absolutely charming to watch these wild critters so close at hand. Anyone who's seen *The Great Outdoors* with John Candy and Dan Aykroyd can guess how long we were charmed.

Once the raccoon tribe had found free food, word passed quickly through their world. We had been discovered and the invasion was on. We couldn't take in the dog and cat food bowls or our own animals would have to go without. Night after raucous night, we put up with our invaders. They always arrived at the same late hour on some predetermined schedule. If there wasn't enough food in the bowls to go around, they used their visit to tear up our yard.

Finally, I decided it was time to call a halt to these nightly foraging expeditions. I just didn't know how. Then I remembered my trusty sling shot gathering dust in a closet. It was one of those things I could never quite persuade myself to throw away. I decided to give one of the little devils a sharp rap with a well-aimed marble. This would hopefully send them all running never to return. At least, that was my master plan.

The next night, I was in place at the appointed hour, waiting behind our double Dutch doors. I silently opened the top half, ready to shoot my marble into the crowd as soon as they appeared. Just as I was wondering if this would be the one night they wouldn't show, I heard shuffling noises headed straight for our front door. I snapped on the outside light, pulled back on my slingshot and waited.

The tiniest raccoon I had ever seen appeared in the light. He was only the size of my fist. Approaching the food bowls very slowly, he held one end of a two-foot long stick, the other end was hidden in the darkness of the night. All this time I was poised with the slingshot, but I couldn't shoot such a tiny critter. I held back, frozen in position, waiting to see what would happen next.

The little one checked both bowls. Apparently, he decided the dog food was more to his dining preference. He looked back into the darkness beyond the pool of light and jiggled the stick he was holding. At this signal, an ancient raccoon entered the circle of light, holding the stick tightly with one "hand," and cautiously feeling his way along. His muzzle was white with age and he shuffled along like an old man. When he raised his head so our outside light reflected in his eyes, I saw that he was blind.

My mouth gaped open and I lowered my slingshot while the youngster led this old grandfather to the dog's bowl. The blind one groped his way along the stick until his hands touched the bowl. He felt with his hands until he found the food and slowly ate his fill. Then the little one ate while the old chap waited patiently. They followed the same routine at the water bowl.

After they had finished, the tiny raccoon again took up the stick and started to leave, dragging the stick behind him. When he was two feet away from the old man, he gave him a gentle poke in the side with the end of the stick. Grandfather raccoon grabbed it. Together—the little one leading, matching his pace to the old man's shuffle—they made their way very slowly into the night.

I turned off the outside light and put my slingshot back in the closet. I don't know what happened to their raucous relatives—perhaps they chanced upon a tastier brand of pet food than was offered at the MacKimmie home—but I'll never forget our visitors that night. After that, I put out extra food at night for the little trooper who continued to lead his old blind friend to the food. To me it was a miracle to see such compassion. I thought humankind, in their dealings with one another, could use more of the kindness shown by this little fellow.

———·◆·———

As for my own animal companions, I've had many dogs of all types during my life: big ones, small ones, long-haired, short-haired, purebreds, and charming question marks. But two stand out in my memory because they both taught me important lessons. One was Cleo, a huge German Shepherd given to me by friends after they moved to a smaller house without a backyard. Before they owned her, Cleo had been mistreated as a puppy. They told me that poor Cleo was very skittish and terribly frightened of men.

Indeed, Cleo was scared to death of me at first. However, with constant loving words and soothing tones, she became all love and friendship to me. But if I stamped my feet to get mud from the garden off my shoes, she ran away and hid. Her eyesight was poor so she greeted cars that turned into our driveway by barking ferociously as she held her ground in the center of the parking lot. Her performance drove away strangers but friends just called out, "Hi Cleo." Once she heard these words, much tail wagging followed. Friends and patients were then graciously escorted to the house.

When she first came to me, she was five years old and looked like a huge, walking fur mattress. Her former owners had fed her nonstop ever since they got her as a puppy, perhaps hoping to make up for her unfortunate beginnings. She was so overweight that she panted when I took her for her first short walk. However, in time, we walked for miles on the beach. It did us both a world of good.

At first I had to lift her up into my VW bus to take her to the beach, but soon she was jumping in by herself. She loved our beach walks and lost fifty pounds over the next six months. When her former owners came to pay her a visit, they swore I had gotten another dog, which proved to me again what diet, exercise, and love can do for all of God's creatures. For all the years she was with me, she was all affection, a loving soul who just happened to be wearing fur.

Toby, however, was another matter. He remains in my memory as the most selfish Doberman that ever walked, and I had four of these fine dogs. Completely devoted—to himself—Toby always sought the perfect temperature, whether it was lounging in the shade, or sneaking in front of the fireplace to block the heat from reaching anyone else.

An amazing specimen of his breed, Toby looked like the fiercest guardian of hearth and home that ever walked. If I went out the front door to see what unexpected callers wanted, Toby would stand nobly at my side. He was all savage barking and snapping teeth until I called his bluff by taking a few steps back so that he was facing the strangers alone. Suddenly he realized he was solo on the battlefield and every trace of his bravado disappeared. When he looked around and saw me behind him, he quickly moved back to take his place at my side again. Once he had his reinforcements—me—the show began again.

Luckily God provides humor in our lives, and animals sometimes give us our best laughs. One Sunday I was walking on the beach with Toby when we both spotted a burnt log at the same time. It was near the water and looked remarkably like a huge dog from our vantage point a hundred feet away. I quickly saw the log was not a dog, but Toby was still under the impression that a canine adversary lay ahead.

Toby—normally as cowardly as the day is long—decided to show the "log dog" who owned that section of beach. He started to stalk the log, growling with a low rumbling deep in his chest. Emboldened by the silence of his foe, he snarled and bared his teeth. As he warmed to his mission, his hair bristled. The closer he got to the log dog, the more his hair stood up on his back. Just as his growling approached attack mode, he got close enough to see that his rival for the beach was just a burnt log, and not another dog. He came to an abrupt halt, a look of total disbelief and embarrassment on his face.

Not wanting to embarrass Toby further by letting him know that I had seen his foolish attack and humiliation, I turned away. Toby turned swiftly to look back at me, clearly wondering if I had seen his fierce battle plan fall apart. Luckily, by the time he was looking directly at me, I was wisely looking out to sea so that he could safely assume I hadn't seen his blunder. Once he was sure that his cover hadn't been blown, we were free to enjoy the rest of our walk. Afterward I realized how silly we all are, forever hoping not to appear foolish in the eyes of others.

———•◆•———

Now two wonderful cats own us, marvelously independent creatures. Whisper is the lady of the manor who knows that all life revolves around her comfort as arranged by her faithful servants (us). She spends her elder years in her soft, cozy bed with an occasional trip into the fields for a good gopher hunt. Knowing how to sit perfectly still, she waits for gophers to make any telltale sounds, which result in a swift pounce. Then she brings her trophy to the back door and notifies us of her triumph by yowling loudly before partaking of her hearty meal. So notified, we run quickly to attend her, giving her the praise and petting befitting a great huntress.

We rescued Buddy, our other cat, from the animal shelter. We gained a cherished companion although Whisper was not pleased to share her domain. Being owned by Buddy is a different experience. He is more aloof and may or may not come when called, depending on whims to which we are not privy. A nonstop silver shadow of activity, he's the longest cat I've ever seen. It's like having a living accordion around the house when he stretches out in a lion-like pose to relax. When he investigates anything, he raises his head high on his long neck like a periscope to look around. Although he has claws like sabers, he always withdraws them in a gentlemanly fashion when we play. He roams so swiftly over our property that we think more gophers have fallen due to pure luck than to his hunting skills.

We know our cats are at risk each night in coyote and bear country. However, we don't want to hamper their natural nocturnal habits so they are free to be in the great outdoors via their private in/out access door. One night we heard coyotes calling; they sounded as though they were in our front yard. We only had Whisper then. We rushed out on the front deck and called for hours until we tearfully gave up hope. About that time, Whisper came sleepily out of a box that was under the deck. She stretched, yawned and looked bored as we petted her and gave her treats. No doubt she thought she had already reached her idea of heaven since her minions were fawning over her in the middle of the night.

—— •◆• ——

As we go through life, our pets have a way of leaving their stamp upon our hearts. I was surprised when my first father-in-law, who was a no-nonsense person, shared an experience he had after being in a terrible automobile accident in the '30s. He told me that he lay in a coma for weeks until he "woke up" on the other side, back on his family's farm in Imperial Valley, California where he had grown up. He was standing on one side of a stream. Ahead of him across the water, all the colors were bright and beautiful, but when he looked behind him, everything was like an old black and white photograph.

On the other side of the stream, Dale saw not only his family and school chums who had passed on, but all 40 of the wonderful farm dogs he had loved over the years. The dogs were all jumping with excitement, and calling out to him, "Come on, Dale, come on over."

Dale was amazed that he remembered all their names, but said he never gave it a thought to question that his dogs were talking to him. Just then his father stepped forward and said, "Come on over, Son."

"I can't . . . I'll get my shoes wet," he answered.

"Take them off," his father encouraged.

After taking off his shoes, Dale put one foot in the water, but quickly pulled it out when he felt the ice-cold water. His father smiled and said, "Just grab my hand, Son. I'll help you come over."

Dale tried again, but the bone-chilling water stopped him once more, "I can't."

His father said, "Well, Son, evidently it's not your time yet. But when you wake up, you just make sure to get Dr. Smith to operate on you. He just moved into town, but he'll fix you right up. Now don't you let anyone else operate on you. It's important. Don't forget."

Dale came out of his coma minutes before the surgery, which had been scheduled to amputate his arm. He grabbed the anesthesiologist's arm, and, remembering his father's words, quickly demanded that the doctors call in Dr. Smith to perform the surgery. Once the operating room staff recovered from the shock of Dale's awakening, they argued that they had never heard of a Dr. Smith, but Dale insisted. Sure enough, Dr. Smith, who had just moved into town the day before, was found and he saved Dale's arm from amputation. I found this story all the more remarkable because Dale never believed in anything he couldn't see or touch.

One thing I know for sure is that all our cherished animal companions will be waiting for us on the other side when our time comes to cross over. I have seen it. No one ever really dies, even our beloved pets. They just go on to another plane where they—like us—are once again young and vital. There they happily dash about having a great time playing with all the other animals that have been in our lives while they wait for us to join them.

How very blessed we are to share our planet with these loving beings. They are perfect examples of unconditional love, living in the moment, and finding joy in life's simplest pleasures. We would find the world to be sorely lacking without them. Our pets, whatever species, open our hearts to a closer connection with the Creator's love for all His creatures, great and small. If love is the frosting on the cake of life, our dear animal companions give us some of the sweetest frosting we could ever hope for.

Bob and Winnie MacKimmie

Winnie, already in charge at 13

My first official MacKimmie portrait
(at least it's not on a bearskin rug)

Age 4, visiting friends with Reddie in Canada

Age 54, kayaking and fishing off the California coast

Arriving in Redlands, California

In the orange groves of southern California

Dressed for my leading role in a school play

A California landlady and her trusted assistant

Time marches on . . . and yes, that *is* a genuine Buck Rogers ray gun

J. C. Hugh MacKimmie

At home in Pescadero

Home on the range in Montana

Andrea and Jim

PART III

MY CALLING

12

OVER THE YEARS

⎯⎯⎯⎯◆˙˙◆⎯⎯⎯⎯

While it is one thing to read about healers, it's quite another to be one. Being different from the rest, healing is as natural to me as breathing, and I do a lot of that too. I have always listened to a different drummer, one distant and far away, whose rhythm and power awakened within me hidden memories of past lives.

As the angelic beings of the Power revealed other levels of existence and consciousness to me, I had no choice but to follow their guidance as given. My ordinary life ceased to be. Other realms—as real to me as this dimension—became a major part of my daily life. I wish you could do what I do for a few days, just to know what it feels like when I'm hearing and seeing the angelic beings as they heal and teach.

Although I didn't know what to call it when it began, the Spirit that moves within all things made its presence known to me when I was a child. Everything around me was strongly influenced whenever this energy flowed through me; however, I had no control over when it would flow, where it would go, or what it would do. As a child, I didn't understand what it was or how it was to be used until the angels of light awakened within me the power that inspired me in this lifetime of healing and teaching. Then it moved me into a world of healing that few others would understand.

People are born with all kinds of talents, mine being as an energy runner, an energy that heals, transforms, and awakens soul patterns within others. Once born, there are a million distractions on the path we choose in life. I could name them, but so can you. However, the Power has never let anything stand in the way of my healing gift. A sometimes baffling way to make a living, but for me there is no other choice.

In following my heart's song, I welcomed the loving guidance of my heavenly companions. These angels shared with me the peace that passes all understanding, and explained that every experience in my life was essential for my awakening. This inner knowing is what I offer to all those who come to me for healing. And my senior partners in this mission are the healing angels of the Power itself.

As Ben Franklin wisely said, "God heals, the doctor takes the fee." Mighty fine words for keeping the ego at bay, and for many years I had a sign on my wall with Ben's quotation to remind the ego that it does not lead the parade. While the ego longs to be recognized as the star player, the heart waits patiently to be of service, its resources remaining, for the most part, untapped.

My goals in healing have always been the same: to relieve pain, to encourage people to adopt life-changing health practices, and to help people awaken to their unique spiritual path. I want to empower patients who are willing to change and take responsibility for their health. To this end, I seek natural approaches in healing and teach my patients how they can give the body every possible chance to heal itself. Of course there are times in life when broken bones or accidents call for medical intervention. However, in everyday living, I find such help is usually not required if we take our health back into our own hands—where it belongs—and follow Mother Nature's guidance.

Over the years I have seen that happy people are usually healthy people. Patients can eat, drink and be merry as long as they have mastery over *what* they eat and drink. Our bodies serve faithfully and remain wonderfully balanced if their owners learn to treat them with loving, conscious care. Therefore, I campaign for organic foods, plenty of clean air and water, moderate exercise, early hours of sleep, and prayer. Prayer is the most powerful force in our lives. Through prayer we can bring about magnificent changes for the betterment of ourselves and human-kind. By praying for what is best for *everyone* concerned in any situation, we allow the Creator's grace to flow healing at whatever level each person is ready to accept and receive this heavenly gift.

——— ·◆· ———

From the beginning of my practice, I have enjoyed talking to patients about the Creator and His perfect design of a body that has the awesome ability to heal anything. It has been God's great gift for me to treat patients' children, who grew up, married and later brought in children of their own to see me for healing and guidance.

In California, my patients came early for their appointments in order to meet other patients who were also seeking better health. My waiting room was a place of joy where patients could share their healing experiences with each other. I welcomed as cosmic family all who found the Power's healing energy to be exactly what they had been searching for. Patients were always friendly and helpful to each other. As soon as patients realized that a change in diet and habits could improve their health and transform their lives, they got behind our program 100 percent, and made wonderful progress. Before long, they were enthusiastically encouraging other new patients to follow the health guidelines.

As one big family, my patients often behaved like one. I recall one afternoon when an obnoxious teenager was brought in by his mother. He held forth in a voice that penetrated the walls of my treating room with language that would make the proverbial sailor blush. I didn't want my other patients to be offended, but I couldn't leave the patient I was with at that moment. Then I heard the voice of one of my favorite elderly patients. She asked the boy sweetly—but loud enough to stop the teenager in his tracks—if he would help her outside for a breath of air. His reply was "Sure, lady." I heard no more until there was a loud bang on the outside door.

Five minutes later, when it was his turn, the young fellow walked silently into my treating room holding his stomach with both hands. He looked at me quizzically and asked, "You know that little old lady out there?"

Smiling as I thought of Jan, I answered, "Yes."

He went on "She's not a little old lady at all!"

Intrigued, I asked, "What do you mean?"

"I thought she was just a little old lady when she asked me to help her go outside. She even leaned on me like she couldn't get around too good. But as soon as we got outside, she jabbed me hard in the stomach with her elbow. And when I was doubled over, she banged my head against the door and said, 'No more of that filthy language. Those are nice people in there. Now you go back in and act like a gentleman.' Cripes! What's her problem?"

Laughing inwardly, I said, "I don't know, but it's probably a good thing that you followed her advice before she really did some damage."

When Jan came in, I heard the same story from her. Still incensed by the boy's language, she said, "Well, if his mother can't take him in hand, I *will*. *We're* not going to put up with *that* kind of nonsense around here, *are we?*" I agreed.

———•◆•———

Over the years, my healing gift plus the Old Man's work formed a foundation for the multidimensional healing work I love. Many patients ask what I feel during a session, what state of mind I must maintain, and how the healing works. Throughout the healing process, I ask the Power what I can do to help and what energies are involved to restore the patient to health. While praying for divine healing to take place, I am taken to heavenly realms where I know that Heaven is our only recourse. Serving as a conduit, I release the patient to the Creator, for God is the Ultimate Healer and the key to all healing.

Before I ever touch the body or talk with the patient, I first release any preconceived notions as to the patient's condition. Then I open my own energy field in order to feel the impact of the patient's condition and the overlay of the patient's ego/personality as it contributes to the illness. After this, I feel the effect of any drugs being taken by the patient (currently or in the past) and the results of any x-rays and surgeries. Thus, by the time I touch the body and begin to talk with the patient, I have already sensed the problem areas.

Next, I weave my way into the biofield energy of the patient. At this point, I move into the hidden recesses of the problem. As the energy increases, deeper layers of the condition are revealed. Frequently, I find the original problem has been obscured by medications, x-rays, stresses, a traumatic childhood, or simply the confusion of living on the earth plane.

Eventually, I reach the deepest layers where karmic patterns are found. I never ignore the fact that illness has important lessons to teach. To simply heal the condition—without addressing these lessons—leaves energies at play that can create further illness. Unless we learn the important lessons behind our illnesses, we must face these lessons over and over again until they *are* learned, and the scales balanced.

Healing energy flows like sonar into the body. As it returns to my hands, I can sense those organs that, like drained batteries, are lacking in essential life force. While communicating with the body's cells and organs, I can feel the healing flow as it ripples back to me. This flow sings a precise song of energy, which the cells hear and follow. This energy song—totally different for each person—reflects the soul's covenant with the Creator.

During the first treatment, the angels show me two roads of life ahead for the patient. On one road, I am shown a future with the person healed and in splendid health. On the other road, I am shown what happens if the person lives their life without making any changes. My charge is to encourage each patient to take the higher road of health where the angels gather to offer healing. I've always thought it would be wonderful to treat every person in the world one time. Then I would have the opportunity to present the two roads and pray that the road of health is chosen.

While I'm prepared to teach patients *how* to walk the road of health, it is entirely up to them to *walk* it. This is their freewill choice since the Creator kindly allows us to choose our habits. I explain that they are now at a crossroads and their old bad habits represent a roadblock to future wellness. They can follow instructions and discover new ways of healthy living, or they can follow their old bad habits down the other road, which leads to further pain and disease. In critical cases, they may find themselves looking into the face of death.

———•◆•———

It's too bad we aren't twins. One body could be fed perfectly, given lots of water to drink, and balanced with rest and exercise. The other body could be treated as usual. Then we could observe both bodies further down the road of life, and choose accordingly. I've seen reports stating that 95 percent of a person's medical costs are incurred during the last six months of life. What a sad, desperate attempt to save what's already gone. To lose your health is to lose everything!

How often have I seen ambulances racing at high speed, sirens screaming, rushing to get to the hospital in minutes. Usually the patient in back has spent a lifetime enjoying all the bad habits that preceded this event. Now, of course, every second counts in a mad scramble to get help. Let's face it, poor choices ultimately catch up with us. Unfortunately, by then, it's often too late for people to reclaim their lost health.

Once I actually did come close to performing the twin experiment. Two patients, a man and a woman—unknown to each other—came in on the same day. They both had recently suffered strokes. But I saw in their energy fields that both of them could come out of their strokes completely *if* they followed directions and totally changed their way of life . . .

The man was treated first. His wife had to help him walk into my treating room since his right arm and leg were almost useless. The muscles on the right side of his face drooped, which caused him great difficulty in speaking. I used Creative Healing and then ran energy, focusing on the nonfunctional side of his body. In 15 minutes, God restored his body and his speech completely. He and his wife were astounded. She declared, "It's a miracle." I agreed, "God has healed your husband and we were privileged to see it happen."

After I told the husband to thank God for his healing, I began to lecture him about his poor nutrition. "You are going to have to stop drinking coffee, give up fast foods and alcohol, and knock off all the sugary treats that you love. I mean ice cream, chocolate, pies, cakes, cookies and donuts. You have to do your part on the nutritional end in order to support your healing."

Watching his energy as I gave him guidance for his future health, I saw that he wasn't listening at all. Trying to get his attention, I warned, "If you *don't* change your habits, I'm afraid your stroke will return and your speech will be so slurred that even your wife will not understand you. *Do you get it?*"

Looking bored and edging toward the door, my willful patient grudgingly acknowledged my words by nodding. Exasperated, I said, "If you *don't* change your ways, the healing angels tell me that your stroke will return in nine months to the day. You will find yourself helpless and in a wheelchair if you don't turn your life around. *Do you understand?*" He stopped moving toward the door and nodded nervously. I added, "Now, on the other hand, if you listen and follow my instructions, you'll be just fine all the way." He nodded one last time, grabbed his wife's hand and hurried her out the door.

When my next patient came in for treatment, I had to do a double take. Although my previous patient and this lady didn't know each other, their stroke symptoms were absolutely identical, like twins. Through God's grace, the same miraculous healing occurred for her. In 15 minutes, she was restored to perfect health. There weren't any signs of the stroke that had brought her into my office. She was thrilled and I was fairly bursting with joy and gratitude to God for these two miracles.

Before these two patients left my office, I hammered them both on the changes they needed to make to preserve God's healing. I wanted to be sure they knew *exactly* how to honor their miraculous healings. The lady listened to the same speech I had given the man. However, she actually listened closely to everything I said. She understood and agreed that an attitude of gratitude to the Creator and specific changes in her dietary habits were required to maintain her restored health. A perfect patient, she realized that without these changes her illness would return.

Both patients left in perfect health, but nine months later the man was wheeled in by his wife. She reported that he hadn't followed any of the nutritional guidelines. His wife interpreted his pleas for help because his speech was unintelligible. When I tried to treat the poor fellow, the healing flow refused to enter his body. It bounced back into my hands. (This occurs when people choose *consciously* to ignore their side of the healing contract.) I was saddened to see him leave in the same condition as when his wife wheeled him into my office. However, his condition was living proof that a return to bad habits recreates the original condition.

By coincidence, his "twin" came in the next month. I was thrilled to see that she was in wonderful health. She had totally changed her life in order to follow the guidelines I had given her. I was glad that one of the twins had followed the path of health, even though the other one had chosen the road that returned him to his original disabled condition. This lady is a perfect example of why it's easier to treat 500 women than any ten men. Women, who are the great caregivers in our world, listen and are ready to carry out any and all changes that will help their families and themselves. God bless the ladies!

———— ·◆· ————

The first treatment is my favorite because positive shifts can be so dramatic. It has always puzzled me why a healer can help one person, but not another. Some people I thought I hadn't helped at all told me later that their lives changed in wonderful, unforeseen ways after their first treatment. Some of these folks confided that they had been on the verge of suicide the day they first came to see me. But, as in June's account of *First Love* in Chapter 15, they were shifted completely out of that state by the healing energy.

During the first treatment some patients are taken to the top of the mountain of health where they can view the grandeur and beauty of a healthy life. The effect may last for days, weeks, months, or in rare cases, a lifetime. This time frame depends on God's plan and how willing the patients are to follow the simple health guidelines I give them.

After receiving a free ride to the top, patients who do not make the effort to try and follow the guidelines typically find themselves sliding back down the mountain. *Their* first question is, "What happened?" *My* first question is, "What did you eat or drink of your old favorites?" Then I listen to a round of true confessions: "But it was only *one* cup of coffee and I used to drink a *pot* every morning" or "I guess I shouldn't have eaten those cookies at the Christmas party" or "Gee, my sister was in town and it was *her* idea to order dessert." Believe me, I've heard every excuse in the book. I tell these patients that now they will have to climb the mountain again on their own steam in order to regain their health.

Of course, I will help them by running healing energy to assist them in their climb back up the mountain. However, it is their responsibility to use the information, as given by the healing angels, to learn a new way of life in which they take control of their health. I explain they are now driving on a very narrow road and there is no spare tire in the trunk. If they get even one wheel off this road, they will end up in quicksand. In other words, the final responsibility for healing lies in their hands. Although there have been a few surprising exceptions . . .

I was present when God healed a man who had been confined to a wheelchair for 13 years. Bob was receiving $3,000 every month for his total disability when he came to see me. In one treatment, he was taken straight to the top of the mountain of health. Amazed, I saw that Bob would have a lifetime of superb health from that moment on. As karma would have it, my angelic guides told me there was *nothing* he needed to change in his habits to stay well, something I rarely heard. When Bob walked out of my office pushing his wheelchair, I thought, "There goes a lucky man. Bob caught the brass ring and he's going to have a free ride this time around."

Bob called a few weeks later, "Doc, I want to go back to work driving trucks. I miss it. Besides, I feel guilty about getting disability checks since I'm out of the wheelchair and feel so wonderful every day since your energy treatment."

"Well, call the insurance company and tell them what you just told me."

"Doc, I already tried. They must think I'm a crank caller. They wouldn't believe a word I said. Would you call them?"

"I'll give it a try," I replied.

After my call, the insurance company finally agreed to send someone out to see Bob in spite of their records showing 13 years of proven disability. When the insurance adjuster arrived, Bob was up on a ladder hoisting 14 foot beams—by himself—to position them on posts for a carport extension he was building. The adjuster got out of his car and called out, "Excuse me. Can you tell me if the man who owns this house is home?"

"That's me," Bob yelled down.

"No, no. I mean . . . I need to see the man who's been in a wheelchair for 13 years."

"Oh. Well you can see the wheelchair. It's in the garage over there gathering dust. I don't need it anymore."

After the insurance man got over his shock, he asked Bob for his social security number to be sure he had the right man. Once he confirmed Bob's identity, he wrote up his report. Bob's disability checks stopped and he returned to his old job. My hat is off to this man of integrity. How many people would go back to work and give up that kind of security? After all, the case was 13 years old and the check was sent monthly like clockwork. I'm afraid some people would have just kept cashing the checks and gone fishing. But Bob was thrilled, "Doc, I just want to thank you again. It's a miracle to be active and working again."

———•◆•———

In most cases, I would rather not know what the patient thinks is wrong because I have already seen into the body's biofield energy, which tells me what's going on. However, I ask for a history of their condition, what they think is the cause, what has previously been done for the condition, and why they have come to see me. At times I shudder when I hear the horror stories of what patients have suffered in their search for healing because by the time they come to see me they have usually made the rounds. If they had found help, they wouldn't be in my office . . .

When Ted came to see me, he had to duck to enter my treating room. He was nearly seven feet tall, quite thin, and had the longest feet I'd ever seen. At first glance, I thought he had two gigantic white skis strapped to his feet. Then I saw that he wasn't wearing any shoes, just a mass of white bandaging wrapped around both feet. I didn't know then what a good thing it was that I *couldn't* see the true condition of those feet.

Ted's wife helped him limp over to my treating table. Walking gingerly, he placed his feet carefully as though walking barefoot over hot coals. He explained, "My feet have burned day and night for the past six months. It doesn't seem to matter what medications the doctors prescribe. I've had shots, taken every pill, and applied every ointment known, but nothing's helped. The ulcerations just seem to get worse. Now the doctors tell me that my feet will have to be amputated. So if you can't help me, that's what's going to happen."

"We'll do what we can to help. Let's see what God has in mind for you," I said.

As instructed by the Power, I ran energy through Ted's feet, one at a time. I held my hands on either side, four inches away while I silently offered prayers for his healing. After the treatment, we talked about his curious condition and his career. Ted reported that his feet felt better now and that the burning sensation was gone. Ted walked out of the office without his wife's help.

When Ted returned to my office in two weeks, I was happy to see he was now able to wear shoes, which were an astonishing size 16. He casually asked, "Would you like to see the original Kodachrome photos of my feet before I came to see you?"

"Sure," I replied. I was shocked and horrified when I saw the photos. His feet had been horrible, black, gangrenous things that hardly resembled feet at all. The pictures showed feet that were covered with huge oozing ulcers the size of silver dollars. The ulcers were filled with pus and went clear to the bone in several places. As I held back from gagging, I thanked God that I hadn't seen these pictures before I treated him, or I might have turned him away as completely hopeless.

Ted and his wife began grinning from ear-to-ear. He removed his shoes and socks and wiggled his toes happily, "Look at this, Doc." The skin, which had been black in the photos, was pink with normal circulation. Then he jumped up and gave me a big hug. Ted was 55 and thrilled to return to his active lifestyle. He said, "You should have seen the doctors' faces when they saw my healed feet. They wanted to find some scientific explanation. To me it's plain and simple. It's God's miracle!"

I smiled and said, "I guess you and I both know that God heals."

"Are there people you can't help?" Ted asked.

"Well, I do the best I can for everyone, but the results are always in God's hands." To this day, I shudder when I think that I treated his enormous feet without knowing what was hidden under all those bandages.

———— • ◆ • ————

Patients are usually referred by their family or friends who have received healing through my treatment. If the energy almost blows them off the table, they will tell friends who then expect similar results. Unfortunately miracles have one drawback: the people who hear about them come to see me because they want the same or *greater* miracles for themselves, often without making any changes in their diet or their way of life.

However, we are all different and have different lessons to learn. God always has been, and always will be in charge of the Miracle Department. Miracles only happen when God wants them to happen. Whenever this is about to occur, I feel the energy in the room shifting and changing in preparation for miraculous events to come. The transforming winds of change blow through the room and I know that soon the patient and I will be lifted into a higher state of being through the increasing voltage of the healing flow . . .

Gloria, a bright, energetic lady I had known for years, phoned me on a Sunday to ask for help. She was staying at the hospital every night to be with her daughter who was in a peninsula hospital with total kidney failure. Debra was only nine years old, but she was already having dialysis treatments since she hadn't urinated normally for three months. The doctors planned to remove both her kidneys and put her on dialysis for the rest of her life.

Gloria said, "I woke up in the middle of the night and remembered your healing work. Do you think you can help her?"

"I'll be right over and we'll see," I answered.

When I entered Debra's hospital room on Sunday evening, she was bravely sitting up in bed talking to Gloria. They both looked exhausted but greeted me with smiles and hugs. Debra was obviously in a lot of pain so I began running energy on my little patient right away while I prayed for divine assistance. Since both mother and daughter were familiar with my work, they thought nothing of me standing a few feet away from the bottom of the bed to run healing energy into her feet.

Debra closed her eyes, her body relaxed, and her breathing became slow and steady. The energy began to move into her feet and legs, and then into her torso. Debra looked up and smiled at me when she felt the energy moving through her body. Suddenly, the energy began building rapidly. Seconds later, the Power swept into the room, filling Debra with golden light.

When the energy reached Debra's kidneys, vibrational signals returned to my waiting hands. It was clear that her kidneys were out of sorts and on strike, sitting on the sidelines like football players waiting it out on the bench. Trying to sort out the problem, I began talking with them. They were grumpy and said that poor food choices and lack of water had created the original damage. In an effort to get Debra's attention, they had gone on strike since the only way for the body to get the owner's attention is through pain, disability and disease. I understood their side completely and promised to straighten out the food and water situation with Debra and her mother.

As the kidneys started getting friendlier, I asked them if they would please come back on line. After a ten minute conference, the kidneys said they would operate perfectly the next morning if Debra would drink lots of water during the night ahead. The Power told me that if she honored her side of this contract, full kidney function would be restored at 9:00 A.M.

Passing on this information, I explained, "The kidneys are willing to function perfectly again, but, Debra, you're going to have to drink lots of water tonight. And you're going to have to straighten up your food act and *keep* drinking water after you're released from the hospital. If you keep up your side of the program, the kidneys have agreed never to bother you again."

"I can do it! I *know* I can!" Debra exclaimed with a big smile on her face. Gloria hugged her daughter, overjoyed to see her smiling again. Knowing the doctors would be anxious to test the kidneys when they discovered they were functional, I suggested that Gloria request only a simple urine test. Now that Debra's kidneys were in balance again, I wanted to be sure nothing disturbed their energy fields. I hated to think of any further invasion of the kidney itself. Those innocent organs had been insulted enough for one lifetime.

Gloria called me the next day at noon. Sure enough at 9:00 A.M. Debra's kidneys were functioning perfectly. She was pain free and urinating normally. Her doctors were astounded, but Gloria kept me out of the picture as I requested. Many patients in the past, anxious to help others, told their medical doctors about their healing experiences with me. This information rarely helped anyone but it did heap burning coals on my head and labeled me as a quack and a charlatan. So my part in Debra's healing remained a well-kept secret.

The next week Gloria and Debra came to my office. Debra was flushed with excitement. She pulled out a plaque she was hiding behind her back and proudly presented it to me. The plaque read: "To Doctor MacKimmie, he works with God." Gloria smiled, "It was all Debra's idea and she paid for it with her allowance." I couldn't have been more pleased. With hugs all around—a habit in my office from the beginning—they thanked me once more. And I told them again that God heals, all praise to Him from Whom all blessings flow.

————·◆·————

Over the years I have seen that all healing goes exactly where it is needed according to a pattern of priorities established by the Creator, which may or may not correspond with what the patient and I would choose. Patients are often curious as to what control I have over the outcome of their treatment, and how long it will take to be in wonderful health after we begin. I explain that all is in God's hands, not mine.

First, healing has to neutralize toxicity in the system. If a person is very toxic, they may have to bump around a bit and go through detoxification before moving into better health patterns. Then the energy works to clear karmic patterns, which block awakening. Everything the patient can change (nutrition, emotions, attitudes and life patterns) to help restore the body is presented by the angelic beings. The miracle is that the wisdom of God's healing flow knows the entire story of the patient as it has been lived for all eternity.

When a person is very ill, I find it's like trying to move a car that has been stuck in a mud hole for a long time. The car needs a very strong push at first to get it moving. But once out of the mud, it's much easier to roll it along. Eventually, it starts running on its own energy. As soon as this happens, we back off and see how it runs. Finally, the car goes faster and runs at its best under its own power. And this is the ultimate goal of healing as I see it: for people to have the vitality to reach top speed and feel energetic and enthusiastic in their lives.

Ninety percent of my patients feel the energy flow strongly during their treatment. They may have sensations of heat, tingling or both. Occasionally a patient feels intense cold, even to the point of shaking. When this happens, turning up the heat in the room makes no difference in the experience of cold because it is the healing energy at work. A few patients say they feel as if they are about to rise off the table and float in the air. Most feel relaxed and peaceful.

However, I recall one angry man who abruptly confronted me before his treatment. His energy bubble flared violent red as he shouted, *"You fake! You're taking my wife's money for quackery!"*

The infuriated husband then got on my treating table. "Go ahead. Do your phoney baloney healing. I know you've been hypnotizing my wife so that she imagines she feels better after your treatment."

Hoping to calm him down, I started speaking, "Well . . ."

"Well nothing! You can't hypnotize me! And after you're through, I'm going to get up and punch you in the nose for stealing her money!" he yelled.

Noting his clenched fists, I had no doubt he meant it. I found new meaning in the phrase "heartfelt prayer" as I prayed to God to defuse this volatile situation. The Power instructed me to run energy into the bottoms of his feet. Praying that this would calm the man, I did so.

In a few seconds, he moaned and his face turned white. I asked, "What's the matter?"

"I . . . I feel tingling . . . all over. I'm going to *float* off the table! What the *hell* are you doing to me?"

"I don't know what you're talking about. I'm not doing anything," I replied.

He moaned again, "I . . . I think I'm gonna faint. What are you doing to me?"

"I don't know what you mean. I'm not doing anything. Besides . . . didn't you say I'm a quack? Maybe it's just your imagination."

In another minute, the husband started laughing. He jumped up, gave me a hug, and said, "By God, you're the real thing. I thought my wife was crazy when she talked about feeling such things in your presence and how wonderful she felt now after all her years of sickness. Well, Doc, she can come see you any time. You're the man!" I breathed a sigh of relief and offered prayers of gratitude as he paid me and left my office still laughing.

Like this man, some people are skeptical before the treatment. But when I tell them in what ways their body is at risk, they are amazed and open to accept the healing energy. Some people soak up healing energy like giant sponges. Others—while they would say they came for healing if asked—lock and bolt the castle gates against any changes in their lives.

Surprisingly, these patients do everything in their power to keep the energy from reaching the areas where healing is needed most. At times, it is possible to sneak around these blockades and shift the energy to peripheral roadways in the body. In this way, we bypass the major freeways, which are being blocked by the patient, and then we can make an end-run to bring in health-giving energy where it is needed.

While I am running energy, the Power taps into the source of universal knowledge. I am shown a panorama of the patient's life, and the healing angels give me information to guide the patient. There are times when we have to deal with past lives or colliding energies from parents, grandparents or other family members; sometimes we have to take on the whole family tree.

When instructed by the Power, I explain to the patient that before birth we all choose exactly the life we are living right now. We could have chosen wealth, or fame, or anything else we desired. However, from the infinite plane of wisdom that knows our higher purpose, we choose the precise life that we are living. Only this life serves the purpose of the soul and balances the credits and debits in the great book of life.

13

RULES OF THE ROAD

⸺◆••◆⸺

When I first began healing, all I knew was the thrill of helping others. However, if there were blockages in the patient's body—from poor food choices, drugs, lack of water, etc.—the flow of energy would be restricted. Once these blocks were out of the way, I would feel the revitalized energy loop return to me when the healing session had completed.

I wanted my patients to be partners with me in their healing, and I asked them to join me in a program of proper nutrition, drinking lots of clean water, early hours of sleep, relaxation and exercise. The more cooperation I received in following these health guidelines, the faster and better the results. Without these changes in nutrition and lifestyle, I knew that it was only a matter of time before disease would pay them another visit. Disease is simply doing its job. Dr. Pain is our ally; it's the body's only way to tell us that something is terribly wrong and needs to be corrected.

Realizing the importance of providing my patients with enough information so that they could make healthy choices, I taught them about proper nutrition, which brings me to . . .

Rule Number 1:
The body must be fed and fed correctly.

When a person's body is nourished with real live food, healing energy flows harmoniously throughout the body. Once patients experience the gift of enjoying life in a healthy body fueled with proper nutrition, they can use the renewed life force received during the healing process to fulfill their destiny. But I've discovered that it's never easy to be the bearer of nutritional news in a world addicted to junk foods . . .

I recall a woman, weighing at least 250 pounds, bringing in her five-year-old son. The boy had purplish lumps the size of golf balls all over his body. All the hair on his head was gone, and his feverish eyes had dark circles underneath them. As soon as I touched him, waves of sugar and sheer exhaustion swept back to me from his energy fields.

Fearing the worst, I turned to his mother and asked, "What does Larry eat and when does he go to bed?"

Without batting an eye, Mom replied, "We eat chocolate bars and drink sodas. That's what we like so I don't bother with anything else. And Larry loves to stay up with me to watch the late shows on television. That's our favorite time together."

It was hard to believe, but I saw that it was totally true. I began by saying, "Your boy is very ill." Mom shot me a tell-me-something-I-don't-know look. Braving her disapproval, I continued, "I'd like to help Larry but he's going to have to eat only real, organic foods. Plus he'll need to drink a quart of water every day—just water with nothing in it, not a squeeze of lemon, *nothing*—and go to bed at 8:00 P.M. Do you think you can handle this?"

Surprisingly, Larry's mother nodded and agreed to enforce this new program. I gave Larry several more treatments. The lumps went away and his hair grew back—thick, black, and curly. I was delighted to see him become a very handsome, healthy little boy.

Mother and son were fine for five years. When Larry was 10, Mom brought him in again. His hair was still thick and black but hidden underneath were the telltale purple lumps. Tapping her foot impatiently, his mother said, "He's back eating chocolate bars, drinking sodas, and staying up late so that he can watch television with me."

"Hmm. Have *you* stopped eating chocolate bars and drinking sodas?" I asked her.

Astonished, she protested, "What are you talking about? *I'm* not the patient. *I'm* not sick. If he wants to be healthy, he should eat foods that make him healthy."

Hearing those words, I knew that all Mom wanted was to be left alone to eat the way she pleased and stay up all night. I turned away and rolled my eyes. "That takes the cake," I thought.

Biting the bullet, I turned back to Mother and son. I put my hand on Larry's shoulder and said, "You know you're going to die if you don't stop eating junk food. Your body just can't take it."

His eyes filled with tears. "Doctor Jim, I don't care. I just want to eat like my mom and stay up and watch TV with her."

Since they were unwilling to follow a good nutritional program, I told them they had to seek help elsewhere. Sometimes I wish I had been a psychiatrist. Maybe then I would have understood this mother and son duo. Fortunately for my sanity, most people want to get well, stay well, and are willing to follow the nutritional program after they see it works . . .

A concerned Russian family brought little Boris to my office, and I mean the whole family, including various aunts and uncles. Simply put, he was a five-year-old holy terror. I was their last hope because they couldn't cope with him any longer. For the good of the family, they were ready to place him in an institution on whatever drugs were necessary to calm him.

Watching in horror as his father fought to hold Little Boris in his lap, I wondered how the family had put up with this violent behavior for five years. Little Boris kicked and screamed like a wild beast while his father tried to hold him still. Suddenly, he punched his father in the stomach while he ferociously kicked his father's legs. Then he tore his father's glasses right off his face, and threw them to the ground. I'd seen a lot of wild children long before A.D.D. (Attention Deficit Disorder) became a popular diagnosis, but never anything like this. Little Boris made Linda Blair in *The Exorcist* seem quite charming.

Dreading the predictable answer, I asked the father—between kicks and screams—my standard question, "What does little Boris eat?"

His father raised his voice above the screams, "Sodas and chocolate bars."

"I'm sure he does! What *else* does he eat?"

At this point a chorus of voices from the rest of the family chimed in: "No, no, Doctor, you don't understand. Our little Boris won't eat anything else."

Having gone through this with Larry, I was outraged, "Of course, that's what *any* child wants to eat given half a chance. Take away all the sodas and candy *now!* From this moment on he is only to eat meat, vegetables and fruit. Don't you *dare* give him *anything* but *water* to drink until this madness *stops!*"

The father raised his eyebrows and said, "But Doctor, he'll starve. Sodas and chocolate bars are all he likes. He refuses to eat anything else."

Faced with this insanity, I figured I had nothing to lose by getting little Boris out of my office before he got loose and destroyed the place. I shouted over the rising decibels of his screams, *"Then tie him up if you have to! But don't let him eat anything until he starts eating good healthy foods!"*

Certain I'd never see this family again, I was shocked when six weeks later, I saw the infamous name, little Boris, on the schedule. I thought of closing the office and hiding but that seemed unfair to the other patients who were scheduled on that day. When I saw the family arriving for their appointment, I steeled myself and waited for the uproar to begin. But when they entered my office, little Boris was an absolute angel. I held my breath. Little Boris smiled innocently in my direction.

Could this be the same child? I could only think that he was taking some very welcome, tranquilizing drugs. I asked the smiling family what they had done to bring about this change. The family members looked at each other in surprise. The father answered, "Why Doctor, we just followed all your instructions to the letter, exactly as you told us." Over the years, Boris grew up to become a fine, healthy young man, an asset to society, and a pleasure to know. But at five he had shown perfectly that we are what we eat at *any* age.

Unfortunately growing older doesn't necessarily make us wiser in our food choices. There was a charming old Japanese man who came to see me when he was 72. He had just been released from the hospital and was taking five drugs for chest pains. I asked him about his diet. He told me he *loved* cookies, which he pronounced "coogies." We talked further and that was his diet: coogies and his prescribed drugs. I stared him down and said firmly, "No more cookies." He was very unhappy but within a month his heart was fine and his pot belly had disappeared. However, each time he came to see me, he looked at me with mournful eyes and asked, "Coogies ok now?" Shaking my head, I said firmly, "No. No more cookies."

Once recovered, this elderly gentleman went back to work at the family's nursery. His family was concerned at first but the old chap thrived as he worked hard all day in the lush greenery. I told the family that he'd enjoyed a lifetime of hard work on the land and now he'd found his place in the world again. They relaxed, happy to see him happy. He stopped taking his pills on his own and was wonderfully healthy for years.

However, five years later—without asking me—he returned to his beloved coogies and started having chest pains again. When the family asked my advice, I told them to get him started on the nutritional program we had given him originally. They did and my coogie friend had no more trouble.

———•◆•———

I have spent a lifetime researching sound nutrition for my patients. It turned out to be a very simple diet with minor adjustments made for each person. Eliminating junk foods entirely is the first step. And it *can* be done. If you're looking for trouble ahead, just grab a bite of "whatever" when you're hungry. If you're seeking health, you can't plant cabbages, and expect roses; you become what you eat.

My patients are used to me preaching to them about caring for the body and the wonderful benefits that come from feeding the body correctly. Good wholesome foods are paramount. Stop and consider the price we pay for the chemicals that blanket our foods and preserve their shelf life. I suggest that my patients purchase only organic foods. Organic foods saved my life. For me, there is no choice. When folks complain about the higher cost of organic foods, I tell them it's cheaper than paying for drugs and surgery.

The energies of the body are beautifully organized into three primary levels: physical, mental, and spiritual. To enjoy life to the fullest, all three must work in concert. If we focus too much on any one aspect, our lives get tangled and lopsided. By focusing on the physical, the body's musculature can be developed until it is awesome, but we must attend to *all* aspects of life. Those who devote all their energy to the mental plane refine their intellect, but the body and spirit also need appreciation. In the circle of life, *balance* is the key.

A few people challenge me with the ancient teaching: "I am not this body." Although these words point to a spiritual truth, we still have to live in this rental body until the light body comes along. So why not take care of it? As we progress in our spiritual lives, there comes a time when we are required to bring our mind and body into partnership with our spirit. A tall order, but together these three aspects form a synergy of supporting energy for our earthly journey.

Our physical bodies require clean foods, pure drinking water, and fresh air and sunshine. They also need movement of the muscles and tissues to send nutrients to the cells and flush waste out of the body. The more natural the movements (Yoga, Tai Chi, Qigong, etc.), the more perfect the flow of energy. Early hours of sleep charge the body's energy batteries, and allow time for the body to repair itself. Ben Franklin was right: "Early to bed and early to rise, makes a man healthy, wealthy and wise." While there's no guarantee of worldly riches, if you feel that health is wealth, then pick up the ball and run for the goal line of health.

My joy has been to teach people—those who will listen—to be responsible, to take charge of their habits and do what it takes to reclaim their health. Too many people will spend 100 dollars to get out of a dollar's worth of work. Julius Caesar said, "Give me responsibility, I want freedom." Caesar also said, "Take no counsel of your fears." Don't think about how difficult the task is before you. Just *do* it. Take action now!

Until one is committed, there is hesitancy, the chance to draw back, always ineffectiveness, concerning all acts of initiative and creation. There is one elementary truth the ignorance of which kills countless ideas and splendid plans: that the moment one definitely commits oneself, then providence moves too. All sorts of things occur to help one that would never have otherwise occurred. A whole stream of events issues from the decision, raising in one's favor all manner of unforeseen incidents and meetings and material assistance which no one could have dreamed would come their way. Whatever you can do, or dream you can, begin it. Boldness has genius, power and magic in it. Begin it now.

— Johann Goethe
(1749–1832)

———•◆•———

If I had a flat tire and wanted it fixed, I wouldn't get in the repairman's way and steal his tools. Yet some people go out of their way to sabotage their healing, and balk at following instructions. After years of energy work, I now expect patients to complain when I take away their coffee, chocolate, sodas, etc. Then I listen to a but-these-are-a-few-of-my-favorite-things speech.

However, if patients listen and follow, real miracles can occur. The first miracle is if they *do* listen. I explain that I won't carry *both* ends of the stretcher. They have to pick up *their* end when I pick up my end. When patients argue on behalf of their favorite addictions, I think of a sign, which hung in my office for many years: "The success in your case, may depend on which one of us is the doctor." However, some people cling to their addictions as if their lives depended on it . . .

Andrea and I were staying with friends one summer when they asked if I could possibly help a friend of theirs who was quite ill. After I agreed, they phoned her and she came over. Before I could say anything, she grabbed my arm and said, "Doctor, you're looking at a desperate woman. I'm in terrible pain all the time. It's been going on for *years*. I've been to *everyone* but *no one* has been able to help me. I've heard *wonderful* things about you. Please help me. I'll do *anything* to get well."

After her speech, I looked further into her energies. I saw that she was actually attached to her desperation, and proud that no one had been able to help her. I also saw a major addiction to coffee. In her case, it was simply destroying her. I said, "If you will give up coffee, I believe we can eliminate all your pain."

She gasped, turned white as a sheet and whimpered, "I didn't think I'd have to give up *coffee* to get better. I *need* my coffee. I have a *very* stressful job and couldn't *possibly* get through the day without coffee. If I'd known that you were going to ask me to give up coffee, I wouldn't have come over." Choosing to keep her pain rather than give up coffee, she left, another lesson in what people are willing—or *not* willing—to give up in order to get well. In her case, this desperate woman was not so desperate after all. But at least she was honest.

Another honest lady was Claire. When I first saw her many years ago, she was walking down the street with the aid of a cane. Since she was so young, I stopped her to ask how she had injured her leg. She explained, "It's not an injury. My hip joints are disintegrating. The doctors say I need both hips replaced because the bone has deteriorated so badly. But they told me to hold out for as long as I can since I'm so young. I'm supposed to wait until the pain becomes intolerable so I'm taking lots of drugs for the pain. You see, the hip replacements won't last for my lifetime, and they can only be replaced two or three times. After that, I'll be in a wheelchair for the rest of my life."

Stunned by her words, I couldn't imagine someone so young faced with such a grim future. I said, "This may sound strange but I do energy healing. Perhaps the energy and a change in your diet might help your condition. If you'd like to give it a try, I'd be happy to run energy on you to see if it helps."

The young lady agreed and came in the following week. At thirty, youth was on her side, but she was a chocoholic and a true junk food junkie. Anything with sugar was the mainstay of her diet. As I ran energy, I explained all the changes in diet that she needed to make in order to help her body heal while it built new tissue and bone. With relief from her pain and the joy of walking without a cane, she became an enthusiastic patient. She gave up coffee, chocolate and all the sugary goodies she loved. After three energy treatments, Claire could ski, hike for hours, dance and do whatever she pleased without pain.

For three months Claire followed the recommended diet strictly. However, one day she came in and I knew from her energy that there was trouble on the horizon. She looked into my eyes and said, "I'm going to have the surgery. I just couldn't hold out. I have to have my chocolate and my morning lattes. I'm sorry, but I have to eat the things I love. And I don't want you to waste your time when I can't follow the diet." Her cravings had won.

"I appreciate your honesty, Claire. You gave the program your best try. And now you've made a decision based on what's important to you. I hope the surgery does wonders for you."

Two months later Claire had both hips replaced. Later, I saw her in town walking with crutches. When I stopped to talk with her, she confessed, "There's something I didn't tell you the last time I saw you. I was too embarrassed. After three months of not touching *any* chocolate, I took my first bite. And as soon as I did, all my pain came back instantly. It was unbearable and I knew I had to schedule the surgery right away. If only my desire to be well could have been stronger than my desire for chocolate. Now it's too late . . . but it was wonderful for those three months when I could be totally active without any pain. I don't know what I could have been thinking to have thrown my miracle healing away." I wished her well and blessed her for her honesty.

———•◆•———

Before coming to me, many of my patients began their search for health by taking enough daily supplements to rattle when they walked, or by adding exercise routines that promised glowing health. Unfortunately, they still felt unwell. By clinging to entrenched, comfortable habits not conducive to health, patients were often undermining their own wellness campaign.

Stopping whatever is poisoning the body is the first step, and it will never be easier than it is right now, in the moment. To get my point across to patients, I emphasize . . .

Rule Number 2:
It's not what you *start* doing that gets you well; It's what you *stop* doing that *gets* you well and *keeps* you well.

When severe lower back pain brought a 40-year-old lady into my office, I had no idea that she had just come from the dialysis unit of a large San Francisco hospital. Touching her hand as she lay on the treating table, the energy took over and flowed powerfully into her body. However, as it returned to my hands, it spoke of a strange distortion in the frequency patterns of her kidneys. This clearly signaled the cause of her lower back pain. These frequencies were setting off some of the worst vibrational warnings I had ever felt.

Wondering how much my patient knew about the cause of her back pain, I asked, "Do you have any clues why you are having so much pain in your lower back?"

She shrugged and said, "I don't know, but it's *terrible* and has been for months. Friends said you might be able to help me."

"Hmm. Have you gone to any medical doctors recently?"

"Yes, I was just seen in the dialysis unit at the hospital. The doctors say I've got total kidney failure. They're going to remove both of my kidneys and put me on dialysis for the rest of my life."

When I checked the kidneys, they were both as dry as two stones on the summer desert at high noon. I steeled myself and asked, "How much water do you drink?"

"Oh, well, I don't like water. I only drink coffee and sodas."

"OK . . . other than what's in your coffee and sodas, how much *water* do you drink?"

"None. I told you. I *hate* water. Never drink it. I drink coffee and sodas."

"All right . . . so when was the last time you *did* drink water?"

"Oh heavens . . . let me think . . . maybe 10 years ago?"

I groaned inwardly, surprised that her kidneys had held out *this* long, "So, Nancy, what did the physicians in the dialysis unit have to say when you told them what you drink?"

"They didn't say anything. No one at the hospital ever asked me what I was *drinking*. I don't see what *that* has to do with *anything*. They did all the tests and said I should schedule surgery and have my kidneys removed right away."

"I suggest you call an insurance company and ask them to send you the statistics on how long a person lives after going on dialysis when both kidneys have been removed."

"Listen, I'm not worried about this *kidney* thing. I came in to get away from my *back* pain. The painkillers I'm taking aren't helping much. I'll do anything to get away from the terrible pain."

"I'll treat you *if* you agree to stop the coffee and sodas *immediately* and drink a gallon of water a day instead. Each of your kidneys is only the size of a human ear. Every day each hardworking kidney has to clean thousands of quarts of blood. These small organs have to juggle all kinds of chemical toxins—dumping the bad and retaining the good—to perfectly cleanse your blood. The kidneys are God's incredible recycling plants."

My patient looked dubious so I continued my pitch for the kidneys. "If we didn't have these organs, we would have to drink a thousand gallons of water every day to do the same job. I suggest you apologize to your kidneys for mistreating them. Talk to them. Like every cell in your body, they are super-intelligent. Tell them that you love and appreciate them for their wonderful work. Promise them that you'll drink enough water so that they can do their job."

As soon as the energy treatment brought relief from her back pain, she was ready to give up her traditional drinks in favor of water. After she had three treatments in one week, she had no more back pain. Much to her surprise, both kidneys now worked perfectly, and she happily canceled the surgery.

Six months later, Nancy called, "I was wondering if it would be all right for me to start drinking coffee and sodas again?" I shook my head in dismay. I knew she was calling with the hope that I would give her a free pass to drink her old standbys. Before I could answer, she added, "I'm so tired of water. I think I'm going to throw up if I drink one more glass."

Knowing that her mind was made up, I realized it would be useless to review the kidney information that I had given her before. I said, "You know, Nancy, it was stopping the sodas and coffee that got you well, and that's what will keep you well. But it's your choice. You'll have to make this decision for yourself." After I got off the phone, I apologized mentally to her kidneys for the coming disaster.

———— • ◆ • ————

Nancy's story reminds me of three beautiful young girls who worked at a produce store in the Bay area. They all looked like the flawless beauties on television exercise programs who hint to the rest of the female population that physical perfection is easily attained by jumping about charmingly in the privacy of your own living room. The produce girls were lively and chattered away happily as they stocked the bins.

One afternoon while I was shopping in the produce section, another girl came in with a case of sodas. She tossed each of the girls a can. The girls caught them on the fly with practiced ease, popped the tops, and drank them down. I couldn't resist asking the girls if they ever drank water. They burst out laughing. "Are you *kidding?*" *"Not likely!"* "Water tastes *terrible!*" The soda "tosser" laughed too and joined in, "These girls *never* drink water. The *only* thing they drink is at least a dozen sodas each during the day."

That summer, one of the girls injured her back and came to me as a patient. Forgetting the scene I had witnessed at the market, I told her to drink as much water as possible to help her healing process. She gave me a disgusted look, "You're kidding right? I *hate* water. I really don't get why people drink it. I *never* do. Neither do my girlfriends. We all like sodas."

The soda scene came back sharply to my mind in every detail. Before I could suggest that she was going to have to change her ideas about water. She casually explained that they were all going to the dialysis unit at a big hospital to get dialysis by vein for their kidney problems. Having met an Australian M.D. long ago, who instructed people to drink a gallon of water each day for their health, I saw how much trouble the girls were heading into. Thinking that I might get over the wall of soda stacked in her energy field if we talked further, I said, "So . . . tell me about your dialysis experience."

"Oh, it's *fantastic!* We go twice a week. The hospital dialysis unit has the most *wonderful* recliners and we get to watch new movies. They have *thousands* of movies to choose from. And there's a *huge* screen that hangs right in *front* of us. Gosh, it's just like being on vacation. And . . . you want to know the best part? Our insurance *pays* for it."

Studying her wide-eyed enthusiasm, I took a deep breath and plunged into an uphill battle. "Dialysis—or any other mechanical device like a lung machine—will never be as efficient as the human body, which was designed perfectly by the Creator. Because of the dialysis machine's lower efficiency, the body tends to slowly build up toxins."

My patient didn't seem to care. The only response I received was a bored "um-hum" issued between closed lips. I went on to explain how the kidneys function and that each kidney requires a certain amount of clean water in order to function properly. Whenever I paused, she nodded and um-hummed me. I asked her to pass on the information to her girlfriends so that they could think it over. She yawned, "OK . . . sure . . . I'll tell 'em."

Later, when I saw my reluctant patient at the produce store, I found out that the girls were still enjoying their dialysis days, happy to relax, watch videos, and let their insurance pay for it all. By this time, I realized they were ready and willing to be dialysis patients for the rest of their lives. We moved away from the area before this insanity destroyed their health. Frankly, I dreaded seeing the final outcome of their choices.

Despite facts to the contrary, I've heard some "experts" insist that we don't need to drink water at all. The theory is that we get enough water in our daily foods. But a chap in California lived to be 117 years of age and drank two gallons of water daily. I've never suggested drinking *that* much, but adults need, at the very least, two quarts of clean water every day. This is water without any additives—not even a squeeze of lemon—to help the kidneys cleanse the blood. It's like a car wash, the more water, the easier the job.

When eminent physician Alexis Carrel won the 1912 Nobel Prize in Medicine, a major portion of his research was in the transplanting of tissues and whole organs. He theorized that kidneys were designed to last 400 years if they were fed properly and continually cleansed of all toxins. Water anyone? He also suggested that the human body needed only one tenth of one kidney to survive. Of course, he lived before toxins could be found in foods, drinking water, even the air we breathe.

Keep in mind the only thing holding up the kidneys is the layer of fat that surrounds these delicate organs. The kidneys do *not* like to be chilled. Just imagine going into a delightfully cold lake on a hot summer afternoon. The water feels exhilarating to the feet, invigorating to the legs, stimulating up to the waist, but you feel like you're going to pass out when the icy water hits the kidney area. For one horrible moment, you wonder if you'll ever get the rest of your body submerged. Luckily, once you're in, you're in.

I flinch when I see teenagers wearing the latest fashion craze of jeans about to fall from their hips and short tops that expose the midriff. This may have the stamp of glamor, but they are risking their health in later life. Still, I know it's of little use to tell teenagers anything. At least I never wanted to be told anything when I was young. What adults in my life called "wisdom," I called "boring." But, believe me, the urinary system is one part of the body to keep on your side. Any malfunction in this area gives more pain than any other area of the body as far as I've seen in my practice.

The body works day and night for only one reason: to bring you abundant health every moment of your life. It will heal anything, if it gets cooperation from the owner. Why not love and appreciate your faithful servant? Most people work better when the boss acknowledges and appreciates them. Our bodies are the same. Appreciation of your body and all its organs will do wonders for your health.

———— ·◆· ————

When a person is in severe pain, it's truly remarkable how willing they are to change. They're ready to cooperate and follow the diet, that is, until they feel better. Then it's anybody's guess what they will do, and I often saw patients caught by . . .

Rule Number 3:
With the relief of pain, patients return to their old bad habits, which caused their problems in the first place.

I have watched patients return to their prior bad habits more often than I care to remember. They felt so invincible in their renewed health that they returned to the addictive goodies of civilization, which first made them sick. Whenever possible, I headed them off at the pass before they ran wild with the thrill of their healing.

On the other hand, a few patients refused to cooperate or follow *any* guidelines for their health. Although I treated them as instructed, some of the heart goes out of healing when I realize I'm trying to change someone who doesn't want to change. I hate to bail out the patient's boat at one end, and then see the patient bailing water *in* at the other end.

Time and time again, I carefully explained to my patients that the average diet creates stress in the body, which eventually leads to sickness. To emphasize that small habits can be enough put them under, I liked to use the example of a nail. It may be small, but once embedded in a tire, it can bring a 3,000 pound automobile to a halt.

However, as I tried to reinforce changes in diet, lifestyle and hours of sleep, some patients simply threw a fit. They wanted help, but only as long as it didn't inconvenience them in any way. I found I could lead a patient to better foods but I couldn't make them eat those foods against their will. Suddenly they were back into their favorite junk foods and down they would go. Fortunately, these patients have been very few over the years . . .

Bart was a crusty, ill-tempered man in his 50s who came in complaining of a weak heart and circulation problems in his legs. Disabled by his condition, he had to lean on his daughter's arm to get into my office. However, as soon as I began flowing energy, Bart felt better. While I was treating him, I gave him information about the nutritional program, explaining that by making these changes he could maintain his healing. Looking into his energy fields, I saw that he thought he was far above all this information. No one could tell him anything. He apparently knew it all from birth.

With energy that bristled with selfishness, Bart was about as open as a bank vault at midnight. When I saw that he believed God *owed* him his healing, I was shocked and disgusted. I didn't like him as a patient, or as a person, but whether I liked him or not didn't matter. After one energy treatment, he could walk without assistance for the first time in months. And he did, straight out of my office, leaving his daughter to hurry after him.

Two months later, Bart's daughter brought him in again. He wasn't any worse than the first time I had seen him, but he had clearly returned to his former sick condition. His daughter informed me that once back home, her father didn't follow any of the dietary instructions. This didn't surprise me in the least. I told Bart that it was time to listen up or he would find himself worse than before. My rebukes fell on deaf ears. He stared me down, proud to have followed his own rules.

For reasons I couldn't fathom, God kindly healed him again. Had it been up to me, I would have left him to enjoy his poor health. But after 15 minutes of energy flow, he was completely restored again. He got off my treating table and walked haughtily out of my office without any thanks or even a backward glance in my direction. His daughter stayed behind to thank me and apologize for her father, but the patient himself was long gone.

Sure enough two months later here came Bart for the third time. His daughter must have given up on him since this time he stumbled into the office on crutches. Clearly, he had embraced all his bad habits once he was home. It is very rare for the Power to agree to heal someone who has turned their back on healing twice. Astonished when the healing angels said this pompous fool would be healed once again, I gritted my teeth and ran energy as directed. Before my eyes, he was restored to health immediately. Briskly heading out the door, crutches tucked underneath one arm, he left without so much as a nod or a thank you.

By this time I'd had it. I thought, "If Bart screws up again surely even the Power will agree that he doesn't deserve to be healed." How wrong I was! Two months later here was Bart for the fourth time, leaning heavily on his crutches for support. Like an arrogant dictator, he *commanded* me to heal him.

"All right Buddy," I thought. "Now I'm going to be allowed to tell you what I *really* think of you." I waited for the Power to tell me we had reached the three-strikes-and-you're-out ruling. But no! The angels directed me to run energy for the fourth time. I took a sharp intake of air. How could this be? I was shocked but followed the Power's guidance. Bart, restored to perfect health once more, walked haughtily out of the office smiling smugly as though he had done me a favor.

A few months later, I heard what happened to Bart from his daughter who told me that once he was home, he continued all his old bad habits. However, this time he became so ill that he went in for a medical examination. His heart was so bad that he was given two choices by the doctor: surgery or death. Heart surgery was scheduled.

When Bart woke up in the recovery room, the surgeon and his daughter were standing by his bedside. Still feeling the blissful effects of the anesthetic, Bart told the surgeon he'd been to a chiropractor who had put him on a strict diet of meat, salads, fruit, and lots of vegetables. Studying the surgeon's unchanged face, Bart added that he had been advised to stop drinking coffee and sodas and drink plenty of water instead. When the surgeon still said nothing, Bart went on to say that this healer also advised exercise, getting to bed early and prayer.

The surgeon calmly responded, "Why, Bart, it doesn't matter what you eat. You can eat whatever you want, stay up late and watch television all day and all night if that's what you want."

Relief swept over Bart's features. He reached up and grabbed the surgeon's hand, "Doctor, why are you so *good* to me?"

The surgeon said, "To tell you the truth, you might as well eat anything you want . . . with your condition . . . and at this late date. Your arteries are terrible, the worst I've ever seen. Any of them could blow the next time you get angry or excited. Too bad you didn't listen to that healer. He was perfectly right. You should go back to him. Tell him not to waste his time on people like you. Tell him not to be a fool and care more about you than you do about yourself."

After Bart's daughter described this event, I felt vindicated. Although she always claimed that her father loved me dearly for what I'd done for him, she was sadly mistaken. His energy fields clearly revealed that he hated me because his healing had not been under his control. He resented me to the day he died, which happened exactly as the surgeon predicted. One day he got off the couch, screamed at his wife, and dropped dead on the spot. If allowed, Bart is now in heaven drinking coffee and shoveling in cake and ice cream just as he loved to do in this life.

———•◆•———

Some patients feel more comfortable on a medical drug program. Having made this karmic choice, they are happy turning over the responsibility for their health to the medical professionals, who stand ready to prescribe drugs for symptoms and perform surgeries. And who can blame patients who want instant relief from symptoms with no effort on their part?

But the right to choose, no matter what type of practitioner is involved, is important. You wouldn't want to be forced to take your car only to a certain mechanic, or to have your wardrobe limited to one store. We should be able to make the choices we feel are best for us at the time. And if we change our minds, and decide to go with alternative care, then we should be able to change horses; after all, it's our health that's at stake.

Some patients opt for surgery after telling me their surgeons told them diet had nothing to do with their condition. However, it's not smart to go swimming with rocks in your pockets. Poor eating habits may be all the rocks needed to sink your boat of health. I often hear patients say: "my problem is genetic" or "everyone in my family has the same thing." Maybe so, but eating patterns are also inherited. Just as emotional dysfunctions are passed on from one generation to the next, so it is with our food habits, which brings me to . . .

Rule Number 4:
You can feed *into* your sickness or *out* of it.

If you realized that running over nails every day caused flat tires, wouldn't you figure out that *not* running over nails would be a better solution than fixing flat tires all the time. Better yet, you might stop throwing nails out in front of you as you drive through life. In short, get both horses on the same end of the wagon pulling toward health, instead of having a wagon with a horse on each end pulling in *opposite* directions . . .

When Minnie first came to see me, she had horrible radiation burns. They were worse than any I had ever seen in my practice. The left pectoral area, where the breast of this 42-year-old woman had been removed, was now only skin stretched as tight as a drum over her ribs. But worse than this disfigurement, the entire area looked as though it had been burnt and sizzled like a steak on a grill from strong radiation treatments. She had survived the standard procedure for a mastectomy in the early 1950s, but the results were appalling. Her left arm and hand were withered and curled tightly to her chest like a chicken's claw. She was unable to move her left arm at all.

Over the next six weeks, I gave Minnie energy treatments once a week. She also had to correct her terrible diet from top to bottom. I convinced her to drink a gallon of water a day, and instructed her to go to bed early and walk for a half hour each morning. It was thrilling to watch the tissues of her left arm begin to fill out. After the third treatment, she was able to use her arm for the first time since the surgery and radiation two years before. Minnie couldn't have been happier. When she received an invitation to visit her family back home in the deep south for a couple of months, she was feeling so good she decided to go.

Two months later, Minnie came into my office overweight and depressed. Her left arm curled to her chest once more. While the arm had not withered, the tissues were angry, red, swollen and painful. After I heard what she'd eaten on her sojourn south, I gave her both barrels, "Minnie, you must realize that you cast aside the good diet that brought you back to health. You made the choice. You fed yourself right back into your old sickness."

Offering a feeble defense of her actions, she said, "Oh, Doctor Jim, you don't know how it was. I tried to protest and stick to the diet. But my family told me I was plain crazy to believe that food had anything to do with my condition."

After we went back and forth on this issue, I told her I would try to help her again because as Andrea says, "We live and we learn, but *mostly* we live." My thoughts went back to the Old Man who would never have spoken to her again after her lapse from the diet. However, I know that—being our weak and wobbly selves—we all make mistakes.

Before I began her treatment, I warned her, "The Power won't always flow healing to those who don't keep up their end of the healing contract. You've got to promise me that you'll eat right from now on. And if you are fortunate enough to be healed again, I'd advise you not to throw away the gift this time."

"Oh, I understand. I promise."

"Then let's pray together for another healing," I said and we both bowed our heads and asked the Creator for His grace.

After six weekly treatments, Minnie was fine. Then she went to Canada to visit more relatives. When she came dragging into my office two months later, she was horribly depressed. And no wonder. Her weight was up again and her arm was back to its old position, curled tightly to her chest. Again, the tissues were angry, red, swollen and painful. Her energy fields were muddied and clogged by what she had eaten in Canada.

Shaking my head, I asked, "How could you do this to yourself after your *last* experience?"

"I'm so sorry. My relatives wanted to celebrate my recovery and prepared tons of food for my visit . . . none of it on your diet of course. You have to understand that since I was staying with them, there was nothing else to eat except what they offered me. I tried to explain the diet to them. I *really did*. But they told me it was all nonsense." As she looked down at the floor, waves of discouragement surged from her energy fields.

When I put my hands on her shoulders, Minnie raised her head. Looking deeply into her eyes, I counseled, "If you go down that road again—unwilling to stand up to people and fight for your health—please do not to come back to me. The angels have told me they will heal you one last time. But this is the end of the road. I won't be allowed to help you again. I like you and I don't want to see you die."

Minnie got tears in her eyes and said, "I swear I'll stay on the diet for the rest of my life, no matter what. Thank you for your help and thank your angels for me."

Once more we embarked on the road of healing, and once more Minnie was healed through God's grace. The further miracle was that this grateful patient never stepped away from the diet again in all the time that I knew her. She finally understood how far off the track she had gotten in the food department and what it took to hold the line against all odds, especially relatives. Most people—unless it is life and death—continue to eat the wrong things and pretend there's no such thing as water; they stay up late, hang on television, sit too much and wonder why they don't feel good.

It is inspiring to see patients empower themselves by making a conscious choice to rethink their lives and habits. By choosing healthy patterns, these patients are rewarded with good health and well-being. However, change the way you eat and all hell breaks loose around you. I warn patients that they will very likely encounter unbridled animosity from family and friends when they change the way they eat. Suddenly you are the target. People do not like their comfort zones challenged. If you change your eating habits, it implies that *their* habits are unhealthy, and such a thought makes them uncomfortable.

14

FORCES BEYOND RULES

———— ·◆··◆·———

The soul's desire for spiritual lessons is a powerful force far beyond our understanding and any earthly rules. It is our only purpose for incarnating. We come to the earth plane as students, learning as our soul progresses on its chosen path . . .

Julie had been told her case was hopeless. She wanted to see me for an energy treatment to ensure that a planned medical procedure would go well. Her doctor in Hawaii was sending her to a large medical center in New York. There she would have a small pump inserted into her liver. After she returned to Hawaii, drugs would be put into the pump to introduce them into her liver. These drugs would circulate through her liver and then throughout her body. She interrupted her flight from Hawaii to stay in the Bay area for one day so that she could have an energy treatment before flying on to her destination. Because of these unusual circumstances, I agreed to see her on a day when I didn't have other patients scheduled.

As soon as Julie came into the office, I saw the dark, ominous energy of approaching death around her. I hated to see those particular ghostly, gray clouds at any time since it meant the person was headed down a path of self-destruction, but it was especially disconcerting to see them gathered around someone so young. Only in her early thirties, serious illness had already taken its toll. I wondered if her inner being might be ready to change course and avoid the fatal path she had chosen.

After my silent prayer, I ran energy, focusing on her unsuspecting liver, which had no inkling of the coming pump. After 10 minutes, her face changed from death's ghastly, gray mask to a beautiful, rosy hue. Her eyes sparkled. She laughed, jumped up and capered around my office in wide-eyed wonderment.

"What just happened?" she asked with amazement.

"God has healed you," I said.

"I know this is going to sound crazy, but can I run up and down your driveway?"

"Help yourself."

Julie ran out of the house and dashed down the long driveway. She returned, whooping and hollering. When this wasn't enough for her exuberance, she took off running around my two-acre field. I heard her shouts from the house. Luckily, Pescadero was out in the country so there weren't any close neighbors to wonder what was going on.

After several laps, Julie stopped. Never tiring of God's miracles, I was as excited and delighted as she was. Then I voiced my thoughts, "How wonderful, Julie. You can just turn around now and head back home to Hawaii where I see a long, healthy life ahead of you."

Julie frowned, "But I promised the doctors in New York that I'd let them put the pump in. I don't know *what* my doctor at home would say if I came back *without* it. It wouldn't feel right to just go home. I mean . . . after all . . . I've got to keep my word to my doctors."

"Well, for your own sake, you'd better make an exception this one time. I hate to say it, but you're crazy if you go through with this pump procedure."

Julie bit her lower lip and said, "I'm sorry you feel that way but the hospital paid for my flight to New York. I think it's some kind of experimental surgery. And it's just that . . . well, I just don't think it would be right not to show up now after I said I would. Besides, you said I'm healed. God's not going to take that away from me."

"No, you're right. God won't. But *you* can take it away from *yourself* by not listening to what I'm telling you." We argued back and forth until she left saying that she'd think about it. I was saddened to see in her energy that this pump implant was a done deal.

Julie stopped by again on her way back from New York to Hawaii.

She pulled up her blouse enough to show me the small tube protruding from her liver. It had been folded over and taped to her stomach. The drugs would be put into the pump by shooting them through this tube. For me it was—and still is—eerie to see anything not "of" the body made a part of the body. (In my opinion, always a disaster in the making.)

Julie said the doctors in New York hadn't put the drugs into the pump. She was carrying a carefully packed flask, which held the mystery drugs. Her doctor would administer these when she got back to Hawaii. In a flash of light, the Power revealed a vivid picture of Julie's grim future if she went through with this procedure. Knowing I had this one last chance to convince her not to go through with it, I said, "I'm glad you stopped by. I'm sure the pump is an amazing piece of modern technology, but how are you feeling?"

"Oh golly . . . never better. I feel like I'm bursting with energy, and I'm so happy. I feel like I love the whole world and the whole world loves me," she said, beaming happily.

"Julie, don't you want to keep that wonderful feeling?" I said gently.

"Of course. But nothing's ever going to make me feel anything but *wonderful* again." Certainty radiated from her smiling face.

Again I felt the pain of her bleak future if she started the drugs. My heart hurt when I saw the possibility of her life—now brimming with joy and vitality—fading away. My mouth went dry. I paused before I spoke, praying for the right words. "Julie, I want you to listen very carefully to the words I'm about to say to you. The Power has told me that within a minute of the drugs entering your liver, you will feel far worse than you have ever felt in your life. What you felt before can't begin to compare with the pain you will suffer. The angels say that you will call me after it's done. You will speak these words: 'Oh God, what have I done? God gave me the gift of healing and I turned my back on His gift.' Please, Julie, think about the magnificent gift of health that is yours . . . right here . . . right now. Don't throw it away by putting those drugs into the pump."

She pursed her lips and gave me a don't-rain-on-my-parade look. She laughed nervously and said she had to leave for the airport. Then she smiled and took my hand in both of hers, "Don't worry, Doctor Jim. I know I'll *never* be sick again, no matter *what*. Thank you for your help and God's healing." After she left, there was nothing more I could do except pray for her.

Two days later, Julie called me from the hospital in Hawaii just before the drugs were to be administered. She said, "I'm sorry that I have to go with the drugs." I replied, "I'm sorry too. Good luck with your choice." Then we hung up. I will always remain mystified as to why she made that last minute call. Was it to hear another plea not to do it? I was all out of pleas. Was it to get my blessing on the procedure? That was one thing I couldn't give.

When the phone rang ten minutes later, I knew it was Julie before I ever picked up the phone and heard her voice. She sobbed, "Oh God, what have I done? God gave me the gift of healing and I turned my back on His gift." It was word for word as the Power had given. She moaned and asked, "How could I have been so stupid? How could I have thrown away my healing? Why didn't I see my wonderful health was a gift from God and it was my job to keep it? Why couldn't I have just come home and lived the long, healthy life that you saw for me?"

I responded gently, "Don't worry, Julie. Karma had its way. But all things come together for good and out of this will come the highest good for your soul. I've been told you won't suffer much longer."

She asked softly, "Can you pray for me so that my passing will be easy and soon?"

"Of course," I answered. And I did. And it was.

What do any of us know about life and its purpose? We muddle our way through life until we have an experience that shocks us out of our unconscious state. Maybe we change our ways and maybe we don't—that decision is directed by our soul.

———— ·◆· ————

When I ask patients about their conditions or their lifestyle, I expect to hear the truth. Only truth lets us stand on firm ground and see the lay of the land . . .

A friend asked if I would help a woman in her early sixties who was renting an apartment in a large complex. Ann was in terrible pain and from all reports her continuous screams were alarming the neighbors. It wasn't hard to find her apartment; we could hear her screams echoing through the complex.

Ann's studio apartment was the kind of dingy place rented by those down on their luck, sparsely furnished and barren of cheer. When my friend introduced us, I was dismayed to see certain peculiar energies had set up camp in Ann's biofield. I recognized these murky shadows surrounding her; they meant a serious condition had been caused by unresolved emotional issues. While Ann tossed and turned on her bed, trying to get away from the pain, death waited impatiently to claim her. Since my friend told me that Ann had rented the apartment after being in the hospital, I asked Ann about her diagnosis.

Between screams muffled into her pillow, Ann said, "The doctors couldn't find any reason for my pain. I mean it's not cancer or anything like that." Although her assurance didn't mesh with what I was sensing, I began to run healing energy. After a few minutes, I felt soothing energy vibrations moving into the areas of her pain.

Ann took a deep breath, and her face and body relaxed. Once her energy settled, she stopped screaming. With the relief of pain she smiled and thanked me for coming. Ten minutes later, Ann fell asleep. My friend and I left quietly. The troubled waters had been calmed, and Ann's neighbors would get some sleep that night.

The second time I treated Ann I sensed aluminum strongly in her energy field. It rose up to fight the normal flow of healing. When I asked if she had any aluminum cookware, she was irate. *"I'm not stupid! As sick as I am, I'd never cook in aluminum!"* she yelled.

Glancing over at the pots and pans stacked to dry in the kitchen, all I saw was aluminum. "What about those pots and pans?" I asked.

"Those are *all* stainless steel," she said emphatically. "I got them when they were on sale and the package said stainless steel."

"Can I take a closer look?"

"Go ahead! See for yourself! It's all perfectly good stainless!" she hissed.

After I checked them, I informed her, "Well, the handles *are* stainless, but the pots and pans themselves are solid aluminum." Horrified, Ann told me she purchased the set on sale at a camping store because they were so light and easy to pack. She'd been cooking in them for years.

I saw Ann once a day. Although she improved and was out of pain, I could still feel the darkness around her associated with a fatal condition. However, each time I questioned her, she insisted she had no serious illness. We continued the energy work but finally progress came to a halt.

The fifth time I saw Ann, I decided to go deeper and weave my way around the walls she put up every time I treated her. In the inner-most recesses of her being, I found a hidden, horrifying, seething mass of Anger. Knowing the answer, I casually asked Ann if she was upset with anyone. The dam burst. With a venomous look, she launched into a long story of all the wrongs she had suffered from her family. As she told her tale of woe, her rage appeared like a sea of angry red flames around her bed. Now I knew why there were no family pictures on display.

When Ann finished testifying to all the wrongs done to her, I gently placed my hand on her arm and asked, "Do you think you would be willing to give up this anger and forgive them in order to be healed completely?"

"Never!"

Startled by her hatred, I stepped back. Her anger was a carefully constructed wall, designed and fortified over many years to protect her from the outside world. "Unless you can surrender your anger and open to forgiveness, your condition will not heal further. I'm afraid we've reached a plateau in the healing work and it's up to you now," I said.

Her body stiffened, "At least I can *count* on my anger. It's always with me, like a close friend I can rely on, which is more than I can say for my family. My anger is comforting and familiar. I *can't* give up my anger."

Wanting to show Ann that her only hope was to move past her an-ger, I went to see her again, but she continued the tirade of hatred toward her family. I saw that Ann was unable to help herself by releasing these past grievances. After this explosion of anger, I found the healing energy would no longer flow into her body. Instead, it bounced back into my hands so I had to stop the treatments.

Over the next few weeks, Ann's pain slowly returned. The owner of the building finally had to ask her to leave before she emptied the entire complex with her screams. After her son came to get her and took her to a hospital in the city, he called to thank me for trying to help his mother. He asked, "Did you know that my mother has terminal cancer. It's spread throughout her body."

"I thought as much, but your mother always denied that she had cancer when I saw her."

"Oh, she's been denying that anything's wrong with her for years."

Two months later, Ann's son called again to tell me that his mother had died. I felt certain that she continued clinging to her hatred right to the very end, as though it was a raft keeping her afloat on the ocean of life. Just as the cells of the body cannot dictate what foods are eaten, neither can they control what food for thought is offered to the mind, and *both* are equally important. If only Ann had realized that by allowing love and forgiveness to guide our lives, we can discover healing in every moment.

I can only hope that Ann learned her lesson before she crossed over and will return in another life with more compassion for herself and others. But her soul will make this decision and who can question the soul's wisdom in guiding our lives?

———•◆•———

It has always surprised me that a patient's belief as to whether or not I have healing powers doesn't seem to affect the outcome of the healing. And after a while, I stopped worrying whether patients had faith in healing or not. Too often I saw people—who were *sure* I couldn't help them—totally transformed by the power of healing and God's grace. Their energy shifted in the twinkling of an eye, and then they were gifted with enough faith and trust for a hundred patients.

While many patients think it's necessary to have faith, I couldn't care less as far as the healing goes. As for personal faith, it's a great blessing to have faith and trust in one's Creator. For without belief in a loving, compassionate Creator, humankind seems lost. Still, I have to report that on a few occasions, the patient's faith in my healing abilities was stronger than *mine* . . .

Suzanne Caygill, who wrote *Color, the Essence of You,* had been a patient for years when she called me from Palo Alto. She explained she was scheduled to give a color palette seminar the next day, but she was having so much heart pain that she was sure she couldn't drive to my office. I agreed to drive over to her hotel and treat her there.

Suzanne was a woman with a commanding presence. Whenever she entered a room, everyone knew it. She was tall and imposing with meticulously coiffured red hair that no other woman could have carried off. But Suzanne's famous flare was gone when she answered the door of her hotel room. She was so weak I had to help her back to her bed. I listened to her heart with my stethoscope, hoping to hear the comforting "lub-dub, lub-dub" of a heart functioning normally. Instead I heard an unsettling "swoosh-swoosh, swoosh-swoosh." Her heart was as bad as I had ever heard, and I've heard more than fifty years' worth. There was no valve closure at all. The valves were flapping in and out like swinging barroom doors that didn't meet in the middle.

Swallowing hard, I gave her the bad news and concluded by saying, "I think we'd better get you to the emergency room right now. I know one of the top cardiologists and you may need immediate surgery on those valves. I'll drive you over and then I can notify your friends and the seminar people what's happened to you."

However, she was adamant; she refused to go to the hospital and insisted that I run healing energy through her heart. "I'll be fine after your treatment and a good night's sleep," she insisted.

"Suzanne, you're crazy. You don't seem to realize how serious this is. You could die! We've got to get you to the hospital *immediately!*"

"*Absolutely not!* Don't even *talk* to me about it anymore. There's *no* way I'm going. Just run the energy. Where's your *faith?* I'll be fine. You've never failed me."

When she wouldn't reconsider, I ran energy until the healing angels told me the healing was complete. I left her the phone numbers of the hospital and the cardiologist in case she came to her senses or had any problems during the night. I left shaking my head at Suzanne's legendary determination.

The next day I was sweating bullets. I called the hospital first to see if Suzanne had been admitted during the night, but they had no patient by that name. Then I called her hotel. They said she could be reached over at Stanford Plaza where she was giving a color workshop.

All day long, I worried about her. Waiting until that evening, I drove to the hotel and knocked on her door. Relief swept over me when Suzanne opened it, looking her usual extraordinary and majestic self. When I asked to listen to her heart, I couldn't believe what I heard. A cheerful "lub-dub, lub-dub" greeted my stethoscope. The beat was as strong and steady as any 16-year-old's heart. It was God's miracle. Seeing my amazement, Suzanne smiled and said, "I told you I'd be fine after you ran energy on me."

To this day, I think it was Suzanne's faith in my healing abilities that got her well. The only faith *I* had on the previous night was in my driving ability to get her to the hospital for surgery. But once again, God was right in there pitching. Suzanne lived on and on for many years and whenever she asked me to listen to her heart, it was perfect.

———•◆•———

As I look back, I recall how many women came to my office with abdominal distress. It's common for women to have congestion and pain in their lower abdominal area, particularly after childbirth. The treatment is simple but it takes time to return the lymphatic system to a normal energy flow if their system is loaded with toxins. Some ladies had huge lymphatic nodes that felt like golf balls inside their distended abdomen. Their bodies had created these "garbage cans" to hold poisons, which were being stored in the body. In such cases, I always found it necessary to treat the low back before treating the abdomen.

Early in my practice, I discovered that the healing energy restored normal function in most abdominal conditions, including endometriosis. I found this out accidentally when lady patients became pregnant after their endometriosis had been healed. Some of the ladies were thrilled but others were extremely upset because they had counted on their pelvic condition as a permanent fertility block. However, suffering from this disease is one tough way to stop pregnancy. I clearly remember one lady who was tickled pink to have this condition removed . . .

For several summers my wife and I camped in Montana before making this state our home. On every trip, Andrea tried to get together with a gal pal she had worked with in San Francisco who was now living in Montana. But our plans to meet never worked out. I was anxious to meet her because whenever I commented on the beauty of any woman,

Andrea scoffed and told me that I would see a really beautiful woman when I got to meet her friend, Diana.

In the summer of 1992, we finally got together with her and I was forced to admit that Andrea was right. Diana was 36 and very lovely indeed. As we sat out on her deck overlooking the Big Fork River on a perfectly beautiful day in big sky country, the ladies caught up on their lives since leaving San Francisco. Andrea shared stories of our travels in the southwest, and Diana talked about her passion for cross-country skiing and summer kayaking. We were just getting up to leave, when Andrea said, "Gosh, Diana, it's wonderful to see you looking so healthy."

Diana exclaimed, *"Healthy?!?* I've been bleeding vaginally for three years. I'm scheduled for a total hysterectomy in a few days." She went on to express her sadness because she would never be able to have any children after the operation. Her only consolation was that she had been told she would never have been able to get pregnant anyway because of her endometriosis.

Andrea and I looked at each other for a few seconds and silently agreed to take the next step. Andrea quickly explained that I was a healer and asked if I could run energy that might help her body to heal. Surprisingly, Diana accepted this sudden turn of events, but said she had to leave in 15 minutes for an appointment.

After I finished running energy, I predicted that she would be pregnant within two weeks. When she told me this was impossible, I told her that God can do anything. I said she would have a little boy, the light of her life. To keep the healing energy on track, we took a whirlwind tour of her kitchen. We told her to get rid of her aluminum and nonstick cookware and to give up coffee. She agreed to do it all. After hugs all around, we parted.

Two weeks later, we were back in Washington state when we received a phone call from an excited Diana, "Boy, do you guys work fast. Twenty minutes after you left, the bleeding stopped completely. And guess what! I just found out that I'm pregnant!" Again, I said she would have a little boy, which she did. Her son is now a wonderful young man heading into his teenage years.

———— •◆• ————

As the years rolled by, my healing days were never routine. Every day I looked forward to new and interesting cases coming into the office. I learned to expect the unexpected and to enjoy God's wonderful sense of humor, often at my own expense . . .

One afternoon, a new patient came in, having been referred by a friend. Before I could say anything, she sized me up with narrowed eyes, and said, "I've heard you can see where a person's problem is without that person ever telling you where the pain is."

"Well, sometimes that's true. It depends on what God has in mind," I answered.

Opening her mouth to speak, she started to point to her right shoulder with her left forefinger. Suddenly she clamped both arms stiffly to her sides as though they were glued there and declared defiantly, *"Oh no!* I'm not going to tell *you* where my pain is. *You* tell *me!"*

Once she was situated comfortably on my treating table, I said solemnly, "You're having pain in your right shoulder."

She gasped and exclaimed, "My God, it's *true!* You just *know* what's wrong and where the pain is without a person saying anything at *all."*

Sure she was joking with me, I laughed, but when she did not laugh with me, I decided it was best to get on with the healing. Surprisingly, she spread my fame far and wide after this incident. Hopefully, because she left without any pain in her right shoulder, and not because I had proved my remarkable intuitive abilities.

My practice also taught me that God works in strange ways to teach us life's lessons . . .

There was one memorable morning when a peculiar headline in the local newspaper caught my attention. I didn't subscribe to the paper but a patient happened to leave that particular edition in my office. In bold letters, the headline read: *Local Woman Saved From Cremation Under Mysterious Circumstances.* I was intrigued. Nowhere in the article— and I studied it carefully—was there a clue as to the identity of the woman or a hint as to what these "mysterious" circumstances were.

I continued puzzling about this story until my first patient, a woman I had never treated before, came in. The newspaper story had so captured my imagination that I couldn't help mentioning my interest in it to my new patient. The lady turned several shades of red. Curious, I asked, "Do you know the woman in the story?"

She covered her face with her hands and said softly, "It's me."

My curiosity kicked into high gear. I'd hit pay dirt. "No *kidding*. What *happened?*" I asked.

She lowered her hands so that I could see her face once more. "I'll tell you but *only* if you promise not to tell anyone else for 10 years."

I quickly drew a cross over my heart with one finger and swore to keep the story to myself. Since over 40 years have passed, I'm on safe ground now. And her story is too intriguing to keep it to myself any longer. So here is her story as she told it to me that morning . . .

"It all started when I heard our alarm go off at 6:00 A.M. As usual, my husband, who was lying in bed beside me, didn't get up. I knew he'd be late for work again, but when I tried to tell him, no words came out of my mouth. I screamed as loud as I could but there was no sound. When I tried to move, I realized I was paralyzed. My eyes were staring straight up at the ceiling. I waited for this horrible feeling to pass. When it didn't, I started to panic."

"How awful," I said, pulling my chair closer.

She nodded and continued, "About this time my husband rolled over against me. He woke up and screamed. I must have been stone cold because he ran to the phone and called the doctor. Then I heard him tell the doctor he thought I was dead. All the time he was talking, I was screaming at the top of my lungs, but I guess it was only in my head. In reality, I couldn't make a sound. While I tried desperately to move, I lay as one dead. When the doctor finally arrived, he examined me, pronounced me dead and closed my eyes."

Her voice trembled as she went on, "After the doctor left, my husband called the local mortuary. I was taken to the mortuary where I was placed on a cold slab and covered with a sheet. Another doctor came in, pulled the sheet off my naked body and examined me for signs of life. He verified for the mortician that I was dead. Suddenly, I thought of my will, in which I had stipulated that I didn't want to be embalmed. I was to be kept in cold storage for three days and cremated on the fourth. You can imagine the thoughts that ran through my mind. In a few days, I would die in the fires of cremation unless something or someone could break the spell of my strange state of suspended animation.”

“You must have been terrified,” I said.

“Oh I *was!* On the third day, my family held a wake. You can’t imagine how horrifying it was to have someone dress me, make up my face, and put me in a coffin. I continued to scream: *I’m alive! I’m alive!* I screamed and screamed. But nothing came out of my mouth. It was like being in some gruesome, grade B horror movie, or a terrible nightmare that I couldn’t wake up from, but it was real.”

“I showed no signs of life at the wake. And believe me, I tried. But I heard everything going on in the room during the wake. I learned *exactly* what people thought of me. My husband was in shock and mourned me deeply. However, some people I supposed were dear friends gossiped about me and joked about my early passing since I’m only 31. Other people I barely knew said how much they’d miss me and how important I’d been in their lives because of things I’d done for them, things I’d forgotten long ago. I swear if everyone could hear what others really think of them, our lives would be totally different.”

“If they only *knew* what you *heard!*” I exclaimed.

“You’ve got *that* right,” she agreed. “On the fourth morning since my ‘death,’ I was totally exhausted from screaming. But just when I thought I couldn’t be more afraid, reality set in. In a few hours, I would be burned alive. I could already feel the flames licking at my body. My cremation was scheduled for 6:00 A.M. and I wondered desperately what time it was.”

“By this time I’d given up screaming as completely useless. Instead, I listened. Suddenly I heard the sharp click of the door to the cold room where I lay on my slab with a sheet over me. From conversations I’d overheard among the staff, I knew the teenage janitor arrived at 4:00 A.M. Only two hours left! Still, there was some small comfort in knowing a living being was in the room with me. But on this fateful morning, I heard more than one person. Female giggles echoed in the stillness of the morgue, and I realized that the janitor had brought along a friend.”

“What happened next?” I urged.

“Well, after further laughter and much discussion about how to proceed, the janitor and his girlfriend lifted the corpse off the slab next to mine, put it on the floor, and spread a blanket over the slab. The next thing I knew they were in the throes of a lively, passionate lovemaking session. I was shocked. In fact I was so damn furious at their disrespect of the dead—including me—that I sat up and shouted out, 'You little bastards!' For one brief moment, they stared at me—the newly risen dead—and I stared back at them—frozen in mid-passion—then they bolted from the room stark naked, running for their lives."

"Oh . . . I would have loved to have seen that!" I laughed.

She laughed too, "I understand the police saw them running down El Camino in the buff and picked them up. Naked and terrified, they told an unbelievable story of the dead coming to life. When the police accompanied them back to the mortuary, they found me wrapped in my sheet, wandering around in a daze. Thank God the newspapers didn't use my name or give any details about what happened."

"What an incredible story," I said. "You were going to die, but terror wasn't enough to wake you up from your sleep. Imagine. The horror of your situation didn't bring you back to consciousness. Only righteous indignation snapped you out of it. You owe your life to the amorous habits of those two teenagers."

My patient was silent for a minute and then said, "By golly, you're right. I hereby forgive them both for their sins." We smiled at each other briefly and then burst out laughing. We went on laughing until our sides hurt.

"So what do you think you learned from your experience?" I asked.

"My second chance at life gave me a first class opportunity to shift my friendships according to everything I heard at my wake. Not everyone gets to die, find out who their true friends are, and return to life. My new philosophy is to treat everyone better because we may never get a chance to know who our true friends are—until it's too late."

"Good for you. I think God must have really enjoyed your part in His Divine Comedy."

———•◆•———

Although healing sometimes feels like riding a dragon through the sky while eating sushi with chopsticks, I would not trade my healing life for any amount of money, power, or any other gift this material world has to offer. My fulfillment comes from surrendering to the Power as God heals those who are ready for their lives to change. My heart rejoices and I feel blessed to complete the healing contract as given by the Creator for each person in this dance of life.

Curious, I once asked my heavenly companions how many angels took part in the healing. Hearing their heavenly laughter, I imagined they numbered in the thousands. And then they revealed, *"Although we are many, all things are one thing. The oceans are many . . . we are many . . . still, we are One, even as individual drops of water merge in the ocean's vastness. The ego loves the dance of separation, but in truth, all are connected, woven together in the great tapestry of life."*

While healing has not always been an easy path, I am always in the best of company with angels who are closer than the beating of my own heart. Early in my career, I pondered, "Why me?" But with the passage of time and the opportunity to live a life of healing, I simply appreciated the gift and thought, "Why not me?" My years of healing have clearly shown me what God and Mother Nature can do when invited into the picture.

Having seen thousands of miracles in my lifetime, I can only be amazed by the splendor of God's loving concern when He blesses His children with healing. Seeing people released from the bondage of pain— whether physical or emotional—through God's grace, is a constant miracle in my life. I feel joy in the deepest part of my soul to see people make the changes that bring the delight of living back to them. When the healing angels instructed me to become a minister, I was not surprised since healing is always a deeply spiritual experience. I was ordained as a minister on October 18, 1990.

I could go on for days about the beautiful gift of healing and the way of the healer. That any gift from God would have a heavy aspect may surprise some people. However, everything in life has a price tag. To be married has a price tag. To be single has a price tag. Everything has its price. Sometimes I ponder why the Creator loaded me up with healing, but kept the control of that healing in His hands. I have the privilege of acting the part of "Healer" as one would play a part in a play. But while I move around the stage of life in my minor role, I never forget that the Creator directs the play from beginning to end.

I searched the world over to find greater healing. But in the end, I returned home to my own heart where God's song is familiar. I hear it when I listen in the silence of the moment. To stop living my life of healing would be like standing under Niagara Falls and telling the thundering torrent to stop. My heart sings the song I was born for when I run the healing energy.

Following my heart's desire to become a sea of wisdom as the Old Man was before me, I have walked the inner path, happy to receive bits of wisdom from time to time as they drift by. Now in my seventies, I feel I've learned so very little of what there is to know. When I think of how much there is still to learn and experience in life, I realize that—no matter how long I live—I will never grasp even a fraction of this world's knowledge. This is one of the reasons I believe in reincarnation. How could one ever learn enough in one lifetime?

And when this journey ends and I cross over, you will not find me sitting at the side of the road, revving the motor and waiting for the light to change. I plan to find the next gear and move on down the freeway of my new life. I will launch into God's starry heavens, and find my way home once more.

15

IN THEIR OWN WORDS

·••◆·

Many of my patients have been kind enough to share their healing stories with me over the years. I wanted to include a few of these to allow the reader a glimpse into healing from the patient's point of view. I am grateful for their contributions to this book. We have all come to the earth plane to love and help each other. Within these accounts is the expression of that love and the intent of these patients to help others by sharing their healing stories.

Healing, whether of self or others, is a grand mission. I hope these stories encourage all healers and patients in their spiritual quest for divine healing. May these narratives bring hope to all those who are searching. You *can* be healed. Let healing flow through every cell in your body as you read these stories. Enjoy!

·◆·

MY MEETING WITH JIM MACKIMMIE
Dr. June d'Estelle, Ph.D., author of *The Illuminated Mind*

My introduction to Jim MacKimmie was one of the most fortuitous events of my life! Only because of that meeting, am I here today.

Suzanne Caygill, the world's leading authority on color, called me one day many years ago, asking if I would drive her to San Carlos, since her car was in the garage, leaving her without transportation. She was feeling ill, and wished to see Dr. James MacKimmie, a chiropractor and spiritual healer who always came to her rescue when she was in need of healing. She suggested that I might wish to have a consultation also, since I was coping with severe allergies. I was glad to take Suzanne, but was dubious of Dr. MacKimmie's ability to help me. I was married to a medical doctor at that time, was immersed in traditional medicine and its organizations, had never heard of spiritual healers, and had been treated (unsuccessfully) by the country's leading allergists.

In addition, the allergies, while debilitating, were of secondary concern to me, for I had another much more serious health problem, which was known only to my husband, my parents, and my consulting physicians. I was being treated by the head of orthopedics at the University of California Medical School in San Francisco for bone cancer. My whole left shoulder blade was so riddled with lesions that it resembled a piece of porous Swiss cheese. No treatment had been given, for the medical school was referring me to Mayo Brothers to consult a specialist in this rare form of cancer. His first step would be to surgically remove the scapula, along with my left arm. The U.C. orthopedist warned me that I would not be coming back, since this particular cancer was always rapidly fatal, so I should plan accordingly. This was a particularly distressing prognosis, not only for me, but for my family, for I was the mother of seven young children.

I entered Dr. MacKimmie's treatment room with itches, rashes, sniffles, sneezes and wheezes, carrying my ever-present box of facial tissues. When I left a half hour later, my allergic symptoms were gone, never to return. I hadn't mentioned my cancer, since I had discussed this situation only with my specialist physicians, and it didn't occur to me that this unknown chiropractor might have any new opinions.

However, I was so profoundly impressed with the alleviation of my allergies, that a week later I brought my daughter, Mary, to see Dr. MacKimmie, for Mary was also beset with allergies. I sat quietly to the side while Mary was on the treatment table. When Dr. MacKimmie requested her birth date, which was in April, he asked if she ever had headaches. To her reply that she had frequent, painful headaches, he commented that Aries often had headaches when they were run-down. I asked him what symptoms Geminis (my sign) had when they were run-down. He replied that Geminis tended to have problems with their arms, hands, and shoulders! I remarked, "Dr. MacKimmie, nobody ever has anything seriously wrong with shoulders, do they?" He answered, "You do, but don't worry about it. In a month you will be well."

When I went to San Francisco the next week to have final X-rays taken before leaving for the Mayo Brothers Clinic, the orthopedist gave a shout of excitement, exclaiming, "June, come look! Something amazing is showing on the X-rays!"

Even I, with my untrained eyes, could see that the holes, or lesions, were half the size of those photographed two weeks previously! Not only that, but new bone growth was filling in all the cavities!

"I have never seen anything like this," marveled the doctor. "We will postpone the surgery and see what develops." Two weeks, later, the X-rays showed no signs of cancer!

"What did you do?" asked the doctor. "We haven't given you any treatment. I have never heard of this virulent form of cancer simply disappearing! In fact all the instances we have known about have invariably resulted in fatalities."

"I didn't do anything," I replied. "Oh, I did go to see a spiritual healer."

"You go back to that spiritual healer and tell him that he saved your life," instructed the doctor. "That is the only possible explanation. It is an absolute miracle, and you are the most fortunate person I have ever known."

When I walked into Dr. MacKimmie's office a few days later, he greeted me with, "How is your shoulder?"

"You knew all along that I had bone cancer?" I asked.

"Oh sure," he replied. "It's healed, isn't it? I told you that you would be well within a month."

Then I asked the most important question I could have asked, "Dr. MacKimmie, what caused my bone cancer?" His reply instituted a major turning point in my life, altering my eating habits completely and indirectly influencing countless other people.

"Your underlying problem is nutritional," he replied. "You are a coffeeholic and a chocoholic. Right now, your body is absolutely saturated with chocolate and coffee. Both are extremely toxic for you. Your father has liver problems, and you have inherited that tendency. At this very moment, your liver function is down 25% because of the chocolate in your system. In addition, you cannot tolerate any dairy products except butter, nor can you handle refined sugars or grains."

"You also have severe aluminum poisoning from cooking in aluminum, and using aluminum products such as aluminum foil. Go home and throw out everything aluminum in your kitchen, never drink another drop of coffee, avoid dairy products, chocolate and refined foods, and you should be fine."

I was stunned, for he was absolutely correct. My dad did have liver problems. I was drinking coffee around the clock, even traveling regularly to Carmel to a coffee importer, where I bought special gourmet roasts and grinds. Many of my favorite recipes included coffee. He was right also about my addiction to chocolate. During the current Christmas season, I had just consumed a whole five-pound box of fine chocolates, a gift from my husband's office staff who insisted it was for me alone. And all my cooking utensils were of heavy aluminum. I took pride in always having available freshly baked cookies, cakes and other desserts rich with sugar, chocolate, dairy products and refined grains.

I had been convinced that I was feeding my family a healthful menu, as I scrupulously followed the medical guidelines of the time. I carefully balanced starches, proteins, fruits and vegetables, and made sure we used lots of dairy products. No authorities, to my knowledge, had voiced any objections to unlimited use of sugars, processed or refined foods. Until Dr. MacKimmie's recommendations, I had no idea our way of eating was harmful.

Deeply grateful, and shaken with the knowledge that I had just had a miraculous reprieve from certain death, I went home and did exactly what Dr. MacKimmie advised. I discarded all my aluminum cooking ware, bought stainless steel, cast-iron and Pyrex utensils. I substituted whole grain products for refined grains, raw sugar for refined sugar, discontinued all dairy products, chocolate and processed foods, and followed his dietary recommendations precisely. Coffee became forever a mere memory of the past.

I was so saturated with caffeine that I was in a stupor for almost two weeks. If I had consulted Dr. MacKimmie further, he would have advised me to use caffeinated tea to taper off coffee, and to add vitamin supplements to assist in cleansing my system of toxins. Nevertheless, I stayed with the regime, despite falling asleep at the most awkward times. I reaped a marvelous reward. One sunny morning two weeks later, I awoke to fleecy clouds, singing birds and a wonderful sense of well-being that I hadn't felt since I was a child. For the first time in years, my body was cleared of destructive toxins, and was in a state of homeostasis, or healthy balance. It was the most incredible, joyous feeling imaginable.

That sense of inner harmony and well-being has stayed with me ever since, too precious to jeopardize for indulgence in the appetites of the moment. Whenever I do occasionally succumb to holiday hospitality or tempting tidbits when away from home, the resultant discomfort and mental fuzziness quickly bring me right back to the wholesome, totally satisfying diet and lifestyle recommended to me by Dr. MacKimmie so long ago.

Since that time, I have recommended to my students in the workshops I teach that they schedule a consultation with Dr. MacKimmie for any health problems they may have. Over the years, many hundreds have sought his advice. If they faithfully follow that advice, an amazing percentage of them are completely healed of physical, mental, emotional and seemingly incurable problems.

Equally important as his incredibly powerful healing work, is the spiritual counseling and wisdom this gifted man shares with us. Many of us call upon his inspired insights and caring to help guide us through the turmoil of our lives. He walks closely and intimately with the Divine, bringing the highest teachings to humanity with clarity, authority, and his own personal whimsical humor. He truly is the beloved spiritual mentor for hosts of us. I perhaps feel more deeply blessed than others to know him, for not only has he lightened my life with his love and counseling and healing, but he and his close partner, God, actually returned that life to me.

————— • ◆ • —————

CONNECTING THE DOTS
Dolora Deal, co-author of *Incidents Beyond Coincidence*

Healing comes in many forms. You don't have to have a devastating physical disease to need healing on other levels. And I fell into this category. It wasn't even my idea to go see Dr. MacKimmie. My husband, Steve, was the one who wanted to see him. That in itself was unusual. Steve didn't believe in many of the things I had explored while seeking emotional and spiritual fulfillment. However, in the last three years he had been plagued with a physical ailment. Seeking help through conventional medicine, he had been on antibiotics for a year and a half. Each time he went off the antibiotics, he experienced a flare-up in his condition. Not choosing to be on antibiotics for the rest of his life, he started exploring herbal treatments, diet changes and exercise programs to heal his body.

Every year our hometown of Sun Valley, Idaho holds a Wellness Festival in May. I've been a guest speaker at this conference since its early days. In my talks, I communicate how Life is a Gift, The Purpose is Joy. I was speaking again in 2002, scheduled across from Caroline Sutherland, a medical intuitive. I had wanted to hear her lecture but due to scheduling problems that was impossible. When I asked my husband if he would be interested in hearing what she had to say, he decided to attend her lecture.

Steve arrived home from the lecture with a flyer about the healing ability of Dr. James MacKimmie. He said he felt drawn to Dr. MacKimmie and would like to see him. I was shocked that he really wanted to take this step. I jumped at the opportunity to make it happen. Besides, it sounded like a great adventure.

I called Dr. MacKimmie's number in Montana on June 1. "Dr. MacKimmie's," Andrea answered, "How may I help you?" I explained to Andrea who I was and said we wanted to schedule two appointments. Andrea said Dr. MacKimme was going to be at a radon health mine outside of Butte, Montana and could see us there in July. The drive would only take five hours from Sun Valley so we decided to book appointments on July 8 at 11:00 A.M. and 11:30 A.M.

We began our journey with no expectation of what was to come but with great anticipation. I was looking forward to the meeting because I had felt a spiritual connection with the MacKimmies when I talked with them on the phone. I had a feeling of trust. They were not strangers although we had never met.

The weather was lovely as we drove into Montana. We arrived at the Merry Window Health Mine on July 7. I was just walking into the office to register when I heard the MacKimmies ask the manager, "Have the Deals checked in yet?" I answered, "No, but we're ready to." The connection was instantaneous and we all agreed to meet later.

Saturday night action in downtown Basin, Montana is mighty slow, but we found a good restaurant and had dinner. Then we went back to our motel room to settle down with a couple of good books. At 7 P.M. the MacKimmies arrived at our door along with Dr. June d'Estelle and her daughter Carole. We were going through the initial getting-to-know-each-other conversations when I asked, "June, how did you meet Dr. MacKimmie?" She told me her amazing story and I was in awe.

Now it's impossible for Dr. MacKimmie to be in the same room with you and not see the imbalances in your energy field. He kept looking in my direction. Finally, he said, "Let's go into the other room. I need to do some work on you."

My appointment wasn't until the next day, but I was interested and open so I followed him into the next room. He started checking my energy fields by touching different areas of my body with gentle pressure. Then he started telling me my most hidden thoughts. Thoughts I had never shared with anyone. "How could he know that about me?" I wondered.

I immediately saw there was no way to hide anything from him so I just relaxed and allowed myself to be open and receive the energy he was flowing to me. I asked him about the sexual abuse I had experienced as a three-year-old. Was it real? He told me it was real or the intent had been so strong that I had experienced it as real on some level. It wasn't just a bad dream. He put his hand on my lower abdomen over my missing womb. (I'd had a hysterectomy while I was pregnant at the age of thirty-five.) He touched my lower rib cage and said, "So you don't burn out." "What did that mean?" I asked myself. Now I believe it referred to the increase of kundalini energy I was about to experience. Dr. MacKimmie worked on me for about 15 minutes that evening. Then he gave me a big hug and said, "See you tomorrow." Sleep was not something that came easily that night.

Early the next morning, we all met at the mine for radon treatments. Dr. MacKimmie said to me, "You held the connection all night, didn't you?" I answered, "Yes." But I wondered how he knew. When eleven o'clock came, Steve went for his appointment and came out feeling lighter as though something had shifted for him. (Steve has not had a problem since.) When I went in, Dr. MacKimmie picked up where he had left off with me the night before. He continued using the energy to heal my emotions and spirit.

Before my session with Dr. MacKimmie, I had always had a deep longing within me to go home, my spiritual home. In times of solitude, I would sob and plead with God to please take me home. I wasn't sure where home was, but I knew it wasn't here on this planet. This ache existed in me as if a part of myself was completely missing and I didn't know where to find it. Finding this missing part of my emotions or my spirit has been a driving force all of my life. I had been searching for decades, wanting to feel whole. My healing with Dr. MacKimmie shifted me into a vibrational level that healed the connection with that part of myself that I had been missing for lifetimes.

It has been almost two years now since that first healing with Jim. I have to tell you I don't have any missing parts. I feel whole. I no longer look at the stars seeking a missing part of myself. I no longer cry in anguish for God to take me home. All my dots are connected. I am whole and joyful in my life. I will stay in this place and do my best to bring joy. Thank you Jim for healing, and for removing my pain and filling in the missing parts. Love, Dolora

———— • • ————

LIFE'S ENDLESS ADVENTURE
    Josette DePendragon

I first met Dr. James MacKimmie in 1963 shortly before the Kennedy assassination. When he foretold this assassination would take place, I found it difficult to take his prediction seriously! After it took place, he warned that a massive earthquake would take place in Alaska in the next few months. On March 28, 1964, Alaska had the largest quake in their history, 9.2 on the Richter scale. Maybe he could see into the future after all.

Then I moved 200 miles away from the doctor to Morro Bay. An unhappy divorce left me feeling very insecure. I called Dr. MacKimmie in great distress. He told me to sit down and keep holding the phone for five minutes by the clock. In spite of my "but . . . but . . . but," he hung up. A massive jolt of non-electrical energy immediately surged out of the phone and down my arm. The energy flowing through me dissolved my physical and emotional distress! From that point on whenever I would call out mentally to Jim the room would be flooded with a particular scent and I would be filled with well-being, peace and joy!

Perhaps the most startling experience came about in the following manner. When I was 11, I had a very vivid dream of running frantically through convoluted underground passages while being chased by an angry mob. Seeing a bright light in the distance, I raced towards it and soon found myself in bright sunshine, next to a natural pool, which in turn was very near the ocean. There were four Greek columns behind the pool and a long beach stretched off to my right, ending in a headland. A boy of my age was playing with a gold colored ball. We started to throw it back and forth until it fell into the pool. I dived in after it but when I broke to the surface I found I was holding a skull. I woke up in shock! I never forgot this dream.

In the nineties I took a trip to Cancun. When I sat down at the picture window of the hotel's restaurant and looked out, there was the pool (manmade) with the four columns behind it, a beach stretching off to my right with a headland in the distance but now covered in condominiums! The memory of the skull returned and I felt a chill. Upon returning to Mount Shasta I became quite ill. My energy receded more each day. Mentally I called out to Jim, asking him where he was and telling him please, I could sure use some help right NOW.

The next morning the phone rang. It was Jim saying he and Andrea had just arrived in Mt. Shasta and were on their way over to my place! When I opened the door, he took one look and asked me what the heck I had been doing to myself and did I know that I was DYING? He promptly started treating me, which he continued to do for several days and in no time I was back on my feet feeling wonderful.

I believe that our thinking, feeling and doing aspects tend to get unbalanced. Whenever this happened to me, I turned to Jim for help. Quickly and without fail, he restored my body and my spirit for another go at the endless adventure we experience as LIFE!

Thank you Jim for your unconditional and unfailing help!

CHESTER'S EYE SURGERY
     Dr. June d'Estelle, Ph.D.

     Our family was very worried. At the Eye Clinic in San Francisco, my dad, Chester, had been diagnosed with a large tumor behind his right eye. All of the tests had been taken the day before, and he was scheduled for surgical removal of the tumor the next day. We all knew that the problem could be serious, including the fact that a condition with one eye could cause the other eye to react the same way in sympathy.

     I had volunteered to drive him to San Francisco from Watsonville to check him into the hospital in preparation for the surgery the following day. I suggested we drive up the coast from Santa Cruz, a beautiful drive along the ocean, instead of coping with freeway traffic. I also had a sneaky plan in mind, for Dr. MacKimmie's office was in Half Moon Bay right along our route.

     Most of my family has been fully supportive of my involvement with metaphysics and holistic medicine, but a couple of family members were so dedicated to traditional medicine that they looked askance at anything which deviated from its dictates. My dad had listened to their viewpoints, so questioned some of my less than orthodox activities.

     When we reached Half Moon Bay, I casually mentioned that I would like to stop for a few minutes to have a consultation with Dr. MacKimmie, if he wouldn't mind waiting. Dad was agreeable, and started to relax in the car as I stepped out in front of the office.

     "It is so cold out here," I remarked. "Why don't you wait inside in the warm waiting room?" This seemed sensible, so Dad accompanied me inside and soon became engrossed in a magazine.

     When I had my session with Dr. MacKimmie, I told him of the situation with my dad, and asked if he thought he could help him to go through the surgery more comfortably. I also explained Dad's skepticism about non-traditional healing, so asked if we could manage this indirectly.

     "Sure," said Jim. "We will run a little energy, which should help."

     As I left the treatment room, Dr. MacKimmie stood in the doorway, turned to my dad and said, "You're next. Come on in."

     Dad looked around startled, and said, "You mean me?"

"Yes, we'll just give you a little extra energy and charge your batteries to help you while you are in the hospital," said Jim. "It will only take a minute and might make you feel better."

Dad gave a sheepish grin, scratched his head, and followed Jim into the office. When he came out 15 minutes later, Dad was delighted, for he actually did seem to feel calmer and more energized. He thought Dr. MacKimmie was a most interesting, very wise man. He had enjoyed the stories Jim told while Dad relaxed on the table, unaware that Jim was quietly directing powerful healing energy to him while they visited.

My sister, Marilyn, a registered nurse, arrived at the hospital in San Francisco just as we did. We helped with the ritual of getting Dad checked in as a patient, then Marilyn and I waited together as the staff ran final tests in preparation for early morning surgery. I told her about the little game Jim and I had played on Dad, and Dad's good-natured acceptance in going along with the fun. Marilyn appreciated Jim's gift of healing energy, and knew it would help with the stressful ordeal the next day.

The tests seemed to be taking an inordinately long time, and Marilyn became more and more concerned. "What could they be finding wrong?" she asked. Eventually a doctor came out to explain the delay.

"We are totally confused," he stated. Turning to Marilyn, he continued. "Here are the pictures and the results of the tests we ran yesterday. See the large tumor and its hazardous location . . . You can see why we recommended immediate surgery." Marilyn nodded in agreement, sharing his sense of urgency.

"Now look at the results of today's tests." said the doctor. "We were so shocked that we ran the whole battery again. We can't figure out what happened! There is no question of errors in either set of tests, but look at the results!" All of us could see that there was no tumor in the second set of images!

"It looks as if the tumor either exploded or evaporated," puzzled the doctor. "Here, you can barely see the remains of the stem where the tumor was anchored, but the growth itself has simply vanished! The whole hospital staff has been in consultation about this, and none of us has the faintest notion what occurred. None of us has ever seen anything like it! We will be writing this up for the literature, but all we can say is that it is a miracle of some kind. You might as well take your Dad home, because we won't be doing any surgery tomorrow."

Marilyn knew what I had only suspected, that surgery itself would have been a serious drain on the vitality of a man in his eighties. She had known all along that the nature of the problem could have resulted in blindness in one or both eyes, in painful and extended series of therapies, in various other complications or in actual loss of his life.

As the doctor walked away with an expression of bewilderment on his face, Marilyn and I looked at each other in awe and dawning recognition of what actually had occurred. With an overwhelming sense of joy and gratitude, we acknowledged that God and Dr. MacKimmie working together were responsible for the incredible miracle which had taken place in those few minutes of "charging Dad's batteries."

As we drove home, Dad was equally as bemused as we were, hardly able to grasp the beautiful reprieve which had been given to him. Every time any of our family speaks or thinks of the miraculous event, we are filled with humble thankfulness that Dr. MacKimmie and his partner, God, are part of our lives.

————•◆•————

WHEN THE STUDENT IS READY, THE TEACHER APPEARS
Jeanie Lawerence

By the time I got to Dr. MacKimmie in my mid-twenties, my body had just about given up on me and my spirit was not in great shape either. In the year prior to being referred to Dr. MacKimmie, I had undergone two major abdominal surgeries to remove ovarian cysts. The surgeries were extremely painful and frightening. It took months to recover from each of them. In a follow-up visit to the gynecologist, he discovered that I had yet another grapefruit-sized cyst on my right ovary, the badly scarred site of the first surgery.

I felt terrified, hopeless, and doomed to a third major operation. I asked the gynecologist for some time to deal with this information and he gave me a stay for a maximum of three weeks before going under the knife again. This is where the grand and glorious Dr. MacKimmie enters my story.

A friend told me about Dr. MacKimmie who at that time resided in a small coastal town on the Northern California coast. I made the trek to his office, sixty miles from my home, for a "treatment." At that point, I had no idea what a treatment was nor did I know what to expect from this mysterious sojourn. After waiting for some time amidst a room filled with other patients, I met Dr. MacKimmie. His treatment room was warm, quiet, and calm - a reflection of him. I explained my dramatic life situation to him and he continued with the treatment in a very nonchalant manner. He was completely confident that I would not need surgery again and he outlined a few simple tasks for me to do at home between treatments, not the least of which was to have faith in The Power and to live life just one day at a time.

Dr. MacKimmie applied castor oil to the area above the cyst and held his hands over my body creating a tingling sensation that streamed from the bottom of my feet to the top of my head. These treatments were brief and pleasant but had an impact far beyond my greatest hopes. After a few short weeks of treatments, I returned to the gynecologist for an assessment of the large cyst. The doctor examined me and sat back into his chair before saying a word. I looked at him and he exclaimed, "It's gone, there is nothing there." I was as elated as he was shocked. I walked out of that office and into freedom, the freedom to dictate what would and would not be done to my own body.

When I called Dr. MacKimmie's office with the thrilling news, his response was, "Did she ever doubt me?" I can assure you, I have never doubted him since.

———— • ◆ • ————

JOY'S STORY
Helen Wainess

It all began in May, when Joy started to complain that her foot hurt. I was driving her back and forth to Portola School. As soon as she got in the car, she would take off her shoe and say she could hardly walk on her foot. I would scold her and tell her it was because she wore sloppy moccasins and her feet had no support.

She was very tired all the time and as soon as she got home from school would climb into bed and rest and watch TV. She kept saying to me, "Something is very wrong with my foot." I would say, "Oh, Joy, if I take you to a doctor what will they *do?* We'll just start in on a big thing. Just rise above it."

On the Saturday before Mother's Day we went down to Saks. Joy bought me an orange nightgown. She was very, very worn out from shopping. The next Tuesday she went to school. Mr. D., her P.E. teacher made her jump rope on her foot 51 times. She was too afraid of him to tell him it hurt. The next day she couldn't walk and her right big toe was red, swollen and throbbing with pain. I figured she had broken a small bone somewhere, so I kept her out of school on Thursday and drove to the Palo Alto Medical Clinic. I told the girl at the desk I wanted to see a doctor who could have a foot x-rayed.

We were sent to Dr. C., who looked at the toe, then sent us to x-ray. When we returned to him, he said no bones were broken. So I said, "Well, what's the matter with her foot then?" He asked us a lot of questions. He said it looked like gout to him, and we should see a gout specialist. There was only one in the clinic and he was busy. He said he'd try to get an appointment for Joy and to have her stay off her foot entirely. Joy went to the lab to give samples of blood and urine. By this time, her foot was one big ache. We got crutches for Joy and she went to school on them.

On May 28, Dr. K., the specialist, saw her. He said it looked like gout, but it was very rare for a small girl to have it. He sent her to be completely x-rayed for osteoporosis, a bone disease. Then he gave her two shots of ACTH. He told us to put her in bed for a week and pack the foot in ice—over , under and around it. We did this, and it was only while it was frozen that she could stand the pain. After two days, the expected sensational improvement did not occur. So he gave her a dose of Butazolidin. We discovered later that this was the drug given to the horse, Dancer's Image, for sore legs, which caused a scandal at the Kentucky Derby. By this time, I felt that we'd do just as well taking Joy to a vet.

On June 4, we saw Dr. K. again, and he had us take more x-rays. He said if Joy were his daughter he would send her to the Mayo Clinic. He didn't know what to do with her, so he sent her on to an orthopedic man, Dr. C.

On June 7, we saw Dr. C., who without much ado shot a tremendous dose of cortisone right into the sorest part of Joy's toe. Joy screamed and yelled and we had to hold her down on the table. Then he gave us aspirin and codeine pills for the pain.

Joy was in such excruciating agony that on the way home I stopped and bought her an expensive monkey, named Casanova, she had wanted and I had said I could not afford. I felt so guilty because I had allowed that doctor to torture her.

Over the weekend the pills drove her practically out of her mind. Her eyes rolled up into her head. She fainted and was terribly sick. On my own, I stopped the pills. When I called Dr. C., he was surprised that she would get such a reaction. She was truly in agony from this experiment. We didn't know what to do next. All this time she was visiting the lab periodically giving more samples of blood. One doctor thought she might have tendonitis and that an operation might help. Another suggested putting her toe in a cast.

On July 8, we were sent to Dr. F., an endocrinologist. His personality was even more unpleasant than the others and he was no help at all. He made out a lab slip for still more tests. While we were waiting outside his office, we stared at a big oil painting of a torn window shade with a dead rat hanging from the shade pull. Suddenly it did something to me. I said to Joy, "This is it. No more tests. No more stupid doctors." So we went home and didn't go to the lab.

I decided to really clean house. I worked like a dog and then I sat down and said, "Now the house is so clean that Alice will come to see me." Alice was one of our dear Ventura neighbors and the best housekeeper I knew. I had not seen her in a year.

William, my son, was posing for me as I drew his portrait. He had been sitting for only a half hour when the bell rang. It was Alice and Hal. We laughed a lot about our ESP and enjoyed their visit. Alice suggested that we try a pail of cold and a pail of hot water and stick Joy's foot in each one briefly. She said it helped athletes when they were injured.

Sometime after Alice and Hal left, I said to Joy, "Perhaps we had better ask the Ouija board what to do about your foot. It will probably help as much as the doctors."

Joy had wanted a Ouija board for Christmas but had never really used it. So we got it out and right away there was action. The speaker said his name was Sirge Guhrub and he had lived in Persia 507 years ago.

We asked him to tell us what color our dresses were. He got it right. Then he said, "Flow hot water." We asked if we should do what Alice suggested and he said, "Yes." We asked if he knew what Joy's favorite animal was and he said, "Monkey." He volunteered that his was a snake. Then he said, "Quit Now Spirit." That was all we could get.

The next day, July 9, we asked for a message. The board spelled out: "Get Joy bunk beds. Go down store today sale. Go to sale. For Joy."

We said we couldn't understand how bunk beds would help Joy. The answer was: "Comfortable. Make Joy better. Please I beg new bed. Get the beds for Joy."

Later that day we tried again. The message came: "We want Joy to get better. Buy beds now. Take sage advice. Cure Joy."

July 10, Joy and I searched through all the papers to see if any bunk beds were advertised. Our little local paper, *The Town Crier*, had some advertised at a second-hand store, called Furniture Faire, for $29.95.

We went to the board and asked if we should get the beds. It said, "Get bunk beds for Joy please. Bunk beds needed for Joy for me go get beds now." We asked, "Shall we get beds at Furniture Faire today?" The answer was: "Yes."

We phoned Joy's Dad and he thought that we were a little nuts. He said go ahead and buy them if you want. Joy and I drove down to Furniture Faire. We asked the proprietor where the $29.95 bunk beds were. He showed us. We went in the corner and looked at the beds and then looked at each other. We didn't know what to do. He came over and asked, "Is this what you want?"

I said, "I don't know."

"Are you having company?"

"I don't know."

"Do you *need* bunk beds?"

"I don't know." Then I blurted out, "You wouldn't believe why we're here if I told you."

He replied very calmly, "Oh yes, I believe *anything*."

So I said, "We were sent here by the Ouija board to buy bunk beds." He didn't appear surprised.

"Yes, you were sent here so I could help you. That little girl is a channel." Then he looked appraisingly at Joy on crutches with her foot all bandaged and asked, "What's the matter with her?" I said, "We don't know." He nodded, "I know, you've been to all the doctors and no one can help you." He wrote something on his card and gave the card to me. He said, "Here is the name of a doctor. Go to him and ask for healing. He will help Joy."

I wondered, "What do we do about the beds?" He said, "That was how you got to me. Forget them." We thanked him, went home and called Joy's Dad. He still thought we were going crazy.

We went to the board again. We said, "We have been to Furniture Faire and the man there told us about a healer. Can you tell us the name of this doctor?" It spelled out the doctor's name. We asked, "Are we supposed to buy the beds or has this served its purpose now that we have met this man?" They replied that we didn't have to buy the beds now.

"Shall we make an appointment to see this doctor?"

"Yes."

"Will he help Joy?"

"Yes, he is helping us to help Joy."

For several days I waited before I called the doctor. It all seemed too fantastic and ridiculous. Finally one morning Jerry, my husband, was talking at breakfast about our upcoming vacation. He said we couldn't go anywhere with a small girl on crutches who needed an ice bag on her foot day and night. Then I figured, what have we got to lose, and in desperation phoned for an appointment.

On July 17, off we went, feeling a little silly and a little scared about the whole thing. We had never even been to a chiropractor before and thought he might break Joy in two!

We found a very pleasant lady receptionist who was a welcome change from the picture of the dead rat in the other doctor's office. While we waited, we told her about all the terrible times Joy had been having with her toe and how all the important doctors couldn't help her. She just smiled and said, "Don't worry, Dr. MacKimmie will help you."

Finally we were inside. We told how we happened to come to him, feeling a little embarrassed. He accepted our story in a matter-of-fact manner. Joy got up on the table. He did a few things to her. Then he said, "Put your foot on the floor now, Joy."

"I can't."

"Yes, you can, Joy. Walk to your mother."

"I can't."

"Walk to your mother, Joy."

So Joy put her foot down and walked. She put away her bandage and her crutches and just walked. We drove down to Menlo Park to her friend's house. She tore in the house shouting, "I'm walking . . . I'm walking." And she was. And she is. And this whole story is the absolute truth.

We returned to Furniture Faire. Joy walked in. We said, "See . . . she's walking!" He replied, "Yes, I told you he'd help her."

I asked, "How can we ever thank you for this?" He said, "Forget it."

We went back to the board. We said, "Thank you for helping Joy to find the doctor." The board said, "Forget it. Forget it."

But we never can.

———•◆•———

FIRST LOVE
Dr. June d'Estelle, Ph.D.

My dear friend, Jed, was under a lot of stress. He was carrying a heavy load his first semester in college, he was in the first stages of flu, and he had just broken up with his girlfriend. I knew that Jed was deeply in love with Pat. They were discussing marriage, had opened a joint bank account, and were driving together to college each day in Jed's car. When Jed was in class, Pat used his car for errands.

One morning I decided to stop by Jed's apartment on my way to an appointment with Dr. MacKimmie. I found Jed staring out the living room window with an air of sadness and depression. He blamed his mood on the flu. But I later learned that Jed had just discovered that Pat was using his car as a trysting place for romance with another student and had stripped their bank account in order to buy gifts for this other student.

Devastated from the shock of her actions, Jed had stayed home from classes that day.

"How about driving with me to see Dr. MacKimmie?" I asked. "You haven't met him, but he always makes me feels so much better when I have the flu. It is such a beautiful drive along the ocean, and I'd love your company."

Jed hesitated, then finally agreed to come. He was very quiet and introspective as we drove to Half Moon Bay. Dr. MacKimmie glanced at him in the waiting room, then beckoned for him to come in first, ahead of all the other patients. The session seemed much longer than usual, but when he came out, Jed was completely transformed. He was smiling and cheerful, and walked with a bouncing step.

When it was my turn to see Jim, his greeting was serious, "It is a good thing you brought him here to see me this morning. He was so depressed and distraught that he was planning to commit suicide tonight. I knew it the minute I saw him, although he didn't say a word about it. I think we have pulled him out of danger, and he has a whole new perspective."

Jim continued his explanation, "The feelings of first love are extremely intense, and should be honored. Also, Jed has unusually strong emotions, is highly sensitive and very idealistic. This betrayal has been shattering for him. He had put Pat on a pedestal and committed his total loyalty to her. It is a serious shock to discover her unworthiness for that devotion. He should be all right now, though."

On the way home, Jed happily recounted his experience. "We talked a little bit about the flu, then, while I was lying on the table, Dr. MacKimmie suddenly started telling me about the first time he was in love. His girlfriend cheated on him and finally threw him over for another guy. Dr. MacKimmie was so enamored of this woman, and so upset when she left him, that he even considered committing suicide."

"Dr. MacKimmie explained how strong our emotions are when we are adolescents, that we feel everything intensely, our joys and triumphs, our sorrows and our disappointments. These seesaw emotions tend to level off as we get older, and become more balanced, but while we are going through this emotional time, they can be harrowing."

"Dr. MacKimmie told me he saw that first girlfriend ten years later, and couldn't believe he had even looked twice at her. He was so grateful that she had found someone else when she did, for now he could see all her faults that had been obscured in the glow of romantic love. He told me to enjoy the thrills and discoveries of falling in love, to have the fun of pursuing lots of fascinating women at this period in my life. This was the time to try my wings and explore the world of romance before becoming too serious about any one person."

Jed continued, "I told him then about what Pat had done and guess what he told me." I waited.

Jed cheerfully quoted Dr. MacKimmie: "Wasn't it lucky that she did this now? What if you had actually married, and then she decided to run around with someone else! She needs to explore falling in love with lots of different people right now, just as you do, so it actually is all right. Besides, would you really want to be committed to someone who behaved in such an unkind, underhanded way? She doesn't have the same standards you do, so you would have discovered before long that you couldn't live together harmoniously. You certainly owe her a vote of thanks for taking the initiative and pulling away from your relationship before you became any more involved."

"I felt so much better as he explained," said Jed. "Suddenly I can see how silly I was to let her actions get me down. I can see her objectively now . . . it's as if I had been under a spell before, where I just saw her good points and wasn't even aware of her other qualities. Boy, I am so lucky I'm out of that relationship. It's so lucky that we went to see Dr. MacKimmie today."

"Would you believe that I was so depressed that life didn't seem worth living, and I was actually ready to commit suicide tonight? I had it all set up. How could I have been so stupid as to let a situation like that end my life?"

"There isn't any way I can thank Dr. MacKimmie enough for opening my eyes and putting me back on track. And thank you for persuading me to go see him!" Jed chattered happily the rest of the way home, his normal outgoing self, involved with plans for activities with his friends.

My heart was filled with gratitude for Dr. MacKimmie's clear insight, his wise and tactful way of lifting a soul from deep depression, his act of divine intervention, which averted a needless tragedy that would have haunted a family for the rest of their lives. With flair and ease, he heals minds, emotions, relationships, souls and destinies as well as bodies.

————·◆·————

FAREWELL TO CHOCOLATE
Toni Taylor

My friend, Minerva, called to tell me that a healer was coming to town. Did I want an appointment on Sunday? Of course I did. I live in Santa Cruz, California, one of the alternative health hot spots on the globe. I'd been complaining about my knee for years. I've played tennis and skied for 50 years and had unsuccessful arthroscopic surgery. Although I'm part of the conventional medical community (I've been a nurse for 25 years), conventional medicine had not done well by my knee.

My MRI showed degeneration of the bones due to bone-on-bone contact. We tried $1457 worth of Synvisc injections to create an artificial meniscus without luck. A famous local icon orthopedic surgeon said he could fracture my femur and realign my knee to give it a few more years of service. And then Minerva called.

On Sunday, June 16, 2002, Father's Day, I drove up to the three white crosses church on Highway 1 in Scotts Valley. I knocked on the door of a nearby house and was invited in by Jim MacKimmie. He looked me in the eye and led me back to the room he was working in.

He told me stories of people he'd helped, people who were skeptical and critics. He interspersed these stories with suggestions to help my healing: no coffee (even decaf), no pork, no battery watches, soak your feet in Twinnings Earl Grey tea every day, drink three cups of blueberry leaf tea, rub your knees daily with olive oil, eat a piece of fatty red meat. Then he said no chocolate. I looked at him and said, "I don't think I can do that." He returned my gaze and said, "It will be easy."

At the time, I was eating chocolate candy every day. Chocolate was the only food I wanted. It was why I got out of bed in the morning. A latte with shaved chocolate and a chocolate croissant, then I'd exercise, stop by the candy store and buy chocolate to snack on all afternoon.

I walked out of the session with Jim pain free. I haven't eaten chocolate or coffee since, except at a birthday party when I was helping cut the cake and unconsciously licked my finger. I quickly washed my hands and rinsed my mouth, hoping my miracle wouldn't be rescinded. I live in a chocolate world: the hospital report room is always full of chocolate gifts from patients. The other thing that calls me is the Christmas catalogs with things like dried Seckel pears dipped in Belgium chocolate. And I resist.

Without dieting, I've lost 23 pounds. I used to say I'd be normal weight if I didn't eat chocolate and it's true. The true miracle for me is the cure from my chocolate addiction. Jim MacKimmie, I thank you a million times for a thousand reasons.

———•◆•———

MEETINGS WITH REMARKABLE JIM
Leland Montell

My first encounter with the good doctor was in my early teens. My mother had tried all types of new age "cures" for my teenage angst, but to no avail. Although I did not know what to expect (I did not even know what a chiropractor was and I thought a healer was a breed of dog), I saw our trip to Dr. MacKimmie as another mother-driven episode in the airy-fairy progression that did little to cure my chronic adolescence.

The office was simple with lime-green shag carpet and dark wood paneling on the walls. Over the door into the treatment room was a plaque that read "God Heals, The Doctor Takes the Fee." Well, I thought, at least he's honest about it. On the reception counter was a picture of the doctor standing between the branches of a large tree that had fallen over. He was posed as if steering the trunk, a wide grin on his face. Below the photo a caption read something like "Jim tries his hand at dowsing." I was not sure what to make of it. I thought that the search for life's meaning was serious business, and here was this guy acting like a clown.

My first treatment gave me a start. The old boy put his hands out a few inches below my feet, and my feet began to tingle. This sensation moved slowly up my legs. Then he put his hands above my head and chest. More tingling. "Balancing your energy," he explained. All the while, he was chatting away about nothing in particular: his house, family, car accidents, cowboys, people acting crazy, or whatever seemed to pop into his head. Then he adjusted my spine and neck, and sent me on my way.

The appointment lasted about 15 minutes, and I left feeling lighthearted— a remarkable sensation for me at that time in my life.

Over the course of several years, I made regular visits to Dr. MacKimmie at his office in San Carlos and later in Pescadero when he moved his office into his home. I would arrive with a few questions about health, karma, the hereafter, or any one of a million questions about my greater purpose. Upon entering the office, he would begin talking, and I would promptly forget what I meant to ask. Then as I lay on his treating table, he might say, "By the way, karma is not simply a cause and effect system." This would lead to further discussion or he might hand me a book to read. It would be too simple to say that he always said the right thing at the right time. Occasionally, when my confusion was urgent, I would reach him by phone for a few words of practical advice and spiritual encouragement. I would usually end up laughing and feeling lighthearted once more.

After college, I spent two years serving in Africa as a Peace Corps volunteer. Africa exposed me to a number of alternative interpretations of life in the universe, and the big question began to work on me again. So, upon my return I went to see my wise old Master determined to get the full story this time. After the usual greetings and sharing a few wild Peace Corps stories, I worked up the courage to ask my burning question: why are we really here? I was certain that I was finally prepared to receive the truth . . . Dr. MacKimmie's response stunned me: "Who the hell knows?" We both burst into laughter. Then he looked me in the eye and said, "But remember, God wouldn't waste your time."

———•◆•———

A TALE OF MIRACLES AND ADDICTIONS
Dr. June d'Estelle, Ph.D.

My husband and I arrived at Stanford Hospital on a very distressing mission. We had just learned that Wanda, one of our dearest friends, was here with inoperable cancer and had but a short time to live. Our personal and professional relationships with Wanda and her family extended over many years, commencing originally with our mutual involvement with Arabian horses. Wanda was the capable business manager of a highly successful Arabian horse breeding and training establishment, as well as a wise and powerful voice in many other endeavors.

The Stanford physicians shared with my physician husband the details of her illness. Despite their most stringent efforts, her cancer had metastasized, they said. From the original lesion, it had spread throughout her entire body, saturating her blood and even invading her brain. Nothing more could be done for her medically, they decreed, and she had but a brief few days of life remaining.

Her devout wish was to go home to die. I volunteered to return the next day and drive her to her family home. The nursing and medical staff sadly installed her in my large station wagon, wheelchair and all, and loaded her with medication to ease her discomfort. As we drove away from the hospital, I had a sudden inspiration. Palo Alto was very close to San Carlos, where Dr. MacKimmie's office was located. Would she be receptive, I wondered, to taking a slight detour and paying him a brief visit?

"Would you be interested in going to a spiritual healer?" I asked.

"At this point, I will try anything," she replied.

When we wheeled into Dr. MacKimmie's office, he graciously escorted her right into his treatment room, explaining to the clients who filled his waiting area that this was an emergency. I accompanied them, lending my moral support as she was prepared for examination and treatment.

As he checked her carefully, the doctor asked, "Exactly what is your problem?"

"Well among other things," she replied, "I have rheumatoid arthritis."

"You have much more than rheumatoid arthritis," said Dr. MacKimmie. "I guess you know your real problem has spread through your whole body, including your blood and your brain."

"Yes, I know," she answered. "Is there anything you can do to help me?"

"How badly do you want to be healed?" was the reply. "I don't know if you are willing to do what must be done in order to become well and remain well."

"Doc, I will do anything," she said. "Just tell me what I must do."

"From this moment on, you must never again drink a drop of coffee or smoke another cigarette," he instructed. "If you have the strength and determination to follow these two rules, you can be healed."

I really wasn't surprised at his assessment, for I had never seen her without a lighted cigarette in one hand and a cup of coffee in the other. However, I had strong doubts that she would be able to overcome such deeply ingrained habits all at once.

"I will do it, Doctor," she promised.

As she reclined on the treatment table, Dr. MacKimmie began channeling healing to her. I was sitting on a stool close to her shoulder, when suddenly I became overwhelmed with dizziness, and slid off my stool onto the floor.

"June, you get out of here," commanded Jim. "I am giving her a blockbuster and it is too much energy for you."

I couldn't stand, so I feebly crawled on my hands and knees over to the door, managed after several tries to turn the doorknob, wobbled and crawled out into the center of the waiting area, where I collapsed in front of a dozen people. You can imagine the consternation my appearance caused!

"What did he do to you?" I heard the horrified receptionist asking, over the babble of concerned voices.

I groggily reassured them that all I needed was to take a little nap on the carpet and I would be fine. Which I proceeded to do, awakening when Wanda reappeared. As everyone helped her into the car, she seemed to be more optimistic and chipper, while I gradually recovered my equilibrium sufficiently to deliver her to her family home.

Two weeks later, since she seemed to be even stronger, I drove her to Stanford Hospital so the surprised doctors could do a checkup. To their absolute amazement, the cancer was completely gone! "Which of our treatments do you suppose healed her?" they wondered, while Wanda and I chuckled knowingly and didn't enlighten them.

She returned to her busy life managing their large Arabian Horse program and participating in her other extended activities, feeling better than she had ever felt before.

I was out of touch with the Arabian horse world for some time while I was immersed in college affairs, but five years later I visited the large Southern California Arabian Horse Show in Santa Barbara. I soon found my friend's beautifully decorated stalls and tack rooms. And there was Wanda, capably handling all the intricate details of her family's successful performance at a major horse show . . . with a glowing cigarette in one hand and a steaming cup of coffee in the other!!!

"What are you doing?" was my appalled greeting. "You know Dr. MacKimmie said you must never smoke cigarettes or drink coffee again!"

"Oh June," she replied cheerfully. "I am completely well now. I feel so wonderful that I know it is all right for me to indulge in my special little pleasures again. And I do enjoy them so much! It has only been two days since I decided to start smoking and drinking coffee once more, and I derive so much satisfaction from them. Don't worry. I'll be fine."

My pleas to reconsider her decision had no effect.

Exactly one month later, we received notice of her funeral, due to her death from cancer. We were deeply saddened, for having been given the priceless gift of life itself, she broke the only two minor stipulations required to retain that blessing. With his profound wisdom, Dr. MacKimmie had known.

———•◆•———

STUMBLE INTO GRACE
Kiyoko Hancock

My future husband, Michael, had terrible sciatica when we first met. Whenever he had an "attack," he limped and spent a lot of time lying on a heating pad being grumpy. He was in a lot of pain. One day when his back was particularly sore, he told me that he was going to go see Dr. MacKimmie. I had never heard this name before. I asked, "Who?"

Michael explained that Dr. MacKimmie was a chiropractor and psychic healer who helped a lot of people get well. Although I prided myself on being open-minded, I was skeptical. Michael was hardly a person to be easily fooled or misled, but I thought "psychic healing" was outright quackery. My lip curled with disdain. I was not convinced.

Michael laughed, "I know. I know what you're thinking. But really, Dr. MacKimmie is the only one who can help my back. Come with me and see for yourself."

That week I went with Michael to Dr. MacKimmie's. His office was warm, clean, and friendly. As I sat in the waiting area having a cup of tea, I began to think, "Maybe, this isn't so bad." Then, I looked up. I was shocked to see a bulletin board covered with tabloid magazine clippings touting different treatments. I was horrified. Was this a joke? I couldn't believe my eyes. I thought, "No one who uses tabloid magazine articles for documentation is going to touch my back! Hah!"

When Michael came out, I shook hands with Dr. MacKimmie. I was polite and civil, but my mind and heart were closed. I marvel now how this Woody Allenesque introduction marked the beginning of a 30-year relationship with a man who proved to be a dynamic, moving force through the ups and downs of my life. I didn't realize it at the time, but I had a lot to learn that day. I was happy when I saw that Michael got better right away, but I didn't really know what to think so I forgot about it.

Six months later I had a horseback riding accident and hurt my back. I was in a lot of pain. When I couldn't get hold of my regular physician, Michael suggested calling Dr. MacKimmie. Amazing as it sounds, Dr. MacKimmie had moved his office one short block from my house. Because I was in such pain, and with Michael's urging, I made an appointment. What could I lose, right? After all, Michael did get better right away. With this reassuring thought, I took the intuitive leap of faith and went to my first appointment.

That first appointment with Dr. MacKimmie changed my life forever. Through his work I felt a door open into the deepest part of my being. He showed me how to access my own inner knowledge and intelligence. By pointing the way, clearing obstacles and illuminating and purifying the path with his "light," Dr. MacKimmie healed not only my physical body but forged a spiritual bond between my body and my mind that was beyond space and time. I became healthier, happier, more creative and confident. I felt new stability in my life. I felt connected and centered in every aspect of my life.

After that first appointment, every time I fell off my horse, every time I got sick, I would go see Dr. MacKimmie. I started thinking of Dr.

MacKimmie as my "first line of defense," knowing I could always go to a medical doctor if Dr. MacKimmie's treatment didn't work. Finally, I started seeing him once a month—physically sick or not—as a preventive "tune-up." I was a believer. I didn't know how it worked. But I had experienced his healing gift in every cell of my body first hand. I knew it worked because I could feel it in my physical body and experienced tangible results.

Then one day Dr. MacKimmie asked me to help run his office. I was happy to have the opportunity to work with him and learn more about his wonderful work. I said yes immediately. During the time I worked for him, I saw people of all ages, illnesses, complaints and conditions come through his doors. I saw chronic disability and acute illness. People went into his office looking pale and drawn. They came out with color in their faces and new life energy in their bodies.

I witnessed hundreds of people healed before my eyes. It was a truly humbling experience that affected me deeply. I saw large and small miracles with so much regularity they seemed like normal happenings. This experience opened my mind and inspired me to be a more compassionate person. Dr. MacKimmie gave me weekly treatments. After a while, I felt like I could glow in the dark. I was functioning at peak performance levels in every aspect of my life. It was a wonderful period of my life. Then one day, Dr. MacKimmie decided to retire and leave the area.

After our paths separated, I didn't see him again for 15 years. During those years when different health issues came up, I tried to find someone to replace Dr. MacKimmie and couldn't. I only stayed healthy because all the treatments Dr. MacKimmie had given me were like putting money in the (body) bank. Over the years, I made withdrawals. As my account balance went down, I began to feel ill. I went to other chiropractors, various healers and medical health workers, but I felt worse and worse.

Finally I developed a serious health crisis. I was diagnosed with colon cancer. Subsequently, I had surgery followed by five months of chemotherapy. This was a defining experience in my life. I survived, but the process left me physically weak and emotionally traumatized. I was grateful to be alive, but I felt like a burned out shell. Nothing I tried really helped. Some things I tried actually made me worse. I realized surviving cancer was going to be a long-term issue. In my darkest moments, I knew there were some things worse than cancer. I needed to heal my body *and* my mind.

At my lowest moment, I had a dream. I was walking along railroad tracks. It was a beautiful day. I was out in the country, fresh air and blue skies. I could see in the distance a man walking along the tracks toward me. As he came closer, I realized it was my old friend, Dr. MacKimmie. I was beside myself with joy. I cried and hugged him. I was just so happy to find him. "Jim," I said, "My God, where have you been? I've been looking all over for you. I've been having a terrible time. I'm completely lost." And I started to cry.

"Don't worry kid," he said. "Everything will be ok. Take it easy." He lifted his hands and started flowing healing energy into me. I felt this incredible tingling warmth flood my body until I felt completely electrified. The physical sensation in my body was so strong in my dream that it actually woke me up. Fully awake, I felt the energy continuing to flow down through my legs and feet. It felt exactly like the treatments I used to get from him. For a moment, I had a glimpse of my former healthy self. I had forgotten so much, I hardly recognized myself anymore. It was a real awakening.

I thought about this dream for weeks. I believed that Dr. MacKimmie must be alive somewhere. I knew he could help me. I became determined to find him. Amazingly, I found him with the help of a private investigator. When I met Dr. MacKimmie again after 15 years, it was more dreamlike than any dream. Like a Twilight Zone episode, it seemed as though I had just talked to him the week before, as though there had been no time of separation at all. I was very happy. I knew Dr. MacKimmie was the one to help me on the next leg of my journey. And I was right.

I had been feeling lost for so long. I had forgotten who I was. But Dr. MacKimmie still remembered and reminded my body/mind by pointing the way home. With Dr. MacKimmie's help I am learning to trust my body again, to listen and respond to my inner voice. My confidence is slowly returning and I am starting to feel like myself again. In turn my body is becoming more stable, as it learns to trust that I will listen and take care of its needs.

Cancer is a powerful and exacting teacher. I can now honestly say the process of surviving cancer proved to be a bittersweet blessing in my life that helped to make me a better person. My life energy has new brightness, intensity and joyfulness. My self-awareness has expanded and my appreciation for others has grown. I am lucky to be alive and I know it.

Thank you, Dr. MacKimmie.

————•◆•————

THE UNINVITED GUEST
Andrea MacKimmie

Spring seemed the perfect time for getting together with my single gal pals. I had traded my maiden name (Blatchley) to become Andrea Rosenberg years before, but I still had more single friends than married ones. I asked my husband, Russ, if he would mind going out for a few hours on Sunday while I had my girlfriends over for brunch. Once he agreed, I moved into Virgo planning mode with no idea that this brunch would change my life forever.

Looking out the window on that fateful morning, I saw an unfamiliar woman walking with my guests as they approached our condominium complex. I assumed she was simply arriving at the same time to visit someone else. However, when I heard a knock on our front door, I opened it to find a stranger standing in front of me. A jumbled chorus from my friends, who were standing behind her, explained the presence of this uninvited guest. They all spoke at once. "We knew you wouldn't mind." "We brought Helen along." "She's an astrologer." "You'll just love her."

Helen's astrological inclination surfaced when she saw the large, dramatic painting (owned by my husband long before I knew him) hanging above the fireplace in our living room. Russ loved this painting and had hung it front stage center. I thought it was depressing and had learned to ignore it. The primary colors the artist used were black, black, and black with a few swirling galaxies of light spattered here and there. Helen was a lovely person with the exception that she had an affinity for this painting. In fact, she wanted to *buy* it for her office. "What an opportunity!" I thought. Keeping my expectations in check, I told her that it was my husband's painting, but she could certainly count on me to ask him if he wanted to sell it.

After the ladies left, my husband arrived home. I told him there was actually another human being in the universe who not only liked his favorite painting, but wanted to buy it. Russ was thrilled. He called her immediately, not to sell the painting (as I had hoped), but to arrange a meeting with this kindred spirit. When they got together for lunch, Helen told him about a series of seminars on meditation that were changing her life.

Before I knew what was happening, Russ and I were taking June d'Estelle's series of Illuminated Mind Seminars. At each seminar, June stressed that anyone on the spiritual path *must* see Dr. MacKimmie. However, she also handed out a sheet with his recommended nutritional guidelines: ". . . no milk, no chocolate, no soft drinks . . ." I thought, *"No Way!"* If only I could have imagined the incredible healing awaiting me, I would have been at his office the next day.

Poor health had been mine for as long as I could remember. I had seen countless doctors and specialists over the years in my search for healing. By the time I heard Dr. MacKimmie's name from June, I had Hashimoto's Thyroiditis (an autoimmune disease), severe asthma (I lived on a "puffer"), endometriosis, diverticulosis, and fibrocystic breast disease. My gynecologist was going to do a biopsy due to the rapid enlargement of one of the cysts. I started coughing up blood and sometimes collapsed from idiopathic (meaning the doctors could find no cause) pains that felt like burning knives were being stabbed into my legs.

Today I would have also claimed the diagnosis CFS (Chronic Fatigue Syndrome) for my own. On weekends—when I could sleep in—it was usually early afternoon before I could drag myself out of bed. I recall one afternoon when I was so tired that I couldn't hold a pen in my hand. I kept picking it up but my fingers had no strength and I kept dropping it. Finally I gave up and just went back to bed. By the time I first heard about Dr. MacKimmie at June's Alpha class, I was taking 13 medications three times a day. None of them seemed to help, but I kept on trying. At night I cried into my pillow, praying for God to take me.

Apparently I needed to suffer a while longer because I waited another two years before making an appointment with Dr. MacKimmie. The last thing I wanted in my life was one more doctor, especially one who was an hour and a half away. Russ finally convinced me to make an appointment by assuring me that we wouldn't have to follow any of the doctor's peculiar dietary advice that June introduced in her classes. With that understanding, we headed south on a sunny Saturday afternoon.

Three miles inland from the coastal town of Pescadero, we found the doctor's office. As we drove up the tree-lined driveway, I was surprised that I didn't have my usual case of nerves about seeing a new doctor. The waiting room was warm and inviting. Everything felt very familiar and comfortable. The energy of his loving concern for his patients filled his office.

In the treating room, the doctor had me lay face up on his treating table. He told me that he was checking my body's "energy" (a new term for me). Then he announced, "Your body's screaming that you're poisoning it with milk. You're going to have to stop *all* dairy products if we're going to help you."

Dismayed, I blurted out, "I don't think I can give up drinking milk."

Dr. MacKimmie smiled knowingly, "Oh, don't worry. It's not going to be a problem for you." And it never was.

In my mind, milk instantly became a slimy glue-like substance that I had no interest in drinking. When he held his right hand a few inches above my throat, I had the sensation of an electrical charge passing from his hand into my throat. I asked what had just happened. He said my thyroid was "coming back on line."

As he continued running energy into my body, I felt as though every cell in my body was coming alive for the first time. The tingling sensation throughout my body reminded me of sparkling champagne bubbles. Experiencing the joy of healing, tears ran down my face. The healing energy had taken me to a heavenly place of restoration. When I left his office, I was filled with a sense of sweet, overwhelming peace.

By the time we got home, I could hardly keep my eyes open. I went right to bed and slept for 18 hours straight. However, in the days that followed, Russ was stunned to discover me up early every morning working in the kitchen or doing laundry. Together, Russ and I banished all the foods from our pantry that the doctor's diet listed as no-nos. We sold our new microwave oven, another item on the no-no list. Russ pitched in and helped me follow the new dietary guidelines to the letter.

I often wonder why none of my other doctors ever asked me what I was eating and drinking. Dr. MacKimmie certainly made the critical importance of eating correctly crystal clear. Each day I experienced the glorious energy of newfound health pouring through my body, and optimism filled my life. After that first treatment, *all* the cysts in my breasts vanished and my thyroid began functioning normally again. The other conditions cleared during the next two months.

It was so exciting getting well that I happily made the three-hour round trip once a week for the next six months. For the first time in my life, I had incredible health and energy. When concerned friends suggested that I'd better go to a medical doctor and have more scans and tests to see what the doctors would find, I laughed and said that I could never doubt God's wonderful healing. After six months, I celebrated by throwing out all my medications. The miracle of health was mine. I had truly been given back the gift of my life.

————•◆•————

THE POWER OF HUMAN TOUCH
The Reverend Dr. Rodney R. Romney, author of *Wilderness Spirituality: Finding Your Way in an Unsettled World*

In March 1996, I went for a consultation after my annual physical exam. The examining doctor informed me that it was possible I had prostate cancer, due to an enlarged prostate, an elevated PSA reading, and a suspicious lump on the gland itself. He then recommended that I see a specialist in that field. I, who had never been seriously sick a day in my life except for an occasional cold or bout with the flu, was suddenly confronted with what everyone faces sooner or later in life, a sense of one's vulnerability and mortality as a physical being.

Reluctantly I went to see the specialist and after the examination, I was advised that I should submit to a biopsy. After he explained to me the possible aftereffects of such a procedure, none of them pleasant, I said I wanted some time to think about it. Clearly this doctor did not like his patients temporizing or disputing his advice. His final words to me, as I left his office, were threatening and blunt, "Don't wait too long. Death from prostate cancer is not pretty."

The next Sunday in church (I was then the minister of a church in downtown Seattle), I found myself, during the course of my sermon, sharing with the congregation that I was dealing with a prognosis from a doctor that was disturbing as well as depressing, and that I would like them to hold me in their prayers. At the conclusion of the service, a woman approached me and suggested that before I agreed to surgery or anything else, she would like me to see a healer who had been an effective agent of healing for herself and several family members and friends through his discernment and his healing power of touch. I learned that he was a retired doctor who now worked as a spiritual healer in his home, but only on those cases that were referred to him. I called Dr. James MacKimmie the next day and arranged an appointment for later in the week.

While driving to his home, I listened to a tape by Deepak Chopra on the subject of spiritual healing. I admit to being a bit of a skeptic when it comes to persons who set themselves up as spiritual healers, but at the same time I am aware that true healing has a mental and spiritual component that cannot be denied, and that the mind can be a strong influence on the body. I cannot say that it was what Chopra said that stirred me as much as it was the music that was played at the end of his talk. I was so moved that I pulled off into a roadside stop and wept unrestrainedly. "God, I need your help," I prayed. "Let me be open to receive it in whatever way it comes."

When I arrived at Dr. MacKimmie's home, I was encouraged to find a warm, smiling and engaging man, with no airs whatsoever, in contrast to the other doctors I had recently encountered. After listening to me describe why I was there, he shared a bit about himself, his background, and how he worked. Then he had me lie down for the healing session. He began to move his hands across my lower back and abdomen. When he found what I assumed were organs or glands that emitted low levels of energy, he would press there with one hand while touching my shoulder with the other hand. In the area of the kidneys, pancreas, and prostate, where by touch he discovered high levels of toxic congestion in the tissues and low energy, he would press gently but firmly for several minutes. As he did so, I could actually feel the pain and discomfort in those areas begin to dissolve and disappear. Gradually I began to feel lighter and freer than I had in a long time.

As he worked on me, Dr. MacKimmie talked about what he sensed was going on in my body. He suggested that I should eliminate my consumption of caffeine, since he felt it was likely responsible for some of the problems in my kidneys, pancreas and the urinary tract. After his treatment, which I can only describe as gentle but forceful pressure with one hand touching specific areas of my lower body while his other hand touched my shoulder, he suggested that he had pumped about as much energy into me as I could assimilate at one time. I got up feeling a hundred percent better physically than I had felt in some time, and he invited me to return if I ever felt I needed to.

What I learned from Jim MacKimmie that day went beyond experiencing the spiritual gifts certain people seem to have. Clearly that is true in his case; he is a person with rare insights and unusual gifts in the area of healing. However, I also learned from him that each of us can assist our bodies in healing themselves of illness or discomfort. There are times when we can be our own healers.

Nearly ten years later I am still well and healthy and living in gratitude that this man, Dr. James MacKimmie, entered my life at a time when I needed him most. We have remained friends and stayed in contact. I know that if I ever needed his help again, he would be there for me, as he has been for many others. He is a man with rare and unusual gifts of discernment and healing power, which he uses lovingly and gently for anyone who comes to him.

PART IV

THE POWER

16

MY ANGELIC COMPANIONS

W hen I raise my hands, the Power flows and lives change. But what is this energy that flows through me when I raise my hands? And how does it work? These are the questions I have asked for a lifetime.

After the Power's first visitation, I imagined a life in which I would help others regain their health and find their place on the spiritual path. I envisioned healing energy flowing from my hands to all who were in need. My heart knew this would be a life well-lived, and I embraced this calling in the center of my being.

By focusing my attention on healing day after day, it became the center of my existence. Thoughts of healing lived in my consciousness every moment. At first, I energized everything—the sun, the moon, the stars, mountains, lakes, trees, clouds, rocks, the earth, animals—everything that crossed my path. Whenever the Power began to move through me and flow out into the universe, it felt as though my hands were being pulled toward a great magnet, an all-powerful force that could not be resisted.

Once at the aquarium, I stood admiring a school of yellowtail circling gracefully in their tank. Gliding around and around through the water in perfect formation, they seemed to be following a dance choreographed by some mysterious inner guidance system. I chose one and raised my hands to run energy into it.

My recruited patient immediately leaped into the air and began swimming vigorously in the opposite direction of the school. His companions were forced to dart in all directions in order to dodge this unexpected oncoming traffic. Excited onlookers crowded around the tank and asked each other what would make this one fish swim contrary to all the others. Turning, I walked away with my hands in my pockets. I went back the next day and was happy to see the yellowtails once again circling peacefully in their watery abode, all swimming in the same direction.

After more than 50 years as an energy runner and healer, I do not speak lightly of the Power's energy flow. Like any miracle, it just is. Since I am merely a fascinated observer when the transcendent flow takes over, I could never begin to explain what actually takes place during a healing session. But if I could transform the healing flow into some other medium, I believe it would be like hearing the grandeur of a magnificent symphony, or feeling the first warming rays of a glorious summer sunrise. Then again, it might be like watching the shimmering aurora borealis dance across the heavens to light the winter night sky.

"The Power" has always been a comfortable term for me since this group of angels has been around me forever, like old friends. These powerful beings from the angelic healing realm never interfere, but are ever available for guidance. With their wonderful sense of humor and love of words, they have been ideal companions on the road of life. The essence of my heart and being is centered in the mysterious flow of the Power that heals as it wills. This energy flow is a living force, radiating from a point of light, which connects humankind with the Source in God's loving heart.

From the beginning, the Power made it clear that all healing was from God and that judgements about others or myself would block the healing flow. Healing energy was never to be used to impress others and I was always to acknowledge that my own healing abilities came from a higher source. I feel blessed to be an observer while the Power runs the show from a higher plane of wisdom and truth. They teach, I listen, and so it has always been.

I serve as a conduit for the healing energy as it is given for each patient. The rest is left up to the Power. But living in the Power is not like reading about it, or seeing it on television. As soon as I connect with the

Power, angelic energy begins raising the vibrations for those who are ready and ask, consciously or unconsciously, to enter the golden door of the Creator's infinite healing love.

Angelic beings surround us at all times, existing in perfect harmony with the infinite energies of the universe. They influence us—and we them—through the vibration of thought. When we lift our thoughts to higher realms of consciousness, we attune ourselves to angelic frequencies. Like eagles soaring higher and higher on thermal updrafts, the higher we fly in consciousness, the more we can flow effortlessly with divine intention. And so it is when I connect with the Power.

Once the connection is made, the Power is totally in charge. While bringing in this orchestra of living light, I am guided and directed by the healing angels, a role for which I volunteered before entering this present life. I have learned that I can either get in the way, or surrender to the divine presence that exists within all of us.

While I minister to the body according to angelic instructions, the Power flows healing into each patient. This energy flow goes exactly where needed, regardless of what I think or say. Healing takes place while I chat along with the patient about their problems or their family. (At times, these are one and the same.) I am neither the engineer of the healing flow, nor the pilot. God's healing moves through me for reasons unknown to me.

Of course I would love to say that I'm in charge and know everything about everything. When you are young, it seems there's nothing you don't know, but as you grow older, you learn ever more, until you finally graduate into the genius class of knowing that you know nothing at all. As Lord Goring says to his father in Oscar Wilde's *An Ideal Husband,* "I love talking about nothing, father. It is the only thing I know anything about."

However, I do know that healing takes place on many levels when I'm working with people. And physical problems are actually the least important aspect of healing. Once pain is relieved and the life force restored, deeper healing can take place. I rejoice when I see healing on these deeper levels renew a patient's faith and trust in a higher power. As a minister, I have seen that it is difficult for any life not spiritually centered to hold its course. We are, after all, Soul creatures.

As we move through our lives, no matter how far-reaching our adventures, we long for something greater in our lives that we can't quite define. The Creator placed a presence within our hearts that loves us as a mother loves her child, only more so. Our secret yearning is to contact that inner presence, which waits quietly for our invitation to come forth and manifest in our lives.

Through the ages, saints have spoken of the light of the Creator's love that burns within us. When asked to describe God, the saints proclaimed: how loving, how holy, how beautiful, how perfect, how giving, how sweet, how kind, how joyous. When the church fathers asked for further enlightenment, the saints could only repeat the words already spoken.

Embraced by God's constant presence, the saints knew that mere words were feeble descriptions of the Creator's glory. Any attempt to describe their bliss could never reveal the Creator's grandeur. Just as words fail to describe the sweet scent of a rose to one who has never been in the presence of that heavenly flower, so it is with God. Only through the experience of God's love, can we be immersed in the Creator's grace.

None have left directions to the City of God that lies within our hearts. We are required to find our own way there. Not an easy task while living in a world sadly lacking in silence. For it is in silence that we contact the heart's loving flow and hear the gentle whispering of inner worlds unknown to our outer senses. To contact that love, that essence, our eternal soul, is to contact the divine spark from the Creator's heart, which resides within us all. Once contacted, living a life of love becomes an effortless process.

Through the Power's loving instruction, I saw that we all sleep within God's heart. In our search to learn more about ourselves and our Creator, we imagine that we live on the earth plane, separate from our Creator. In truth, we have never left God's heart. Before the Power lifted the veil, I had been blind to our destiny as spiritual beings. But once given a glimpse of eternal truth by the Power, I saw that life is perfect in every way. Every event in our lives—even the most painful—is totally necessary for our soul growth. It is all part of a Divine Plan.

Once awakened to the truth of our existence, I understood that we are multidimensional critters, whose consciousness is everywhere. The grand illusion, called life, is our dream. During the day, we are in reality asleep. We alone can turn the dream into a nightmare by our belief in its reality; the solution is to wake up.

Each night we awaken from our "day" dream and burst forth into millions of light patterns of vibrational energies, fully conscious and alive in every sense. Once in our light body and conscious of our oneness with All That Is, we join our star families and perform our true function as Eternal Beings of the universe. We travel to other worlds beyond vision and thought. In myriad other dimensions, we are busy performing the perfect work of the cosmos while our bodies remain at rest, sleeping peacefully.

In the morning, covered with dreams, we awaken to the illusion of our earth life and prepare to sleepwalk through this seeming reality. Quickly forgetting the glories of other realities and other lives, our memories retain only bits and pieces of our nightly adventures, which return with us as dreams.

Once back in the world of the physical body, we quickly remember our role on earth as we learned to play it. We pick up our identity and our story once more, ready to sleepwalk through our daily life. However, if you are observant when you awaken in the morning, you can actually feel your other selves come zipping back into your awakening body. Nothing to worry about. It's quite natural.

———•◆•———

When the healing angels first appeared and asked how much power I wanted for living my life of healing and teaching, I was only seven years old. I didn't realize I couldn't simply put a saddle on the healing and ride it to my destination. Envisioning powers like Superman, I boldly asked for "everything" without a moment's hesitation. The angels wisely counseled me against this choice, advising me that this choice meant I would have to travel straight up the mountain of God and encounter more difficulties than I could possibly imagine.

The angels described another gentler path, which spiraled around the great mountain, slowly gaining altitude. Although it would take longer to reach the summit, there would be fewer hardships along the way. Since youth knows all, I chose to climb straight up. Oh, foolish youth. In the passing years, I occasionally complained to the Power about the chaos and confusion that tangled my life as healer, husband, father and traveler on the road of life. But at age seven, there was no doubt in my mind.

After being in practice for a few years, my only real complaint was about money. I had made other people, who listened and took action on my forward vision, very wealthy. However, my ability to see the future—while it worked quite nicely for others—was doing nothing for me in the financial arena. One day I complained to the Power, "It would be nice for wealth to come my way for a change."

There was an overwhelming silence. I waited while an angelic conference took place. At last they spoke, *"You have never asked us for great wealth. Is that what you want?"*

"Well, it would make for a nice change don't you think?"

"Are you able to pay your bills? Are you lacking the comforts of life? Do you not have food and clothing?"

I had to admit that I lacked nothing so I tried another approach, "I'm living comfortably but it would be fun to buy what I want and not just what I need."

"This can be arranged. If you want worldly riches, then we will make it so."

Their tone made me nervous. I interjected, "Please understand . . . I don't want to give up healing to have abundance."

"Then we shall leave things as they are." And so it was.

I began to count my many blessings and realized that I loved healing above all other activities in my life. My work has never been work, but pure pleasure although I sometimes wonder why the Power—always on tap for helping others—usually ignores me completely as it surges into the patient's body. I asked the Power, "Why is it that I can heal others, but I can't heal myself?"

They answered, *"You have awakened to the journey that never ends. You must travel onward driven by energies beyond your current understanding. Whether you enjoy superb health or poor health is of little importance. It has nothing to do with what we see as your progress."* Not what I wanted to hear—since I would have preferred superb health—but I accepted their judgment.

———— ·◆· ————

A few patients—thank God very few—ask if the healing comes from the darker forces. They cautiously remind me that Satan can imitate the light. At my age, I am really not fond of hearing that what I do could be the darker side at work. If Satan heals, he surely does not do it through me. I am aligned with Our Lord and have served as a willing and grateful servant of the Creator for more than 50 years. God heals, period. I believe we are here on the earth to love and help each other. Anything else is nonsense.

I vividly remember locking horns with my second mother-in-law, a staunch Christian Scientist, who is now in her 90s and still going strong. On the day we first met, I saw her awesome and unshakeable faith in the power of the mind. In her eyes, my healing was Animal Magnetism (a term used by Anton Mesmer in the eighteenth century). She firmly notified me that she, *and* Phineas P. Quimby, the father of New Thought, *and* Mary Baker Eddy, the founder of Christian Science, did not approve of Animal Magnetism. Her beliefs bristled with conviction. Under the gaze of her stern visage, I recognized that we were never going to find common ground on the subject of healing.

This indomitable lady was rarely sick, but when she was, I had to rub it in. "My, my," I sympathized. "You surely look sick to me. I can only hope you live through this virus." She would glare back with feverish eyes and say firmly through gritted teeth, "Divine Mind knows no Disease." By golly, a day later she was up and running, ready to gloat about her conquest over disease as soon as I appeared. I admit that I was truly impressed.

Some patients feel compelled to explain my healing gift to me, certain they have it all figured out. I find this interesting since I've spent a lifetime trying to understand the Power's healing mysteries and still can't explain it, but I will do my best. In each session, the healing does what it has come to do. It cannot be steered. The thought of mastering control of the healing remains a joke of the highest order to me. If I attempt to steer it, it soon jumps ship and goes where it is needed most in each patient.

I couldn't possibly guide a patient through all the chaos and confusion of life. But the Creator knows exactly what each person needs.

Whatever takes place is God's will. The physical and spiritual changes taking place are wrapped up in God's loving concern for each patient's current life force and what karmic patterns remain to be worked through.

God's healing angels work on so many levels at once that I can only watch as people change when their energies shift to higher patterns. First, the Power flows into the biofield energy and probes each level before moving through the patient's body, mind and soul patterns. As the Power fills each "battery," as I call the specific energy storage centers within the body, I see the patient's inner radiance begin to glow. During this process, the Power downloads as much energy as the physical vehicle is capable of holding at that moment. Then each person has a contract with the body to nourish what has been given by following a program of proper nutrition, loving thoughts and an attitude of gratitude.

Some patients feel the energy running through them like 220 volts of electricity, others feel it less, and some feel nothing at all. Some patients feel heat, some deep, penetrating cold, while others feel tingling, floating sensations, or that invisible cotton batting is around the area being treated with energy. Others sense a magnetic pull on the area involved. Patients may feel relaxed or sleepy after a session, or they may be so energized that it's hard to sleep that night.

When I first began healing, I used to think all this was important, but it is not. Healing takes place all the same. And over the years, I've learned to accept that reactions are as different as we are as individuals. However, most people sense that something is happening, and usually find their perceptions of life shifting to a higher level.

———— • ◆ • ————

When a life is saved by the Power, the feedback returning to me from the energy flow carries such bliss that I feel I am the most fortunate being in the world to be of service in this way . . .

I had been out on a D-5 tractor plowing our two-acre field in California when I was called to a hospital to see a five-year-old boy. Since time was of the essence, I drove to the hospital still wearing my jeans and a work shirt. I arrived quickly, but looked more like a farmhand than a healer. The boy's father, a pathologist, was in the room crying. He told me the doctors held no hope for his son's recovery. Diagnosed with the big disease, the boy's lungs were so distressed that he had been placed in an oxygen tent.

Trying desperately to breathe, the child's face was pale and strained, and his thick, dark hair clung to his damp forehead. His head was turned toward the wall; his eyes were closed. Standing at the foot of his tented hospital bed, I raised both hands and began running energy. Soon I felt the glow of the Power's healing moving through the boy. Within a few minutes, his breathing calmed and he turned his head to look at me. I smiled and continued the flow until his breathing was free and easy and he fell asleep.

The boy's father called the next day to tell me the doctors had removed the oxygen tent. I was called to treat him once more at the hospital after the boy said he wanted to see "the funny man who held up his hands." At the end of that treatment, his color and vitality returned, revealing a healthy, vigorous child who was anxious to go home. When the lab tests came back clear, his parents joyfully took their son home.

A month later, I dropped in on the family. Obviously enjoying his new health and freedom, the little boy was happily pedaling his red tricycle all around the yard. The father thanked me profusely. I said, "God surely performed this miraculous healing. Let's give our thanks to Him."

How I wish I could say the story ended on such a happy note. But a month later, I was asked to pay a visit and see the boy at home. Arriving early, I saw him sitting on the porch with his head down. He was enveloped in dismal, gray clouds of energy. I knew from these distinctive clouds that a drug was overwhelming his body's defenses. I noticed the little boy's red tricycle was turned over on the grass, no longer ridden. As soon as his father came out of the house, I asked, "What drug is your son being given?"

At first the father insisted his boy wasn't receiving any drugs at all. I took a deep breath and said, "Don't tell me that. I see the drug in your son's energy field. The healing angels who guide me say that this drug will kill your son in six weeks if it isn't stopped immediately."

The father was furious but finally admitted that his son was getting daily cortisone injections. It was the medical consensus that this would prevent any further problems in the future. I was stunned because I knew that all the boy's tests were clear before he was released from the hospital.

The Power quickly explained that underneath this drug, the boy was healthy. However, the angels told me the cortisone would soon cause the boy's lungs to close down and he would choke to death from cortisone mold. As soon as I gave this information to his father, he threw me off his property and told me never to come back.

Six weeks later, I attended the boy's funeral. The father was overcome with grief. He showed me the death certificate, which stated that his son had died from cortisone mold in both lungs. His eyes filled with tears and he asked me, "Why? Why couldn't I have listened to you?" In my heart, I knew his son's death had been determined by karma, but I also knew that this was no answer for a grieving father. I said, "I'm sorry. I have no answer. But I do know your son is resting in God's heart now and our prayers for his soul will help him to be at peace."

———•◆•———

A few months after the funeral, I was once again out on the tractor when a call came in from the same hospital. I was told that an eleven-year-old girl had been rushed to the hospital by her parents. They had been out for a Sunday drive when their daughter, who was riding in the back seat, suddenly screamed, clutched her head and passed out. X-rays showed half of her brain had hemorrhaged. The pathologist whose son had been in the oxygen tent heard about it. He told me later that he quickly sought out the parents and said, "Don't miss seeing this guy from the beach. I didn't listen. If I had, my boy would still be alive. Call him right away!"

Once more, I arrived at the hospital in my jeans and work shirt, fresh off of the tractor. My heart went out to the anxious parents who met me at the door of their daughter's room. The young girl lay on her back looking very small in the stark hospital bed. Her head had been shaved for possible surgery, and a strap across her forehead kept her head from moving. The doctors were afraid that even the slightest movement might cause further hemorrhaging.

Placing my hands a few inches from each side of her head, I began running energy. As the healing flow increased, I felt the Power reach through the flow and fill this young girl with the gift of life. Her pale cheeks flushed and her eyes fluttered open. She looked up at me and smiled, no longer under the influence of what *had* been her condition before the healing energy.

Ten minutes later, the healing flow ceased. I turned to the parents and repeated what the angels told me, "She's fine now."

The nurses and her parents looked at me as though I was totally crazy. Her mother, who was a RN, handed me the x-ray again. I handed it back, "I'm sorry but this doesn't matter since it was taken before the Power healed your daughter."

The parents looked at each other in confusion and asked, "What should we do for her now?"

"Well, if she was my daughter, I'd take her to Great America and let her ride the roller coaster," I answered.

"You're crazy!" they both exclaimed at once.

At this moment, one of the hospital's great surgeons entered the room. Glancing at the x-ray, he pronounced, "The girl will not live through the night. If she does, she will never speak again."

Before I could think, I blurted out, *"Nonsense!"*

The nurses gasped. The startled surgeon looked me up and down, and asked "Who are you?"

"Nobody," I answered. Taking in my appearance, he said, "That's very evident." Then he turned his back on me, repeated his evaluation and left.

On the following day, the parents called to report that their daughter had wiggled out of the restraints and was in the hallway talking with visitors. The father, who was a cardiologist, informed me that they were taking their daughter to Switzerland for brain surgery. He acknowledged that his daughter might never move or speak again after the surgery, but at least she would be alive (if you call that living).

"This surgery will never take place," I said firmly.

"You're wrong. We've already scheduled her appointment," he insisted.

However, the next day, the father called to tell me that the famous Swiss brain surgeon had called and said he would not operate on their daughter. Then he requested that they never contact his office again and hung up. Astonished by this puzzling turn of events, they took their daughter to a clinic where the doctors drilled a hole in her skull just over the area that was hemorrhaged according to the first x-ray. Much to their surprise, everything was perfectly normal. Another victory for God.

———•◆•———

Early in my practice, a patient asked if I was going to give her husband the "rays." Surprised, I asked, "What are you talking about?" She looked at me as though I was not too bright and firmly repeated, "The rays, Doc. You know. Give him the healing rays from your hands." I liked that. It was a clear picture that I could appreciate and enjoy while I was running energy. I could imagine those rays flowing into patients and bathing them in the warmth and love of healing radiance.

My patients developed their own language to describe the many aspects of the Power, no doubt based on what they experienced during a session. Some patients, like the lady above, spoke of the "rays" of healing. Others asked to be "zapped," "jump-started," "balanced," "charged up," "zoned in," "given the juice," or "loaded up"—whatever suited their experience. I still smile when a patient comes in and says, "Doc, hit me with the rays." For me, the healing flow is beyond any words.

A few clairvoyant patients see the healing energy in all its glory. I remember when a lovely Japanese couple came in for treatment. As I was working on them, the wife became quite emotional. She began shouting excitedly in rapid fire Japanese to her husband. He interpreted since his wife could not speak English. She described huge leaves of energy, which spread out around me in every color of the rainbow. Then she saw energy streams flowing from my hands like Fourth of July sparklers. Every shift in the energy, she saw and described in detail.

It was thrilling to hear the wife, via her husband, describe the various energies in the room during the healing. Unfortunately, the husband saw nothing. He felt tingling and heat, but otherwise, his healing experience was uneventful. Even though his well-being improved, it was clouded by his anger over his wife's remarkable visions. I happened to look out the window as they were leaving. He was yelling at her in Japanese so I couldn't decipher the content but it was clear that he was criticizing her for having her incredible experience while he was relegated to the lowly role of an interpreter.

If patients felt "spaced out" after the treatment, I always suggested they take a little time to rest before driving. I recall one new patient who, after the treatment, stood in the parking lot staring at his car for 20 minutes. Every time I looked out my office window, I could see him still standing beside his car. About that time, another patient left the office, took a key from his pocket, unlocked the door of his car, got in, started his car and drove off.

I saw Ralph dig in his pocket, fish out a key and open the car door. But even after he was inside the car, he didn't drive off. A few minutes later, he started the car and drove away very slowly. I couldn't imagine what this strange performance was all about.

When Ralph came in the following week, I asked what was going on last week. He laughed and explained, "Doc, you're not going to believe this, but after your treatment my car might as well have been a flying saucer. It was a complete mystery to me. I knew the car belonged to me, but that was about it. Then I saw another guy come out and get in his car using a key from his pocket so I fished around in my pockets and found a set of keys. Once inside, I was completely baffled by the big round thing (steering wheel) in front of me. I looked all around until I found a key hole in the steering column. Once I found a key to fit, my memory started returning. By the time I started the car and drove out, I was myself again. Strange, huh?"

———•◆•———

Many patients told me that they had to pull over to the side of the road and cry before driving home. A few patients reported that it took them hours to get home because they felt compelled to stop along the way to sleep, meditate or pray. Whatever happens, it is beyond their control. A few patients have told me that their bodies refuse to buy food from the regular store. Their bodies shuffle them off to health food stores in spite of every effort to resist this impulse. Once there, they find themselves buying the foods that I told them they should eat . . .

My oldest and dearest friend, Jack, referred a friend to me. Elle had been everywhere but had found no help for her condition. She explained that x-rays and blood tests revealed bone density and circulation in her right leg were down 90 percent. The doctors warned her to be cautious since her bones were so porous that they could break quite easily. All the procedures and drugs to date had changed nothing. It was July when she came to see me and the doctors had told her that by Christmas she would be in bed for the rest of her life. She came in on crutches, keeping her weight off her right leg to avoid spontaneous fractures.

Elle was a complete skeptic but Jack told her that I had helped many people and he was convinced I could help her too. As soon as I touched her, I knew that by September 1, which was two months away, she would be totally healed. The angels showed a vision in which she was perfectly well with bone and circulation restored 100 percent to her afflicted leg. After passing this good news on to her, I was rewarded with a look of total disbelief. In my mind, to accomplish the miraculous angelic vision, I would have to treat her once a week for the next eight weeks. And I did see her once a week for five weeks, and then she suddenly stopped coming.

Elle didn't return to my office until September 1 when she strolled in wearing jeans and a work shirt. Seated at my desk, I felt a presence and looked up to see her standing in the doorway. The energies were in perfect balance on both sides of her body. Her leg condition had been healed. She smiled broadly and said, "Guess what?"

I smiled back, "You're completely healed, aren't you?"

"Yes, but how could you know that? I just came from my appointment at the hospital. The x-rays and blood work show that my leg is perfect now," Elle said. "I've been using a cane whenever I work in the garden, but this morning I was out pulling weeds when I realized I had forgotten my cane and a wonderful sense of well-being came over me. Suddenly, I knew I was healed and that Jack was right about you. When I realized it was September 1, I remembered you told me two months ago that I would be well on the first day in September. I decided to get x-rays and tests to confirm your prediction and my feeling of perfect health."

On the day of her first treatment Elle was blessed with a miracle, which I did not learn about until later. She had two large tumors, one in each breast, which had been there for quite some time, but she was afraid to have them removed. After my first treatment, they were gone by the time she arrived home. No doubt God saw that this miracle was necessary to help her see the wisdom of continued treatments for her leg.

Many years later, Elle sent in an old family friend who was a medical doctor. Medical doctors are usually difficult to treat. After all, instructions are for their *patients,* not for *them.* In addition, the majority are skeptics who have a difficult time allowing the healing process to take place. It's hard for them to simply accept healing as part of God's plan and get on with their lives. They tend to analyze the healing process, reassemble it, and pin it down in keeping with their own medical approach.

Darin was taking drugs (of course) for his heart condition and he had a terrible low back. Immaculately dressed, he carried the weight from his excessive lifestyle gracefully. He made it clear that he wasn't interested in making any dietary changes. He just wanted to be healed. Water was never his drink of choice, and he loved ice cream, cakes, coffee, etc., etc. In short, he ate and drank what he darn well pleased. I despaired of moving him even one inch in the right dietary direction.

I was told by the Power that I was to treat Darin three times. He made it quite clear that his time was precious and he wouldn't appreciate being kept waiting. Arriving in his large, black Cadillac, his presence could be felt before he ever entered the waiting room. During his second treatment, I found that he was much *worse* in some areas than before. Puzzled and concerned, I asked, "Darin, what have you been eating? I'm afraid you're much worse in some areas."

"Well . . . I guess it might have been the cherry ice cream and chocolate cake I brought home to share with my sons. You see, they told me they don't eat that kind of junk so I had to eat it all *myself* . . ." His voice trailed off and he shrugged his shoulders when he saw my exasperation. Heaving a deep inner sigh, I decided to get on with the treatment.

After the third and last treatment, Darin stood up and stuck out his hand to shake mine. He said, "Doctor, I want to thank you for your help. My heart is fine now and my low back pain is totally gone. I feel wonderful. And, I owe it all to you and your marvelous treatments." I was pleased—and more than a little surprised—to learn that he had found his healing in spite of his poor nutrition. I shook his hand and wished him well.

17

WORKING WITH THE POWER

――――・◆・"・◆・――――

Although the Power is not mine to command, the angels will listen to reasonable requests. One sunny afternoon, a friend took me flying in his plane; it was remarkable to see that my Pescadero home wasn't at all where I thought it was in relation to the coastline. When we headed back to the Half Moon Bay Airport, heavy fog began rolling in, which is typical for the coast. When Ted spotted the huge gray blanket the ocean was sending our way, he panicked and said he would fly us to Oakland Airport where he could pick up his car and drive me home.

I wasn't in favor of Ted's plan since my car was in the Half Moon Bay airport parking lot so I asked the Power to roll back the fog so we could land on a clear runway. When the Power agreed, I asked Ted to prepare for a normal landing, just as if the fog wasn't there. Ted flashed a frightened look in my direction, "Are you *sure?*" "Yes," I assured him. "It's going to be fine." Sweating, he gripped the controls hard and did as I asked.

As we made our approach, the fog rolled back perfectly like the Biblical parting of the Red Sea, and held as a massive gray wall at the sides and end of the runway. Ted expertly dropped the plane down on the runway and landed. I quickly jumped out of the plane. As soon as my feet were on terra firma, I turned to thank Ted. "Screw that," he shouted. "I'm out of here!" And he was, climbing so fast the manager of the airport rushed out, "My God, if he climbs any steeper, he'll stall and crash."

"I'm sure he knows what he's doing. He's just a bit nervous about the fog."

The manager eyed the wall of fog surrounding the runway, "Well, I can't blame him."

While the manager and I watched, the plane leveled out and headed toward Oakland. The manager shook his head, "It's hard to believe the fog had already taken over this whole area, *including* the landing strip, but then it rolled back, leaving just the landing strip perfectly clear. I've never seen anything like it before." At this moment, the fog moved in again, reclaiming the runway for its own and reducing visibility to zero once more.

———•◆•———

When the Power gives me an unmistakable message, such as clearing the runway for Ted, I can always count on it. These messages come in loud and clear, without a shred of hesitancy like the one for Myra . . .

Myra first came to see me after a stint in the hospital. She had been in traction for a month to relieve her low back pain, which started after a night of sleeping on her stomach. The next morning, she was in agony and couldn't move without excruciating pain, but traction didn't help and a friend referred her to my office. Within a few minutes of energy treatment, she was pain free. After that treatment, she could sleep comfortably in any position.

In the years that followed, Myra sent in her husband, her children, her grandchildren, and many friends. When her husband moved to Alaska with their two grown sons, Myra stayed in the Bay area because of her job. After a month, her husband came from Alaska for a visit. Myra sensed at once that something was wrong. She insisted Kurt go to the hospital for a checkup. Although his test results were fine, Myra was still concerned and brought him to see me.

As soon as I saw Myra and her husband, I received a strong message from the Power. I took Myra's hand. There was no easy way to tell her. "I'm sorry, Myra. You must call the boys immediately. Tell them that if they want to see their father alive, they'd better come home right now.

Kurt's going to die from a heart attack two weeks from today and there's nothing I can do to stop it."

As soon as Myra's sons arrived, they arranged for their dad to see three different cardiologists. All three gave Kurt a clean bill of health. The two boys arrived at my office boiling with anger and told me that my prediction of their father's death was crazy. I begged them to enjoy their time with their dad while they were in the Bay area. The family had a wonderful reunion but the boys remained angry at me for wasting their time. A few days later, they headed back to Alaska, still simmering over what they considered a wasted trip. But Kurt died from a heart attack on the exact date I was given. The boys later thanked me for having them come home to see their father before he passed on.

———•◆•———

There are times when messages from the Power can be all business, especially when a life is at stake . . .

Lila's mother called me early on a Sunday morning after she suddenly remembered how I had helped her family in the past. Gloria asked if I would see Lila on an emergency basis. When I asked what was wrong, she told me that Lila had been in a health crisis for a month and was now in the emergency room of a Nevada hospital. According to her doctors, she was dying. I remembered first treating Lila when she was 11 years old. She was now 18. I said, "If you can get Lila to my office, I'll do all I can to help her."

Gloria and Lila flew to San Jose Airport and came right over to the office. When Gloria helped Lila into my treating room, I was horrified to see that the lovely girl I remembered now looked like a skeleton with skin; even so, she was still beautiful. Slowly, the energy coaxed the life force back into her body. At last, the stark white color of her skin glowed with pink and she smiled. After the session, she walked out on her own, and her mother took her home to San Jose.

The next day, Lila walked into the office, sparkling with vitality, vivacious and laughing. This was the Lila I remembered. After three more treatments, she looked completely like her old self. Thrilled to be well again, she asked, "So, when can I go back to Nevada?"

The voice of the Power spoke firmly and I passed on the message,

"I'm sorry to tell you this, but the town you are living in is death for you. It's imperative that you move from that city immediately and never go back."

Lila stepped back, shaking her head in surprise, "But my job . . . besides, I *love* living in Nevada's high desert country."

"I know, but the Power has spoken and they're never wrong. To argue with their message would mean your death. Where you live, either feeds your energy or drains it, according to what is known as the power of place. Others can live there in health, but *you cannot.*"

"But how . . ."

"I want you to phone the family where you're staying in Nevada. Ask them to pack up your things in boxes and put them out on the front lawn. When you arrive at their house, load the car as fast as you can. Then immediately drive out of town. Once you're past the city limits, you'll be safe. You'll understand when you get there."

Lila bit her lip, sighed, and left the office shaking her head. I knew she thought I was crazy so I waited to hear what happened. She phoned the next day and reported that as soon as she approached the city limits, she began to get sick to her stomach. As she approached the house, she felt worse and worse. Her belongings were in boxes on the lawn, just as she had requested. She pulled up and the family rushed out and helped load her car. As soon as the car was loaded, she said goodbye and headed out of the city. Once she got beyond the city limits, she felt fine all the way back to San Jose where she moved in with her parents.

We would all be wise to search for our individual place of power, which nourishes and feeds our soul. That place *does* exist. Once I advised a woman in the Bay area, who had been sick her entire life, to purchase a cross-country bus ticket. I told her to get out at every stop and see how she felt. I knew there would be a town in another state where she would feel as if she had been reborn into a new level of energy. She called a few weeks later to say that she was happily living several states away. Thrilled with her newfound energy, she said, "You know, Doctor Jim, I never would have believed this, but I've found the sense of peace here that I've been searching for all my life."

Occasionally the Power uses my appearance in dreams or visions to pass on messages even when I am completely unaware of it . . .

I once treated an airline pilot who moved to Hawaii with his 18-year-old son, Henry. One night Henry called from the islands to tell me that I had appeared to him in a vision the night before. In this vision, he was visiting friends who lived three blocks from where he and his father lived. His friends were using gasoline to clean a large generator in a room made from palm fronds when one of them accidentally started the motor. A spark ignited the gasoline, which burst into flames and turned the room into an inferno.

In Henry's vision, the other boys ran down the hill to get the fire department. Henry started to follow them, but I suddenly appeared in front of him and stopped him. I urged, "Go out through the window and dig down in the old pile of leaves next to the house. You will find a bright green hose connected to a faucet, which nobody knows is there. Turn on the faucet and put the fire out; otherwise, the entire house will be lost."

After putting the fire out in his vision, Henry turned to thank me, but I had disappeared. Twenty minutes later, the fire department arrived, fully expecting to find the place burned to the ground. To their surprise, Henry was inside reading a magazine. And here the vision ended.

Henry asked, "Did you know you were with me in Hawaii? What do you think it means? It was so *clear.*"

"No, I missed that one," I said. "We'll have to wait and see what it means."

A week later, Henry called, "Guess what, Doc? Everything happened just like in my vision. As soon as the fire started, I jumped out the window and dug under the pile of leaves. And there it was, a bright green hose already connected to a faucet. I turned it on and put the fire out before the fire department arrived. When the fire department found the owner of the house, he said he never knew the green hose and faucet were under that old pile of leaves. So I guess my friends and I have a lot to thank you for."

"Henry, you've heard me speak of the Power. Your thanks should go to them."

"I'll do it. I never told the guys since it all happened after the fact, but I wish I'd shared my vision the week before the fire. Pretty amazing stuff."

"Yes, it is. The Old Man appeared in many places while he was sleeping at home, but I don't know how I appeared to you. I'm just glad that you were there to put out the fire and save the day."

———•◆•———

When I was 33, I begged the Power to hit me with *all* the Power just once, and not just bits and pieces, here and there. Every morning for a year, I made this same request during meditation. I was enjoying my healing practice, but being typically human, I wanted *all* the Power, not dibs and dabs. After a year had passed, I hardly even thought about my request anymore; it was simply a customary part of my prayers. However, early one morning as I prayed—anticipating that my request would be ignored as usual—the gentle voice of the Power spoke, *"Very well."*

I looked up to see the Power sweeping down from the heavens toward me; it was a dynamic, omnipotent, whirling vortex of energy that I knew would carry me away. Instantly, I realized that I wasn't ready or prepared in any way to receive what was coming upon me. I shouted, *"Stop!"*

But the Power was in motion and not about to stop. When it reached me, it struck with the intensity of its pure and absolute force. When it released me, I felt like I was going to die. I found myself lying on the floor, completely helpless, my body unable to move. It was hours before I felt any semblance of normalcy.

In the months following this event, I was a spiritual wreck. If anyone tried to discuss metaphysics around me, I had to leave. If I tried to read spiritual topics, I became so nervous that I had to put the book down. Grabbing onto anything that made me feel connected to third dimensional reality, I watched television whenever I wasn't healing. I stopped meditating and I certainly had no further desire to reach for higher powers.

After six months passed, I finally had a grip on life after contacting the ultimate force of the universe. Ready to reconnect with the angelic forces, I sat in meditation. As soon as the Power appeared, I spoke of how foolish I had been in my request and how unready I had been for their blast of absolute power. I was taken aback by a chorus of unexpected laughter. The Power said, *"Dear One, we only released the slightest fraction of the Power, so small as to be insignificant."* And so I survived yet another blow to my ego.

My experience in making my request to the Power reminds me of a conversation I had with a friend many years ago about meditation. My friend said he had meditated faithfully every morning for years. Day after day, he had asked to speak to God. Finally, one morning, a commanding Voice spoke, *"What do you want?"*

My friend was terrified. He never expected to hear from God, or anyone else. Again, the Voice commanded, *"We have listened to your prayers all these years. And now we say again, what do you want?"*

Quickly gathering his wits, my friend answered, "I . . . I would like some wisdom . . . just a sentence I can offer to mankind to bring peace to the world."

The Voice responded, *"Tell mankind to try the Golden Rule. In truth, it has been overlooked. Try this rule and get on with your life. See if using the Golden Rule brings the changes you seek."* Then there was silence, the silence from which all things come, and my friend realized that he would only need the silence from then on.

———·◆·———

When I was 39, the Power announced, *"There will be two times in your life when you can ask us questions about anything or anyone. The first time of knowing is fast approaching. Gather your questions and prepare. The second time will come much later in your life."*

I was thrilled. Anxious to learn everything about life in all its phases and patterns, I started typing my questions at once. At last I would find out why we are here, where we came from and our purpose in life. I would also have a golden opportunity to ask about everything in my life and the lives of those closest to me.

Soon, the ego jumped into the game and encouraged me to ask when and how I would pass from this world into the next, how to make tons of money, and how to become the greatest healer in the world. Nothing was left out. When I was finished, I had typed 2,000—brilliant in my opinion—questions. As I reviewed them, each one seemed to glow with promise on the paper.

On the appointed day, I was told the session would begin at high noon and last 20 minutes. As I waited alone in my office, I was as anxious and eager as a young race horse at the gate. When the angels came, they lifted me to their lofty plane of existence where I was held within a loving cloud of light. The Power spoke, *"Let us begin."*

"How can I know God?"

"Beloved One, the way is already prepared. It is each person's birthright. Go into the silence where you are already one with All That Is and you will know God."

"But how can I know God with certainty when I'm going through difficult times in my life?"

"If you do not know God totally in every moment, it is because you are too much focused on your outer life. By focusing on the outer, you are not allowing the love of God to flow through your life in the moment. God is always with you."

"What should my goals in life be?"

"Attend to each moment of each day with love by accepting everyone and everything in that moment as perfect, exactly as they are."

"How can I learn to love in this way?"

"Just be. For you are total love when you can just be in the moment."

As I basked in the loving presence of the angels, I looked at the remaining 1,996 questions. They suddenly seemed so petty. I threw them in the wastebasket and asked the angels to guide me in meditation. The Power counseled, *"Dear One, you will regret throwing away your questions when you return to the normal energies of the body."*

"No, I only want soul wisdom, not ego personality information."

"So be it."

Embraced by their heavenly presence, I was taken into a deep state of meditation. Joined in the Creator's love, we flowed on and on until the angels told me that our time together had ended. Slowly, I returned to the normal state of being on the earth plane. Filled with love and peace, I took a long walk and moved through the rest of the day as though in a dream. I didn't look at the questions again that day and slept wonderfully well that night.

When I got to the office the next day, I thought of the questions and pulled them out of the wastebasket. Oh, no! They were not petty, stupid questions at all! Reviewing them, I wanted to weep for my loss. How could I have been in their Heavenly Presence and not ask the questions that any fool would ask? Before I could go over the edge, the Power came to me and said, *"Do not regret your time with us, for once in that higher state, everything took place exactly as needed for your soul growth."*

It's been 37 years since that first 20 minute session and one day, the second session, as promised by the Power, will come. I wonder what I will ask then. What would you ask? Are there right and wrong questions? Can we shortcut across the fields of life and arrive at our goal sooner than arranged by our higher self before birth? Is it wise to know these things?

We do know that everything flows together for the good of all. In this life, we are always guided as we journey home to God's heart. And, although we have forever to get there, the Old Man told me not to dawdle at the side of the road, but to remain ever focused on the journey itself.

———•◆•———

Let me take a moment and thank the Power for saving my life so many times. Only divine intervention has kept me on the planet this long, for which I am truly grateful. And I must admit I've often given the Power a run for their money in accomplishing this task. I clearly recall one time when a group of teenage friends decided, with the recklessness of youth, to see just how fast our cars could go. We had a new section of freeway, which was going to open the next morning, all picked out. It was a seven-mile downhill run, perfectly straight and ideal for our purpose. Those enticing four lanes with no traffic looked almost too good to be true.

We planned to take turns racing to clock our speed. As anxious as we were, we had the wisdom to wait until late at night to avoid any meetings with the local authorities. The hours of the day crawled by while visions of our speedway danced in my head. Finally we met at 11 P.M. I could hardly believe my luck when I was voted to go first. I went to the starting point with the next two racers, who would follow my run. Meanwhile, the designated clockers drove to the end of our improvised speedway.

After a day of impatient waiting, I was more than ready for my run. With my friends cheering me on, I tromped down the throttle of my souped-up Oldsmobile Club Coupe, oblivious of any consequences. What a thrill to hear the engine roar at full power. The outer world flew by in a blur. My heart pounded with excitement. Suddenly, in the middle of my run, my car—without my turning the steering wheel—was miraculously shoved over one lane to the right by a mighty, unseen force. I gasped as a monstrous, black shadow shot past me on my left, in the lane I had just been in.

When I reached the finish line, my excited friends reported clocking me at 110 mph. I turned the car around and headed back to the starting line to signal the next racer. However, when I reached the spot where I had seen the shadow in the road, I saw the police were there talking with a trucker whose rig was now pulled over on the shoulder. Since the officers paid no attention to me, I stopped to find out what was going on.

The officers were ticketing the trucker for sneaking onto the new freeway. He had an oversized load—an enormous palm tree—and was trying to avoid side streets. Shortly before I took off, the trucker came onto the freeway using a ramp approach further down from our starting line. As soon as he turned onto the freeway, the palm tree, which was being transported with its roots bound in burlap, rolled off his truck and landed in the lane I had chosen for my run.

Looking over at the tree, I saw the impenetrable root sack was at least 6 feet in diameter. I suddenly realized what the gigantic shadow had been to my left. Had I remained in that lane, I would have had a head-on collision with that massive tree. I knew that neither my Club Coupe, nor I, would have survived. I realized the Power had once again stepped in to save my life. Thanks to the intense interest of the police in the trucker's illegal activities, I was able to alert the other racers. We quietly left the scene and our racing dreams behind.

Much later in life, the Power saved me again. Having finished a long, tiring climb on a narrow deer trail along the face of California's Big Sur headlands, I was exhausted and grateful that I only had 15 feet to climb before reaching the top. Then I saw that six feet of the trail had collapsed just ahead of me; only faint traces of it were left, clinging to the face of the cliff. When I looked below me, I understood why climbers are advised never to look down. There was the missing six feet of trail scattered far and wide over the enormous, jagged rocks 200 feet below.

Cursing my bad luck, I wondered if I could make the climb down and still have enough energy to climb back up some other way. Then I saw it. Across the gap, was a gnarled, sturdy root the size of my wrist sticking out from the cliff. What luck! I could jump across the six-foot gap, grab onto that root, pull myself up, and be home free.

Exhilarated by my new plan, I backed up to get a running start. Adrenaline pumping, I ran as fast as I could. I leaped across the gap, ready to grab onto the hefty root protruding from the cliff. To my astonishment, my hands were forcefully redirected and I found myself clinging to a scrawny root a foot to the left of my stout friend. I had previously discounted this root, which was the thickness of my thumb, because it didn't look nearly strong enough to support my weight.

Fortunately, the little root held. I pulled myself up onto the remaining trail and continued my climb to the top of the cliff where my curiosity got the best of me. Finding a long branch, I returned to the edge of the cliff, leaned over, and used the branch to push on the large root that I had mentally chosen for my rescue. As I watched, the root casually fell out of its hole and down the cliff to its doom, 200 feet below on the rocks. Shaken, I realized that root could have been me. Once again, the Power's divine intervention had spared my life.

18

TEACHINGS FROM THE POWER

———— ·◆··◆· ————

I am ever grateful for the Power being present to instruct me when I open to the healing flow. Otherwise, I would surely rely on my mind, which is a dead end for me. By using the mind for what the mind does best, I can take care of everyday tasks, like taking out the garbage. But for life's higher patterns, I have learned to turn to the heart, which has been perfectly designed to guide us on our path of awakening.

From the Power I learned that we burst forth countless eons ago from the Creator's heart. And now we are on our journey home. Until each and every one of us returns to the heart of God, this journey never ends. We are all—no exceptions—destined to return home for we will not be complete until we rest once more in God's heart, in perfect peace. Until then, we are asked by our Creator to live a life of love for ourselves and our fellow creatures.

The Power likes to illustrate life with the following story: imagine you own an old car, which only goes 10 miles an hour on the freeway. Day after day, you watch other cars zipping past you at high speed. Frustrated, you save your money until you can afford to buy the latest, fanciest car with a top speed of 210 miles an hour. Once you buy your new car, you can hardly wait to get out on the freeway and have at it.

However, as soon as you ramp onto the freeway, you find yourself stuck in traffic so heavy that you can only go 10 miles an hour. And so it is in life. Too often we use our energy in getting up to full speed, only to discover that our ideas—about where we should be headed and what we should be focused on—were slowing us down, instead of moving us forward. For that matter, we might be on the wrong road altogether.

Without inner guidance, our energy can be misdirected. We all have inner communication, but, unfortunately, the clamor of outer life can overshadow it. The Power often reminds me to let God be the driver and illustrates this principle with the following story: imagine we are riding in a car, enjoying our journey. The road ahead is lined with beautiful trees; the sky is blue; in fact, everything is perfect.

If we are wise, we let God drive while we sit in the back seat, where we belong. But, being human, sooner or later we ask God if we can sit next to Him in the front seat. God agrees but instructs us not to bother Him as He is driving. He tells us to relax and enjoy the ride. We agree, sitting back quietly to watch the beautiful countryside.

But sooner or later—usually sooner—we ask God if we can put just one finger on the steering wheel. We promise we will place it very gently so as not to bother Him. Acknowledging freewill choice, God agrees. With great delight, we place one finger lightly on the steering wheel. We explain to ourselves that we just want to get the feel of the wheel. Not that we would *ever* want to *steer*, we only want to understand the idea of steering.

As time goes by, we slowly begin to place more fingers on the wheel. Before long, we have both hands on the wheel. Of course, we tell ourselves it's just for a moment so that we can experience the thrill of driving. Then, caught up in our adventure, we open the driver's door and—with a burst of enthusiasm—shove God out of the car. Then we move over into the driver's seat and take off, reveling in our newfound freedom.

However, in this earth life, we are all very poor drivers when we try to steer life's course. Sooner or later—again, usually sooner—we lose control and crash into the ditch. Moaning and groaning, we struggle out of the car. Looking back down the road, we see God dusting Himself off from His forced exit.

As God approaches to see the consequences of our takeover, we fall to our knees and beg His forgiveness. We pray for Him to fix the car and do all the steering from now on. Promising to be perfect passengers, we pledge—above all else—never, never, *never* to bother the driver again and to relinquish all desire to take control.

After God finishes the repairs, He takes His rightful place as the Divine Driver of our life. With humble attitude and effusive thanks, we take our place quietly in the back seat. And what happens next as we journey further down the road? The front seat next to God begins to look so inviting that we can't resist asking to move up front. And then? The circle of life's lessons continues until we wake up and allow God to direct us in every moment of every day.

———.◆.———

Ever interested in learning more, I asked the Power to show me the essence of an atom while I was in meditation. Instantly, I saw swirling galaxies spiraling outward into the cosmos. Objecting, I said, "You went the wrong way. I wanted to go microscopic, not macroscopic. I wanted to see the atom and the subatomic worlds within it, and what lies beyond the proton, neutron and electron."

The Power replied, *"You have just been shown the subatomic world. The universe goes both ways, micro and macro, in complexity and order. It is endless and forever."*

That night, I learned that the force fields in, around, and through everything are totally intelligent and that love is the underlying cause of everything in the universe. Love is a living intelligence, which invests everyone and everything with its powerful energy. Love knows all: the Alpha through the Omega and beyond. In trying to solve the mystery of life, we open a door that leads to a thousand doors, and each of these opens onto a million more gateways into the universe. How infinite is Creation. How grand our Creator.

Although the Power has revealed many other realms to me, I especially remember when an angelic guide took me on a narrow, winding path, high atop a mountain ridge. On both sides of the path, the sheer face of the mountain was impossible to climb from below. In the darkness of the valleys, which stretched out below us as far as I could see, were millions of naked human beings writhing together in frenzied coupling. Dark, thunderous clouds overhead prevented any sunlight from reaching those below. Frozen by the horror of the hellish scene below me, I didn't want to go on, but the angel encouraged me to continue on the path.

At last we arrived before a shimmering veil of golden light, which hung suspended in the air before us, preventing us from going on or seeing what lay ahead. Stunned by its radiant beauty, I inhaled sharply. My angelic guide waved a hand in front of the veil. Instantly, two circular openings, each one-foot in diameter, appeared in the veil of light. I looked through one opening and my guide looked through the other.

The breathtaking scene before me filled my heart with joy. Seven golden beings were tending a green field of vibrant, living grasses, which stretched to the horizon. In this idyllic world, the grasses broadcast a loving energy to the golden beings and these heavenly ones received this blessing and showered it upon everything around them. Magnificent oak trees, strong and purposeful, grew on the banks of a clear, sparkling stream. These trees were conscious and communicated with us as did the living waters of the stream. The air itself was totally alive, dancing with brilliant colors. Pleasing, harmonious tones filled the air.

Everything I saw on the other side of the veil was totally alive, fully conscious, and interconnected in one loving, sentient presence. My guide touched me gently on my arm and said, *"What you are seeing is a reflection of a life as yet unknown to your present mind. Beyond the veil, that is reality. That reality also exists on this side of the veil, but humankind cannot see this at their present level of consciousness."*

Sensing we were about to return, I longed to stay, but knew this could not be. The Power continued, *"What you have seen is humankind's future. If you wish to be a part of this compassionate world when it comes into being, you must decide and make your choice in this moment."* As soon as I gave my word, I was told not to speak of this coming world vision until permission was given, as it finally was for this book.

———•◆•———

When I receive visitations from the Power or experience phenomena, I consider them to be gifts from the Creator for further learning. There was one winter when I was permitted to see perfectly even though the house was in total darkness. For months, whenever I woke up during the night, I saw large pools of colored light playing across the ceiling.

At first, I just lay in bed and enjoyed the show. However, the light made the room so bright I decided to get up and move around to see what would happen. Although all the lights in the house were off and it was pitch dark, I could move easily through the house. The colored pools of light followed me and the walls themselves seemed to glow wherever I walked. There were no shadows anywhere, just a soft glowing light. It was as if all the lights, which were off, had been turned on to the lowest setting of a nonexistent dimmer switch. However, as soon as I began to take this "seeing" for granted, it ceased. I realized once more that I must never take my healing gift for granted.

Then summer arrived. One afternoon, I left the office to eat my lunch in the park. The sun was so warm and comforting that I promptly fell asleep on the grass right after eating my lunch. When I woke up, I was startled to see fuzzy, colored energies wrapped around everyone and everything. My first thought was that beach fog had moved into the area and was reflecting the sunlight in some strange manner.

When this glow suddenly disappeared, I was left sitting on the grass looking around on a normal, sunny afternoon. Then I realized I had been seeing auric fields. For six months, auras were clearly visible to me. Initially, this was fascinating since it was so different from seeing the energy bubbles and biofield energies visible through my inner vision. But after a few months, the appeal of auras wore thin. Their constant presence was not only tiresome, it distracted me from my healing work. I asked the Power to kindly remove this ability and it ceased to be.

Soon after this, I met another chiropractor who told me about being able to see everything going on inside the physical body. When I expressed my desire to do this, he paled. I asked, "What's wrong?"

"Don't," he warned.

"Don't what?" I asked.

"Listen to me. Don't try to see into the body. I worked months and months to do it. And the day I succeeded, I regretted it immediately. You can't imagine how horrible it is to be constantly confronted by people who appear to you as a collection of organs. Once this started, my patient's normal appearance was transformed into an anatomical display that I couldn't block out. I would only see the outer body for a few seconds before it turned into brains, floating eyeballs, coils of intestines, beating hearts . . . I felt like I was living in some horror movie."

"I never thought about it like that . . ."

"Let me tell you. I could hardly stand to *look* at people. What's *worse*, I had to work *twice* as hard for two *years* to get *rid* of this ability. Frankly I don't want anything to do with these extra talents ever again. Believe me. I'm perfectly content to remain an ordinary human being now. And I suggest you do the same."

After listening to his impassioned speech, I decided I would follow his advice. It seemed the wiser path to honor the gifts I had been given and stick with sensing energy, observing the bio-fields, and serving as a conduit for the Power.

———— • ◆ • ————

When I was in southern California, a close friend asked me to speak at her home to a group of 100 people. Having never given a speech in my life, I agreed without giving it much thought. But as the day grew closer, I found myself getting more and more nervous. On the appointed evening, my throat suddenly got very sore. I could hardly speak. Grateful to have an escape route, I had just decided that I was too sick to go through with this speaking engagement when the phone rang. It was Gina reminding me to be on time.

As I launched into my excuse, Gina shouted, *"Are you crazy?* There's a hundred people coming to hear you at 7:00 tonight. I've already told them all about the Power and the healing energy."

"Really, Gina, I'm sorry. But this is *serious,"* I croaked. "I feel awful."

"You're not kidding it's serious! I'm *not* going to cancel your talk. You've got to get over here *right now."*

After we got off the phone, I downed some Vitamin C and drove over to her house. There were cars parked everywhere. I spotted Gina out in front waving me to a spot she had reserved for me. As I got out of the car, Gina rushed up to me, "Don't worry. Everything's going to be just fine."

I managed an affirmative response, and discovered that my voice was scratchy and unrecognizable. Once inside, my knees felt like they would revolt at any moment and refuse to hold me up. Gina introduced me and the audience applauded. When they stopped, I began, which is to say I froze. There was no stage but I most certainly was experiencing a severe case of stage fright. My mind was a complete blank; I had no idea what to say. I bowed my head to gather my thoughts.

When I looked up, every head in the audience was bowed. They had assumed that I was praying. "What do I do now?" I thought. Then I realized that prayer *was* my only salvation. I bowed my head again, this time in earnest, and prayed for God to help me, or let me faint and fall unconscious to the floor. At this point, I wouldn't have objected to being carried out on a stretcher to a waiting ambulance. Anything would do, just so I didn't have to carry on with the lecture.

To my surprise, I lifted my head and began to speak without any sign of my sore throat. Listening to the Teacher who spoke through me, I felt that I too became a student during that first lecture. As the Power flowed through "my" words, the entire room lit up, and a sense of well-being filled each person in the audience.

An hour later, the Power and the voice that spoke through me ceased and I was once more on my own. The sore throat returned so I said a few quick farewells and hurried to my car. Gina ran after me to thank me and tell me that everyone wanted me to come back and give more talks, which I did every two weeks for many years to come.

After that, whenever I was before an audience, I would speak for a bit—rambling and joking about anything that came to mind—while I waited for the Power to take over and speak through me. I just provided the vocal cords, another way for the angelic ones to squash my ego. It was apparent—at least to me—that I was merely a tool. Without the Power in the driver's seat, the car would never have moved at all.

When I moved to the Bay area, I continued giving monthly talks on nutrition, life in general, and anything else that popped into my head. My lectures were always freewheeling. As soon as I began speaking, my mind would race around like a squirrel gone mad. Then, in the middle of sharing that explosion of thoughts, the Power would take over. That was the fun of it, to go on stage and begin speaking about anything at all. Suddenly, I would feel that first surge of the Power flowing into me and out into the audience, filling the room and almost pushing the walls out.

I love speaking before large audiences about health, nutrition, and the spiritual path. When I speak about the potential of the inner flame that never dies, it gives the Power the opportunity to explain how to strengthen that flame in our daily lives. I begin and The Power takes over with wisdom that continues to astound me even now after so many years of instruction.

The larger the crowd, the stronger the Power flows in order to touch each person. There are no limits since it is as easy to flow energy into thousands of people at once as it is to flow energy into one person. As the Power reaches out and focuses energy into the entire audience, the flow lights me up like a Christmas tree. Many have told me later that they not only felt the energy but that it changed their lives in ways they could never have imagined. We all have the possibility of change by allowing the Higher Self that lives within us to guide our lives, and the Power seems to facilitate this process.

At the conclusion of my talks, I always raise my hands, palms facing outward, to send the healing flow into the silence. This touches everyone in the audience who opens to the flow. First, the Power fills my hands until they begin to feel as if they are close to electric heating coils on a stove top. However, there's no feeling of heat, only the glow of energy and the presence of the Power's healing. The energy then fills my body and begins to move outward from my hands, investing the space in front of me with the Power. Gradually this builds in strength until it fills the auditorium. I sense each person downloading the energies as they open to receive the higher frequencies emanating from the Power.

As this symphony of light and color continues, I sense it building and I start to feel like an enormous light bulb whose job is to radiate the ever increasing flow of loving energy from the Source. The essence of love floods the auditorium—now quiet and still—until each person in the audience is completely filled with as much as the physical body can hold in that moment. This essence fills all the nooks and crannies within each person. People smile, basking in this sea of loving energy, their souls touched by grace.

Then the flow levels off as if our plane has reached cruising altitude and is ready to continue to its destination. This is my signal to retire from the scene to avoid disturbing the balance of the energies. I suggest that people remain silent as long as possible after the talk, to soak in the energies received, for these energies may be sustained for hours, days, weeks, or for a lifetime. It all depends on the openness of the receiver and God's plan. During the 50 years that I have given talks, many people who attended have told me later how it affected their lives and the lives of their families and friends.

Some of those lectures were taped and the tapes seemed to have an energy all their own that touched people when they listened to them. Patients told me that when a friend was depressed and thinking of suicide, they would send this person a tape. After listening to the tape, the person forgot their suicide plans and began life anew.

———•◆•———

A few patients have told me that they have seen the angels while I'm healing or during the talks . . .

When Hal came over to the coast to see me 25 years ago, he was working for the Federal Government. At that time, he was suffering from digestive problems and his low back required treatment. Since his back was reluctant to return to full strength, he came every two weeks for three months until his back returned to its normal energy pattern. During this time, we became good friends. I appreciated his openness, honesty, and his willingness to change his lifestyle according to our health guidelines.

Several treatments down the road, Hal stopped me in the middle of the treatment and said, "There's something I've got to tell you. When I came to see you the first time, five golden, angelic beings appeared behind you as soon as you raised your hands. And I've seen these angels every time I've come to see you. The one in the middle, who seems to be in charge, is at least seven feet tall. The two on either side are shorter. Doc, I'm not the kind of man this sort of thing happens to. I've never seen anything like this before. I've *got* to ask. Do you *know* these guys?"

I laughed and replied, "I always wondered why you kept glancing in back of me while I was running energy. I could tell by the expression on your face that something wonderful was going on, but I've never been aware of anything other than the usual healing energy of the Power. I can tell you that these beings are visitors from the angelic healing realm, which I call the Power."

A few treatments later, I asked, "Are the angels of the Power still with us?"

"Yes, Doc. They're always there as soon as you raise your hands to start treating me."

"Does it bother you?"

"No, of course not. I enjoy *seeing* the angels of the Power as much as I do when I feel their healing energy."

One day I told Hal that he should apply for a government accounting position in a particular town in California. He told me there was no federal office in the town I mentioned. I told him to put his application in anyway and he agreed. His coworkers ridiculed him for putting in an application for a nonexistent job in a nonexistent office. Six months later, when a federal office opened in the town, he was happy to be the first on the list for the openings.

At other times, different beings have appeared through me to my patients. In most cases, patients seemed to take it in stride when this happened although I could never explain how these appearances occurred. Some patients described these beings to me in great detail. While many of their descriptions were quite familiar to me, as though I had been with those beings in other lives, others were strange and unknown to me.

At one evening lecture, I had barely started my talk when a woman got up and stormed out of the auditorium. Before leaving, she complained to the person at the door, "I came to hear Doctor MacKimmie speak, not some old *Chinese* man dressed up in *robes.*" This particular description is the one I've heard most often over the years.

While I was never aware of becoming the old Mandarin, many of my patients saw him. They said he wore silk robes of vivid colors in ornate patterns, had a queue that reached to the floor, and wore exquisite jeweled rings on tapered fingers that ended in long fingernails. All of this was very interesting to me since I was unaware of these transformations; however, I gradually became used to reports of these appearances.

———•◆•———

At times, incredible and miraculous happenings occurred during and after lectures. A neighbor came for the first time to one of my talks when I was speaking at her church. Afterward, while I was busy talking with a few people who stayed after the lecture, I saw her examining the back of the stage just behind where I had been standing. After the people left, I asked, "Can I help you?"

My neighbor said, "Those violet, blue, and pink colors that were on the curtains behind you while you were lecturing were so very beautiful. It was amazing how the colored flood lights followed you when you were moving around the stage. I especially liked it when the colors changed every time you raised your hands."

Knowing that there had been no flood lights, I smiled and asked, "So what exactly are you looking for backstage?"

The lady frowned and answered, "Well, I talked with other people here tonight and they saw the *same* lights. I wanted to get the same color display for the Christmas performance at my daughter's school. But . . . well . . . here I am backstage . . . and there's only an empty plywood wall with a white curtain over it. I don't see any lights at *all.*"

"People often see these lights at my talks. I can't explain them. I don't know where they come from or what they are. I sense them behind me, but I've never seen them. The way I look at it, most of life is a mystery so we might as well enjoy it all."

After one lecture, an old man pushed through the people around me. He wiggled two of his fingers in my face and asked, "Isn't it wonderful?" Startled, I replied, "What's wonderful?"

"My two fingers. Just look at them. They're perfectly normal. They've been twisted over each other since birth. I've had them broken and redone surgically several times. But they were always worse after the surgery and the pain never quit. Then, you raised your hands after the talk. Suddenly, my fingers were normal. The pain is gone now . . . totally gone. Thank you."

Later, I learned that many healings took place even after the talk due to the energies that flowed from the Power. God does heal, always has and always will. And thank you God for your many blessings.

One other talk comes to mind. I was scheduled to speak in a Palo Alto School auditorium. Arriving at 7:00 P.M., I was ready to begin. Unfortunately the student who was supposed to open the building and set up the sound system wasn't there. It was a winter night—California cold, not Montana cold, but still cold—and those who had come for my talk were none too happy to be left outside in the cold, and neither was I.

Luckily there was another function going on at the school so we joined the group heading inside. Somehow the folks who had come to my lecture all managed to crowd into the large waiting area just outside the locked auditorium. Everyone was eager for my talk to begin. Even though we didn't have the luxury of chairs, I started speaking. However, in my mind I was busy berating the miscreant who had shirked his unlocking duty. I was hoping that the absent student would show up before I finished my talk. At least that way, we could conclude the session in the warmth and comfort of the auditorium.

However, the only arrivals on the scene were more people going into the classroom next door to the auditorium where an art class was being held. As my talk got under way, I discovered that our "room" apparently had the only restrooms in the vicinity. Students from the art class would suddenly burst through their classroom door and tromp loudly across the cement floor, heading to the facilities at the back of our room. Shortly, my words were accompanied by a flushing that echoed through our room like Niagara Falls. Next, the students would clomp back to their class. These particular artists must have been water lovers since every few minutes their door banged open and a new face appeared. I was ready to lock their door until I saw it had no lock. And so it went for two hours.

In the midst of this madness, I found myself pushed aside as the Power came through to speak and the energies began flowing to everyone, including the artists in the next room. Many people told me later how inspiring my talk was, but I have to admit that through it all, my ego fumed on the sidelines, angry that the thoughtless, unfeeling, negligent—and other words unfit to print—student hadn't come. Most churches simply mailed me the key and asked me to turn the lights off and lock the doors when we were through.

And as we were leaving, guess who arrived on the scene with the key. No apology of course, just an explanation that he had received a call at home, telling him to be sure to lock up after we left the auditorium. This call gave our brilliant student a flash of inspiration, and he decided to cruise by the auditorium to see the lay of the land. When he asked if we were through so that he could lock up, I informed him that he need not bother since the auditorium had never been *unlocked* in the first place. He shrugged and ambled off.

The only gratification I had was that we did not have to pay for the auditorium nor the anterior waiting room where all those wonderful people sat on cold cement for two hours. Although I would have chalked up the night as a total disaster, I learned later that many healings took place. God doesn't seem to care about working conditions. But next time I would choose an open auditorium, heat, and a working microphone.

———•◆•———

Such has been my experience in witnessing the healing Power at work for these many years. In the movies, I might have a chance to wear a dazzling, electric-blue cape and have a magic wand that sparkles like Dorothy's shoes in *The Wizard of Oz*. Or perhaps wear a rainbow-colored suit, dignified to respect my 76 years of traveling on this spiritual healing journey. I actually do remember a time when I wore a suit and tie with properly polished shoes to greet my patients, but now I'm more casual in my healing ministry. Thankfully, God heals no matter what I'm wearing.

PART V

HEALERS AND HEALING

19

ON THE SHOULDERS OF GIANTS

———— ⋅◆⋅⋅⋅◆⋅ ————

S ir Isaac Newton said, "If I have seen further, it is because I have stood upon the shoulders of giants." Fifty years ago I knew healers who were giants; they were very special and very few. Like the Old Man, these healers truly had the gift. Working in the background, they were dedicated to healing and doing their best to help anyone who came to see them. They held the torch of healing high to light the path for all who followed. It is through their work that we can see further today.

As I walked my own path of healing with the Power as my companion, I sought out these miracle workers. I found rare gems scattered across the country doing their marvelous work, putting their own needs aside in order to devote their lives to healing. There are not words enough to express my gratitude to the incredible healers who came into my life. They generously shared their remarkable skills with me; thus, I was able to grow as a healer and increase my knowledge of the powers that exist within us all.

The great healers that I knew personally have all crossed over, incredible healers, gone in our time. Like the great composers of the eighteenth century—Mozart, Haydn, Beethoven and Bach—these healers were all born in a cluster within a short span of time, and I have not met their like since. I miss these dear old friends whom I knew long ago; they were so magical. They were also remarkably forthright when they talked with me—I loved that.

These healers were willing to answer my questions about healing, but, at times, the healer freely admitted there was no answer to the question I had asked. How refreshing! We seldom hear professionals admit that there is no answer, as though not having an answer to every question is a crime.

How I miss those high-energy giants of the past. As primary healers, they worked in Time Eternal, focusing the infinite power of the universe to heal the physical body and liberate the soul. Lest we forget the work of these early healers, I will tell you about a few that I have known.

———·◆·———

Harry Edwards was one of England's finest spiritual healers. His faith ran deep and he drew inspiration from Jesus of Nazareth. I thoroughly enjoyed my lively correspondence with him. In one letter he enclosed his photograph. As soon as I saw his marvelous face, I thought Harry looked like I imagined God would choose to look, marvelously distinguished with a commanding profile and glorious, silver hair.

During the time we corresponded, I was also treating people at a distance via their photographs. I requested these folks to send me feedback once a month by letter as to how they were coming along. Months and months went by and I received only three letters. I complained to Harry that, although I learned there were many healings, only three out of hundreds had ever written to me. If I had been listening, I would probably have heard his laughter across the Atlantic.

Harry wrote back saying that I was very lucky indeed and should celebrate my fantastic success in hearing from these three people since he treated thousands and had never received *any* communication at all. He added that people tend to forget the healer and go on with their lives once they are healed. This dear healer died in 1976.

———·◆·———

While I was in Los Angeles, I took classes with Dr. Charles C. Hayes once a month for a year. A chiropractor and one of the greatest pendulists and nutritional healers ever born, he told me that his introduction to the power of healing came when his wife was dying. Dr. Charles had tried every medical and alternative therapy for his wife, but she was barely holding on to life. Finally, he had to accept the fact that she was dying.

One day when the minister came to be at his wife's bedside, he couldn't bear to stay in the room any longer.

Overcome with grief, Dr. Charles left the house and went to the park. He sat down on a bench and sobbed into his hands. A man came up and asked if there was anything he could do to help. Dr. Charles said his wife was dying and nothing could help her now. The man asked where he lived and said he would come the next day to see if he could help her.

The next day, Dr. Charles had forgotten his strange encounter until the man from the park knocked on his door. Dr. Charles took him into the bedroom where his wife lay in a coma. After the stranger studied Mrs. Hayes for a few minutes, he said he needed to leave but would be back shortly. When he returned, he brought an herbal "tridosha" formula, which he placed on her tongue. In Ayurvedic medicine, tridosha refers to the three doshas (Vata, Pitta and Kapha). These three dynamic forces, which are constantly shifting within us, influence the body's state of health. The goal of the formula was to bring these powerful forces into balance.

A few minutes later, Mrs. Hayes jumped up, looked around, and started giving Dr. Charles the very devil for allowing her house to get into such a mess. After this scolding, she got out the vacuum cleaner and started to restore her house to its proper order. The astounded Dr. Charles excitedly followed the miracle man back to his home. The other chap was also a chiropractor and he taught Dr. Charles the wonders of using a pendulum as an instrument of diagnosis and treatment.

Dr. Charles became a master pendulist and taught penduling all over the world. The pendulum was used in ancient Egypt and in many cultures as a tool to interface the left side of the brain (analytic/conscious) with the right side of the brain (intuitive/subconscious). The pendulist can then access Universal Knowledge, which is the cosmic storehouse for all information.

It was a gift to meet Dr. Charles and take his work. He gave classes once a month teaching tridosha analysis, penduling and E.D.T (Energy Distortion Technique). I'm sure he was the best in the world at that time. He could locate energy distortions all over the body and correct them within minutes. At every meeting he cured crowds of sick people using a pendulum. I would have thought this method unbelievable if I had heard it from someone else, but I saw it all first-hand.

Dr. Charles saved my life several times. In one case, I had been deathly ill for months. I knew I was losing ground rapidly in my battle for survival so I drove 250 miles to see the good doctor. I was the third person to be treated that day. He placed the tips of his fingers gently on my body, one hand on the upper portion of my back and the other on my head. He held this contact for a few minutes. Then he told me to walk outside for 15 minutes and to notice when I felt better.

Earlier that morning when I was on my way to the doctor's office, I had walked past a schoolyard. The laughter of the children absolutely rubbed my nerves raw. I wanted to scream at them to be quiet. After my treatment, I was striding right along when I checked my watch according to the doctor's instructions; the 15 minutes were up. Then I became aware of the pleasant warmth of the sun on my face. Looking around, I realized I had arrived back at the school playground. The laughter and shouts of the children were like the sweetest music. I found myself enchanted by the joyful faces of the children at play.

Back at the doctor's office, I walked into his large waiting room. Everyone turned in my direction. I was bewildered when the other patients began shouting. They jumped up and wanted to hug me. Dr. Hayes came into the room to investigate the uproar. He smiled and told me to go into the bathroom and look in the mirror. When I did, I saw that there was not a line on my face. The gray pallor of illness that had been mine for months was gone, replaced by a wonderful, healthy pink glow. I felt reborn.

For weeks afterward, people on the street would stop me and ask what had happened to me. I glowed with health and good humor. I simply loved everybody and everything. A month or so later, this glow began to fade. I was shocked, but grateful to have been in that place of peace and joy for even a little while.

Early in my career, I sent many patients to see Dr. Hayes and they all got well. A genius in his healing work, he held workshops for other healers to share his techniques. Some of the information he taught us was so strange that we hesitated to share it with others, but it always worked. I learned many things from him, but he told me the energy I used in my healing practice was quite unique and said he had never experienced anything like it before. He advised me to follow wherever it led.

Dr. Charles and his wife, Liz, were very kind to me. He stressed the importance of organic foods, which he declared were responsible for maintaining his perfect health. He loved working in his garden where nary a weed ever appeared and was happy to show me how to grow organic fruits and vegetables. Whenever he worked outside, he wore a broad-brimmed hat, dressed all in white, and wore white gloves. Carefully protected from the sun, his skin remained lily white and there was not a line on his face at 90 years of age.

Dr. Hayes has crossed over now, and I hope he's enjoying the fruits of his fine work. I remember once hearing that he paid for 28 young men to take their college training in chiropractic. Thank you, Dr. Charles, for your generosity in teaching so many of us your wonderful work, and for saving my life.

———·◆·———

Dr. Neil Bruscolini was a chiropractor in southern California. I watched him help many people in his long career as a healer. A dear friend of many years, he was a kind, sensitive man, and one of the most brilliant men I have ever met. A bit older than myself, Dr. Neil was the first to alert me 50 years ago to the effects of fluorescent lighting. I changed the fixtures in my office to full spectrum lights as soon as he shared his new research with me. I recall that once, for six months, he received specific healing instructions for his entire day during his early morning meditation. Although his patients might not be injured until later in the day, he received clear, healing instructions for them before he left for the office. Who knows why this was so, but it was very handy while it lasted and all who came to him were healed.

It was through Dr. Neil that I met the remarkable Dr. Hayes whose technique saved my eldest son's life. My adventurous son, Robert, was four years old when he climbed up on our roof and fell off. We rushed him to the hospital, but the doctors gave us no hope and told us to take him home.

Within a few hours, fine lines appeared all over Robert's face, like the wrinkles of an eighty-year-old man. His beautiful, sparkling eyes dimmed, and he was unable to eat or drink anything. Desperate to save him, I tried every treatment I knew, but nothing helped. (Unfortunately, this is true for most healers. Concern for our family makes it difficult to remain in the open, receptive place required for the healing flow.)

Forty-eight hours after Robert's accident, my wife Helen and I had exhausted every possibility we could think of for helping our son. (I had not yet met the Old Man.) Robert was dying before our eyes. Suddenly, I thought of Dr. Neil. We hurried to his office with our son.

I placed Robert gently on Dr. Neil's treating table. Neil quickly explained that we were going to use a specific contact, which Dr. Hayes had taught us just the week before. In the exact manner given, we applied the contact with all of us (Dr. Neil, his wife Jenny, Helen and myself) hooked together in a series to make a living battery of energy. After six minutes had passed (and Dr. Hayes had told us that three minutes would be considered an eternity for this treatment), a blast of heat passed through all of us and nearly melted us into the ground.

And presto, Robert was instantly up and smiling. Tears welled up in my eyes to see his eyes sparkling with life once more. He looked at me and said, "Daddy, I'm thirsty." We gave him the biggest glass of water that we could find. He drank it all and more. Then he said, "Daddy, I'm hungry." We prepared a huge meal and he ate it all. Within an hour, his wrinkles disappeared totally. Here was our dear boy of the quick smiles and ready laughter back again. Dr. Neil lost the ability to heal in that particular way six months later. But I thank God that he saved my son.

———•◆•———

Attempting to meet Dr. Leon Truscott for the first time, I arrived at his home early one morning. When I knocked on the front door, it was opened by a large, imposing woman wearing a white uniform. She glared and demanded to know what I wanted. I told her that I had come to see Dr. Truscott. She emphatically declared that he was not there and ordered me not to come back again. Behind this intimidating personage, I saw a shadow-like figure waving to me. Looking closer, I saw a short, white-haired old fellow who signaled me toward the back of the house before he disappeared. Under the watchful eyes of a wife turned security guard, I backed away from the door, which closed firmly in my face.

Rounding the corner of the house, I headed toward the garage where Dr. Truscott met me. He pulled me into the garage and escorted me to a large room at the back where he had his treatment table and instruments. He told me his wife disapproved of chiropractors and thought very little of the energy work that he loved so well. I instantly thought of another chiropractor in Glendale whose wife was a registered nurse and hated chiropractic. As his office nurse, she ran patients off at an alarming rate by referring them all to local medical doctors. And so, poor fellow, my friend gave up his office and took only house calls.

Dr. Leon was so sensitive he could feel changes in the atmosphere whenever there was an atomic test in Nevada. He could tell the exact hour and minute the bomb was detonated. After hearing the news from him, I would hear on the radio that a test had been performed just as he had said. In his view, this testing was detrimental and would create great sickness in future generations.

An accomplished healer and teacher, he was delighted to pass on his unique muscle testing method to interested healers. I observed his patients being treated with his gentle touch and saw the wonderful results. I hope God reserved a special place in Heaven for this sweet man.

————•◆•————

Dr. Floyd Dudgeon, a chiropractor in Oakland, California treated several hundred people every day. He was a tiny, frail 70-year-old when I met him. Although he looked as though the slightest breeze would blow him away, he worked from dawn to midnight. He was truly one of God's miracle workers.

Dr. Dudgeon healed a neighbor of mine who was in the hospital and scheduled for breast surgery. A family member told her to call him from the hospital. When she called, he told her to leave the hospital immediately and go home. He ordered her not to answer her door under any circumstances.

Later that day, she heard pounding on her door. Remembering Dr. Floyd's instructions, she ignored the knocking. By the next morning, the lumps in her breast were gone, and she never had any further problems with the condition. She told me that when she called to thank Dr. Dudgeon, he told her that the pounding she heard at her door had been the police, sent to bring her back to the hospital. She told me that she was later able to verify this fact.

People waited hours to see Dr. Dudgeon. I talked with dozens of his patients who willingly shared the miracles he had performed to heal them. A close friend of mine was saved from cancer by Dr. Dudgeon after the hospital had given up on him following a round of chemotherapy. As a part of his treatment, Dr. Dudgeon told my friend to recite Romans 8:19 from the Bible several times a day for two weeks: "Creation waits in eager expectation for the sons of God to be revealed." Within a month, the cancer was gone. For all the help he generously gave his patients, I'm sure the good doctor has been given some prime real estate in God's heavenly kingdom.

———•◆•———

Joe Jessel of Ashland, Oregon was an incredible healer, but all he ever wanted from life was to be plain, old cowboy Joe. He had no interest in healing. His mom had always healed so Joe grew up knowing all about it and hated the whole idea. Joe told me that his hatred started when his mother, Suzie, described her life as a healer.

It all began when Suzie's parents made the startling discovery that people who held her as a baby were healed of every illness, including cancer. After that, Suzie's parents passed her around from person to person for healing treatments. For 10 cents, people held their baby girl on the site of their disease for a few minutes and all were healed. Suzie told Joe that she had a hard time growing up because most people regarded her as a freak. As a young boy, these stories disturbed Joe. He knew one thing for sure: he didn't want to be a healer like his mother. Besides, he had his heart set on being a cowboy.

When I talked with Suzie, she said that in her early twenties she decided she was through with the healing business. She walked into the hills to tell God that she was going to stop healing right there and then. But Jesus appeared and proclaimed, "You will not stop. You will heal." Suzie was deeply religious, but even after this appearance of the Master, she continued to question her healing. Should she stop healing? Was it against her religion to heal? Finally she decided again that she was going to stop. Jesus appeared to her again and said, "Heal my sheep." Mom Jessel told me that she never again questioned her calling.

Joe told me that his chance to escape his healing career ended when he was 13. He was at a baseball game when one of the other boys got hit in the nose, which started a serious nosebleed. He asked Joe to take a look at it. As soon as Joe touched him, the bleeding stopped. "Damn!" Joe exclaimed. "I've got the curse too!" As a soldier in Korea, he stopped bleeding for wounded soldiers coming into the field hospital. But he hated healing so much that he sometimes drank to escape from "the curse." Back in the states and out of the service, the highway patrol would often rush him to the scene of an accident. All Joe had to do was touch the victim and the bleeding—no matter how severe—stopped.

Like his mother, Joe decided to stop healing at one time. He planned to ranch and raise cows like a real cowboy, but his cattle all laid down and wouldn't get up unless he was healing. So he sold the cattle and went on healing. When Joe told me these things, it struck me as very strange that so many people want to be healers, but Joe hated every minute of it.

If Joe or Mom Jessel put one hand on your body, you would feel nothing. However, the moment they put both hands on, it felt like your body was baking in a hot oven. It was all the heat a person could stand, but at the same time it felt quite wonderful. They only spent a minute on each person, no matter what the condition. I sent every cancer case I came across to see them and they all got well within two weeks. The Jessels didn't deal in nutrition or give any other advice for health. When I asked Joe about the blood sugar problem I was having at that time, he said, "Doc, eat regler." Of course he was right on target.

I noticed that some of the Jessel's patients went through severe pain before they got well while others simply got well in a week or two without any pain. When I talked with their patients, there seemed to be one common denominator. If the person had been taking drugs for their condition, they experienced pain when the healing energy brought about a cleansing reaction, or healing crisis. Other patients urged the sufferers to sweat it out. If they did, healing was their reward.

Back then, each treatment was a dollar, which you put in Mom Jessel's apron or in Joe's shirt pocket. Both Joe and Mom Jessel could tell how many treatments would be needed to heal you. Mom Jessel would lightly touch the back of your hand. When the healing was complete, a large capital "H" would appear, like the welt of a brand; this sign lasted for 10 minutes before disappearing. If more healing work was needed, the "H" would be incomplete; for example, one leg of the "H" would be missing. Joe couldn't do that, but as soon as he looked at a person, he knew how many treatments would be needed. They treated all day and long into the evening. Together, they saw hundreds of people on healing days. There were small places to stay and a cook served up hamburgers. A rough, simple operation but those two were genuine healers who served humanity and God.

After observing the Jessels at work for three weeks, I returned home to the Bay area. Back to work at my office, I had a new patient come in who was only 45 years old, but he was on a downhill run in his health. At every appointment, I carefully instructed him about good nutrition, exercise, drinking lots of water, meditation, and early hours of sleep, but Ken was one tough case.

Although I continued to explain the beating his body was taking by not making these changes, Ken didn't want to listen. Death energies began to gather around him; I saw that he would die soon. Since he was unwilling to make any changes and take responsibility for his health, I sent him north to the Jessels.

Joe told my patient 25 treatments would heal him completely; he took 24. Ken felt so good after treatment number 24 that he returned to the Bay area to show me how healthy he was. Indeed, he looked incredible and simply glowed with health. I warned him, "No matter how good you feel now, go back for your last treatment or you're inviting your condition to return. If Joe told you 25 treatments, then 25 it has to be."

Ken strutted around the room while he thought over my warning. Finally he stopped and announced, "Doc, don't worry. I'm totally healed and the hospital said so too when my test results came back."

"I'm trying to tell you what the angels are showing me," I countered. "If you don't take that last treatment, you will be a dead man. I can't put it any plainer." But he smugly refused to go.

Three years later, Ken came dragging in to see me at my office. He was a physical wreck, and his old disease was in full swing. When I touched him, I felt deadly toxins stacked in his body. I asked. "Are you drinking any water?" He stared at me blankly and repeated, "Water?"

Ignoring the wave of frustration I felt, I gave it another go and started reviewing the health guidelines. While I was speaking, I watched his energy field quickly build an impenetrable wall of resistance. Once I saw that he was still unwilling to make any changes, I advised, "Forget making these changes. If you want to live, leave for Oregon tonight and see Joe."

Finally, many months later, Ken headed north to see Joe for healing. Joe died the day before my patient arrived. And my patient soon followed him. Surely karma, knowing that this man would only learn from further pain, kept my patient from making that trip in time to see Joe.

Michelle's was a happier story although it didn't start out that way. She was 18 when she came to see me. Admiring her long blonde hair, I could see that she had once been stunningly beautiful, but her youthful beauty had since been stolen by leukemia. Her first words to me were, "I'm dying."

While I was running energy, the Power told me to send her to Joe so I described how Joe Jessel healed his patients. I guess my story was the last straw. Giving me a grief-stricken look, she said, "My sister just died from leukemia."

"I don't believe your sister's fate has to be your fate," I said earnestly. "Make the trip to Oregon and see Joe." Michelle left quietly. I saw in her energy that she had already resigned herself to her sister's fate.

Two months later, I received a phone call from Michelle to thank me for telling her about Joe. She was at the hospital and her test results showed that she was now perfectly healthy. After hearing her good news, I said, "From the look you gave me when you were leaving my office on that first appointment, I never thought that you would go to see Joe. That look told me that you thought I was a nut case."

Michelle laughed, "Oh, I thought you were crazy all right. But let me tell you what happened and why I changed my mind about your advice . . ."

"It was Christmas Eve, a month after I'd been to see you. My boss and I were at her clothing store in Los Gatos. We had just finished working all day without taking any breaks. It's hard to believe that men actually leave their Christmas shopping until the very last minute. We were totally exhausted and decided to have a couple of drinks to celebrate the end of our hectic day. After sitting down, we had just put our feet up when a woman started rapping on the store's glass doors with a large key."

"My boss rolled her eyes and said, 'Michelle, run to the front and get her to stop that before she breaks the glass.' So I put down my drink and ran to the front. I yelled, 'We're closed!' through the closed doors. I was hoping that would be the end of it, but the woman yelled back, 'I just want to buy that coat on the rack nearest the door. I looked at it earlier today and have the exact amount to buy it. You won't even have to make change.' I turned around to look at my boss who raised her eyebrows and nodded."

"After this last shopper paid for the coat, she asked if we had a box so that she could mail the coat to her niece in Oregon. I went digging around in the back and found a box that would fit. After I checked with UPS, I told the woman that a driver would pick it up and deliver it to the Oregon route that night. She was thrilled and I finished packing the coat."

"Then I asked the woman her name for her return address. I nearly fainted when she said 'Jessel.' I must have looked like I was going to pass out too because she asked me what was wrong. I told her 'Jessel' was an unusual name and that a chiropractor had told me a month ago to see a healer named 'Joe Jessel' in Ashland, Oregon to cure me. The shopper laughed and said, 'That's my brother Joe. I'll write you a note so you can stay at the ranch and get healed.' And that's exactly what happened."

After serving God's mighty work in this life, Joe, a reluctant healer, died at 52. Perhaps next time around, God will let him be "Cowboy Joe."

———•◆•———

Never was there a more cranky healer than Chris Lawson of Depoe Bay, Oregon. His biting comments on life were interrupted only by the ring of his chewing tobacco striking the inside of his brass spittoon. But he was totally dedicated to his healing practice. I remember the sign planted on his front lawn that boldly proclaimed: "MY NAME IS CHRIS LAWSON AND I CURE CANCER." When the medical authorities took him to court, thousands of his patients came to court with before and after medical reports that proved his healing ability. He told me the court's decision allowed him to continue his healing work.

For my first meeting with Chris, I went to his office in an older home on a cliff overlooking the ocean. Anxious to meet this healer, I was the first to arrive that morning. Having heard that Chris hated people to park in his spot, I drove as far as I could to one side of the lot, drove off the asphalt, went past several large mud puddles, and parked under a dying tree.

While waiting, I congratulated myself on avoiding any trouble. As more patients started arriving, another car pulled up next to mine. The driver glared at me, got out, slammed the car door, and stalked toward the house. I asked another man, "So, who's the old codger with the attitude?"

"Oh, that's Chris Lawson. You're parked in his favorite spot."

For the next few days of my visit, I tried to ingratiate myself with him and smooth his ruffled feathers, but with little success. Eventually, I gave up this hopeless cause and quietly observed while he treated his patients. I saw dying people carried in; in a few days, they were able to walk in without any assistance. Within two weeks, they were totally healed and left for home restored to perfect health. People came from all over the world to be healed.

Once Chris decided to accept me as a fellow healer, he shared his favorite fishing story with me. One day he was on a commercial fishing boat along with 30 other die-hard fishermen. Like many other coastal areas, Puget Sound was often home to heavy fog, and this day was one of the foggiest so the skipper was navigating by compass. But when the fog lifted, he was startled to find that he wasn't out in the ocean at all; he was still in the bay. His boat had been going around in circles.

The skipper couldn't imagine what was wrong until he saw Chris had taken a seat near the compass. The skipper shouted, "Damn it Chris, I told you to always sit in back, away from the compass." (Having stopped clocks and crashed our computer, I could easily understand that his healing energy created some unexpected side effects.)

Shortly after I returned from Oregon, Steve came into my office for the first time. His wife was with him; they were both 28. A fast car and worn brakes had resulted in a terrible accident. Steve was now a quadriplegic in a wheelchair with no control over his bowel, bladder, arms and legs. I felt especially sorry for his young wife who was totally responsible for the care of her husband and their two children. Although the energy helped, the Power told me that his lessons involved going to see Chris Lawson so I persuaded Steve to go north for healing.

After one treatment from Chris, Steve called me, his voice filled with excitement. He could stand for the first time since his accident, had bladder and bowel control, and the use of his arms. I was so happy for him and his little family. He reported that Chris said that if he would stay for two weeks and take treatment every day, he would be totally healed and completely normal in every respect. I said, "If that's what Chris told you, then you can count on it. I've never seen him wrong."

On the third day of their stay in Oregon, Steve's wife called me in tears. I heard Steve yelling in the background, "I have to get home to Palo Alto." He was screaming this over and over like a madman. "Put Steve on the phone," I told her. When he picked up the phone, I said, "Do whatever you have to do to stay in Oregon. Chris is never wrong. If he said you'll be normal in two weeks, then you will be completely healed if you stay there under his care." Steve yelled, "I don't care. I've got to get home." And back they came to Palo Alto.

Every time Steve came to see me, I urged him to head north since the Power continued to declare that Steve's lessons and healing were with Chris. He always agreed but casually said he'd get to it later on. For two years, I tried to persuade Steve to return to Chris. One day, Steve called and said, "I'm ready to go back to Oregon to be healed, for my family's sake." I said, "You know, Steve, Chris is getting up there in years. You're lucky he's still alive."

The next day, Steve called from Depoe Bay to tell me that Chris had died the day before. I think Steve's sudden urge to be healed had surfaced because his subconscious mind knew the old healer was gone. Since God is always in charge, Steve must have had more to learn from his condition than from further healing. He did retain the use of his arms, and control of his bowel and bladder, for which he and his wonderful family were very grateful.

During the next week, 50 other patients that the Power had directed me to send to Chris called and asked how to get in touch with "that old healer in Oregon" I had mentioned to them. They all said they were now "ready" to see him. Coincidence? I had told them about Chris for years, but now it was too late. Surely karma had a hand in the fate of these patients who knew about Chris, but never received his healing gift.

Otherwise, why would so many people suddenly wake up to the healing energy this old healer shared during his life, only after it was gone. I saw this same sudden interest in the Old Man's healing after he died.

I spent many weeks in Oregon observing these wonderful healers, and saw dying patients restored to perfect health. During the '60s and early '70s, I sent cancer patients unwilling to make any changes at all up to Oregon to see the Jessels or Chris Lawson. It amazed me that these healers accomplished miraculous results without any effort on the part of the patient—without dietary changes, or meditation, or anything at all. These healers were just plain folk and not highly educated, but, by George, they could heal all the incurable conditions that I had ever come across.

To this day, I have never found anyone (except the Jessels, Chris Lawson and the Old Man) who could heal fatal conditions without requiring patients to make changes in their lives. Perhaps there are others out there, but they wisely keep their mouths shut and continue their wonderful healing work. With the death of Chris Lawson, the last of the three Oregon wonder workers was gone.

———•◆•———

Dr. T. J. Bennett, was a chiropractor in Burlingame, California. Elegant and fastidious, his students surmised that he must sleep wearing a tie. His debonair appearance was matched by the classic car he drove, which he kept spotlessly clean and polished at all times.

Maintaining strict discipline in his classes, Dr. Bennett set incredibly high standards for his students and his profession. His technique was to hold contacts on specific reflex points in order to trigger healing in certain centers of the body. Since Dr. Bennett had exceptional results with his patients—even when his reflex points seemed to stray from where he carefully taught his students—we declared amongst ourselves that he had to be a healer. However, when we mentioned this to him, he fumed and denied it in no uncertain terms. He made it clear that he thought healers were quacks and any reference to such an idea was utter nonsense.

When Dr. Bennett passed on, his methods seemed to disappear. But I still use the Bennett Reflex technique, which he taught us with such demanding precision, to balance the body's energy fields. Thank you, Dr. Bennett, for your magnificent instruction.

————•◆•————

Bill Gray of San Francisco, a fine healer with an excellent reputation, treated people in Hollywood, Washington, D.C. and everywhere inbetween. When I talked with him, he ascribed his healing abilities to the solitude of his early life growing up around Lake Tahoe. He confessed that when he moved into the peak healing period of his life, he was often so busy that he sometimes fell asleep from sheer exhaustion while he was treating.

There was no doubt about it; Bill had a unique and distinct energy, which created incredible healing results in the physical body. He had the strongest hands-on current of energy I have ever felt. When he treated me, it felt like 220 volts of electricity were passing right through my body. I loved to have these treatments and talk with him, but there was one problem: after his treatment, I could have easily eaten a dozen 10-course meals at one sitting.

After going to Bill, I finally understood why some patients told me they got the "munchies" after my treatments. My personal solution, after a treatment from Bill, was to head immediately to a nearby restaurant where I ordered (and rapidly consumed) a huge meal, one that would have made a lumberjack blush. Then, I would go to another restaurant down the block where I did the same. Finished there, I hit one more restaurant and pumped down another bounteous meal.

Amazingly, I never had a hint of indigestion, or gained any weight from these meals. I thought about ordering the three huge meals at one restaurant, but I didn't want to answer embarrassing questions about my enormous appetite. Where did all that food go? I never asked Bill about it while he was alive so I'll have to wait until I see him again on the other side.

————

These were the healers I knew personally who helped me on my path as a healer. And what colorful characters they were. I remember one elderly chiropractor in Los Angeles who treated his patients in an old hearse. He had painted it white with a huge red cross on the side. His treating table in the back of the old Cadillac was where the casket would have been. Patient and D.C. had to crawl in for treatment. He told me the reason for this odd arrangement was that his wife, an R.N., ran his patients off to any M.D. she could find; thus, he was forced to run his practice as a mobile adjustment unit.

———·◆·———

Healers have always fascinated me, and I never tire of hearing their stories. I read of an eighty-year-old healer in Texas who saw little people come into the room when she was healing. They wore hard hats (like those miners wear) with head lamps, which they focused on the area of the body she was to heal. Needless to say, her patients were unaware of these visitors.

———

Then there's a group of healers called "bonesetters" who are specifically skilled in bone regeneration. I remember a classmate in high school who broke his arm, but after several surgeries, his arm still wouldn't heal. He was in a cast for two years before he heard of Bonesetter Reese. My friend traveled to the Midwest gingerly holding his arm in a sling since he had been instructed to have the cast removed before his healing appointment.

According to my friend, Bonesetter Reese just held the broken arm between his hands for a few minutes. That was it. When my friend returned home the next day, he told me he thought that he must have been crazy to have made the trip. But when he checked in with his orthopedic doctor, the new x-rays showed that the bones were finally knitting perfectly and clearly stronger.

———

Edgar Cayce was a remarkable healer and psychic, and, like Harry Edwards, found his great inspiration in Jesus. Cayce is the most well-known healer and seer of the twentieth century. As a Sunday school teacher, he shared his deep faith in Jesus with his students. He read the entire Bible every year of his life. Although Cayce faced adversity most of his life, he remained optimistic and cheerful. Called "the sleeping prophet" because he did his readings while in a self-induced sleeping state, Cayce said anyone could do what he did, but mysteriously no one ever has. Today everyone looks for a Cayce to diagnose and treat them, but once he passed from this dimension in 1945, they broke the mold. There is no other Cayce.

Cayce's gifts were awesome. He was a fine spiritual diagnostician, but people took advantage of his kind and loving nature. While many profited from his readings, he remained poor. The readings he did for himself said his life of suffering was to prepare him for a higher level of consciousness in his next life. During his readings, the lessons behind the condition were identified.

It was Cayce's belief that the condition would return, or a worse one would appear, if there wasn't a change in the person's attitudes and life patterns. He wanted those he helped to understand the lessons—and therefore the blessings—within their sickness. Otherwise, the most important aspect of healing would not take place.

Mankind owes Edgar Cayce a great debt for his lifetime of service. His own poor health never slowed him down. He died in the saddle, leaving us an important legacy of healing modalities such as the castor oil pack. It's no wonder people bless Cayce for his remedy to alleviate painful muscles, tendons and joints by rubbing the body with cold-pressed peanut oil.

———

I heard many tales of "The Goat Doctor" who lived in the gold country of northern California where he tended his goats and healed people. I've talked with many of his patients who also came to see me. They said he spoke little or not at all while he treated the hundreds who came to see him every day. For his wonderful healings, he required payment in silver dollars. When he died in 1959, reports of his buried treasure known as the "faith healer's hoard" soon followed. Is there anything quite so intriguing as stories of buried treasure? It was reported that over $200,000 in coins was dug up on his property—at least that's the sum that was reported.

———

Born in Texas, Magnolia Ellis, who was half Cherokee, had her healing practice in New Mexico in a small town called Hot Springs. (In 1950, the town was renamed Truth or Consequences after Ralph Edward's successful game show.) She healed through laying on of hands, and hundreds of people came from all over the world to see her. The streets were filled with the horses, wagons and cars of the people waiting to see her. Considered one of the great healers in this country, I spoke with people who had been treated by this lady. They said she was kindness itself and never let her healing powers go to her head. When Andrea and I visited Truth or Consequences in 1990, all that remained of her fame were old newspaper articles and a building with a large sign on top bearing her name.

———·◆·———

Years ago, it was not easy to find a healer. It was like prohibition. You had to have connections, or know someone with connections to find a natural healer. It was strictly word of mouth. Patients who didn't respond to drugs or surgery hunted desperately for healers who were hidden away, far below the surface of everyday life. Healers were afraid of being called "quacks," "fakes," "frauds," "charlatans," "witches," or other similar labels. These names were generously stamped on those who did not march in step with the accepted authorities. It sometimes seemed as though those authorities were not in place to protect the public, but to hound any healers who tried to get people well outside the medical establishment.

When I first started out, alternative healing methods were just beginning to appear on the horizon. God help you if you were a natural-born healer and answered the call to help people regain their health. "Real" healing by "real" doctors was only sanctioned in the medical arena. The country was called Disease, and the medical populace firmly planted their flag there. They did not take kindly to anyone trespassing on their territory.

But over the years when I looked into the careers of people like Harry Hoxsey, I saw only the magnificence of "real" people trying to help other people. The well-researched, eye-opening book, *When Healing Becomes a Crime: The Amazing Story of the Hoxsey Cancer Clinics and the Return of Alternative Therapies* by Kenny Ausubel, gives the reader an inside look at what was labeled "quackery."

Jesus was not the only one who braved the powers of the establishment to speak the truth. Sometimes I wonder who the quacks are. Is a quack anyone who goes against the accepted medical dictates? I would fear for the world if one group had complete control over our health choices and the dietary supplement industry.

With profound insight, Benjamin Rush, M.D., one of the signers of the Declaration of Independence, declared:

> *"Unless we put medical freedom into the Constitution, the time will come when medicine will organize into an under-cover dictatorship . . ."*

And his statement was made more than 200 years ago. It's a different world now. I cheer with enthusiasm when I see alternative healing coming into acceptance. Every step to recognize and integrate all healing methods into the mainstream of patient choices will benefit all of us.

20

PHILIPPINE MYSTERY

———— ◆ ·· ◆· ————

As you know by now, my joy has been to search out other healers while I travel through life. In 1983 I planned a trip to the Philippines to see the psychic healers I had heard so much about. However, the week before my trip, I was seriously considering all the advantages of staying home. Then, the night before my planned departure, an unexpected call from a dear friend convinced me to go. He had just heard of a blind man recovering his eyesight by going over to the Philippines for treatment. With this recommendation, I finished packing my bags and headed for the San Francisco Airport the next morning.

Our tour group had thirty people, half were terminally ill with "the big C" and had been given up by their doctors. Ready for takeoff, our seats were in an uncomfortable, bolt upright position. Once in the air, we all anxiously waited for the pilot to turn off the seatbelt sign. Finally, over the Pacific Ocean, the closely watched sign turned off. It was time to get comfortable and gear ourselves for the coming 14-hour flight.

All the passengers eagerly pushed the designated button to recline our seats. What a shock! The reclining option didn't exist, not at all, not even one degree. That bolt upright position was ours for the entire grueling trip. I'm sure the airline made a bundle by pushing the seats together as close as possible. There wasn't an inch of wiggle room. It didn't take long before we discovered the organizer and director of our group was reclined and comfortably settled in her first class seat, which was in the upper reaches of the 747. A first class ticket would have cost

$1,000 more, but had I known what was waiting for me in my coach seat for 14 hours, I would have gladly paid every penny.

Desperate for the flight to end, I kept asking the woman seated next to me for the time. In my mind, I waited hours before asking again. But each time I asked, she insisted only minutes had passed since my last inquiry. Finally, she whispered, "If you ask me for the time *once more,* I'm going to put my watch where you can't see it. And, believe me, it's going to be in a place that you'll personally find far more uncomfortable than these miserable upright seats." I nodded and settled back to sweat it out.

At last, the saving grace, a movie (singular) came on. Yes, just one. After all, no sense in spoiling the passengers. It was a helicopter thriller called *Blue Thunder,* which was played over and over for the entire 14 hours. By the time we touched down in Hawaii for refueling, the whirring of the movie helicopter had definitely lost its thrill. We rose from our seats, painfully square-bottomed. My posterior felt as though I had been sitting on a cement block through a lengthy, and particularly boring sermon. Never was a stop so appreciated.

We staggered forth from the plane desperate for a breath of fresh air only to be greeted by all the heat and humidity that Hawaii could offer, reminding me of a certain, hot, sweltering, summer day in southern California many years before. Let me share what happened back then before I continue my Philippine adventures . . .

———•◆•———

On that particular blistering morning, my wife excitedly surprised me with tickets for a house tour, which had been organized as a charity benefit in Redlands. Two hours later, as we waited in a long line outside the historic house, the temperature rapidly climbed to over 100 degrees. I groaned when I checked the tickets. Our tour, the last of the day in deference to the summer heat, was scheduled for high noon.

The line advanced with agonizing slowness toward the entrance. I held our two-year-old daughter, Marilyn, in my arms. As the line crept forward, she felt more and more like a large, hot water-bottle. Thanks to wearing the required black suit and tie for this momentous occasion, sweat trickled steadily down my back while my watch ticked ever slower.

The July sun moved higher in the sky until there was no shade to stand in anywhere. I prayed for a breeze, but as the long line inched forward, the Santa Ana winds refused to heed my call. Twelve o'clock came and went without our advancing any closer to the entrance. No doubt the visitors inside were leisurely admiring the huge oil paintings hung especially for this exhibition.

By my calculations, the interior of the house had to be cooler so I told my wife I'd be back and headed to the entrance of the house. I explained to the suspicious security guard who blocked my way, "I need to take my daughter to the bathroom." Luckily Marilyn was asleep with her head on my shoulder so she didn't contradict me. I showed him our tickets and assured him that my wife was still patiently waiting in line. After I promised to return to my place in the outer realms, he grudgingly let me inside.

One step inside the house confirmed my theory. Although the temperature couldn't be considered arctic, the house was infinitely cooler. As I made my way through, I found the thermostat hidden behind one of the huge oil paintings. Without hesitation, I turned the dial to high. When I returned to the end of the line, I remarked to my wife, "I think the line will speed up shortly."

"My God, I hope so," my wife sighed. "I don't know how much more of this heat I can take." And Helen was a Redlands gal who enjoyed the heat of summer.

Soon, people in line began to stroll toward the house as people in the house began to come out more rapidly. Soon, people fairly flew in— and more particularly out of—the now stifling house. Our own passage through the house was made in record time. Clearly the guards didn't know where the thermostat was, nor was I at liberty to tell them lest I reveal my part in the mass exodus.

The next day, our local paper reported that the owners of the historical house were vacationing in Panama during the exhibition. The news article lamented that the owners couldn't be contacted to tell the officials where the offending thermostat was located. Somehow the heat had inadvertently been turned on, a terrible oversight, which had driven the roasting visitors out. What a shame! I sincerely hope I rescued other men in black suits, coerced by well-meaning wives into attending this fiasco. However, back to Hawaii . . .

Our layover was brief, just long enough to tell friends that we had been to Hawaii. Unfortunately, the plane was fueled in record time. All too soon we were crammed back in the plane, weary, worn, and bolt upright. Passengers started aging before my eyes until their faces had so many lines that they began looking like dried apple dolls. Out of desperation, people began to lie down in the aisles and under the seats. If you moved through the cabin, you had to be careful not to step on this carpet of people. The stewardesses could not have been nicer, smiling cheerfully as they stepped over the horizontal bodies in their path.

The flight attendants finally served food. The excitement of a meal—interrupting the third or fourth viewing of the movie—helped for almost five minutes. Then we wilted again while the movie "chopper" relentlessly repeated its adventures. Einstein said the simplest explanation of his theory of relativity was that time flew by when you were talking to an attractive, attentive woman who hung on your every word. But faced with a self-centered, unattractive woman, the clock stopped. Had he been on our flight, he would have arrived at his theory much sooner with an even better illustration of relativity.

Dazed and exhausted, we landed in Manila. Our tour guide descended from first class, obviously rested and ready for action. She moved briskly ahead, pointing us toward the baggage claim area. We easily identified our bags by the bright yellow, yarn pompoms, which our guide had given to us in San Francisco to tie onto our luggage.

Miss Energy took us in tow. With flashing smiles, she moved us through customs. Efficiently giving money to the appropriate officials, she whisked us through the airport. Everything was a blur. Still, we forced ourselves to stumble on in her wake.

Once we regained consciousness in Manila, we realized that Hawaii had only been a practice run. Nothing had prepared us for the stifling, hot, sticky air of Manila, filled with the pungent fumes of diesel and gasoline engines. After a short wait, we were herded onto a smaller plane for our final flight to Baguio.

What a relief to step off the plane in Baguio, the summer capital. The temperature was in the low 70's and the weather was perfect—what a change from Manila. No wonder the American airbase was located here. On the drive to our hotel, we had a chance to admire the many luxurious homes dotting the hillsides. When we finally reached our destination, we were grateful to see a modern, four-story, luxury hotel built in an A-frame style.

The next morning, our group gathered in the hotel's ground floor restaurant to eat breakfast. The central interior of the building was open above the restaurant all the way to the top floor. High above our heads were beautiful tropical plants hanging in huge baskets. As we were eating, I got bumped by a flash of intuition. I looked up and said, "I feel an earthquake coming."

All 30 people froze, forks in the air. After a few seconds, they all laughed nervously and continued eating. Five minutes later the whole building shook. Several of the huge hanging plants crashed to the floor while we ducked. After that, if I even cleared my throat, everyone stopped and waited to see what I would say next. But that earthquake was the only intuitive flash I received on the trip.

Everything in the hotel was spotlessly clean. The glasses in our bathrooms sparkled, each sealed with a reassuring, sanitary paper cap. It was all very impressive until I went back to my room because I had forgotten my wallet. As I entered, I heard a noise in the bathroom. I peeked in and spied the room service gent inspecting my drinking glass.

As I watched, this conscientious fellow held my glass up to the light. Apparently, it was not up to his standards. After spitting generously into the glass, he went on to polish it smartly with his cloth. Smiling at his success, he carefully positioned the sanitary paper cap over the sparkling glass and replaced it on the bathroom sink. When I returned to breakfast, I shared my recent discovery with my fellow travelers. After that, when the hotel staff assured us the hotel water was perfectly safe to drink in sanitized glasses, we declined with knowing smiles and continued to order bottled water.

Later that morning, we took our first jitney ride. Everywhere we went in the islands, a never-ending parade of color filled the streets due to the gay banners and glittering reflectors on these jeep-like vehicles. The hoods and tops were covered with shiny, silvery metal statues of horses. One jitney might have 100 horse figures mounted on it.

Our guide warned us to keep our elbows inside the jitney. Elbows outside the window risked being smashed by oncoming jitneys since the thrill-seeking drivers came within inches of each other. Our jitney took the countryside hills in stride and we soon arrived at the treatment center of one of the great healers in the islands, Jun Labo. A handsome man of about 35, he was rightfully called "King of the Hill." This was the healer we had traveled so far to see.

We changed into bathrobes for the healings about to take place, leaving on only our underwear. Things moved very quickly; each person was on Jun's table for only a few minutes. Once it was your turn, you dropped your robe and lay on your back on his treating table. Jun put his fingers on and then deeply into your gut. It became obvious very quickly why Jun wore short sleeves for his work; as soon as he began, there were loud slurping sounds and blood flew everywhere.

When I was on the table, I looked down at my gut and watched as Jun plunged his hands deeply into my abdomen. I could only see his knuckles. Blood gushed out and poured down my sides onto the table. He pulled out something from my gut that looked like a bone with tissue and cartilage on it, and chucked it with authority into a bucket on the floor.

The pail was nearly full of similar pieces from the patients before me. An assistant periodically and efficiently emptied the pail. For one awful moment, I stared nervously at the open bloody wound in my stomach. Then Jun swiftly wiped the blood away with an old towel. Lo and behold, the opening was no more. It was quite a first day. After returning to the hotel, we were eager to talk about our experiences and share stories of our reactions to these strange events.

Unbeknownst to me, a police chief in the group told the lovely young ladies serving us in the hotel dining room that I was a famous doctor from California. He added that I had a large rice plantation and had come to the islands specifically to find a Filipino wife. The petite girls flocked around me, happily chattering that they were ready to return to California with me. I was flattered but confused when they promised to take care of my rice plantation back in the United States. After I found out what was going on, I tried to convince them that I had no rice paddies. Unfortunately, I never could convince them; they were all raised on rice so it made perfect sense to them that I would have such a farm.

The next day, my matchmaking friend helped his mother, who was close to death, onto Jun's table. He remained standing within a few inches of his mother. The healer's fingers disappeared into her gut and blood flew everywhere, hitting the ceiling and walls. We heard a crash. The officer had passed out cold and lay unconscious on the floor.

However, by the next day, we were all eating snacks while we watched Jun work. It was amazing how quickly we became accustomed to gushing blood and the sound of those inexplicable tissues slopping into the bucket below the table; it was soon very familiar and casual. We were all astounded to discover that, while pounds of heavy tissue were taken from our bodies every day, none of us ever lost an ounce.

Most of our group had been given up by their medical doctors in the States; this trip was their last hope. About half of these folks got well after their sessions with the island healers. When I followed up on this later, I found that half of those who got well, stayed well for years, while the other half returned to their previous condition within their first year back in the States. Like Cayce, all the healers we saw in the Philippines said changing to a positive attitude was required, or the condition would return.

One enterprising lady preserved her tumor after it was removed by the Filipino healer. Years later when the tumor returned, she had surgery in the States. She showed me the two tumors and they were exactly alike in size and shape. One surgeon, who brought his father over to be healed from cancer, asked the assistant for the tissue that Jun removed from his father's abdomen. The doctor preserved this tissue in a jar, and brought it back to the States. Later, he told me, "I had my father's tissue from Jun's surgery analyzed by our pathology department. Our pathologist told me that he'd never seen any tissue like it; it was neither fish, nor fowl, nor animal. No one could classify it."

Our wonder grew every day as we observed the continuing miracles in Jun's healing theater. I saw a huge wad of cotton pushed right into my gut. I actually felt it inside my abdomen. Then the "surgeon" used two fingers to pull out the now bloody cotton from a different place while I watched and felt pulling in my intestines. It was amazing. None of us knew what to think. Illusion? Mass hypnosis? The real deal? Who can say?

One dear, older lady had hemorrhoids and the bouncing jitney rides were absolute torture for her. One afternoon, the surgeon/healer removed the hemorrhoids. It was wonderful that she could now ride in comfort, but she nearly drove us crazy for the rest of the trip when her missing hemorrhoids became her favorite and only topic of conversation. After her years of suffering, I couldn't really blame her.

The police officer had terrible ringing in his ears from time spent on the firing range. After his first treatment, the ringing stopped, and he was ecstatic. The next day, Jun arranged for a brass band, the best in the Philippines, to play for us. They traveled 150 miles for this special concert. We gathered outside in a handball court enclosed by high cement walls on all four sides.

Our group of 30 stood in the center of the court where we were entertained by the loudest brass music I ever hope to hear. It bounced and echoed off the cement walls in a deafening crescendo of decibels. Poor Bob's ringing came back within seconds. I asked, "Why didn't you cover your ears?" He replied, "I just couldn't offend the musicians or hurt Jun's feelings after he went to so much trouble." I wondered how many of us suffer needlessly because we fear to hurt another's feelings.

We all had cameras and snapped hundreds of pictures standing a foot or less away from the "surgery." I witnessed a six-month-old baby with the healer's fingers in her head while the baby cooed happily. We had three appointments a day for 10 days. It was mind-boggling. Surely what we witnessed was occurring on some other dimension beyond our current comprehension.

Although no sanitation was observed, there were no infections. Being trained in public health and sterile techniques, I had a hard time watching conditions that should have caused peritonitis and rampant infection. It reminded me of the book *Arigo: Surgeon of the Rusty Knife*. Arigo was a Brazilian peasant and world-famous healer who operated under the most primitive conditions. A sweet and gentle man, he healed hundreds every night using unsterilized knives and no anesthetics without any sign of infection or pain. How? One more mystery to ponder.

During our stay, I was asked to treat several Filipino women for gut trouble. I quickly discovered it was aluminum in every case. They had thrown away their cast-iron pots, which had been used for generations. Now they used aluminum because it was light weight and so easy to clean. I asked why they didn't use stainless steel cookware. They said stainless steel was only used for the jitneys, which would otherwise deteriorate from salt in the ocean air.

Jitneys were their livelihoods. Health was secondary. Sound familiar? Once I discovered that all our hotel meals were cooked in aluminum, I existed on canned salmon and crackers three times a day. Luckily, I was able to supplement this austere diet with the island's incredible tropical fruits.

The local people were all smiles and extremely charming. On every block, older women, who were friendly and soft-spoken, gracefully and efficiently swept every bit of dirt and litter into little folding pans. Their industrious efforts kept the streets immaculate at all times. At a factory we visited, we saw young women of 18, or less, sitting on the floor, nimbly weaving brightly colored thread on shuttles into lively patterns for long linen runners. Their feet were deformed from holding the finished runner tightly in place on the large looms hour after hour. Smiling readily, they stopped their work to speak to us in soft, gentle voices. These lovely ladies were some of the most beautiful women that I had ever seen. Although they worked 10 hours a day for low wages, they appeared to be cheerful and content.

The presence of soldiers was an unnerving sight everywhere we traveled. They grimly noted our departures and arrivals at the hotel. When I went to the bank, I learned that only one customer was allowed in at a time. Once inside, I glanced up. Perched high above me on an interior balcony was a soldier who held a sawed-off 12-gauge shotgun, cocked and pointed directly at me. He was a fierce-looking fellow who followed my every move with his gun, which could have taken the teller and me out in one blast. I put my hands in the air and smiled at him. He glared back in response. It was perfectly understandable why the bank hadn't been robbed in 20 years.

The healers I met in the Philippines instantly recognized me as a fellow healer. However, they insisted that my healing was far different from theirs and that they wanted no part of my type of healing. When I asked what they meant by these comments, they declared that their healing was a simple mechanical process. They insisted that my energy work healed not only the body, but also healed on soul levels, which they said was not within their energy focus.

Once I understood what they were talking about, I agreed and explained that my healing was (and is) tied in with teaching patients about the higher path, past and future lives, karma, and soul growth. Patients of mine who also went to my friend, Dr. Thomas Hanna of "Somatics" fame, told me that he always told them: "Dr. MacKimmie is a Doctor of Souls." I always meant to ask Tom about his statement, but now he too has crossed over, so my question will have to wait until I meet him again on the other side.

Finally our trip came to an end. The return flight was delightful because the plane was half empty and we could each occupy several seats. Stretching out to sleep was sheer heaven. And what made it so easy to sleep? Give up? *Blue Thunder* played over and over on our flight back. By this time, the roar of the helicopter was like a familiar lullaby to us. And we never had to look at the screen—the story was always the same. From time to time, Andrea has generously offered to rent this movie for nostalgia's sake, but I always pass.

In spite of jet lag, it was wonderful to be home where I had my own organic food, wonderful clean water, and time to think over what had happened on my trip. Once my photographs were developed, I showed the pictures to friends and people in town. Some of the old timers nearly fell over seeing all that blood and tissue spilling out of people. But one fellow looked bored and made no comment.

Surprised, I took this fellow aside and asked him why. He said, "Oh, I've seen it all before. When I was in the Navy, we were stationed off the Philippines for three years. If a surgery done by the ship's doctor failed, we carried the patient ashore to one of the healers. It only cost 25 cents for the healer to perform psychic surgery, and the patients always got well immediately after the healing session."

A year later, I showed pictures of my trip to some pathologist friends. They all insisted the pictures had been faked. I said, "But I was there. I saw these surgeries actually taking place before my eyes and took the pictures myself." However, they still argued that the whole thing had been faked.

Finally, I threw all the pictures away since most people would not believe they hadn't been faked in some way. Well for them, perhaps that's true. I recall the old adage: those convinced against their will are of the same opinion still. However, seeing is believing. And I saw what I saw. While I still don't understand what I saw in the islands, to this day, I remain fascinated by what took place in the healing rooms of the Philippines.

21

THE HEALER'S PATH

————◆·"·◆·————

What makes a healer? Having been a healer all my life makes it easy to explain: I haven't the foggiest. Many of us flounder through life until something greater takes hold and pulls us into a different pattern. There is a Presence, a power within all of us, that magnetizes events and people to us. That power, the Source itself, is the observer of our life, and waits patiently within until we awaken.

Within this Presence is the knowing of our entire existence forever. You will find the Source in the Present Moment . . . the Now . . . the land of the Soul. If you are wise, when it leads, you will follow. Then miracles will pour into your life. Miracles are with us every day. They are concealed in the unseen but powerful forces that bring change into our lives. However, like children, we sometimes need to be pushed and pulled into those moments in our lives that are truly miraculous.

The greatest healer ever known had no medical degree and never dispensed a prescription. Although He died more than 2,000 years ago, He still blesses all who surrender to the Christ. In a life that personified compassion and healing, He walked the talk—and not just on Sundays.

I recall one patient from India who told me he was delighted with his new Christian faith. He proudly informed me that he had found a loophole in the workings of karma. By repenting on Sunday, he could start the week with a clean slate. I tried to explain otherwise to him, but he thought he had a firm grip on his new religion and was thrilled that karma was no longer a factor in his life.

Once when a patient asked where Jesus fit into the healing picture.
I said, "Jesus is a class act and a great all-around guy." I studied her
puzzled face as she considered my reply. When she broke into heartfelt
laughter, I told her about my cousin in Canada who was taken to church
for the first time when he was a precocious four-year-old. At dinner, his
father asked Eddie what he thought about church. Eddie looked thought-
ful and replied in solemn tones, "I believe this God-fellow is going to
work out nicely. He seems to be all right." Everyone at the table had to
bite their lips so as not to laugh upon hearing his youthful wisdom.

I always tell my patients that Jesus is a great master whose place is
at the top of the pyramid of light, expressing all creation. Jesus never
forgot that He was His Father's child. This knowing was the ballast that
kept His ship afloat in the midst of the mighty storms and betrayals of the
world. By centering himself every moment in the Light of the Creator,
which is the truth of our being now and forever, Jesus played His part
lovingly from beginning to end. And the end of His life was, in truth, a
new beginning in the everlasting life of His resurrection. His life served
as the greatest teaching ever given to humankind. And His work lives on
through the ages in His teachings.

———•◆•———

Being a healer is a great mystery. It was to Edgar Cayce and it
surely is to me. In healing as in life, each healer must dance to his own
tune. In the beginning we dance to the tune of parents, teachers, friends,
movie heroes . . . any song but our own. However, as we wend our way
through life, we finally reach a place where we discover our own song,
the song that has been singing in our heart forever. When all manifesta-
tions of outer power fade away, then the inner road of heart—found in
the silence of the self—will show the way.

The great Persian poet, Jalal al-Din Rumi (1207–1273), wrote: "Feel
yourself being quietly drawn by the deeper pull of what you truly love."
While it's not difficult to follow your heart, there is always the temptation
to imitate others and fit into a mold not of your own heart's design and
choosing. But true healing cannot be taught, it must be felt in the heart.
By being yourself, you trust that sweet place in your heart where the
Creator's healing energy flows through you to your patients. There you

have the freedom and the knowing that you are serving as an instrument of a higher healing power.

We healers are a strange lot, a band of brothers and sisters dedicated in spirit to serving the Creator. Called by a powerful force that will not be denied, we must heed the words of our inner guidance. Whether you are a beginner or an old-timer, wise in your chosen field or still pondering your decision, your future is assured. A grateful world thanks you for answering your soul's call and stepping forward to heal.

If you are drawn by an inner desire to heal, get on with it. Jesus said, "He that believeth on me, the works that I do shall he do also; and greater works than these shall he do . . ." Why not take Him at His word. If you are willing and open, opportunities to heal will be presented to you. If you do not feel the healing energy flow at first, just be and pray to be of service.

I encourage you to embark on your journey. Your heart will lead you to do and say the right thing in every circumstance. Choose to be with those who make your heart glad. Speak the truth and know that divine protection is promised by the Creator. After all, healing is very natural and has been going on for millions of years. You, and you alone, will discover if your inner desire to heal is a true calling from the higher realms. If it is, I can assure you that this call is a wonderful beginning to an adventure that knows no end.

————•◆•————

I've never known anyone in healing who was not deeply committed to helping others. I know many healers in the beginning stages who are working conscientiously to relieve the suffering of humankind. Healers have to begin somewhere. If today healers are everywhere, perhaps that's what is important.

As you begin your adventure in healing, realize that most people seek help from a healer only as a last resort. After all other avenues of healing have been exhausted, they seek a natural or alternative healer. They arrive in pain, exhausted from their search for help, but usually expecting instant healing with little or no effort on their part.

One healer I knew told me he carefully weeded out those who were, in his words, "human wreckage." I never did, and sometimes I heard so many different symptoms from a new patient that I thought I should have been an undertaker. However, I told God if He sent people to me, then I would do my best for them no matter what the condition. But I also asked that if He did not want them to come to me for healing, to let them find their help elsewhere.

We all know that pain is not normal. It serves as a warning that something is wrong. If that pain is expressed on the mental or emotional level, it does not diminish the person's experience of pain. Usually holding a patient's hand will start the healing flow. You may find that surprising changes for the better can occur within minutes. Healing is the most natural thing in the world. The relief of pain is a grand happening, and you may be the instrument that God uses to take that pain away.

By the time a patient comes to you, you will be seeing a person who is usually discouraged and depressed. Of course, these attitudes interfere with the healing process. Multiple drugs, surgeries, x-rays, poor habits and God knows what other assaults on the body have already taken place. Nothing has helped and now you are presented with a body that's like an old car, almost gone, barely lasting long enough to break down in your parking lot. One kick of the tire and the whole car would collapse, but the patient is ready for you to right all wrongs and get the car back on the road . . . "Can you get it fixed in 20 minutes? I'll be back."

Your job is to neutralize the toxins, x-rays, drugs and poor habits. Inspire your patients to *stop* focusing on sickness, and *start* focusing on the body's powerful ability to heal. As the healing unfolds, both the patient and the healer need to have patience and honor the process. Strangely, some people fight the healing process tooth and nail, clinging to the old habits that caused their sickness in the first place. As people in our highly civilized world load up on junk food goodies and embrace the latest drugs, there will be more than enough sickness to go around. So never worry about having enough people to work on.

The medical brethren have their problems too. Patients expect their doctor to untangle all their problems from birth on. Then the patient insists on being given a prescription for the latest drug to cure their ills. In the movies, the little blind girl is seen by a famous Swiss surgeon, who happens to be vacationing near her home. Touched by her blindness, he performs the surgery right there in her home, without any fee. The wee tyke is restored to perfect health and perfect sight without any follow-up visits or complications. Ah, if only life was that simple.

——————•◆•——————

If you educate yourself about health and nutrition from the wealth of books available, you can apply these principles in your own life. That done, you can suggest to those who come to you how they too might change their lifestyle—as you have done—by eating correctly, exercising, drinking water and getting enough sleep.

Can it be that simple? It seems so to me since such a program returned me to health after being diabetic and having cancer. Which reminds me, the health of the healer is another peculiar card in the deck. I've seen miraculous healings in my office on days when I felt unwell and wanted to stay in bed. I've also discovered that the same energy flows to heal even when earthly situations upset my emotional balance. The healing energy carries its own separate power far beyond my comprehension. A fellow healer once told me that even if my body died, he thought the energy was so powerful that I would go on healing just the same. Who knows? Personally, I'm looking forward to a little rest after this life.

Is a healer's life difficult? Yes, it can be. You must produce results. You can't just give a person a pill, pat them on the head and send them home. People come because they expect to feel better right away. However, each healer works differently and the results vary. Just because your treatment worked for Aunt Tilly doesn't mean that it will help Aunt Tilly's mother, son, niece or nephew. Unfortunately, if your treatment doesn't help in *exactly* the same way, then you are judged accordingly. Sorry but it's true.

So take a reality check. It would be wonderful if we only saw those fortunate people who were ready to be healed. But that seems forbidden. And I don't suggest looking for the glamour of miracles since miracles cannot be repeated on demand. Let them find you. The truth is that no healer can help everyone who comes in for healing. Unfortunately this can stress the nervous system of any healer whose one desire is to heal everyone who comes seeking help.

Healers, especially beginners, are disappointed when they cannot help everyone. They often feel like failures. Luckily, the simple cure is to remember that healers do not heal; God heals. Healers simply open themselves to a higher power through prayer and meditation. This allows the miraculous flow of the Creator's healing to come through and help the body heal itself. When healing takes place, it is because the body has accepted the Creator's healing. Healers remain facilitators and observers. The rest is up to the Creator and His healing angels.

Is a healer's life rewarding? Yes, yes, and yes. Healing is the most difficult *and* the most pleasurable assignment in the world. Healers are given powers and energies that must be expressed through a life of healing. To do otherwise would be to deny your soul's journey. To turn to the material world for your rewards would be like eating dirt for sustenance. Healing is a calling beyond our control. It simply *IS*, an inner drive of the soul that must be answered, or there is no rest. Not to heal would be to stop living. It is not a life of choice. We have no choice. We follow an inner spiritual light that burns brightly like a star, calling us inward, onward, upward and God-ward.

We are all healers in one way or another. Our paths may differ, but we are all one great cosmic family. Communication with the Power is effortless once we are willing to let go of the steering wheel and let God begin to live through us. The real you is inside, waiting to be born, ready to radiate healing energy into the universe and beyond. It is your destiny.

The road less traveled is always waiting for you. There are few footprints here, but there are clues left by those who have gone before. I encourage all who are healing, who aspire to heal, who seek healing for themselves and others, to stay the course. It is surely time now for natural healing to lead us back to the timeless wisdom of Mother Nature.

True healers recognize that we are all here to love and help each other. In doing so, we serve all life. Healing energy is always ready to flow through us to help others when we open ourselves to it. One of the finest experiences we can have as a healer is the feedback from patients when they feel the renewing flow of life and vitality flooding their body. When patients are healed, you then share a spiritual experience with them that is beyond any words. To be a participant in returning abundant life, to those who have lost it, is to feel the deepest joy in your heart of hearts.

I have always believed that all healers are helped by great healers who have crossed over to the other side. These dedicated healers now work from another dimension to act as guides and helpers. To be a healer is to belong to the grand healing circle of all healers: past, present, and future. We are privileged to be the ones now working on the physical plane as servants of humanity. In time, we find ourselves on the other side, supporting the healers working here on the earth plane.

I don't know what it takes to become a great healer. I only know that all healing is an apprenticeship that goes on lifetime after lifetime, a contract signed before birth. These lifetimes are like planting a garden. The steps cannot be rushed. Finding fertile ground, preparing the ground, planting seeds, watering and picking weeds, all must be done in their proper order, one step at a time to reach our goals in life.

Tend your garden and you will see it flourish. Hold a positive attitude. Ask for divine help. The higher our thoughts fly, the greater will be the heavenly response. If the healer is inspired, the patient's energies will respond to those higher frequencies. Know that all results belong to God. Do your best to bring people good health: that is the top line, bottom line, and all the lines in between. Your rewards of the heart will be beyond measure. So relax and enjoy the ride. Let yourself flow effortlessly into your work, hand in hand with God.

22

THROUGH A HEALER'S EYES

---•◆••◆•---

A fter a lifetime of healing, I rarely ask the "whys" of healing anymore. I simply observe the process and appreciate its blessings. Of course I understand the curiosity that many of my patients have had about why it works, whom it works for, and all the details involved—things I have puzzled over for more than half a century. After all, how can we know the vastness of the cosmos when we live within a tiny point of light? Like a prisoner who only has a peephole in his cell's outside wall, we see almost nothing. Yet we are ready to declare that the limited world we see must be all that exists. However, if we are taken up to the roof, we experience a 360-degree view, which instantly frees us from the limitations of the mind. Having been blessed with the opportunity to live as a healer, I will try to answer those questions that have been asked most frequently by my patients over the years.

---•◆•---

What is the basis for healing?

What brings about multidimensional healing? I have to laugh when I think of "scientific" explanations. All theories about healing are pure speculation, even those presented by healers themselves. The closest I have come to an answer is that healing is love in all its aspects, a gift from our Creator as part of a divine plan beyond our knowing.

Love's opposite is fear and these two emotions are the key players on the earth plane. Fear is a function of human thinking. But love has its own agenda, closely bound to the eternal timing of the soul. To love and be loved is the ultimate energy in the universe. In reality, nothing else exists. When we surrender our lesser self to the great love within, then love and fear are free to dissolve into one another. This allows healing on every level of our being.

Within our hearts is an All-Seeing, All-Knowing Presence, longing to be set free. This presence is not found in the outside world. It is found through an inner search and rescue mission. By resting in the stillness of the heart, we reconnect with this loving presence. Thus, we begin to discover how to live and express the love that abides within us all. "Sometime," wrote Pierre Teilhard de Chardin (1881–1955), "after mastering the winds, the waves, the tides and gravity, we shall harness for God the energies of love—and then for the second time in the history of the world, man will discover fire."

In the office, I have had many opportunities to watch the power of love heal more than the physical body . . .

Walt was a school supervisor who came in once a month for maintenance energy treatments. Over the years, we developed a close friendship as he shared his troubles at work, his failing marriage, and a difficult divorce. After the divorce, Walt's wife painted him as the very devil incarnate to her young son. Walt knew what she was doing, but had no way to stop her. He eventually stopped seeing his son because of the pain it caused them both. During the long, hard years of struggle before his life made sense again, I came to know the depth and integrity of this fine man.

Many years later, unbeknownst to me, I began treating Walt's son who was now 35. (His son's last name was different due to his mother's remarriage, so I didn't connect the two of them.) One day Walt's son came in for treatment and saw his dad waiting for an appointment. An uncomfortable chill filled the waiting room while father and son sat across from each other in stony silence.

The son's appointment was first. He marched into my treating room bristling with anger. He told me his father was a monster and I was *never* to schedule them on the same day again. Before he could continue, I stopped him in his tracks, "Son, I've known your father for 25 years and he is one of the finest men I've ever had the privilege of knowing."

Braving further hostility, I went on, "I want you to wait for your father until he's had his treatment. Then I want you to forget everything you *think* you know about him and talk with him. I promise you that you're in for a total surprise if you'll just trust me and talk with him." With further mumbled misgivings, he grudgingly promised. I learned later that he and his dad went down to the beach and spent the rest of the day together.

From then on, Walt and his son met once a month at my office. After their treatments, they always spent the day together at the beach, catching up on their years of separation. These monthly meetings took place for one joyous year. Watching the flow of love between them filled my heart with joy. Their souls basked in their love for one another and their love filled the office each time they came in.

One day, Walt's son came in and said, "My dad won't be coming in today . . . he died last night." After the son tearfully thanked me for reuniting them, I said, "I'm glad to have played a small part in your reunion. Mending fences always occurs in God's perfect timing. Through God's grace you were open and willing to make peace with your father. That second chance blessed you both."

Edgar Cayce said that, while healing can come from many sources (surgery, drugs, therapy, manipulation, herbs, plants, attitudes, etc.), the love of the Creator and our love for each other are the foundation for healing. For some people, medical intervention would be an insult to their soul. To find themselves in a hospital where drugs are doled out, would be abhorrent to these people. They want to stay with natural healing therapies and natural foods, no matter what happens.

Other people prefer drugs and surgery, no matter what happens. They are wedded to traditional medicine, happy to walk down the aisle hand in hand with their allopathic doctor. They seem completely uninterested in exploring or hearing about any natural therapies or other possibilities. Which is the right road? The one that rings true in your heart. And what a blessing that we all have the right to choose what type of healer or doctor we want to help us.

Why is healing such a mystery?

Why not? All of life is a mystery. Even in our modern scientific world, instrumentation still hasn't given us the information as to what happens during the healing flow. In the medical arena, people are grouped into categories by disease and treated accordingly. However, we are all so different that it's hard to tailor one accepted treatment modality to fit the needs of every individual. While billions are spent on orthodox medicine, more people are turning to alternative therapies, which focus on each person as unique individuals.

In my practice, I would say that no two people have the same problem, no matter how similar their cases might appear. Vibrational patterns tell a different story for every person I see, and the lessons locked into the condition vary tremendously. In each case, the information flowing to me about the condition is as different as the individual. And as individuals, we all react differently to healing no matter what form that healing takes.

In southern California there was a VA hospital with 300 veterans in wheelchairs. Therapies of all kinds had been tried, but these vets remained bound to their chairs year after year until a horrendous earthquake occurred. When it hit, the top two floors of the building crashed down inside the building with a mighty roar.

Before the structure collapsed, half of the veterans confined to wheelchairs leaped up and took off running on spindly legs, which were unused to even walking. They managed to run all the way outside and away from the falling building before their legs gave out. Of these fleeing men, half retained the use of their legs and never returned to their wheelchairs. But the other half had to be returned to their wheelchairs, unable to move as they had when they first ran for their lives during the quake. More mystery.

Who gets healed?

People with total faith may travel thousands of miles and cross oceans to seek healing miracles. They may—or may not—receive that healing. Or, healing may be waiting just around the corner, without their ever pursuing it. When the Old Man died, his neighbors gathered to share their memories of him. One family had a paralyzed son. The other neighbors asked why they never took their boy next door for healing. They replied, "We never thought about it."

Some people, whom I considered scoundrels, have been healed instantly, right in front of my eyes. Other people, who seemed so saintly and deserving, weren't always healed. For that matter, why are some people healed completely in a matter of seconds while others may need many treatments? All in all, healing is a confusing undertaking. As I was told long ago, God heals who, why, when, and how, for reasons I can never know. And so it is today.

I do know that healing is granted to each person from a higher power far beyond our comprehension, in ways as unique as our individual fingerprints. I often wonder what it takes for people to wake up and seek the healing that will change their lives. Usually Disease comes knocking at our door with a message that can't be ignored. It's the Creator's way of saying, "Excuse me, but you're headed in the wrong direction."

Rhonda had been a patient for many years, coming in whenever she felt like a treatment. She often skipped months at a time and then I'd see her name on the appointment schedule. No matter what calamity struck her friends in the way of illness, she would casually remark, "Oh well, ya gotta die sometime." These shallow words of consolation didn't go over well with her friends who complained about her unfeeling words when they came to see me. I heard these words repeated many times over the years. When Rhonda told me that a friend had been diagnosed with cancer, she added her stock observation, "Oh well, ya gotta die sometime."

When I noticed Rhonda's name in the appointment book, I realized it had been five years since I'd seen her. On the day of her appointment, she entered the treating room in a total panic. Before I could say anything, she blurted, "I've got cancer." I couldn't possibly pass up this opportunity to see how she liked hearing her favorite phrase, "Oh well, Rhonda, ya gotta die sometime." She immediately snapped back, "Are you *crazy?* Screw *that* noise! I'm gonna *die!* You gotta *save* me!"

Rhonda agreed to come in once a week. In three weeks she was gaining weight and feeling stronger. When she returned to the hospital six weeks later for examination, they told her she was in remission. Wonderful words for any cancer patient to hear. After that when her friends got sick, they never again had to hear her ya-gotta-die-sometime remark. Rhonda had learned the lesson of compassion the hard way.

It takes whatever it takes, for as long as it takes, for the soul to progress and healing to take place. I would love to understand the many mysteries of healing. Perhaps when the smoke clears after this lifetime, the angels will kindly explain what my life as a healer was all about.

What's the best way to find a healer?

By the time a person seeks a healer, they have usually tried and given up on most of the traditional methods of healing. Although finding a good healer can be difficult, each person will find the "right" healer in God's perfect timing. There are no mistakes. It's an adventure, like going on a treasure hunt. What you dig up may turn out to be priceless . . . or not. It's impossible to know until you see what results are forthcoming in your search for healing.

Today people are seeking to develop the elusive gift of healing in growing numbers. Hundreds of people call themselves "healers" after learning the basics of healing through videos, seminars, expensive courses, personal instruction and the like. I see "new" healing techniques springing up everywhere. Every time you turn around, you run into "channels," "mediums," "mystics," "energy shifters," "facilitators," and "intuitives" of all types and descriptions.

The healers you discover in your search will differ in their style and approach to healing. Some use methods learned from other healers, others develop their own techniques. In a state of grace one may meet a wonderful healer who is ready to treat somebody just like you, in fact, it *is* you. And there you are.

There are probably as many ways to find a healer as there are individuals, prayer being the most common. But one of the most unusual approaches was told to me by a young lady of 30 who came to me for treatment and was extremely sensitive to the healing energy. As soon as she told me that she had just flown in from Hawaii and was moving to Arizona, I asked, "Who referred you to me?"

She casually replied, "Oh, I used the finger buzz method."

Completely lost as to what she meant, I asked, "And just how does that work?"

"Oh, whenever I need to find someone to help me, I go to the yellow pages of the local phone book, look up the proper category, and run my finger down the listings until my finger buzzes. Then I dial the phone number under my buzzing finger. It never fails. I always get the help I need."

Now I've heard of many strange methods, but this was a new one for me. I passed this curious method on to a friend who was a fisherman. When he tried it out, he found he could locate fish by moving his finger over an ocean chart until he felt the buzz. Will life's wonders never cease?

———

Once you begin your search, you may run straight into the healer who can help you, or you may be living right next door to a healer and never hear of his work. The essential thing is to keep looking. Become acquainted with the people at your local health food store as they often know the healers in their area. Andrew Carnegie once said, "As I grow older, I pay less attention to what men say. Instead, I watch what they do." These words are important in your search. While there will always be a few ego cases in the mix just to make life interesting, word of mouth is an excellent way to find a good healer . . .

When I think of word of mouth referrals, I hark back to a time when I was suddenly flooded with patients who all came to see me because of their terrible back pain. I was baffled to hear them all parrot the same words when they saw me for the first time: "Simms sent me." Seeing so many patients a day, I couldn't recall a "Simms." I always meant to find out why this mystery man was sending in so many patients. However, being busy with new patients, I never had the time.

For seven years, the Simms's parade of patients continued off and on. Then one day Simms himself came strolling in with his wife, and I thanked him for his many referrals. Curious, I asked, "Can you refresh my memory about what happened when I first treated you?"

Simms replied, "Fate brought me to your office. I've had horrible low back pain for years. Whenever I ran out of pain pills, I'd just call my doctor and get a renewal on my prescription. But one day I called and got the doctor's answering service. He was on vacation. As soon as I heard this, I was frantic. I told the woman at the service that my back pain had never been worse and I was out of pain pills. I told her I couldn't stand the pain and asked her what I should do."

His wife interrupted, "We were desperate. You just can't imagine how much pain he was in."

Simms continued, "The woman who took my call must have heard the anguish in my voice. She said she would give me a name and number for someone who could help me if I swore that I'd never tell anyone. She said she would be fired if anyone ever found out that she'd given me this information."

His wife jumped in and added, "It was one of your patients who took his call at the doctor's answering service. I got four men to help me. Using a sleeping bag like a stretcher, they carried him out of the house and put him in the back of our station wagon. Then I drove to your office with the men riding in back so they could help us out at the other end."

Simms took over, "Riding in back on that makeshift stretcher was pure hell. When we stopped in front of your office and I saw your sign with the word 'chiropractor' on it, I threw a fit."

"He sure did," his wife said. "You should have heard him. He said he wasn't going to any damn chiropractor. I paid no attention. I hadn't brought him all that way just to turn around and go home again. Besides, what other hope did we have? I told the men to carry him into your office. We probably looked like quite a sight to your other patients. When it was his turn, the men placed him carefully on your table."

By this time, I remembered the four men bringing Simms in on his sleeping bag stretcher. Smiling, I took over telling what I remembered of that morning. "Of course, I didn't know anything about your feelings toward my profession," I began. "And when I asked how I could help you, you just glared at me. I could see that further conversation wasn't going to improve the situation so I turned the matter over to God and started running energy. After 15 minutes, the healing energy shut down and the angels said it was done. So, I said you could leave. As I recall, you were so mad when you got up from the table that you grabbed the sleeping bag, and literally stomped out of the room without saying a word to me. A few minutes later, I saw your station wagon drive off with you sitting up in the backseat."

At this point, his wife dived in, "You're absolutely right. But when he *walked* out of your office, I couldn't believe it. I asked what you'd done for him."

Simms laughed and said, "I told her 'not a damn thing' because you just stood at my feet with your hands out. She snapped back 'but you walked out' and I suddenly realized she was right. Not only did I walk out, but I didn't have a pain in my body for the first time in my life."

"And what brings you in this time after seven years?"I asked.

"Oh, I'm feeling great. I just thought I'd get a checkup to make sure I keep feeling great."

After I told him that he was fine and his energy was balanced, he said he would be back in another seven years for another checkup. I thanked him again for all the patients he had sent. Whatever Simms told them about me, they were always 100 percent sold before I ever saw them, and most of them were well in one treatment.

———

By staying open, you will be directed in miraculous ways to find someone who can help you. You never know how or when a referral to a healer may appear in your life . . .

Ruth called from Yosemite National Park to ask if I could possibly see her the next day on her trip back to Los Angeles. She told me she had been in hellish pain for 12 years after a freak accident. Imagine crossing the street at night and falling through an open manhole. That's what had happened to Ruth. The workers had finished for the day, but neglected to put the cover back in place.

When she arrived the next morning, I thought she must have made head's turn when she was younger because she was still stunning at 60. After she made herself comfortable on the treating table and I was seated beside her, she clasped my two hands in hers, shut her eyes and said, "Doctor, I will do *anything* to get well!"

Being a comedian at heart, I couldn't pass up this wonderful straight line. I waited for half a minute, *"Anything* Ruth?" I asked.

Ruth kept her eyes closed for a wonderful, theatrical pause. Then she opened one eye, looked at me, and said, *"Almost* anything, Doctor." We both burst out laughing.

As I started to run energy, I asked, "How did you happen to hear of me?"

"Well, first let me explain that I never eat breakfast," she began. "But yesterday morning, for the first time in my life, I felt compelled to have breakfast. So I went to the dining room at Yosemite's Ahwahnee Hotel. By the time I got there, it was very crowded. In fact, there was only one chair left in the room. It was at a table with three other ladies who were sharing their experiences with a healer that they all knew. I couldn't believe my ears. I finally broke into their conversation and told them that I was desperately in need of healing. They all agreed that Dr. MacKimmie was the man I should see. One of the ladies gave me your card and here I am."

By the time I had finished her treatment, she told me that 90 percent of her pain was gone. She was very grateful to feel so much better. I would have liked to take away the other 10 percent of her pain, but unfortunately, she had to get back to Los Angeles.

———

Having been on my own search for great healers during my lifetime, I know it takes perseverance and fortitude to keep on looking. Never give up. You will find your healer through inner guidance. In some mysterious way, you will be guided to someone open to the higher powers of healing. So follow your heart, and pray to find the healer who is perfect for you. Be willing to follow the clues that God drops in front of you, and He will guide you to those who will help you in your healing process.

One older lady who arrived for healing said, "God guided me to your office." Always interested in such events, I asked, "And exactly how did He do that?"

She replied, "It all started when I went to Florida to visit one of my three daughters. After I got off the plane, my back pain was so bad that I was limping. A man came up to me and told me about you. He took out one of your cards from his wallet and gave it to me. It was old and battered, but the phone number was still readable so I took it."

"The next week, I flew to San Diego to visit my second daughter," she continued. "I was limping across the street when a woman came up to me. She told me about you and gave me your card. This one was newer and cleaner than the Florida one. A week later, I flew to Alaska to visit my third daughter. After the flight, my back was terribly painful.

While I was waiting for my daughter to pick me up at the airport, I cried out from the pain. A man walking by stopped to tell me about you and he gave me your card. By then, it was clear that God wanted me to see you so I booked a flight to San Francisco, took a taxi from the airport, and here I am."

Smiling, I said, "Well, it looks like God wasn't about to give up on pointing you in the right direction, even if it took three times." I treated her once and God took care of the rest; her back pain was healed completely that day.

———

With God in charge, I am never surprised as to who comes for healing or how they find me. Many years ago, I received a small donation in the mail from a Mr. Lum. I had no idea who he was, or how he had found me, but I noticed the postmark was from Hawaii. His note stated that he had severe low back pain and was confined to his bed. The Power directed me to run energy on his note. A month later, here came another donation from Mr. Lum with a note that he was now able to get out of bed and move around. Again, I ran energy on his note. Another month passed and Mr. Lum popped up in my mail once more. He wrote that he was able to leave his house and go on with his life again.

The fourth month, I saw Mr. Lum's name on the day's schedule. When he came in, he shook my hand and thanked me for healing his back. As soon as I started running energy, he said, "Ah, there's that same wonderful energy that healed my back. I've been feeling it for the past three months." And thus, the Power taught me that distance doesn't matter in the least as far as healing is concerned, and that the healing connection is made even if the healer has never met the patient.

———

One busy Saturday morning at the office, my secretary unexpectedly informed me that she had errands to run so I worked alone that day. At 10 A.M. sharp, the mail carrier arrived. When he saw how busy I was, he simply dropped the mail on my desk and headed out to continue his rounds.

It was Sunday morning before I had a chance to look through the pile of mail and opened a letter from a man in New York asking for healing. A few minutes after reading his letter, the man himself called and told me that he was feeling quite wonderful. When he told me that he had been totally healed on Saturday at 1 P.M. New York time, I realized that this was the exact time that the mail had been dropped on my desk in California.

I marveled how the Power could heal him instantly when the mail was on my desk, but not opened until the next day. Regardless of the fact that I knew nothing of his request, he was healed. He called again a few days later, to thank me once more for his long distance healing. We both gave thanks for God's miraculous healing timetable that works no matter what the distance or circumstances.

Can a person help in their own healing?

Do you as a patient have responsibilities? In my book, the answer is "yes." The healer should not have to carry both ends of the stretcher. If a patient is willing to stick to beneficial guidelines for health, then the body will be more open for healing on every level. Whenever patients seem unwilling to carry their half of the stretcher, one of my five-year-old patients comes to mind . . .

Diagnosed with epilepsy, Richie was having nearly 100 seizures a day when his parents brought him to see me. The rest of his brothers and sisters were as healthy as both parents. The doctors seriously doubted that Richie could ever attend public school and had suggested putting him in an institution for long-term drug care since his condition disrupted the entire family.

Richie lay face up on my table while I prayed to help him recover his health. When I touched his hand, the angels told me that he was allergic to dairy, sugar, fast foods, MSG, soft drinks, junk foods, and food coloring. As the Power steadily flowed healing energy into his body, I noticed the flow was especially strong into his liver and pancreas. In a few minutes, he relaxed and smiled. When we talked, I discovered that he was a very intelligent, sweet child.

Next week's appointment brought the exciting news that Richie had only had three seizures all week. The next week he only had two, and within a month, none at all. His parents were elated. I instructed them to continue restricting Richie's diet to avoid all the foods related to his condition.

Richie remained free of epileptic seizures for many months. Then his parents brought him in because he had started having seizures again. I hid my surprise when his mother said, "Richie asked me if he could see you all by himself."

As soon as Richie and I were alone, he started crying. He explained that he had seen his brothers and sisters sneaking sugar and milk into his food when they thought he wasn't looking. Apparently, they thought it was funny when he fell off his chair onto the floor in an epileptic seizure. And, of course, Richie couldn't always catch them to stop them. I was shocked.

After Richie stopped crying, we had a long talk. I told him that if he wanted to be well, he was going to have to take care of himself and take on the responsibility of preparing his own food. He eagerly agreed. All he wanted was to be well all the time and go to school.

After I brought Richie's parents into the office, I informed them that Richie was going to take charge of his diet and his cooking. I told the parents to put a secure padlock on a drawer that would contain only Richie's food. We discussed how he could handle cooking his own meals. At five, he took charge of his life and his health. That ended the problem.

At his next appointment Richie told me that everything was going well. His food was under lock and key, completely inaccessible to his mischievous brothers and sisters, and his father had built him a box to stand on so that he could cook at the stove. When Richie grew up and married, he made sure his own family continued eating healthy foods and taking charge of their own health. Years later, he called and told us about the video, *First Do No Harm,* with Meryl Streep, which also gives a dietary answer for childhood epilepsy.

So, if Richie could take responsibility for his health at five years of age, what excuse do any of the rest of us have for not grabbing onto the wheel of health and steering our lives in the right direction?

———

Through God's grace, the healer connects with the patient and the loving force within the heart of the universe to help dissolve anger and fear. As soon as we let go of our angry, fearful thoughts, we open to the healing flame at the very center of our beingness. In taking this essential step, we move forward in the healing process, and realize that we are loved beyond all knowing . . .

Sally had a large lump centered in her right breast; it made her breast tissue feel like stone. After trying one round of chemotherapy and radiation without success, she heard from others of my healing work and came to see me. As I was treating her, we talked about her life. She and her husband had not yet started a family. Being from a large family of 12 children, she had made up her mind that the last thing she wanted in her life was to be around a large family, even if it was made up of her own children.

However, Sally's husband was an only child and dreaded the thought of his children growing up without lots of brothers and sisters. He hoped to have at least nine children. Sally tried to convince her husband that one child, or at the most two, would be ideal and more than enough to satisfy her maternal instincts. It would have been nice to have settled such a major difference of opinion before marriage, but, as often happens, "true love" intervened. Looking into Sally's energy patterns, I saw that she was filled with anger and fear about her marriage. I tested the waters, "So tell me about your husband."

"Oh, he's a wonderful person," she smiled grimly. "But I know in my heart that he's going to be in a terrible accident and die very young. I've made a promise to myself that I'm going to stay with him until his death. Other than the number of children he wants, our marriage is fine."

Looking past these statements, I saw her deep-seated fear that her husband would *not* die. And while he lived, she would have to continue dealing with his desire to father many children. She was filled with fear about confronting her husband on this issue. Her unexpressed resentment and fear were driving her crazy and quite literally killing her.

During her treatment, I helped her bring her repressed feelings out into the open. After we talked about releasing these negative emotions. I said, "Sally, it's time to flow love into this situation and release the negativity stored in your body. You really need to share your feelings with your husband and reach a compromise about your future. Otherwise, these negative emotions will destroy you."

By the time we completed the energy work, the lump was gone. Sally was amazed that her right breast was now soft as though there had never been a tumor. I said, "God's love is the energy that healed you. But anger and fear are still in your energy field. It's up to you to surrender these emotions to God's love. Don't delay working out these problems with your husband. Talk to him right away. This will neutralize the negative emotions behind the tumor." Smiling, she nodded and left in a blissful state.

When Sally returned the next day, the breast lump was full blown again. She glared at me and asked, "What's the good of healing if the lump comes back?"

Seeing in her energy that she had not talked to her husband, I explained, "Once you were home with your husband again, your anger and fear took over. By not addressing your feelings, the lump returned. If you don't let go of your anger and fear by surrendering to love, I'm very much afraid that you will be facing death."

She started crying and sobbed, "I know you're telling me the truth."

"Remember, you can connect with God's healing energy at any time," I assured her. "It's always there for you." In that moment, I saw her let go all of her negativity and fear. I began running energy again, and the lump disappeared within a few minutes.

The third time Sally came back, she looked daggers at me, and demanded, "What's the point of having the tumor disappear, if it comes back again."

"Sally, your emotional upheavals are recreating the tumor. You must do your part by resolving this situation with your husband. Remain open to love. You have to turn over all your anger and fear to God or Love or whatever you want to call the Higher Power that runs our wonderful universe."

Sally nodded and said, "I understand. I'll never again allow anger and fear to get the better of me. And I'll reach an agreement with my husband." For the third time, the Power flowed God's infinite love into her body. Once again, the tumor dissolved in minutes. Sally was very optimistic and left singing. I prayed that she would have the wisdom to follow through with her resolutions.

Three weeks later Sally called to say that she had consulted a new oncologist who told her that he had a newly developed chemotherapy that would definitely kill her cancer. I could tell by her voice that she was delighted so I wished her all the best in her new healing program. With this new plan, there was no need to project love into her life, no need to give up anger and fear, and certainly no need to challenge her husband's progeny ideas. Just a quick, easy cure while she waited for her husband to have the accident that she was so sure would take his life.

Sally's husband phoned a few months later. "I wanted to let you know that Sally died. I think in some ways she was glad to die. She suffered so much from the new chemotherapy treatments, and she hated losing all her hair. If only we could have had children. I know how much she wanted a family."

———

Often we stay frozen in our thoughts where the mind can lead us around by the nose. But the pathway to healing is always before us, waiting for us to begin the great journey back to health. There's an old saying: "Sorrow looks back, worry looks around, but faith looks up." In my opinion, the body can heal anything, and prayer is a powerful tool to help us in self-healing. Place your hands over the area of the body that needs healing. Breathe slowly and steadily while praying for healing energy to flow through your hands.

No disease comes into our life that does not have the seeds of a divine lesson within it. Face right into the condition, sit it down in a chair and talk to it, and above all learn from it. Visualize white light washing away the bad guys. Send them on their way. Envision a crop of new, perfect cells emerging and taking over the area. As the first light of morning dissolves the darkness of the night, so the healing energy of the Creator's love revitalizes the cells of your body with renewed life. Imagine what you want to do when you are restored and in perfect health. Give your mind and body this joyful blueprint of your healthy future self.

Read inspirational words and stay in the present moment. A positive attitude and loving thoughts will boost the immune system, which is incredibly sensitive, responding to our every thought. Thought is the builder, and we are constantly experiencing the results of our thoughts.

Become the observer of your life. You will see how your life flows and builds upon your thoughts. When we are forgiving of ourselves and others, we bring incredible healing energy into our lives. Compassion for others bathes us in the sweetness of life that is forever born anew in our hearts. In reality, we *are* love, covered by a thin layer of human emotions.

Let humor into your life. Seriousness breaks the strongest oak, but humor allows the branches to bend and promotes healing. I often say, "If God doesn't have a sense of humor, then I'm not going." I have always found that the higher beings and great masters have a wonderful sense of humor and I am certain that God must too. Apache legend has it that the Creator made man to walk and talk, to see and hear, and gave him dominion over all the earth and its creatures. But the Creator wasn't satisfied. Finally, he gave man laughter. And when man laughed and laughed, the Creator said, "Now you are fit to live."

Can you suggest ways for people to improve their health?

Early in my practice, I wrote a handout sheet for people wanting better health. I wanted to give them a jump ahead in the game of health. In California, it was called the Blue Sheet since I had it printed on blue paper, and it has traveled far and wide to my patients and their families and friends over the years. The first paragraph states:

> Today, whether you know it or not, you are in a battle fighting for your health against food processing, contaminated water, and toxins in your daily environment. Wake up and realize that to experience wellness you must become a researcher into your daily foods, read labels, and ask questions. You must listen to the common sense of your body if you are to survive. You cannot afford to let others tell you what to eat or how to live. Most experts are wrong sooner or later. We live in a world surrounded by junk food goodies. Thomas Jefferson: "The price of Freedom is Eternal Vigilance." The price for your Health is also Eternal Vigilance.

I feel that this is as true today as it was when I first wrote it, maybe more so now. It's an old saying, but absolutely correct, that you are what you eat. What you choose to put on your fork will either lead you down a path of ever increasing health, or ever increasing sickness.

On this sheet I also listed the things I have done that were responsible for bringing me from sickness to excellent health. These are the key suggestions from that sheet:

• Drink at least 8 to 10 (8 oz.) glasses of pure water during the day to help your kidneys filter toxins from your blood.

• Drink water at least 30 minutes before, and 3 hours after eating, to allow enzymes to do their work digesting your food.

• Take ½ teaspoon (maximum) of Real Salt daily in your water or on your food.

• Eat organic/natural: beef, lamb, chicken, fish, fertile eggs, lightly steamed or raw veggies, fruit (best when eaten by itself, not in combination with other foods), herbal teas, sprouted grain bread—in other words—REAL FOODS!

• After drinking lots of water, take a ½ hour walk in the morning on an otherwise empty stomach.

• Lovingly accept and give thanks for your life as it is RIGHT NOW!

Also listed on the sheet are things I have personally avoided all my life in order to stay healthy and active. The list has grown over the years as man has continued inventing artificial ways to "improve" life. When you read it, perhaps you will be able to imagine why this list kept Andrea *away* from my office for two years:

ALL, yes ALL milk products/lactose/casein/whey (read labels), sugar, chocolate, soda pop and diet drinks, pork, head lettuce, most commercial teas, coffee/decaff, artificial sweeteners, artificial flavorings/colorings, MSG, foil for cooking, aluminum and "non-stick" cookware/utensils and any foods cooked using them, aluminum-based and crystal-type deodorant stones, beverages in aluminum cans, electric blankets, battery watches, waterbeds, microwave ovens, cell phones, photosensitive glasses, fluorescent lights, fluoride toothpastes, chewing gum, and preservatives.

Am I a wacko? No doubt Andrea thought so when she first read the list. Still, it never hurts to try something new. So as I wrote at the end of the sheet: Decide in the quiet of your inner being what you want for yourself and from Life and get the two of them together.

Do expectations interfere with healing?

It's best not to play the ego's game of expectation. God is in charge all the way so the game of life is really one of learning to relax, let go, and turn your life over to the Creator. Charles Dickens aside, great expectations are not a good basis for healing. The healing process is greatly enhanced when both the patient and the healer can stay in neutral during the treatment.

In that neutral place, there is an inner knowing that the body is all-wise, with strengths and powers of healing that are awesome and available. The healer and the patient can approach healing in an effortless manner by connecting on the spiritual plane. In removing the mind from the equation, it allows the great powers that reside within every cell of the body to focus on healing. Results are released to a higher spiritual power—in whatever form each person recognizes that power—which in reality does the healing.

Therefore, it is wise to wait before judging the results of a healing session until some time has elapsed after the treatment. I have seen people receive total healing in the first treatment. Others need three treatments to get the healing process underway. Your healing will take as long as it takes.

After a few treatments, one lady asked, "Besides physical healing, you're doing other things on a spiritual level to help us change our lives for the better, aren't you?" I answered, "Yes, but don't pass the word around. Most people wouldn't understand what it's all about unless they've experienced it." However, once you have experienced spiritual healing, you are forever on the other side of the fence. You cannot go back. You cannot deny what has happened to you . . .

I remember a new patient who judged the healing effects of the treatment as soon as I had completed her healing session. Unfortunately, she was one of the 10 percent of my patients who feel nothing during treatment. She was irate and complained that absolutely nothing had happened. I told her that not every patient has an immediate physical reaction, but that doesn't mean that there hasn't been any healing. I explained that although 10 percent of my patients don't feel anything, healing can still take place.

The woman glared at me, declared I was a fraud, and left the room.

I heard her complaints continue outside my door as I started treating the next person. Seconds later, there was a loud crash outside the door of my treating room. I ran and opened the door. There was my last patient out cold, lying on the floor unconscious.

With the help of several patients who were waiting, we moved her into a comfortable position away from the door and cushioned her head with a pillow. When she regained consciousness in a half hour, she was a changed woman. She excitedly told all the waiting patients, "Now don't expect to feel a darn thing when he treats you, but for God's sake, sit *down* as soon as you come out." Very few of my patients ever passed out like this lady, but she was healthy from then on and one of my most loyal defenders after her experience.

————

After a healing session, wait a few days to allow time for improvement. Be patient. Wait and see. Results can come at once or may take some time. In some cases, the patient may suddenly notice how much better they are feeling after weeks of gradual improvement. At other times changes are brought to the patient's awareness by the family members or friends who sent the patient in . . .

A new patient was already on my treating table when I came into the room. Mary had been sent in by friends who warned me beforehand that she had no faith in God. They told me that she was the most cynical person they knew. As I put my palm on her abdomen to check her life force energy, the gentlest of breezes drifted in through my open front window. The breeze just barely moved a set of large wind chimes hanging outside, near the front door of the office. This breeze gently moved the chimes, producing their beautiful melody. Before this lone breeze, the air had been still all morning. Hearing the chimes, Mary looked up at me, took my hands in hers, and said softly, "I know you won't believe me, but I heard tones."

I thought my patient was joking since she surely would have seen the wind chimes on her way into the office. I smiled, "Me too."

Mary squeezed my hands harder, "No, you don't understand. I'm not *kidding*. I really heard tones. They were heavenly . . . so beautiful. I've never heard anything so lovely in my life."

After I realized she was not kidding, I waited for her to ask what might have caused these tones. I also waited for another breeze to move the chimes again and reveal the earthly source of the heavenly tones. I was fully prepared to tell her the truth so that we could both laugh at the silliness of the coincidence of a breeze moving the chimes just at that moment. However, she didn't ask and the air was perfectly still just as before, and it remained so all day long.

The Power instructed me to say nothing about the chimes, and to continue running energy because the lady was totally open for change. When I saw Mary leaving the office, I held my breath. Her head missed the clapper by scarcely a quarter of an inch. When she reached her car, she got in and drove away.

All next week, Mary's friends were calling me, thrilled with Mary's new found faith and trust in God and life. Seeing the wonderful changes in Mary since her treatment, they told her that she was a changed woman. Impressed by her mystical experience, her friends encouraged her in her new outlook on life.

I debated whether I should reveal the source of the tones, but the Power reminded me that no breeze had stirred those heavy chimes in the still summer days before—or after—Mary's visit. God *was* the breeze creating those heavenly tones at the perfect moment. I thanked God for the miracle of the chimes, for Mary's new faith, and for her friends who helped Mary recognize the wonderful changes she was making in her life.

————

In every case, all healing is in God's hands. I am only an observer, instructed to stay in neutral whether I receive gratitude or the occasional statement that I did "nothing." At this stage of my life, I have come to the conclusion that none of us knows very much. The results of healing will be what they will be. Some say it is faith on the part of the patient, but I have not found that to be true. It may help but I have also seen great healing occur for people who didn't like me at all, people who called me a fraud and a quack before—and sometimes after—the treatment . . .

Paul, a young man of 15, was furious with me even before we began. His mother brought him in to see me after I had treated her successfully. When I saw this big, muscular fellow sitting in my treating room, I knew that if looks could kill, I was a dead man. As soon as he saw me, he growled, "You're nothing but a quack who's stolen my mother's money."

Ignoring his comment, I asked, "Why do you think your mom wanted me to see you?"

"Oh, I *know* why she brought me here," Paul admitted grudgingly. "For one thing, I'm flunking out of school. Besides that, I have fainting spells. I run cross country and when the school bus picks us up after a meet at the finish line, we can have as many soft drinks as we want. I'm so thirsty after running that I drink as many as I can. But I can hardly make it to my seat on the bus before I pass out. And I never remember a thing about the trip back to the school."

"Sounds serious," I said.

Paul looked at me defiantly and said, "If you can get rid of this fainting thing, *then* I'll believe in you."

"If you do exactly what I tell you, you'll be on the honor roll by the end of the year and will run in every event without fainting. But you're going to have to drink water, and only water. And I want you to give up the soft drinks and everything else with sugar, like pies, cakes, cookies, and ice cream." Silence filled the room as he thought this over.

"I'll do it, you quack," he said finally. "But just so my mom can see you fail. Then at least we'll be rid of you. The whole idea is completely stupid. One thing for sure: it won't help my grades. I'm flunking three subjects." He promised to follow my program exactly for three months, and we shook hands on it.

To my surprise, Paul's word turned out to be as good as gold. With five months left in the school year, he started his new program. At the end of the three months, he felt so good that he told me he was going to stay on the program forever. By the end of the school year, Paul did make the honor roll and he could easily run 15 miles. Instead of drinking soft drinks and riding the bus back after track meets, he drank lots of good old H2O and ran back to school where he met his friends who had returned on the bus.

Later the family begged me to tell Paul not to unfreeze gallon ice cream containers in their freezer, which he then refilled with water and put back in the freezer as a "surprise." After his conversion to health, he was always on his family's case. The next time I saw him, I said, "Paul, everyone in your family has to make their own decisions about their health habits and what they eat." He agreed to stop his unappreciated health campaign at home. After that, his family enjoyed a brilliant scholar and athlete who didn't frustrate them by trying to change their way of life.

———

One of the most difficult patients I ever treated was a surgeon referred to me by a mutual pathologist friend. Although John had been given all the accepted medical treatments currently in vogue, he was clearly dying. The last word his doctor gave on his prognosis was "grave," an apt word considering John's likely destination. His appearance was shocking. Only in his 40s, he had lost so much weight that he seemed like a walking skeleton, just skin and bones.

As John walked into my treatment room, his energy broadcast his expectations, which he voiced as soon as he saw me. Scowling, he said, "I don't believe that anyone or anything is going to help me."

"Here we go again, God," I thought. "Please handle all the negative expectations that stand in the way of this man's healing."

I ran the energy and asked John to cooperate by following some simple guidelines for recovering his health, in case healing was what God had in mind for him. However, John was so sure that nothing and no one could help him that he wouldn't follow any instructions. I saw him once a week for five weeks. By the fifth treatment, he had gained 60 pounds and was forced to acknowledge his healing since all the hospital tests now showed that he was free of the disease. His doctors, puzzled by his wonderful test results, released him as in remission.

However, John was furious and swore at me, "No goddamned quack chiropractor can heal my condition. I wish I'd never met you! I wish I'd *died* and *never* come to see you. How can I go on working as a surgeon knowing that you can heal people? Damn you to hell *and* your healing!"

Underneath all his anger, I saw that this surgeon was truly a caring man who couldn't resolve the internal conflict of his own undeniable healing with his chosen profession. I empathized, "My friend, you were dying when you came to see me. Now you are well after five treatments. I see no problem, John. Your disease is gone. God healed you. I just happened to be in the room. Perhaps it would help you to remember that it's not the garden hose that you owe your gratitude to, it's the water flowing through it. Without the water's gift, the garden hose itself is of little use. I'm just the garden hose. Why not accept the fact that you are well now and get on with your life? I too am puzzled by lots of things in life. But just because I don't know everything doesn't stop me from getting on with my life." John's face brightened; he shook my hand and left.

———

Why even attempt to judge life when nothing occurs by accident? Everything flows in and out of your life as part of a divine plan orchestrated by the heart and drawn to us for soul growth. The heart beats in the moment, in Time Eternal where we live forever. Time temporal is just that: temporary. All the nonsense of the mind exists in temporary time.

Our true being is eternal, existing joyously in each moment as it presents itself. And remarkably, it's never too late to be healed and to take a hand in your healing . . .

Wilhelm was an 88-year-old man confined to his bed. He was a tall man whose body was covered with a mysterious rash. It was no wonder that he couldn't stand; his ankles were very swollen and painful to the slightest touch. I was horrified when his wife, Lulu, showed me his x-rays. They revealed bones so fragile and paper-thin that any pressure on them could have snapped them quite easily.

In addition, poor Wilhelm was totally constipated, and existed by taking harsh laxatives. He admitted he consumed sleeping pills by the box, and complained that he couldn't sleep or get any rest without them. A prisoner of his own bed, he hadn't been outside the house for three years. The only time he left his bed was to make painful excursions to the bathroom.

Yet, in spite of constant pain, Wilhelm possessed a quiet dignity that reflected the upbringing of a gentleman in every respect. When I commented on the many pictures of great sailing ships, which covered the bedroom walls, Lulu proudly announced that Wilhelm had been a naval commander during World War I.

As I studied this couple, I noticed that he and his wife wore dark old-fashioned clothes. Their faces were gaunt and haggard from years of poor health. I wondered how Lulu, who couldn't have weighed 100 pounds all wet, managed to care night and day for this giant of a man. The shades were drawn; heavy, coal-black velvet drapes stood ready to darken the room further. The floors were covered by rugs in dark, muddy colors, which reinforced the sense of gloom in their house.

From talking with Wilhelm, I learned that his condition had developed over seven years of taking a wide assortment of drugs continuously, including broad spectrum antibiotics and cortisone therapy. I couldn't understand why he had been taking so many drugs for so long. Neither he nor his wife could remember why any of them had been originally prescribed. They were both eating foods that made my hair stand on end. I saw that God was going to have His hands full on this one, but, as always, I put aside my own expectations and judgements about what was possible.

And so we began energy treatments. After seeing Wilhelm every second day for a while, Lulu asked me about cutting back on Wilhelm's medications. I told her this would have to be their decision. While doctors usually monitor drug interactions and dosages closely, Wilhelm had been bedridden for the past three years, too sick to get to the doctor's office, and their doctor didn't make house calls, so here we were.

I agreed with Lulu that while these drugs might have saved Wilhelm's life at one time, we needed to question why he was still on them, especially since neither of them knew why he was taking them. We were all very concerned about the large number of drugs he was taking and the length of time he had been on them. Lulu was a very bright lady and decided to slowly back off the drugs, except for the cortisone.

Within a month, Wilhelm was off of all the drugs, except cortisone. Although he felt much better, his skin continued to bleed and ooze. This condition caused him constant pain. I asked Lulu to consider checking with their doctor about stopping the cortisone to see if his skin would clear. She told me she would call their family doctor about this. He was a close family friend from the same village in Germany that she and Wilhelm were from. She trusted his judgement implicitly. She also admitted feeling guilty about having a chiropractor coming to the house to treat her dear Wilhelm without having asked their doctor's permission.

"As soon as you say the word 'chiropractor,' he will hang up on you," I warned her.

"Oh, no, Doctor. You're wrong about that. He's a very dear, very old family friend," she said.

I didn't say anything further and Lulu made her call to ask the doctor's permission for Wilhelm to be seen by me and to stop the cortisone to see if his horrible skin rash would clear. Of course he did hang up on her, but she thought there was trouble with the phone line. She called again with the same result. After she got off the phone for the third time, she was in shock.

Lulu turned to me and said, "I don't understand. I told him Wilhelm is doing much better now, and asked his permission to have a chiropractor continue seeing Wilhelm. The doctor said he would never speak to me again and hung up on me."

After this phone call, Lulu was so upset that she decided on her own to begin the process of gradually reducing the cortisone until it was stopped. Wilhelm improved rapidly. His skin cleared, his swollen ankles returned to normal, and his digestion was perfect. He began walking, drinking lots of water, going to sleep early and getting up early. I got them started growing their own wheat grass and had them change their cookware from aluminum to stainless steel. Soon I had them shopping for organic vegetables and fruits. Three months later, when Wilhelm turned 89, he was walking several miles each day to the surprise of everyone in our small town.

Lulu and Wilhelm began wearing new clothes in lovely, uplifting pastel colors. Soon they moved into a cheery, new home filled with sunshine and light that came in through the large windows on every side. It was decorated with lovely white drapes and pastel rugs that spoke of spring and life and hope, in contrast to their old house of illness where black predominated in all the furnishings. It lifted my spirits to visit them there and see their healthy, radiant faces.

A year later, a few days before Christmas, I received an invitation from Lulu to come to their home at 7:00 P.M. Knowing Wilhelm's fondness for punctuality, I arrived promptly at the appointed hour. Lulu opened the door and graciously invited me in. She took my hand and led me into the living room where three chairs had been placed to face the most majestic, incredibly thick Christmas tree I had ever seen. Lulu asked me to sit in the large, comfortable, middle chair, which also had a foot stool.

I noticed that on this night, heavy, dark velvet drapes had been placed over the living room windows. When I looked questioningly at the many pails of wet sand near the tree, Lulu smiled mysteriously and whispered, "For fire, Doctor."

After Wilhelm sat down next to me, Lulu said, "There are 60 sterling silver candle holders in the tree. As you can see, each one has a white candle in it. They are pure beeswax and burn very cleanly. In a moment, I'll light them and then we'll watch in silence until they finish their performance."

Once the candles were all lit, Lulu sat on the other side of me and we three silently watched the beauty of the candles burning against the dark, green branches. Warmth from the candles increased the pine fragrance that enveloped us. I had never seen such a beautiful sight, or felt so much love and happiness fill a room. After 20 minutes, the candles gracefully retired from their flames, one by one.

Lulu turned to me and said, "Wilhelm and I are so very happy in our new life. We both have such wonderful health now. We wanted to thank you by sharing the Ceremony of Lights. This is just as we did in Germany every Christmas for many, many years. Thank you, Doctor, for all your healing and for sharing with us your philosophy of health. It changed our lives."

I thanked them both for this wondrous experience, which is one of my fondest memories. I told them they were wonderful patients, and congratulated them on participating in their healing by always following directions, exactly as given.

When Wilhelm was in his 90s, he went to Santa Maria to visit friends. While crossing the street in a crosswalk, he was hit by a car running the stop sign. Because of front-end damage, the car had to be towed away. Amazingly, Wilhelm, who had been knocked 48 feet, firmly refused to be put on a stretcher when the ambulance arrived. He insisted on riding as a passenger.

At the hospital, as soon as the orthopedic surgeon heard the age of his incoming patient, he called for an operating room to be prepared in case he had to amputate. Wilhelm arrived black and blue from his waist down to his feet, and was quickly taken to the x-ray department.

Lulu told me later that after checking the x-rays, the surgeon said, "I'm glad we *don't* have to amputate. Your husband's bones look more like a 21-year-old's. I would have been sawing through bone all night." A gruesome thought, but what better proof of the magnificent job Lulu had done in changing their nutrition. They both lived into their late 90s with fine health all the way. They were exemplary patients and it was my privilege to also call them dear friends.

What part does karma play in healing?

If I could heal people exactly as *they* wish, would their lives be better? Would they be happier? If you ask a person going for healing if they want to be healed, they will answer, "Of course. Why else would I go?" Everyone thinks they want healing, but the inner patterns of the soul may not allow the person to make the inner and outer changes that bring about that healing. Karma runs the show.

Each healing session operates under its own rules, and people carry their own healing with them. By that, I mean they allow healing to occur from a subconscious level, which has inner restrictions. These restrictions govern what the healer will be permitted to do; they are a function of karmic patterns. Thus, people are always healed by the Creator in perfect ways and in perfect timing for their soul growth . . .

A man came to see me after a gambling trip to Lake Tahoe where he had slipped and fallen in his hotel bathroom while taking a shower. Hitting his left temple on the faucet handle in the bathtub, he suffered a stroke. He now slurred his words and his right arm and leg were almost useless. I ran energy and through the Creator's love he was restored to total health in 20 minutes. I warned him to stay away from Lake Tahoe for a month as the Power told me it was dangerous for him to be there at this particular time. He promised to stay in the Bay area where he lived.

However, my bullheaded patient went back to Lake Tahoe that very night and stayed in the same room where he fell in the same bathtub. He struck his head in the same way, and suffered another stroke on the same side. However, this time when he came to see me and I tried to run energy, it returned to my hands. I told him that I couldn't heal him, but would continue to pray for him.

Mutual friends told me later that he never recovered from this stroke. Why he went back after his first healing miracle was and is beyond my understanding. But then, why do any of us do foolish things in life? How often do we find ourselves committing the very acts that we have pledged to stop? What interesting critters we are!

Later, I asked the Power why healing wouldn't flow into this man when he came back to see me for the second time. The angels answered, *"This man did not honor his healing by heeding our warning. He consciously turned his back on the healing he had received. He will learn more from being healed and choosing to lose that healing."*

Karma prevailed. And that was that.

—————

However, if it is time, then the patient and the healer join in flowing love to every area of the body ready to accept healing. This healing is perfectly attuned to the patient's soul growth—never to wishes, wants and desires. Each person's condition is perfect for them in time, place and circumstance. There are no mistakes.

Within every disease lie hidden lessons for soul growth, lessons to be learned and lived through. Complete healing occurs only after the patient understands and accepts all the lessons contained within their illness. If the underlying lessons are not addressed, I have seen the condition return or begin in another form elsewhere in the body, all to return the patient's attention to these underlying spiritual lessons once again.

Before we confront disease, our bodies seem to be rolling along and functioning well. Then bang, seemingly out of the blue, conditions arise that may be simple, or may threaten the person with disability or death. However, I have always told patients that disease is not just lurking somewhere out in the bushes waiting to jump on you. If you ignore Mother Nature's approach to health, one day the proverbial straw will break the camel's back. We don't get sick overnight and we shouldn't expect ill health from years of poor foods and bad habits to vanish overnight. In healing as in life, patience is a virtue so give Dr. Time and Mother Nature a chance . . .

Joe came to see me with a diagnosis of cancer. He had tried one chemotherapy treatment at the hospital. He told me, "The chemo made me so nauseous that I got up and left the hospital in the middle of my treatment. A security guard at the exit of the parking lot, stood in front of my car before I could drive out and said I couldn't leave without my doctor's permission. I leaned my head out the window and told the guard if he didn't move out of the way, he was going to get run over. Luckily for us both, he moved."

After talking with Joe, I said, "You're making a mess of your health with junk foods, coffee, no water, no exercise, and you're not getting enough sleep." He agreed to change his ways and get on the program I advised. By the end of the month, he had gained weight and was walking several miles a day. By the end of the year, there was no sign of the cancer when his doctor ran tests.

Two years later, I was giving a talk at a college and saw Joe's wife in the audience. After my lecture, I asked Carol how Joe was doing. She started crying and said, "The hospital called and said Joe could have a free CAT scan. They told him they wanted to check on him because they couldn't understand why he was still alive when he had been terminal. What would your advice have been?"

"Well, if he wants to die, go for it," I said.

"That's exactly what happened," she sobbed. "Joe said he just wanted to show them all that something else works. He died as soon as they turned on the machine. I can't understand it. He was doing so well. Why did he have to do it?"

I gave Carol a hug because sometimes there are no words and no answers. I knew that explaining the part that karma had played in Joe's death, would not ease the overwhelming grief that she felt from her loss.

———

Karma is the final card in the deck, the determining tally of our credits and debits in the great Book of Life. We have all lived thousands of lives here on earth and on other planes. This current life is just a tiny fragment of the vast expanse of our beingness. The Power told me that our present life deals primarily with the karma of our last five lives. Through love, acceptance, and forgiveness, we balance the books. If we awaken to the truth of our inner self, we release ourselves from the wheel of karma, the great law of cause and effect . . .

One of my favorite stories of awakening to the truth of self concerns a cancer specialist. An oncologist, with a flock of interns gathered closely around him, was proceeding on grand rounds at a prestigious teaching hospital. As they moved from one patient's bed to another, he noticed a large black man smiling broadly as they approached his bed. Before the doctor could begin making his comments, this patient began asking the interns how their schooling was coming along, if they were married, and how they liked doctoring.

Several weeks passed. Every time grand rounds came through the ward, this jolly fellow greeted the doctor and interns with smiles and good cheer. The oncologist never saw this patient without a smile. The patient's sunny disposition began to grate on the doctor's nerves. He checked the chart and it confirmed that the man was terminal. As soon as the doctor knew his patient couldn't live much longer, it was even more disturbing to interact with him. The doctor's irritation grew as he brooded over how this man could be so happy and act as though nothing was wrong.

Finally the oncologist determined to get to the bottom of his patient's bewildering, cheery disposition. The doctor thought he would surely see the truth of the matter if he paid his patient a visit during the early morning hours. He planned to look into the dying patient's eyes when no one else was around. It was one in the morning when the doctor shined his tiny penlight on the man's face. The man's eyes blinked open. A wide grin spread across his face and he asked, "Who's you?"

The doctor angled his penlight to shine on his own features, "It's me, your oncologist."

The patient beamed and asked again, "Who's you?"

"Sorry to wake you. I'm the doctor treating you for your cancer."

The patient laughed, looked deeply into the doctor's eyes and asked once again, "Who's you?"

This interchange went on for several minutes back and forth. The doctor kept trying to explain who he was and the patient kept on responding with the question: "Who's you?"

Suddenly the doctor understood the truth. It didn't matter one bit *who* he *thought* he was. He realized that he was of no use to this man as some abstract "doctor" or "oncologist" or "specialist." Through his patient's words he realized that their *true* beingness was one and the same. The doctor started laughing and so did his patient. They laughed uncontrollably until they could laugh no more and tears were running down their cheeks. The doctor left his patient's bedside forever changed.

From that day forward, whenever students on rounds asked the oncologist what drugs should be given, the doctor no longer told them what drugs were appropriate. Instead he said, "I don't give a damn what drugs you give these patients. For God's sake, hold their hand, write letters for them, hug them, tell them you love them, call their families . . . be of some *use* to these people. Give them the loving support you would give your own family. These people are your brothers and sisters who just happen to be your patients. And one day you may be in their place." This story was related to me by a dear friend who was a pathologist at the same teaching hospital and knew this oncologist very well.

———

Before leaving the question of karma, I would like to share another profound story of one woman's awakening. This lovely lady came in as a patient many years ago and gave me her story to share with others. With profound thanks for her insightful gift, her story as it was given to me follows . . .

I awoke in the hospital bed, feeling exhilarated, awed and humbled. I had no words to describe what I had just experienced. I simply lay there, basking in an inner light, an inner warmth, a profound peace. Hospital life moved into gear; nurses, aids, technicians and housekeepers moved through my room. Now, I found that I had become extremely sensitive to what other people were thinking and feeling. Their thoughts and emotions were as clear to me as their physical bodies. With wonder, I thought, "This must be the kind of vulnerability that new born infants must feel. Is this what people mean by being born again?"

A nurse asked, "How are you today?" I began a tentative, "Listen . . . I've had this incredible mystical experience . . ." But whoever asked the question smiled and moved on. I realized my statement was no different than any other psychiatric patient who had lost touch with reality.

But now, more than eight years later, I can look back and say, "Listen . . . I've had this incredible mystical experience" and know it really happened. This experience integrated and made sense of everything that had ever happened to me in this lifetime. It showed me the meaning and purpose of life itself. It was a birth into a state of consciousness I did not even know existed.

The road to this experience started very early in my life. I always knew I was searching for something, but I never knew what it might be.

As an adult, I sought fulfillment in customary middle-class ways—marriage, a family, traditional religion and then when the children grew older, graduate school and a new career—but fulfillment eluded me. A series of illnesses undermined my health and I could not achieve the goals I had set for myself. I became weak and depressed for several years.

Then the downward cycle began and my life got much worse. I was in an automobile accident, which left me in constant pain. Sleeping pills gave me the only relief from the agony of my injuries. I became dependent on them. My wonderful, loving brother died of a heart attack while running on the beach. The cousin closest to me in age and affection died of leukemia after a short illness. I was in an untenable marriage. Although I was a marriage counselor and could urge other people to discover their highest option and follow it, my own heavy conditioning about the bonds of matrimony (for better, for worse . . .) prevented me from taking that step myself.

Over a period of two years, I watched as every effort to maintain control over the life I was familiar with slid away from my grasp. And then—after the final, devastating trauma of being severely beaten by someone I knew and trusted from childhood—another part of me seemed to take over my life. I stopped taking the pills and abruptly began to detoxify. This precipitated what the medical profession calls "psychosis."

On a Sunday afternoon, my family had me committed to a psychiatric ward, and I can remember welcoming the protection of the hospital. At last I was able to relax. No longer would I have to try to hold my life together. Here were people whose sole purpose was to take care of me, and I could surrender whatever control I had tried to maintain. And so I let go of the world I shared with others, and willingly, trustingly, moved into a world of my own.

From Sunday through Thursday, I was out of touch with this reality. I traveled to other planets, lived and moved in other times and places and became other life forms. But mostly, I watched my life pass before me, re-experiencing everything I had ever done, thought and said, often con-densing events with a similar pattern into a single episode. Although some of what I saw was frightening, some amusing, some sad, some beautiful, and some ugly, I viewed it all as an Observer, without judgement and with the awesome insight of: "Oh, that's why I did that!"

Suddenly on Thursday night, I vomited, had diarrhea, my tempera-ture rose, my blood pressure went up, and I screamed out every obscenity I had ever heard. Then both my big toe nails turned black and blue, and fell off. That was what happened to me physically in the outer world where other people could see what was happening to me.

In my inner world, I felt as though every thought, every feeling, every physical or emotional pain that I had ever experienced from the time I was born—everything absorbed over my lifetime as if I were a giant sponge—was squeezed from my body during this one night.

In my mind, I was climbing an incredibly high mountain. Almost to the top, exhausted, I cried out, "Can't somebody help me?" A voice answered, "Everyone else has made it alone. Would you want someone who is already at the top to come back and help you?" While I wanted to scream out "Yes," I suddenly shot up into a place beyond words, beyond symbols, beyond imagery. It was a place of nothingness, in which all the knowledge—of what is and what can be and what will be—exists.

Perhaps "before words" would be a better description of that place, or simply, a place "where there are no words." As I passed through different levels of reality between the material world and pure energy, I saw my body encapsulated in words, defined, restricted and limited by words. Finally, I burst out of these word bonds into an infinity of word-lessness and timelessness: an infinity of love, ecstasy, bliss, and "the peace that passeth all understanding." I was one with the Universe—I *was* the Universe!

I was in this state for three hours. When I returned to reality in the morning, I was completely physically healed and totally emotionally integrated. Everything in my life made perfect sense and all of it had a divine purpose. Everything I had ever done or been in my life had been to bring me to this moment. It took several weeks for me to comprehend the enormity of my awakening experience. But that first morning, as I lay in bed remembering that I had touched a place within myself where I knew everything in the Universe, two things stood out in that knowing . . .

First, this whole experience of existence on the earth is part of an ongoing play directed by an energy of which I am a part. It is a purposeful, totally loving Oneness. I knew that I had lived many times before and that I would live again. Life goes on forever. If I did not accept my life as my own creation, and play my part consciously and lovingly this time, I would face the same issues over and over again in future incarnations.

Second, I knew that the laws of the Universe are Love and Trust. The Universe is a giant grid of power made of Pure Love. Within the consciousness of this awesome power, I am totally taken care of, *IF* . . . I relax and simply flow with what is happening right now in the moment, everything I desire will come to me: solutions follow problems; questions bring answers; and all my wants are filled. All I need to do is to be aware and respond.

With this new, expanded consciousness, I found myself back in the "real world" functioning spontaneously, happily and well. My release from the hospital came within a week. The only obvious effect of my ten-day stay was my continued heightened awareness. But within a short time, I realized that something even more profound had occurred.

In some amazing way, *all* my negative conditioning of a lifetime had disappeared. I had reached a brilliant new state of clarity. During the time that I was delving into the hidden corners of my mind, watching my life unfold, all the contents of my unconscious had surfaced and been released, and in the process I had let go of all that conditioning, which had limited me for so long. It was as if I had condensed years of Freudian psychoanalysis into one brief, intense session, and had discovered that my true inner core is Universal Oneness, an unlimited ocean of love, and I was the Oneness itself.

My first real recognition of how much conditioning I had dropped away came when I found I could go into a store and spontaneously spend money on myself. I had been a child of the depression, so I had learned early on not to want or expect material things for myself. As I grew up, and later on, as my husband and I became more affluent, it was still difficult for me to spend money on myself. I could spend it on others or give it away, but using money for my own pleasure was agonizing. And now, all at once, I could go into a store and buy for myself, choosing clothes and other major purchases without the anguish of indecision, which had been my legacy from childhood.

In fact, all decisions came easily now. I felt in charge of my life with new and previously unknown feelings of competence. I had energy I had not had since I was a child. Gone now were any residual feelings of inadequacy or resentment. The subtle fears that had governed my life disappeared without a trace. I lost my overwhelming need to please other people. Everything I did had new clarity and purpose. It was even possible, finally, to walk out of my marriage and to discover at last who *I* was and what *I* wanted my life to be. I was more efficient in my work, more present in whatever I was doing, and more spontaneous and playful in how I lived my life.

People on a spiritual path would have recognized what happened to me as an experience of cosmic consciousness, but my background had not prepared me in any way for this profound, life-changing experience. I could only look with wonder and awe at my transformation that is continuing even now. I wonder why every mental breakdown, such as I had, does not lead to the path of awakening to a higher consciousness.

———

It was a great privilege for me to receive this story of spiritual awakening, and I feel deeply honored to pass it on. I include it to show that the awakening process, which lifts us beyond karma and shows us the truth of life itself, can come in many forms. It touched me deeply when she first shared it with me and it continues to fill my heart with its message.

How do miracles fit into the picture?

Webster's dictionary defines a *miracle* as "an extraordinary occurrence that surpasses all known human powers or natural forces and is ascribed to a divine or supernatural cause, especially to God." Not bad. In my view, miracles are simply a gift from the Creator to His beloved children. There is a loving energy all around us, in us, and in all beings. It is called God. There is nothing magical about it; miracles are a natural part of life.

Focus on the moment, one moment at a time; forget the future and the past; then miracles can happen. As Will Rogers said, "Don't let yesterday use up too much of today." And I would say the same about the future. In fact, to focus our energy outside of the present moment, is to waste the Creator's precious gift of life. Our job is to do what is directly in front of us, right here, right now. The rest will take care of itself. Life does flow on in divine order, and we flow with it. To live outside of the moment, is to struggle against the reality of our existence.

As human beings we sometimes feel as though we are cast in cement, barely able to move forward in life except to push on through the daily grind. So we pray for a heaven-sent miracle, a genuine, no-doubt-about-it miracle that will shift our focus and propel us toward our destiny. And why *not* pray for a miracle? It may be just the right time and place to have one in your life . . .

Tony was certainly in the right place at the right time. He was camping at the same Montana campground where I was staying on my vacation. He saw me helping a few of the older people in the camp to ease their pain. Most of these ailing elders were taking drugs for pain and couldn't get around very well. This seems to be the case in trailer parks and campgrounds across the country. As folks grow older, they tend to take more drugs and move around less, resulting in more aches and pains, resulting in taking more drugs and moving around less, and so the circle goes on and on.

After watching me run energy on a few people who were in distress, Tony approached and hesitantly asked, "Sir, I have a knee injury from a mountain climbing accident two years ago. Could you please see if you can help me? The pain is more than I can bear." I invited him to sit down and began running energy through his knee. In a few minutes he started to cry. When I asked him why, he said his knee didn't hurt anymore. Tony said it was the first time he had been out of pain in two years.

That afternoon, the old mountaineer and I took a long walk. While we walked and talked, I learned that Tony, fluent in 12 languages, was originally from Czechoslovakia and had escaped from a German concentration camp in 1942. On orders from the Gestapo, a team of crack mountain climbers was sent after him, but he scaled the Alps to make his escape, outdistancing his pursuers.

I asked him to tell me what happened on the day of his accident two years before. I learned that Tony was a world class mountain climber at 62. On the day of the accident, he was leading a group of climbers in the Canadian Rockies. Having already scaled several thousand feet, they were now strung out across the face of the mountain in a line, connected to each other by a climbing rope.

Tony said he wanted to take a picture of a peak that could not be seen from his position. Another climber volunteered to hold him fast with a rope while he took a picture. Trusting her with his life, he leaned out from the mountainside. For one split second, she released her hold on the rope. Tony's knee took the full shock of his weight, bending backward and tearing the cartilage. He had to be roped down the mountain by a rescue team.

I asked if he had experienced a gut feeling about the coming accident on that fateful morning. He nodded and said that he had foolishly ignored it. For two years, he sought a solution to his pain and disability from every orthopedic surgeon he could find, but without success. After being so athletic all of his life, he was devastated by the constant, agonizing pain of his injury; he could hardly walk.

Tony had come to the campground to pray and try to understand why this had happened to him. He had talked with surgeons who worked on professional football players, ones very experienced in putting the body back together. The medical solution for his torn knee was to weld it straight or bent, whichever he preferred. Once at the campground, he knew he would have to make this momentous, life-changing decision soon. And then he saw me running energy on other campers.

By the next day, all the pain and swelling were gone and never returned. Tony thanked me with heartfelt gratitude, and after that day, we camped together many times over the years. He was very comfortable with my healing methods. He told me his father always said, "Tony, when the doctors fail, always turn to Mother Nature, she will heal you."

———

However, miracles are not such a wonderful thing in a healing practice because they are so unpredictable . . .

I could never have predicted what was going to happen for good old Ernie. I knew Ernie from his service station in San Bernardino when I lived in southern California. This healthy fellow came to see me twice when I was first in practice in Redlands.

Eleven years later (a year after I had moved to the San Francisco Bay area), Ernie's wife called me from the southland because she wanted to bring Ernie up to see me. After being in a wheelchair for two years, the doctors still did not know what was wrong. Ernie could stand for a few minutes at a time, but that was it; he could not walk. I was shocked that they were willing to fly up to see me. However, I had learned never to question when God moved people into my life.

They arrived in a taxi from the airport. The driver removed the chair from the trunk and helped Ernie into it. His wife rolled him into my office. This was a very different Ernie from the healthy man I had treated in Redlands. Painfully thin, his skin had a grayish cast, and I could not see any spark of life force in his eyes.

I ran energy for 20 minutes until the Power's healing flow ceased. Ernie smiled and told me that he felt better than he had for two years. His wife called the next day to say they were still in the area. I asked if they had missed their flight back. She laughed happily and told me why they were still in the Bay area.

"When we left your office, Ernie asked me to push him down your street so he could enjoy the air. He hadn't enjoyed anything for so long that I didn't see any harm in delaying our trip to the airport. I was pushing him down the block when suddenly he said he was sure he could walk."

"I can imagine what you thought about that," I said in surprise.

"Oh, I can tell you, I was shocked when he got out of that chair and walked. Then he said he felt so incredibly energized that he wanted to push the empty wheelchair for a bit. After a while, he insisted that I get in his chair so he could push me. He was so full of energy that he just kept on going for miles."

"How amazing!" I exclaimed.

"It sure was. We were nearly to Palo Alto when we turned around and he started pushing me in the other direction. Now get this . . . he said he was ready to walk to Seattle if I wanted to go. He felt so strong and healthy, and I felt utterly helpless before his determination. But I finally insisted that we check into a hotel and get some sleep. We're flying back today, but I had to call and thank you again."

Next week, Ernie's wife called me from their home. Laughing, she said, "I've got to share part two of Ernie's healing. Early this summer, we hired two teenagers to help out at the station. But they've been no help at all. I think they're both just basically lazy . . . and insolent. Ernie was sure they spent most of their time hiding from him and smoking in back of the station because he could hear them talking and laughing through the walls. Of course, he was too slow in his wheelchair to ever catch them at it."

"That must have been awful," I sympathized.

"Oh, it was. But here's the good part. On Ernie's first day back, he wheeled slowly into the station seated in his wheelchair just like nothing had happened. Then he asked the boys to stack some tires that were behind the station. He'd asked them to do this many times, but nothing had ever been done. The boys headed out back to loaf as usual. Ernie quietly got out of his wheelchair, walked around to the back, and came up on the boys as they were sitting on the tires, smoking and laughing."

"What a victory!" I exclaimed.

"It was the greatest day in Ernie's life. After all those months of frustration, to walk up to those boys lounging on the tires and savor the stunned look on their faces was incredible. He said, 'Well boys, the free ride is over . . . you're both fired.' I just wish I could have been there to see it all for myself."

Later, Ernie called to thank me himself. He said he didn't understand what kind of miracle could have gotten him well in a few minutes at my office. I said, "The very best kind . . . from God." We both had some great laughs while he shared the story of his former employees again, first-hand. If only Ernie could have snapped a picture of their dumbfounded faces, I'm sure it would have been a classic.

———

And I could never have predicted what was about to happen when two 70-year-old gentlemen came to my office on a crowded Saturday morning. One poor chap's left knee was permanently fixed in an awkward, 90-degree angle. The other knee was apparently quite normal. It was painful to watch him walk—if his grotesque, crab-like gait could be called a walk. His bent knee almost scraped the floor as he scuttled into the treating room with his friend.

When he handed me his x-ray, I saw that his knee had welded into a solid mass. I assumed I was talking with my patient until he told me that he was only there to drive his friend to see me. Refocusing, I asked the man with the bent knee to sit on a chair to one side and handed back his x-ray. Then I began running energy on his passenger, my real patient.

After a few minutes the guiding voice of the Power told me to run energy through the driver's bent knee. I moved over to his chair and did so. The handicapped gentleman shouted, *"Hey! I'm not your patient!"*

"I know," I said.

"Nobody can help my knee!"

"Fine."

"Listen! I'm not going to pay you for this!"

"I understand," I responded and continued running energy.

To make his point, the fellow shoved his x-ray at me. The bone of his knee glowed ghost-like on the x-ray, a stony mass—white, fixed and permanent. He said his knee had frozen into its bent position over a period of years. None of his doctors could determine what was causing the bone to calcify. For the past ten years, his knee had been immovable. He said he had gone everywhere for help, but there was no hope for his strange condition. The angels whispered, "Watch." Suddenly, his bent leg straightened out completely.

He shouted, *"My God, I didn't do that!"*

I smiled, "Neither did I."

"What should I do now?"

"I'd go out into the field out back and thank God for your miraculous healing."

He stood up and walked around the room. "Will my knee always be perfect like it is now?" he asked in wonder.

After checking with the angels, I said, "Absolutely."

All day long, as I watched through my front office window, the healed man met each car coming in. First, he showed his x-ray to the arriving patients. Then, he demonstrated his scuttling walk as it had been before the treatment. Finally, he walked around the parking area normally to show them how he had been instantly and miraculously healed in one moment of God's grace.

His understanding companion waited patiently for him all day. At the end of the day the driver came in, hugged me, thanked me, and paid for his treatment. In meditation that evening, I gave thanks for the limitless healing that flows through all of us to help others when we allow it. Miracles may be unpredictable, but what joy they bring to both patients and healers when they appear.

––––––

The healing angels have a rich sense of humor, and I seem to give them some of their best laughs. They laugh when I complain in meditation that my "control" of miracles is as poor now as it was when I first started out . . .

I certainly had no control over things when a young lady came in for an energy treatment and brought her girlfriend with her. I was running energy when the girlfriend interrupted, "Do you think there's anything you could do for my finger?"

"What sort of problem are you having with it?" I asked.

"A horse bit it two weeks ago," Cindy said.

I imagined a small nip of some kind until she held her finger out for me to look at it. Shock is a mild word to describe what I felt when I saw the middle finger on her right hand. The tiniest stitches imaginable attached her finger to the joint closest to her hand. It reminded me of Frankenstein's monster. From the hand to the first joint, the finger was a healthy pink. But the remaining two inches to the fingertip—the reattached finger—was a sickening gray. At the sight of this dead-looking flesh, I exclaimed, *"Good God, how did this happen?!"*

Cindy sighed and said, "We were at a horse show, and I was leaning back against a chain link fence. My hands were behind my back and my fingers were sticking out through the fence. A horse on the other side of the fence bit my finger clean off. I went into shock. Luckily, the finger was recovered and surgically reattached. But now it hasn't healed and the surgeon says he'll have to amputate it next week because my finger is going into gangrene." I ran energy into her finger for five minutes until the Power said it was complete. Then I stopped and resumed treating my regular patient.

When the two ladies returned the next month, I couldn't keep my eyes off the famous finger. It was amazing. The surgeon had attached the most lifelike two-inch artificial fingertip I had ever seen. It matched perfectly the pink color of her skin. The flexibility was astounding. I finally asked, "How's your finger?"

Cindy smiled and showed me the finger up close. It was *her* finger restored to living tissue. The tiny stitches were still there but fading. Her entire finger was now perfect in every way with full function. Stunned, I asked, "What happened?"

"Well, we were driving home when I felt like my finger was on fire and I screamed. I looked at my hand and my finger was bright, cherry red at the stitches. We pulled over and parked at the side of the road. While we watched, that red moved slowly toward the tip of my finger. By the time it reached the end of my finger, which took about 15 minutes, I could bend my finger and the color was normal. I couldn't believe it because the surgeon told me that I would never have movement in that finger since he didn't reattach the severed ligaments. When I went in for my next appointment and showed the surgeon my restored finger, he refused to discuss it."

At this point, both girls laughed happily and Cindy said, "If we didn't believe in miracles before, we do now."

I laughed and added, "Fortunately, the word 'impossible' isn't in God's vocabulary."

The difficulty with miracles is that they come when they want to, do what they want, and exit, leaving both the patient and me to ponder what happened . . .

One afternoon a stunning blonde of 28 came into my office. No one could mistake the look of a superb athlete; she moved with grace and power. She was holding her right wrist with her left hand, which kept her right arm pinned securely across her waist. My receptionist showed her into my treating room where she continued to hold her right wrist as though it was a matter of life and death while lying in silence on my treating table.

As soon as I entered the room, I saw enormous, angry, red flames shooting out from her right elbow in great sheets of fire. My first impulse was to put my hands on her elbow to quench the flames of pain. I hurried over and reached out toward her elbow. She shouted, "Don't you *dare* touch my elbow. No damn doctor will *ever* touch my elbow again. I've had three surgeries on that elbow and each time it gets worse. I hate doctors."

While I shared her thoughts on any surgery that would make a condition worse, I asked what had originally happened to make the surgeries necessary. She said, "I'm a speed skier. I was skiing downhill at 60 miles an hour when I saw I was going to crash head-on into a huge tree. I was terrified of destroying my face so I shielded it with my right arm. But the impact completely shattered my elbow. The first surgery permanently froze my elbow in a 90-degree position, just as you see it now. And I've been in constant pain ever since."

Since she wouldn't let me touch her elbow, I stepped back and began running energy into her feet with my hands about 12 inches away. My angelic healing guides said, *"You're always asking why everyone can't be healed instantly. Why don't we heal this young woman instantly? Then you'll be able to see the outcome. Ask her how her elbow is now."*

"How is your elbow now?" I asked.

"How the hell do you *think* it is?" she responded. "The pain's *killing* me like it has for three years and I can't move it at all; it's frozen . . ." At this point, she straightened her right arm and moved it around. "My God, the pain is *completely gone* . . . I can move it . . . I can bend it . . . it feels *great* . . . I don't understand . . ."

The Power spoke again, *"Now you have instant healing. Your pa-*

tient has learned very little—if anything at all—from her pain. She needed to come to you six times to learn the lessons behind her injury. Follow her miracle of instant healing. You will see how complicated her life becomes because of it."

As instructed by the Power I called the speed skier a few weeks later to check on her. She was extremely upset. Her closest friends now agreed that she must have been confused about ever having been injured in the first place. They thought it was some ploy to get sympathy and attention. Her marriage fell apart and she was facing a divorce. The insurance company now declared that her injury must have been psychological, despite documentation from her orthopedic surgeons. She was angry at life, her husband, her friends, the insurance company, the surgeons, and, of course, me. To my astonishment, she said the whole mess was my fault.

Finally, I understood what the Power had been trying to tell me all along. My patient had not learned from her accident. Because of her instant healing, the lessons she could have learned during the healing process would have to be learned later on in other ways.

So I let go of my dream of instant healing for everyone. God in His infinite wisdom would have to decide who was ready for miracles, and who was not. I learned to step back and behold the magnificent rhythm and flow of life as patients moved through their healing process. I joined in celebration with my patients as they accepted the lessons inherent in their conditions and moved forward into new lives of health and vitality.

The Power tells me that if I *never* see another miracle, I have already seen more than enough for many lifetimes. And I have to agree. Then, the angels laugh and declare that if we look around, we will see that our lives are adorned with miracles every day. Inevitably, the Power says, "Let's get back to work." And so I do.

Looking Forward

LOOKING FORWARD

$\cdot \diamond \cdot \cdot \diamond \cdot$

Surprisingly, at 76, I still see myself as 16 and wonder, "Who is that old chap in the mirror?" Only a moment ago, I was a child. Now I have an old man's visage, but the child within looks back from the mirror, laughing at the old fellow staring into the glass. I have given much thought to death as it is surely in my future. Six months ago I had a brush with death. But when the Grim Reaper laid his hand upon my shoulder and I agreed to go, he removed his hand, smiled gently and said, "Later, friend." Then he turned and walked away. So I will continue to shave the old chap in the mirror as a matter of duty and love until Death seeks me out once more when my time comes.

I know when the day comes for me to leave this earthly plane, I will be laughing all the way into the next dimension. Don't you just love to laugh? I do. I love the way humor creeps up on us with punch lines that tickle our funny bone until we double over in laughter. There's something missing in folks who are too serious to laugh. I thank God for the humor in life. It fractures pompous attitudes and makes even stiff, formal folks laugh unexpectedly at times, at least behind closed doors.

Throughout my life, humor has been—and still is—like having springs in the carriage of life. It eases the thumps and bumps along the way. I don't know when I've enjoyed humor more than in this present incarnation. How wonderful that we, as actors upon the stage of life, think that this life is real. This is the greatest joke of all. Of course, while we're here, we each flow energy as an ego personality, which makes the earth plane the perfect theater for experiencing illusion as reality.

In other dimensions, you quite easily pass right though walls, but

469

here—as you may have noticed—it hurts to bump into a wall. One day you will wake up to discover that reality is what you believe and create in the moment. Thrust into other dimensions filled with life, you simply soak it all in. Eventually, you leave your mind at the side of the road because life, in all its fullness, is too great for our small minds; life is the province of the heart.

We live and have consciousness, but are we aware? Within the heart we know all things totally, but we do not know that we know. Imagining ourselves to be otherwise, we heavenly beings of spirit shuffle about in a rental car body, dragging our shining wings of light through the mud of everyday life.

Everything here is so very solid in appearance, Yet, quantum physics tells us there are vast universes of space between every atom. We are in an infinite universe and the infinite universe is within us. Surrounding us, and within us, divine energies and celestial forces are in constant communication with every cell and subatomic particle, all joined in perfect understanding.

This loving connection occurs within the sacred intelligence of a veiled mystery that we can only experience on the inner planes. There our contact with the Creator is complete and perfect, a done deal. There we are enfolded in our Creator's love for all eternity. Within each moment of forever, we have the opportunity to create our lives anew with love, joy and laughter. What more could we ask of our Creator?

————•◆•————

No doubt, I'll soon begin writing about the old, folk remedies I've seen work so well over the years. And, before my razor sharp memory shreds that journey into confetti, I will capture the adventures of our year-long vision quest on the southwest desert. For now, I'm content to pass on what I know about healing and its mysteries. My dream was to write *Presence of Angels* when I began organizing my notes 25 years ago. I had no idea it would take nearly three years to write and another two for Andrea to edit.

At 21, when I first looked out upon the vast sea of human illness, I set out to heal every one of them myself. And so it began. However, as an older gent, my burning desire to heal everyone in the world has faded away. Now I consider that past campaign to be an ego-driven addiction. The Creator heals through all who open to His Love as the Healer, but for any one human being to try to heal the world takes its toll. I finally arrived at a point where I was content to do the best that I could for people, and not worry about those who chose to eat and drink what they darn well pleased. Freewill choice was involved . . . theirs!

More than 200,000 people have come to me for healing. Only three hundred were in perfect health. These lucky folks walked into my office with vibrant energies spiraling out in dazzling rainbow colors that proclaimed health in every cell. Their bodies were like fine Swiss watches. Their only job was to use the best fuel possible and enjoy the ride all the way; God had gifted them with a Rolls Royce this time around.

Of course, there was a time when I thought I would heal everyone who came in to see me. However, the passing years taught me that God heals everyone in His own way and in His own time. I learned that Sickness and Healing are perfect for soul growth; both are a part of the great celestial dance of the cosmos.

Everyone wants a miracle. What they don't realize is that sometimes you create your own miracles through hard work and paying attention to what you eat, drink, and think. So as much as I love miracles, I take my hat off to those people who work diligently in every way to restore their health, people who listen and follow commonsense guidelines for wellness. With the help of the Power's energy, they straightened out their diets and lifestyles. For me, it was always a miracle in its own right to see people reclaim their health. I rejoiced in their renewed zest for life, which they were then able to share with everyone around them.

Listen to your body. It is always whispering wonderful truths to share with you in the Silence of your Inner Being. It will never cease speaking to you. Miracles await you within the Truth of your Self. Listen as if to hear exquisite music, which is playing ever so faintly in the distance. Listen and you will hear. Remember in the deepest part of your being that your Knowing is Always and Forever.

———•◆•———

Life is a grand mystery of infinite proportions. Would I choose a life of healing all over again? Of course. And now I find myself moving into a higher energy in healing and teaching. Commonsense might say, "Why don't you step back after more than 50 years in the harness?" But my inner self says, "It's time to take part in the great raising of spiritual consciousness that lies directly ahead."

As we approach the next step on our journey home, we are opening completely to our intuitive, spiritual nature. Thankfully, many people today *are* open to the deeper spirituality of life. Mother Earth blesses those who have awakened to see that all life in the universe is One Life and reflects the Creator's love for his Creation. This awakening makes all children *our* children, and all of creation dear to us.

Healing is my inspiration and my reason for living. Having retired from my chiropractic practice, I still love to run energy as a minister and healer, especially when speaking to large audiences. To the Power, it makes no difference whether the audience is 300 or 3,000; the energy increases and intensifies to lift everyone's energy. It's pure joy to watch the Power flow from person to person while I behold the awakening of those who are ready to embrace the Inner Light and begin their lives anew in the Now Moment.

The best way I can explain the importance of the Now Moment, which reveals itself more often than we breathe, is to share the following conversation that I once had with the Power. One morning I asked, "So where exactly is this train of life headed and when do we get there?"

"Wake Up, Dear One! You have already arrived at your destination. You have been dreaming. Wake Up! You are here. Now!"

"But where is 'here'?"

"Child, stop pretending you do not know where we are. We are Home. You keep dreaming about trains and destinations and train wrecks. Stop all that nonsense and enjoy the moment. Welcome Home . . . Here and Now."

"But how do I live in this place called Home?"

"Live in the bubble of the moment. Then you will never again be away from Home. Only by staying in the moment can you be at peace in the flow of the Creator's love forever."

"So how do I begin all this?"

"Ah, that is simple. There is no beginning and no end. There is no

starting, no stopping, no trying. Life just IS . . . always has been, and always will be. Open to the Now Moment and just BE."

"Why do I forget so easily?"

"Because you have freewill choice each moment of eternity to judge everyone and everything in your life as good or bad; that ties you to the future and the past. Or, you can simply accept each moment, and all that is in it, as perfect and loving, no matter what its appearance, knowing that we are all one in God's heart. Loving acceptance is the magic key to the Now Moment."

"Is it really that simple?"

"It is. God gave mankind the greatest gift of all: freewill choice. Man has used his mind to imagine he is separate from God's heart. He imagines he has to earn his way back to the Source by traveling a long, difficult road. Man thinks he has to struggle through all the potholes and tangled circumstances that his mind devises. Finally, life becomes so painful that at last man stops reaching for one more answer outside of himself. Then he is ready to accept the Truth hidden in his own heart, and awaken to the joy of the Now Moment."

"You mean reality is waking up to each moment and being in that moment? I guess that would mean forgetting the past and every memory it holds. We'd have to let go of all future expectations, all five year plans, all regrets about the past and fears of the future, and all working and reworking of our strategies . . . right?"

"Yes, Child. Stop your search. God has made it all so simple. The Truth is that only the Now Moment is Real. All else is the dream, which continues forever . . . if you continue sleeping. The Now Moment is life's great gift, and the secret to living life. Do not eat breakfast thinking of lunch, eat lunch thinking of supper, and eat supper planning tomorrow's breakfast. Whatever you are doing . . . do it. Live in the Moment . . . totally, lovingly and effortlessly with full awareness of everything that exists within that moment."

"Well, I've wasted a lot of time. I feel so far back and trapped in my mind. I'm afraid I'll never escape."

"Ah, but the Now Moment waits for you forever. Everything you have ever experienced in your life—everything you have ever thought, said, and done—has been totally necessary to bring you to this moment of awaken-

ing. The bubble of the moment exists in gentle, effortless living of the present moment, which occurs Now . . . and Now . . . and Now. Each 'Now' lovingly gives birth to all the Nows ever after."

"What should I do to stay in the Now?"

"Don't do anything. Just BE and breathe—in the moment of course—one loving breath at a time. Ask for help. God will hear. You are totally loved and cared for, from the beginning of time through all Eternity."

"So what do I call this way of life?"

"Being."

"Just *being?*"

"Yes."

"I'm going to plan my life around this truth and stay in the Now Moment forever!"

"Be careful. You have been at this point many times. You always turn away from the Now Moment to organize and search for strategies. You let your mind 'help' you to BE. Your mind does not know, has never known, and never will know how to just BE. You can never know this through your mind, no matter how hard, how long, or how intense your search."

"The mind remains blind to the purpose of life. The mind's purpose is to help you function in this third dimensional world . . . opening doors, and keeping one foot in front of the other while walking . . . But if you allow your mind to attempt to discover life's divine purpose, it will only confuse, complicate, and make difficult everything in your life."

"Begin the simplest program and in short order your mind will be in the game to help you. You will be swept instantly into the future and the past. Your mind will run away with you like a wild horse with the bit between its teeth. It will drag you madly down the potholed road of your self-created existence."

"On the other hand, your heart waits patiently and lovingly for you to wake up and accept the greatest gift of all . . . Being in the Now."

"Why does it take us so long to learn how to live our life in the moment and love our way through every moment?"

"It has always been your choice. The door to the Eternal Now Moment is always open. Your future is assured. You are held safely in God's loving heart. Nothing can ever disturb or change this. It just IS. So lovingly accept your birthright to Live and Be in the Moment. Know that we are with you every moment of forever."

———•◆•———

A few months after this conversation, at one in the morning, apparently my appointed hour for receiving certain messages, once again an unseen, mighty hand brought me up to a sitting position in bed. Startled awake, I heard the familiar voice command, *"Look!"*

Opening my eyes, I saw before me a point of light. After years of praying to awaken to the totality of life itself, it was happening. In one glorious and holy instant, all that I had ever prayed for during my lifetime was presented in that point of light. The light expanded until it became a radiant star of such brilliance that I knew I would have been blinded if I had looked at it through earthly eyes.

Within that brilliant star, floating in the blackness of the night, I saw the entire universe as it had been before the birth of life and into the future, beyond time itself. Everything and everyone existed within this light. I saw the energies of every being on earth as they lived their past and present and future selves in each moment, the entire panorama of Creation from Alpha to Omega.

I saw all things forever—what would be, wouldn't be, could be, couldn't be—the limitless possibilities of the universe. There before me was my life in every moment of the time ahead and as it had been in past lifetimes. I saw all the people that I would heal, wouldn't heal, all the readers of this book, and the healing of the entire planet and everyone on it when we take the great leap forward in consciousness. All this in one split second of time, in one point of light, never to be forgotten.

This vision swept away any thoughts or ideas about Creation and how it should be or would be; it was all perfect. The intention of the divine was clearly in motion and I saw that we will make it, and to spare, all the way home to God's heart.

The angels of the Power then appeared in the room. I asked what all this meant, all this seeing of everything in its purest essence forever.

Their loving answer: *"All is well."* As I listened, I heard their words echo through eternity and knew these words as ultimate truth, always and forever. I knew then that life continues through eternity, sacred and perfect. I knew that we are all evolving together, even as the earth and other planets are evolving, in the Eternal Now Moment.

As suddenly as it had grabbed me, the hand released me and I fell back down in bed. Basking in the revelation that nothing was out of place in the entire universe and pondering how to ever convey this experience to anyone else, I thought I would never sleep again after this wondrous event. But, although sleep did not come easily, eventually I did fall asleep.

The next morning, I woke up early as usual, headed out for my morning walk, and had completed my morning chores before my vision came back to me. How could I have forgotten? The remembrance of the enormity of my experience jolted me totally awake. At that time, I realized I could not encompass any of it in words. I felt that I could talk forever on any one facet of what I saw and still be trying to express what took place. I was left in the dust of my passage into the Light, with no means to pass on to anyone what I had seen in the starlight that had come and gone. But I did hold fast to the Power's heavenly statement of this vision's message about life itself: "All is well."

———•◆•———

In the Now Moment, which exists in the gap between thoughts, listen and wait for inner knowing. The clatter of the outer world threatens to drown out the still, small voice of truth, but seek this voice in the silence within. The questions that you would ask—Why are you here? What are you here to do?—have all been answered. Those answers are waiting in your heart. Where are you? With God. When? Now and Forever.

Life is in the living of it, not *having* lived it or *going* to live it, but *living* it one Now Moment at a time with loving focus. A seeker once asked the Buddha, "What is your practice?" His simple answer: "We sit, we walk, we eat." The confused student said, "But we all sit and walk and eat." The Buddha smiled, "Ah, but when we sit, we know we are sitting. When we walk, we know we are walking. When we eat, we know we are eating."

As hard as it may be for humankind to believe, everything in life points toward awakening. Therefore, everything is perfect, exactly as it is.

A divine timetable exists for each one of us. We are born at the perfect time into the perfect family and circumstances to further our soul growth. Lessons come to us perfectly arranged to reveal our karma with all the people who join us in creating this fascinating play called life.

As we move through life, floating like leaves on the River of God, it's best not to resist God's chosen course for us. Instead, leave your oars behind and enjoy the uncertainty of His divine, drifting currents. They will always take you exactly where you are meant to be. Just be and enjoy the effortless experience of being moved through your life, accepting everything in your life as perfect.

To embrace the great changes to come, be ready to turn on a dime and follow the energy as it moves you in new directions. Let the past and the future dissolve into nothingness; they do not exist. Live intuitively and spontaneously in each moment of your life, where you are cherished in the everlasting love of the Creator.

Seek within your heart for what you love to do above all things. Your own heart's wisdom will guide your flight into the higher realms of being, and one day you will find yourself living the transcendent life that you thought existed only in your dreams. The Old Man spoke of a Golden Age ahead, an age of heart power, in which intuition flows freely and connects us heart-to-heart through the eternal matrix of love and trust that forms our universe. That is the promise.

Embrace the Now Moment. Let your life flow through you out into the world, and beyond into the universe. Smile and be happy. Yours is the love that lifts up the world. Yours is the shining light of peace and joy that makes all the difference in the outcome. It's time to dust off your wings and take flight. Know that God's angels are ever close to you, willing to guide, direct and protect you on your amazing journey through this life. Seek these heavenly beings within the Silence of your Self.

May God's angels communicate with you through your thoughts and dreams, lifting you to the crystalline cities of light in celebration of your awakening. Let us all join in anchoring a world of love, joy, truth, peace and wisdom on our beloved planet, healing our future for all generations to come.

Namaste*

*The Divinity within me honors the Divinity within you.

To order
Presence of Angels: A Healer's Life

———·◆·———

Contact
Quick Pick Distribution
22167 C Street
Winfield, KS 67156

8:00 A.M. to 5:00 P.M. Central Time, Monday–Friday

PHONE ORDERS:
1-800-214-8110 toll free for continental U.S. only
1-888-281-5170 toll free for Alaska, Hawaii, Canada and continental U.S.
1-620-229-8977 dial direct outside U.S. and Canada

EMAIL ORDERS: qpdistribution@skyerock.net

FAX ORDERS: 1-620-229-8978

Checks, money orders and credit cards accepted

———·◆·———

Ask for
Presence of Angels: A Healer's Life
Author: J. C. Hugh MacKimmie
Publisher: Knowing Heart Publishing
ISBN: 0-9770545-4-3

———·◆·———

For additional information
www.knowingheart.com